ALL ■ IN ■ ONE

Cisco® CCIE™

PRACTICE EXAM
& REVIEW 350-001

ALL · IN · ONE

Cisco® CCIE™
PRACTICE EXAM
& REVIEW 350-001

Michael Satterlee

McGraw-Hill / Osborne

New York • Chicago • San Francisco • Lisbon
London • Madrid • Mexico City • Milan • New Delhi
San Juan • Seoul • Singapore • Sydney • Toronto

McGraw-Hill/Osborne
2600 Tenth Street
Berkeley, California 94710
U.S.A.

To arrange bulk purchase discounts for sales promotions, premiums, or fund-raisers, please contact McGraw-Hill/Osborne at the above address. For information on translations or book distributors outside the U.S.A., please see the International Contact Information page immediately following the index of this book.

Cisco® CCIE™ Practice Exam & Review 350-001

1234567890 DOC DOC 01987654321

Book p/n 0-07-219269-0 and CD p/n 0-07-219270-4
parts of

ISBN 0-07-219268-2

Publisher
Brandon A. Nordin

Vice President & Associate Publisher
Scott Rogers

Editoral Director
Gareth Hancock

Senior Project Editor
Betsy Manini

Acquisitions Coordinator
Alex Corona

Technical Editors
Stephen Hutnik
Peter Mokros

Full-Service Compositor
MacAllister Publishing Services, LLC

This book was composed with QuarkXPress.™

DEDICATION

To my wife MaryJo, whose love and support were my
greatest resources when writing this book

ABOUT THE AUTHOR

Michael Satterlee, CCIE, is a Senior Network Architect at AT&T Global Network Services, where he is responsible for the architecture and design of a Next Generation VPN service. He is a co-author of the *Cisco CCIE Lab Practice Kit*.

ABOUT THE TECH REVIEWERS

Stephen Hutnik, CCNA, is a Senior Network Engineer at AT&T Global Network Services, where he is responsible for development, testing, and training for the Global backbone of the AT&T Network. He is also an adjunct Professor of Telecommunications at Pace University, and is the co-author of the *Cisco CCIE Lab Practice Kit*.

Pete Mokros, CCNP, CCSE, has dedicated his career to networking and security technologies. No longer in the corporate world, he is currently focused on sharing his expertise with a range of individuals and organizations to advance the state of technology under their reach. He is an avid golder and a fan of University of Minnesota's Golden Gopher hockey.

BRIEF CONTENTS

CONTENTS

What Is the CCIE Certification?

This chapter will cover:

- Steps in becoming a CCIE
- CCIE qualification exam structure
- Chapter format
- How to prepare for the exam

Introduction

The Cisco Certified Internetwork Expert (CCIE) certification is the crème de la crème of networking certifications. It is recognized throughout the industry as being the most valued and difficult to obtain of all network certifications. The aim of the program is to make you a Cisco expert.

In today's business world, whether you're on the IS staff of a corporation, an Internet service provider (ISP), or a network integrator, people are asking more and more of you. More network use is the norm. More bandwidth is the constant want. More reliability is expected. Companies are putting their most valuable commodity, information, in your hands.

The CCIE program is well named, because you will be an expert in the multitude of internetworking technologies in use today. Armed with knowledge gained from this book and on-the-job training, you will provide benefits to your superiors or your customers because you will be able to design, implement, and evolve networks more intelligently and efficiently than your colleagues.

Besides the recognition that accompanies your CCIE status, other benefits will come your way. CCIEs have the option to jump to second-level Cisco tech support for any

1

case of technical questions or problems. You can also participate in a special CCIE chat forum, and answer questions on a CCO open forum.

Thinking of Becoming a CCIE?

As stated earlier, the CCIE is an advanced certification program. The Cisco entry and intermediate certifications such as Cisco Certified Network Associate (CCNA), Cisco Certified Network Professional (CCNP), Cisco Certified Design Associate (CCDA), and Cisco Certified Design Professional (CCDP) can provide you with a Cisco certification career path towards the ultimate goal: becoming a CCIE. Cisco recommends that you complete the appropriate course work and obtain significant work experience before continuing on your journey to certification.

If you're looking for rough rules of thumb, Cisco recommends that you have two or more years of internetworking experience. A good understanding of Transmission Control Protocol/Internet Protocol (TCP/IP), local area network (LAN) and wide area network (WAN) protocols, the Open Systems Interconnection (OSI) reference model, the Internet, security, and client/server architecture is essential. The company also recommends you have experience with packet-level diagnosis, plus real-world experience with Cisco and non-Cisco products. Again, the goal of the CCIE certification is for you to become a networking expert, not to be introduced to intermediate networking subjects.

Steps in Becoming a CCIE

So what are the steps to becoming a CCIE? The CCIE exam consists of two parts: a qualification exam and a laboratory exam. The qualification exam is two hours long and consists of 100 multiple-choice questions. The student must score at least 65 percent on this test in order to pass and be eligible for the two-day hands-on lab exam. Immediately after your test is completed, you know whether or not you passed. In addition, your score of each section is broken down, giving you a good feedback tool for revisiting weaker areas before taking the lab exam.

The second part of the certification process is a two-day hands-on laboratory exam. During the hands-on exam each test candidate receives his or her own rack of equipment, cables, and patch panels. The candidate is also provided with a full set of Cisco documentation to use throughout the exam. No other material is allowed in the exam room.

Your first task will be to create a network to specification. This will take up all of the first day and half of the second day. Halfway through the second day, while you are out of the room, the exam proctor will insert faults into your network, and you will have to find and fix them—as well as be able to document the problems and their resolutions.

The exam has a total of 100 possible points. To pass, you must achieve a score of 80 points or better. You must achieve a passing score on each section of the exam to be allowed to progress to the next. For example, a perfect score on the first day would be 45 points. You have to earn at least 30 points to be allowed to return for the first part of day two. Table 1-1 shows the scoring breakdown.

The lab starting time varies depending upon location, but will be somewhere between 8:00 A.M. and 9:00 A.M. each day and run for $7^1/2$ hours. You will have a half-hour break for lunch. A proctor will be in the room to clarify questions and handle any emergencies that may arise, but basically you are on your own.

The failure rate for this exam is high. According to Cisco, only about 20 percent of the candidates pass it on the first attempt. On average, CCIE candidates require two to three lab exams before they earn a passing score. Think of your first time as a learning experience, and if you manage to pass, that is a bonus. The number of times you can retake the exam is unlimited.

As with all certification exams, lab exam content and structure are subject to change, so when you are ready to consider taking the lab exam, it's best to get the latest information from Cisco. Cisco's Web site contains specific instructions about how to prepare for the CCIE lab and qualification exams. It cannot be stressed enough that you must have lots of hands-on practice if you hope to pass this exam. If you do not have equipment to practice on at work, you will have to set up a home lab or find another way to gain access to the equipment.

Qualification tests are administered via Sylvan Prometric, and are graded on a pass/fail basis. Each test costs $300; if you don't pass the first time, there is no limit (other than your pocketbook) to the number of times you can take the test. The lab exam is given on site at Cisco locations. You must score 80 percent or higher on the hands-on lab test to pass. The lab tests cost $1,200 each. If you do not pass the first lab test, you must wait 30 days until trying it again.

Table 1-1   CCIE Lab Exam Scoring

Day	Task	Points	Total So Far	Minimum Score to Continue
One	Build	45	45	30
Two (part I)	Build	30	75	55
Two (part II)	Troubleshooting	25	100	80 or better to pass

CCIE Qualification Exam Structure

The qualification exam is computer based and administered at one of the Cisco authorized testing centers listed in this chapter. The exam consists of 100 multiple-choice questions and is a closed-book exam; no reference materials are allowed in the exam room. The student is given two hours to complete the exam and must score at least 65 percent to pass. The passing score will be given on the Examination Score Sheet at the end of the exam along with your score. A grading of either pass or fail will also be given.

CCIE Qualification Exam Blueprint

The CCIE Routing and Switching exam covers IP and IP routing, non-IP desktop protocols such as Internetwork Packet Exchange (IPX), and bridging- and switching-related technologies. The exam will cover the following areas:

- **Cisco device operation** The student should understand the architecture and operation of the router. The student should also know router commands and be able to interpret the output from these commands.

- **General networking theory** The student should have an understanding of the OSI model with a detailed understanding of the functions provided by each layer.

- **General routing concepts** The student should have an understanding of basic routing concepts. The student should also understand the differences between switching and routing, various summarization techniques, and the differences between link state and distance vector protocols.

- **Protocol comparisons** The student should have an understanding of various networking protocols and differences between them. An example of this would be IP versus IPX or TCP versus User Datagram Protocol (UDP).

- **Protocol mechanics** The student should have a detailed understanding of protocol mechanics such as Windowing/Acknowledgements (ACK), fragmentation, maximum transmission unit (MTU), handshaking, and termination.

- **Bridging and LAN switching** The student should have a working knowledge of various bridging technologies such as

    - **Transparent bridging** IEEE/DEC spanning tree, translational bridging, bridging protocol data unit (BPDU), integrated routed and bridging (IRB), and concurrent routing and bridging (CRB)

    - **Source-route bridging** Source-route translational bridging (SRTB), source-route transparent bridging (SRT), data-link switching (DLSw), and remote source-route bridging (RSRB)

The student should also be responsible for understanding LAN switching and trunking technologies such as VLAN Trunk Protocol (VTP), inter-switch link (ISL), virtual LAN (VLAN), Fast Ether Channel (FEC), Cisco Discovery Protocol (CDP), and Cisco Group Management Protocol (CGMP).

- **IP** The student should have a working knowledge of IP addressing, classless interdomain routing (CIDR), subnetting, Address Resolution Protocol (ARP), network address translation (NAT), Hot Standby Router Protocol (HSRP), Domain Name System (DNS), Bootstrap Protocol (BOOTP), Dynamic Host Configuration Protocol (DHCP), and Internet Control Message Protocol (ICMP).

- **IP routing protocols** The student should have a working knowledge of the architecture and design of today's most popular routing protocols, including Open Shortest Path First (OSPF), Routing Information Protocol (RIP), RIPv2, Intermediate System to Intermediate System (IS-IS), Enhanced Interior Gateway Routing Protocol (EIGRP), Interior Gateway Routing Protocol (IGRP), and Border Gateway Protocol (BGP).

- **Desktop protocols** The student should have a working knowledge of desktop protocols, with a focus towards IPX, such as NetWare Link Services Protocol (NLSP), IPX-RIP, IPX-Service Advertising Protocol (SAP), IPX-EIGRP, Sequenced Packet Exchange (SPX), Network Control Protocol (NCP), IPXWAN, IPX addressing, Get Nearest Server (GNS), and Novell Directory Services (NDS) (routing and mechanisms).

- **Performance management** The student should have a working knowledge of the various traffic management mechanics used on a router, including all queuing techniques, Resource Reservation Protocol (RSVP), traffic shaping, and load balancing.

- **WAN (addressing, signaling, and framing)** The student should have a working knowledge of the addressing, signaling, and framing used by today's most popular wide area protocols. The exam will cover Integrated Services Digital Network (ISDN), frame relay, Asynchronous Transfer Mode (ATM), X25, High-level Data Link Control (HDLC), and Point-to-Point Protocol (PPP). The student will also be responsible for understanding the physical layer framing techniques and encoding.

- **LAN** The student should have working knowledge of data link layer addressing, Media Access Control (MAC), and Logical Link Control (LLC) techniques for all Ethernet and Token Ring technologies.

- **Security** The student should have an understanding of the security techniques used by a router. The student should know the general concepts and differences between Remote Access Dial-In User Service (RADIUS) and Terminal Access Controller Access Control System (TACACS).

Chapter Format

The book is broken into multiple practice exams given one per chapter. The exams cover key areas that the student must master in order to pass the CCIE Routing and Switching qualification exam. The areas include networking fundamentals, routing and switching fundamentals, Cisco-specific technology, and bridging and desktop protocols.

The exam questions are multiple-choice with an answer sheet provided at the end of the questions as a quick reference. A detailed answer and analysis section follows each 100 question multiple-choice test. In this section each question is reviewed and answered in detailed. We not only tell you why a particular answer is correct, but we also explain the technology and review why the other answers are incorrect. We believe this is the most effective study format, allowing you to learn not only from getting the correct answer, but also from understanding why the answer is correct and why the other answers are incorrect.

Chapter 2 (Networking Fundamentals)

Chapter 2 focuses on the OSI model, circuit- and packet-switched technologies, wide area protocols, TCP/IP fundamentals, and protocol mechanics. The exam contains questions on the OSI model, namely the features provided by each layer and a comparison between layers. The exam also contains questions on the addressing, signaling, and framing used by today's most popular WAN protocols, including frame relay, ATM, PPP, and ISDN. Questions are also given on IP addressing, subnetting, and basic operation of TCP/IP. The goal is to test the user's aptitude of basic networking protocols, mechanics, and technologies. The following is a detailed breakdown of the topics covered in this chapter:

- **OSI model**   Layer comparisons and functions

- **Protocol comparisons**   IP versus IPX and TCP versus UDP

- **Protocol mechanics**   Windowing/Acknowledgements, fragmentation, MTU, handshaking, and termination

- **Addressing**   CIDR, subnetting, and ARP

- **Services**   DNS, DHCP, and ICMP

- **Transport**   IP fragmentation, sockets, and ports

- **ISDN**   Link Access Procedure on the D channel (LAPD), Basic Rate Interface (BRI)/Primary Rate Interface (PRI) framing, signaling, mapping, dialer map, interface types, B/D channels, and Multilink PPP

- **Frame relay**   Local Management Interface (LMI), Data Link Connection Identifier (DLCI), permanent virtual circuit (PVC), framing, traffic shaping, forward explicit congestion notification (FECN), backward explicit congestion notification (BECN), committed information rate (CIR), discard eligible (DE), mapping, and compression

- **ATM**   Switched virtual connection (SVC)/PVC, ATM Adaptation Layer (AAL), user-network interface (UNI)/network-network interface (NNI), Interim Local Management Interface (ILMI), cell format, and private network-network interface (PNNI)

- **Leased-line protocols**   HDLC, PPP, asynchronous modems, and compression

Chapter 3 (Routing Fundamentals)

Chapter 3 focuses on routing fundamentals and routing protocols. The goal of this practice exam is to test the user's aptitude on design fundamentals and operation of today's most popular routing protocols. The exam includes questions on OSPF, IS-IS, EIGRP, IGRP, and BGP. The following is a detailed breakdown of the topics covered in this chapter:

- **OSPF**   Areas, virtual links, stub, not so stubby areas (NSSA), area border router (ABR)/autonomous system boundary router (ASBR) redistributions, media dependencies, external versus internal, and summarization

- **OSPF operation**   Designated router (DR), backup designated router (BDR), adjacencies, link state advertisement (LSA) types, link state database, shortest path first (SPF) algorithm, and authentication

- **BGP**   Peer groups, route reflectors, confederations, clusters, attributes, autonomous system (AS) operation, which includes route maps, filters, neighbors, decision algorithm, Interior Border Gateway Protocol (IBGP), and Exterior Border Gateway Protocol (EBGP)

- **EIGRP**   Metrics, route types, and protocol mechanics

- **IS-IS**   Metrics, route types, and protocol mechanics

- **RIP and RIPv2**   Metrics, mechanics, and design

Chapter 4 (Cisco-Specific Technology)

Chapter 4 focuses on Cisco-specific topics including device operation, router commands, router components, performance management, and security. The exam contains questions on nonvolatile random access memory (NVRAM), flash memory, CPU, file system management, and configuration register settings. The exam also contains questions on the queuing techniques, traffic management techniques, command-line knowledge, and LAN switching basics. The goal is to test the user's aptitude on Cisco device operation and architecture as well as the student's knowledge of router commands and his or her ability to interpret the output of those commands. The following is a detailed breakdown of the topics covered in this chapter:

- **Commands** Show and debug
- **Infrastructure** NVRAM, flash memory, CPU, file system, and configuration register settings
- **Operations** File transfers, password recovery, Simple Network Management Protocol (SNMP), accessing devices, and security (passwords)
- **Traffic management** Queuing, weighted fair queuing (WFQ), traffic shaping, and load balancing
- **Authentication, authorization, and accounting (AAA), TACACS, and RADIUS** General concepts and usage comparisons
- **LAN switching** Trunking, VTP, ISL, VLAN, FEC, CDP, and CGMP

Chapter 5 (Desktop Protocols and Bridging)

Chapter 5 focuses on desktop protocols, bridging techniques, and LAN technologies. The exam contains questions on transparent bridging, BPDUs, DLSw, routing information field (RIF) format, IPX, and LAN technologies. The goal is to test the user's aptitude on bridging technologies and concepts, data link addressing, MAC, and LLC. The following is a detailed breakdown of the topics covered in this chapter:

- **Transparent bridging** IEEE/DEC spanning tree, translational bridging, configuration BPDU, IRB, CRB, and access lists
- **Source-route bridging** SRTB, SRT, DLSw, RSRB, and access lists
- **IPX** NLSP, IPX-RIP, SAP, IPX-EIGRP, IPXWAN, and IPX addressing
- **Data Link layer addressing**
- **Ethernet/Fast Ethernet/Gigabit Ethernet** Encapsulation, carrier sense multiple access collision detect (CSMA/CD), topology, speed, controller errors, limitations, and 802.3

- **Token Ring** Token passing, beaconing, active monitor, ring insertion, soft and hard errors, encapsulation, topology, MTU, speed, and limitations

CD-ROM

The CD-ROM included with this book contains interactive software from FastTrak Express. The testing software provides standard and adaptive simulated exams with detailed score analysis, similar to what the student will see on test day.

How to Prepare for the Exam

You realize the need for training of some sort. (Proper training will help you gain the expertise needed to complete your certification goal.) So where do you go, and whom do you talk to about obtaining the proper training? Training comes in many forms and from several sources. For example, you may learn more in an hour of hands-on training than you could ever learn in the classroom. In essence, the type of training you choose depends on your job, goals, and study habits.

Hands-On Training

Hands-on training is just a broader term for on-the-job training. Whenever you think about hands-on training, remember that it involves some type of physical participation by you with the software for which you plan to get certified. On-the-job training is the easiest way to get hands-on training, but it's a little limiting because you don't get to explore the full range of software features and it is difficult to work on a production network. You can also get directed hands-on training using a number of Internet-based remote preparation labs, third-party aids, and sample configurations at the end of each chapter.

Hands-on training could also be the most time-consuming method of learning new skills. Although this type of training will supply you with the most real-world way of performing a task, the amount of time you must invest before you have enough information to become certified might take years. However, no matter how much knowledge you obtain from other sources, nothing will replace the knowledge acquired from on-the-job experience. There's something special about going through all of the procedures for installing, configuring, maintaining, and troubleshooting software and hardware yourself that makes the learning experience more complete.

The best place to acquire on-the-job training is on a live system at an existing company or prototyping labs that offer all the software and hardware necessary to design, install, and configure internetworks without disrupting production networks. All you need to do is find a job that's related to your education requirements. Of course, actually getting hired by a company that can offer on-the-job training before you have a certification in hand is a lot harder than it might seem. Unfortunately, most companies will require you to have the same skills that you are trying to learn before they'll hire you. If this is the case, you may have to work out an arrangement with the prospective employer to work as an entry-level person or to work at a reduced rate. Other times you may be able to work out an arrangement to help out and assist on projects free of charge in return for the hands-on experience. Although this is not putting any money into your pocket, you'll be getting the necessary training that you are looking for. Consider it as a payment toward your education.

Instructor-Led Training

Enroll in a professional education program. The courses will present you with a lot of information in a relatively short amount of time (three to five days for most classes). The instructor will normally present you with a series of lectures, along with oral or written question-and-answer periods, lab exercises, and hands-on experience.

Instructor-led courses are available from a variety of different sources. These sources include Cisco Authorized Training Partners (CATPs), colleges, universities, and different third-party educational facilities. Each of these different educational facilities provides a myriad of services. The services offered by these institutions range from the very general to the very specific. The lengths of classes also range from just a few hours to four or more years. The cost of the different educational services will range from nothing to thousands of dollars.

Because the educational facilities will vary in class size, materials offered, length, cost, and types of services, you'll need to discuss your educational needs with them.

The best place to obtain the required information for the Cisco certifications would be from a CATP education center. Cisco provides excellent training for its certifications as well as for its line of products. Although Cisco does offer some training directly, most of the training comes from the CATPs. Cisco authorizes the partners to teach its courses at a strict quality level. Cisco inspects the centers for proper hardware and software, as well as for the general overall condition of the facility. Each center must a use Certified Cisco Systems Instructor (CCSI) to teach its courses. The instructors have passed a series of competency exams and have attended special courses designed to make sure that they meet the Cisco standards for teaching the course.

CATPs are located worldwide, with the largest concentration being in Europe. Some of the partners are quite large, with upwards of ten classrooms in one location. CATPs are usually smaller. A few partner companies have education centers in different parts of the country. The centers are all basically the same, because Cisco must authorize each one and each center must meet the Cisco guidelines.

What distinguishes the different partners from each other is the quality of the instructors. Although each instructor is Cisco certified, many of the instructors teach only what is in the Cisco course manual. Although this is the base information required for the Cisco certifications, it may not always lend itself to real-world experiences. The extras that the better instructors include usually come from years in the field practicing what they teach. We all have had instructors or professors who really knew the book material that they taught, but if you asked them a question about something that didn't appear in the manual, they did not have a clue. When selecting the center that you want to attend, be sure to ask for references from former students. Talk to these people and get a feel about how the instructor handled the class, subject matter, and questions about related topics not included in the course material. You'll find that most of the instructors will get good reviews.

Cisco has been recognized for a long time by the industry for its proactive approach to training its resellers, users, and systems engineers. You can always count on the course materials written for Cisco software to be current with what's on the market. You can look at Cisco's Web site at **www.cisco.com**. This Web site contains a complete list of courses, current certification requirements, and listing of CATPs.

Self-Study Training

Cisco offers self-study programs, as do other sources. The self-study programs are good for self-starters who have both the time and the attitude to study on their own. By using the self-study programs offered by Cisco and authorized partners, you can save yourself a few dollars. The courses are designed to supply you with the course manuals offered by Cisco and usually include some form of lab training. Most training partners will sell you all the self-study course manuals so that you can study them at a convenient time.

The self-study programs are an excellent way to get some form of training, hands-on experience, and knowledge needed to obtain the Cisco certification. The biggest disadvantage of the self-study program is that you don't receive the instructor-student interaction used in instructor-led courses. If you decide to participate in the self-study program, you'll need to spend the time required to really learn the material.

Other Types of Training

At times, the standard approaches to training, like on-the-job or instructor-led training, won't fit into your schedule or don't meet some personal need (you may not study well on your own). For this reason, alternative forms of education are very popular. The alternative forms of education may include books, audiotapes, videotapes, Web-based training (WBT), and computer-based training (CBT) programs. These are all excellent sources of information that will help to augment your training process. This form of learning is available from a number of vendors providing lab supplements for those requiring hands-on equipment with lab exercises to assist not only in the preparation for Cisco's certifications, but also to provide just-in-time learning for on-the-job project requirements.

From the experienced computer technician down to the beginner, a bookcase with a wide variety of computer books will be a necessity. The library will prove to be a great asset in your quest for advancement in the computer industry. With a well-rounded library, you'll be able to reference the topics and subjects that you may not know very well. You'll find that your library will grow immensely in a short time. Many of the books that you get will have just a few pages on the subject that concerns you right now, but will provide a source of reference on other material in the future.

Many books are available about the Cisco Internetworking Operating Systems (IOSs) on the shelves of bookstores. As a Cisco expert, you'll need to know about the early versions of Cisco IOSs and how they work. You should also know the different commands and terminology that was a part of old versions of Cisco. The versions of Cisco IOSs have many differences. Don't ignore the general networking books. Many of these books have a lot of practical information about how to administer and troubleshoot your internetwork. Although these books may not provide Cisco-specific information, they will help you gain a better understanding of networks in general. Even if you don't use this information immediately, you'll find it essential later.

As you've seen, many different approaches to training are available for becoming a CCIE and for general knowledge of the internetworking computer industry. It's normal to feel a bit overwhelmed because of the vast amount of information that you'll receive in preparation for your certification exams. The secret to making this process work and passing the exams will be to find the style, type of training, and studying techniques that best stimulate your mind.

How to Schedule the Written Exam

CCIE candidates can take the Routing and Switching qualification exam (350-001) through Prometric or VUE. In order to register for the exam you will need an ID number. For candidates in the United States or Canada, a social security number or a social insurance number will be used as your ID. For candidates outside the United States and Canada, the ID number used will be assigned by the testing center. Once assigned, this ID is the identification to the CCIE database record for all certifications and for all recertification exams.

VUE Scheduling Information

Candidates can schedule an exam through VUE online at **www.vue.com/cisco** or via telephone through one of the following registration numbers:

Americas 952-995-8844

Asia—Pacific 61-2-9323-5586

Australia 1-800-356-022

Austria 0800-292150

Belgium—Dutch 0800-74174

Belgium—French 0800-74175

Canada (877) 404-EXAM (3926)

Europe, Middle East, or Africa 31-348-484-632

France 0800-904757

Germany 0800-0826499

Hong Kong 800-930-988

Ireland 1-800-552131

Israel 1-800-9453797

Italy 800-790521

Malaysia 1800-808-578

Netherlands 0800-0235323

New Zealand 0800-445-884

Philippines 1800-1611-0155

Portugal 800-831429

Singapore 800-6161-888

South Africa 0800-995044

South Korea 00308-610-021

Spain 900-993190

Sweden 020-798690

Switzerland 0800-837550

Taiwan 0 0080-611-289

Turkey 0080031929149

United Kingdom 0800-7319905

United States (877) 404-EXAM (3926)

Prometric Scheduling Information

Candidates can schedule an exam through Prometric online at **www.2test.com/ index.jsp** or via telephone through one of the registration numbers listed on their Web site.

CCIE Qualification Exam 1 (Network Fundamentals)

This chapter will cover:

- Open System Interconnection (OSI) model
- Circuit- and packet- switched technologies
- Wide area network (WAN) protocols
- Transmission Control Protocol/Internet Protocol (TCP/IP) fundamentals

Introduction

This chapter focuses on the Open System Interconnection (OSI) model, circuit- and packet-switched technologies, wide area network (WAN) protocols, and Transmission Control Protocol/Internet Protocol (TCP/IP) fundamentals. The exam contains questions on the addressing signaling and framing used by today's most popular WAN protocols, including frame relay, Asynchronous Transfer Mode (ATM), Point-to-Point Protocol (PPP), X.25, and Integrated Services Digital Network (ISDN). The exam also contains questions on IP addressing, subnetting, and the basic operation of TCP/IP. The goal is to test the user's aptitude of basic networking protocols and technologies.

OSI Reference Model

The OSI reference model is a framework for communications between computer systems. It was developed by the International Standards Organization (ISO) in 1978 to promote interoperability between networking equipment. The model is divided into seven layers, each of which specifies particular network functions such as addressing, flow control, error control, encapsulation, and message transfer. This seven-layer model has become the standard for designing communication protocols between network devices and is used widely as a method for teaching and understanding network functionality.

OSI Layers

The OSI reference model is divided into seven layers: application, presentation, session, transport, network, data link, and physical. Each layer is responsible for a different communication task. When two computer systems want to communicate with one another, the information being sent will pass through each layer of the OSI model. The following is list of the OSI layers and each layer's function:

- **Layer 7** The *application layer* provides network services to users of the network. Application level protocols include Telnet, File Transfer Protocol (FTP), and Simple Mail Transfer Protocol (SMTP).

- **Layer 6** The *presentation layer* is responsible for translating text and data syntax, such as Extended Binary-Coded Decimal Interchange Code (EBCDIC) used by IBM systems and American Standard Code for Information Interchange (ASCII) used in most computer systems.

- **Layer 5** The *session layer* assumes that a reliable virtual point-to-point connection has been made and contains specifications for the dialog between the two end systems such as dialog discipline, data grouping, and recovery of an interrupted session. The session layer is responsible for creating, maintaining, and ending a communication session.

- **Layer 4** The *transport layer* is responsible for providing reliable end-to-end communication. The transport layer provides error detection and control at the message level across a network. It handles sequencing, multiplexing, flow control, flow control as well as retransmissions for bad or lost packets.

- **Layer 3** The *network layer* makes routing decisions across the network selecting the appropriate path a packet should take to reach its final destination. This layer contains all the specifications for the transmission and switching technologies needed to build circuits through a network of nodes.

- **Layer 2** The *data link layer* contains specifications for frames, synchronization, and error control. These specifications change the raw bit stream supplied by layer

1 into data and converts data into bits for transmitting by the physical layer. The data link layer also addresses reliability and integrity issues because the data link handles error control within each packet using cyclic redundancy checks (CRCs). The data link layer is broken into two sublayers: Media Access Control (MAC) and Logical Link Control (LLC).

- **Layer 1** The *physical layer* is the lowest layer in the OSI model. The physical layer is concerned with the °of a bit stream over a communication channel. Specifications that define the signal voltages, bit duration, and channel definition are at this layer. The physical layer deals with mechanical and electrical characteristics needed to activate, maintain, and de-activate the physical connections. Examples include RS232C, Token Ring, and Ethernet.

Networking Protocols

Although the OSI model provides the framework for communications between network devices, it does not provide a method for the actual communication. In order for two devices to communicate, they must use a communication protocol. A communication protocol is a set of rules that govern how two end stations transfer information across a medium. Communications protocols generally fall into one of four categories: local area network (LAN) protocols, WAN protocols, network protocols, and routing protocols.

LAN protocols operate at the first two layers of the OSI model and define how devices communicate over a LAN such as a Token Ring or Ethernet network. WAN protocols also operate at the first two layers of the OSI model and in some cases, like X.25, the first three layers of the OSI model. The WAN protocols define communication rules for communications over various wide area media. Routing protocols operate at layer 3 of the OSI model and are responsible for path determination. Network protocols are all of the upper-layer protocols that exist in a given protocol suite and are responsible for end-to-end communications. This chapter focuses on WAN protocols and network protocols, namely TCP/IP. Routing and LAN protocols are covered in subsequent chapters.

Wide Area Networking Technologies

Wide area communication technologies fall into three general categories: circuit-switched, packet-switched, or point-to-point circuits. Depending on the category, various WAN protocols are used.

Point-to-Point Circuits

Point-to-point circuits or more commonly called leased-line circuits provide a pre-established dedicated circuit from one location to another. Point-to-point circuits were largely deployed in the 1980s and early 1990s as a means to connect remote locations together. The problem with leased lines, of course, is that they only provide point-to-point communication. If a hub location needed to be connected to ten spokes, it would require ten physical circuits. As the network grows, the number of leased lines and router interfaces required to connect the network grows by $(n - 1)$, where n is the number of remote site. If a full mesh environment is required, the lines would grow to $n(n - 1) / 2$, where n is the number of locations. As you can see, this quickly becomes economically infeasible. The other major drawback of leased lines is inefficiency. Statistically, not all lines will be used at once; however, because they are point-to-point circuits, no other sites can utilize the available bandwidth. Two common data link protocols are commonly used on point-to-point links today: High-level Data Link Control (HDLC) and Point-to-Point Protocol (PPP).

High-Level Data Link Control (HDLC)

High-level Data Link Control (HDLC) is a derivative of Synchronous Data Link Control (SDLC). It is a bit-oriented protocol; the frame length can be an arbitrary number of bits rather than a fixed multiple of any selected character size.

All HDLC frames begin and end with a flag pattern: a bit sequence consisting of a binary 0, followed by six 1's and another 0. These 01111110 markers are used as reference points to provide frame synchronization. When a line is quiet or idle, these flags are sent continuously for interframe time fill and to maintain synchronization between sender and receiver. To be valid, a frame must have at least 32 bits between its flags. Invalid frames are disregarded. For the sake of economy, a single flag may be used to identify the end of one frame and the beginning of another.

Point-to-Point Protocol (PPP)

Point-to-Point Protocol (PPP) is a standard method for transporting multiprotocol datagrams over point-to-point links. PPP can carry many different types of networking protocols, including IP, AppleTalk, Internetwork Packet Exchange (IPX), and DECnet. It is comprised of three main components: an encapsulation protocol, a Link Control Protocol (LCP), and a Network Control Protocol (NCP).

PPP uses HDLC as a basis for encapsulating datagrams over point-to-point links. It uses LCP to establish, configure, and test the data link connection and NCP to establish and configure different network layer protocols.

PPP Negotiation

PPP goes through multiple negotiation phases before the end systems can pass data. To establish communications over the link, the originating PPP station first sends LCP frames.

The LCP frames establish the connection through an exchange of configuration packets. LCP is used to automatically agree upon the encapsulation format options, handle varying limits on sizes of packets, detect a looped-back link and other common misconfiguration errors, and terminate the link. Once this exchange is complete, authentication will occur. Although authentication is not mandatory, it is almost always used.

After the link has been established and authentication has occurred (if configured), the originating PPP station sends NCP frames to choose and configure one or more network layer protocols. During this phase, the two end stations agree on the layer 3 protocol or protocols that will be used (such as IP, IPX, or AppleTalk). After the NCP negotiation is complete, PPP can carry the corresponding network layer protocol packets.

PPP Authentication

Two common authentication protocols used by PPP are Password Authentication Protocol (PAP) and Challenge Handshake Authentication Protocol (CHAP).

When PAP is used for authentication, the initiating station sends an authentication request to the server containing its username and password. This information is passed in the clear. The receiving station compares the username and password to the list of defined users. If it matches, the authentication request is accepted, and the station sends an authentication acknowledgment.

When CHAP is used, the server sends a request or challenges the remote device to respond. The challenge packet consists of an ID, a random number, and the hostname of the local station. When the initiating station receives the challenge packet, it concatenates the ID, the remote device's password, and the random number, and then encrypts all of it using the remote device's password. The initiating device sends the results back to the server, along with the name associated with the password used in the encryption process. When the server receives the response, it uses the name it received to retrieve a password in its list of defined users. The retrieved password is the same password that the remote device used in its encryption process. The access server then encrypts the concatenated information with the newly retrieved password—if the result matches the result sent in the response packet, authentication succeeds.

The benefit of using CHAP authentication is that the remote device's password is never transmitted in clear text. This prevents other devices from stealing the password and gaining illegal access to the network.

Packet Switching

Packet switching is a WAN switching method in which network devices share a single point-to-point link to transport packets from a source to a destination across a carrier's network. With packet-switching technology, a node only requires one physical line into the provider's network. On that one physical connection, multiple logical connections are used to get to the remote nodes.

Packet switching takes advantage of the fact that not all nodes will transmit at the same time. Statistical multiplexing is used to enable devices to share these circuits. Frame relay, Asynchronous Transfer Mode (ATM), and X.25 are examples of packet-switched WAN technologies.

Frame Relay

Frame relay is a WAN protocol that operates at the physical and data link layers of the OSI reference model. It enables end stations to dynamically share the network medium and the available bandwidth. Instead of requiring separate physical links for each frame relay conversation, each frame contains a Data Link Connection Identifier (DLCI), which denotes which conversation owns the information within the frame. Each frame sent into the network contains addressing information that the network uses to determine its destination. Devices within the network read this information and route each frame to its proper destination.

Frame Relay is only an interface specification and doesn't specify how data will be routed. Instead, the network routes frames using whatever means network builders and providers choose during its creation. In some cases, frames are kept intact as they traverse the network. This is known as frame switching.

Virtual circuits are the mechanisms that address actual frames. Just as typical telephone cables contain multiple pairs of wires (one for each individual conversation), a single physical frame relay interface may contain many individual conversations. However, in frame relay, unlike conventional analog lines, each frame contains a circuit number (DLCI) that denotes which conversation owns each frame of information. If this analogy is taken one step farther, network telephone switches cross-connect physical circuits to other physical circuits until a complete connection is made throughout the entire network. Similarly, frame relay frames are routed by the network to their destination based on the DLCI within each frame. Frame relay uses Link Access Procedure on the D channel (LAPD) frame format because it contains user data and address information, which can then be used to route frames.

The frame relay standards specify the use of either switched virtual circuits (SVCs) or permanent virtual circuits (PVCs). It is important to note that the protocol to establish

SVCs is still undefined. PVCs are defined when the user initially subscribes to the frame relay service. Subscribers establish PVCs between access devices linking LANs across the frame relay network. When PVCs are used, the network operator—whether a private network or a service provider—assigns the endpoint of each circuit. Although the actual path taken through the network may vary from time to time (such as when automatic alternate routing is taking place), the beginning and end of a circuit does not change unless the administrator changes it. These circuits behave like dedicated point-to-point circuits. A PVC does not require a call-establishment procedure and may exist for weeks, months, or even years. All traffic for a PVC uses the same path through the frame relay network. A frame relay network can automatically reroute around failures within the network.

SVCs also comply with frame relay standards. When SVCs are used for frame relay, the actual user of the circuit (the caller) specifies the destination. Like a typical telephone call, there is a call setup procedure (dialing) that takes place to establish a connection. A virtual circuit—using virtual circuit numbers (DLCIs)—is then established for the duration of the call. Although there are standards defined to support SVCs and most frame relay switch vendors support them, SVCs are not generally available from public frame relay networks that still offer only PVCs as a subscription service. Unlike a typical telephone call, multiple logical channels exist within a single physical circuit. Both PVCs and SVCs can share a single physical circuit. Also, no network resources are used when there is silence on the line; therein lies the real power of frame relay.

Frame Relay Addressing

One of frame relay's attractions is the fact that it is very efficient. With only 2 bytes of address overhead, you can transmit up to 8KB of data. Figure 2-1 shows the format of the frame relay frame.

The fields in Figure 2-1 can be explained as follows:

- **Flag**   Each frame relay frame starts and ends with at least one delimiter character of 0x7E. This bit sequence enables the receiver to synchronize on the start and end of a frame. A special bit-stuffing algorithm exists that ensures that this 0x7E character cannot appear in the user traffic.

- **Address**   The address field is either 2, 3, or 4 bytes long. A 2-byte address field is almost always used. The following fields are contained in a 2-byte address field:

  - **DLCI**   This is a 10-bit field that contains the DLCI value that identifies a virtual circuit. For a typical 2-byte frame relay header, this field can take on a value between 0 and 1,023. Some DLCI values such as 0 and 1,023 are reserved for frame relay management.

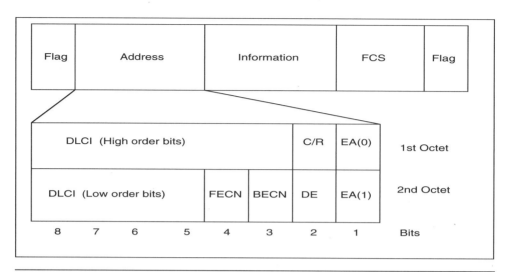

Figure 2-1   The format of the frame relay frame

- **Command response (CR)**   This bit is not used in most frame relay implementations.
- **Extended address (EA)**   This bit is used to indicate whether a 2-, 3-, or 4-byte header is being used. This bit is set to 1 in the last byte of the header.
- **Forward explicit congestion notification (FECN)**   This bit is used to tell the user receiving frame relay frames that congestion exists in the direction that the frame was sent.
- **Backward explicit congestion notification (BECN)**   This bit is used to tell the user receiving frame relay frames that congestion exists in the reverse direction that the frame was sent.
- **Discard eligible (DE)**   This bit can be set by either the frame relay Data Terminal Equipment (DTE) equipment (such as a router) or by the frame relay switch network. A frame with the DE bit set indicates that the frame can be discarded when the frame relay network becomes congested. Whether or not DE-flagged frames are discarded depends on how the frame relay network has been provisioned.
- **User data**   This field contains the actual user payload. The default Cisco frame relay frame size is 1,500 bytes for a synchronous serial interface. Most frame relay equipment can pass larger frames. The largest frame size is 8,192 bytes, although

many frame relay devices cannot pass a frame that large. The main disadvantage of using frames larger than 4KB is that the frame check sequence can no longer detect many types of data errors.

- **Frame check sequence (FCS)**   This is a 2-byte CRC that is calculated on the entire frame except the flags and the 2 bytes of FCS. A frame relay network will discard any frames that have a bad FCS. The FCS is only guaranteed for frame relay frames of 4KB or less; larger frames may not have their errors detected with the 2-byte CRC that frame relay provides.

Local Management Interface (LMI)

Frame relay provides a simple signaling protocol between the frame relay switch and the frame relay DTE (router). This signaling protocol is known as the local management interface (LMI).

The LMI signaling protocol provides for notification of the addition and deletion of PVCs as well as periodic keepalive messages between the frame relay switch and frame relay DTE.

LMI works in the following manner:

1. Every ten seconds the DTE requests status from the frame relay switch. This status request will be sent to the switch over one of two reserved DLCIs: 0 or 1,023 depending on which of the three LMI signaling protocols has been chosen.

2. The frame relay switch will respond to the status request with a status response. This exchange is referred to as a keepalive or aliveness check because its function is to tell both the DTE and the frame relay switch that there is still a communication path between them.

3. Every sixth status request from the DTE is sent as a full status request. A full status request is not only an aliveness check, but it also requests the frame relay switch to respond with a list of all DLCIs that have been defined on the port of the frame relay switch.

4. The frame relay switch responds with a list of all defined DLCIs on the particular frame relay switch port.

Both the DTE and the frame relay switch maintain individual sequence numbers during their exchanges. These sequence numbers can be used to determine if an LMI sequence has been lost.

Asynchronous Transfer Mode (ATM)

Asynchronous Transfer Mode (ATM) was developed as a high-speed networking technique for public networks capable of supporting many classes of traffic. ATM can support a wide array of traffic types such as voice, video, image, and various data traffic over a single physical connection.

ATM is a packet-switching technique that uses short fixed-length packets called cells. Fixed-length cells simplify the design of an ATM switch that enables high-switching speeds. The selection of a short fixed-length cell reduces the delay and, most significantly, the jitter (variance of delay) for delay-sensitive services such as voice and video. These short cell lengths enable the switches to know exactly where to parse the header and forward the cell onto its destination. With shared media networks using variable-length frames and conventional broadcast, the bridge or router doesn't know how many bytes are in each frame, thus introducing latency.

Using ATM, information to be sent is segmented into fixed-length cells, transported to, and reassembled at the destination. Because the length is fixed, the information can be transported in a predictable manner. This predictability accommodates different traffic types on the same network. The cell is divided into two main sections: the header and the payload. The payload (48 bytes) is the portion that carries the actual information—either voice, data, or video. The 5-byte header is the addressing mechanism.

ATM is a layered architecture that enables multiple services like voice, data, and video to be mixed over the same network. Three lower layers have been defined to implement the features of ATM. The adaptation layer ensures the appropriate service characteristics and divides all classes of data into the 48-byte payload that makes up the ATM cell. The ATM layer takes the data to be sent and adds the 5-byte header information that ensures the cell is sent on the right connection.

ATM Layers

The ATM protocol stack is composed of the following components:

- **Physical layer**   The ATM physical layer manages the medium-dependent transmission. It performs tasks such as
    - Converting the 53-byte ATM cell into an outgoing bit stream and converting an incoming bit stream to a 53-byte ATM cell
    - Keeping track of the ATM cell boundaries
    - Electrical and physical specifications
- **ATM layer**   The ATM layer is responsible for establishing connections and passing cells through the ATM network. To do this, it uses information in the header of each ATM cell. It performs tasks such as
    - Virtual path identifier (VPI) and virtual channel identifier (VCI) switching

- Cell multiplexing and demultiplexing
- Flow control
- Header error control
- Cell loss priority (CLP) processing
- Quality of service (QoS) support

- **ATM Adaptation Layer (AAL)**   The AAL is responsible for isolating higher-layer protocols from the details of the ATM processes. It performs tasks such as
  - Segmentation and reassembly of the data
  - Payload error control
  - End-to-end timing

ATM Cell Format

An ATM circuit is based on a connection-oriented, end-to-end link. Addressing information is contained in the ATM cell header in the form of a VPI and a VCI. A virtual channel can be thought of as a transport of cells. A virtual path is a logical grouping of virtual circuits.

ATM cells consist of a 5-byte header and 48-byte payload (Figure 2-2). The 5-byte ATM cell header contains information needed to switch the ATM cell to its next destination. The ATM cell header is examined and updated on a switch-by-switch basis.

The VPI is an 8-bit field that along with the VCI identifies the next destination of a cell as it passes through an ATM network towards its final destination.

Header	Payload
5 Bytes	48 Bytes

Figure 2-2   ATM cell format

Circuit Switching

Circuit switching is similar to point-to-point circuits in that the circuit is dedicated between two points. However, with circuit switching, the circuit is terminated after the data transmission is complete. This enables the carrier to reuse the bandwidth, providing greater efficiency in the core. ISDN is an example of a circuit-switched WAN technology.

Integrated Services Digital Network (ISDN)

Integrated Services Digital Network (ISDN) has been one of the fastest growing telecommunications technologies in the world. ISDN is a digital version of circuit-switched analog telephone lines and is provided by local phone companies or PTTs. This technology supports networks capable of carrying voice, data, video, and other advanced services to homes and businesses.

In data communications, a channel is a unidirectional conduit through which information flows. A channel can carry digital or analog signals comprising user data or network signaling information. In ISDN and time division multiplexing (TDM) environments, a channel is generally a time slot on a transmission facility and is full-duplex (bidirectional).

In today's telephone network, the local loop connection between the user and central office provides a single analog channel used for different types of information. First, the loop is used to carry signals between the user's equipment and the network. The telephone, for example, places a short circuit on the line to indicate that the handset has been taken off the hook. A dial tone from the network signals the user to enter the telephone number. Pulses or tones representing the dialed digits, busy signals, and ringing signals also appear over the local loop. Second, after the call is established, the loop carries user information, which may be voice, audio, video, or data, depending on the application. These two types of usage could be said to represent two logical channels: one for signaling and one for user services.

Organizations are interested in ISDN because of the types of services it provides and its potential for LAN-to-LAN, Internet, remote access, dial-backup, and telecommuting applications.

Basic Rate Interface

The Basic Rate Interface (BRI) comprises two B channels and one D channel designated 2B + D. The BRI D channel always operates at 16 Kbps. The BRI is typically used in one of two ways. First, it can provide ISDN access between a residential or business customer and the ISDN local equipment (LE). Alternatively, it can provide ISDN access between user equipment and an ISDN-compatible Private Branch Exchange (PBX) in a business environment. As a tariffed offering, the BRI can be ordered in configurations other than 2B + D, and other nomenclature may be encountered. If the BRI is to be used only for telephony and no data will be sent on the D channel, the configuration is sometimes called 2B + S (the D channel is for signaling only). If only a single B channel is required, a 1B + D or 1B + S arrangement may be ordered; packet data is allowed on the D channel in the former and not in the latter. Finally, if only low-speed (9.6-Kbps) packet data is required, a 0B + D configuration can be ordered. These configurations enable ISDN to be customized for customer applications and are priced differently based on the number of active channels. It should be noted that in all of these configurations, the interface's physical characteristics are the same; the only difference is in which channels have been activated by the LE and what type of traffic is allowed on the D channel.

The user data rate on the BRI is 144 Kbps (2×64 Kbps + 16 Kbps), although additional signaling for the physical connection requires that the BRI operate at a higher bit rate.

Primary Rate Interface

The Primary Rate Interface (PRI) also has a number of possible configurations. The most common configuration in North America and Japan is designated 23B + D, meaning that the interface comprises 23 B channels plus a single D channel operating at 64 Kbps. Optionally, the D channel on a given PRI may not be activated, enabling that time slot to be used as another B channel; this configuration is designated 24B. This PRI description is based on the T1 digital carrier. It operates at a bit rate of 1.544 Mbps, of which 1.536 Mbps is user data.

Also defined is a 30B + D PRI that comprises 30 B channels and 1 D channel. Based on the European E1 digital carrier, it operates at 2.048 Mbps, of which 1.984 Mbps is user data. The PRI contains more channels than a typical end-user device will use. The PRI is, in fact, primarily intended to provide access to the network by some sort of customer premises-switching equipment, such as a PBX, multiplexer, or host computer.

When a wideband application requires more throughput than that provided by a B channel, the PRI can be configured to provide H channel access. When this configuration is used, the number of available B channels decreases by the number of time slots used by the H channel(s). An example would be a videoconferencing system needing 384 Kbps (an H_0 channel) for a call. The supporting PRI would have extra bandwidth available for a D channel and 17 B channels. If the video system needed a channel, no B or D channel time slots would be available. This flexibility enables the PRI to act as a wideband access system and a narrowband access system, depending on the application active at any time. The same bandwidth (time slots) can be configured for different types of channels on demand.

Internet Protocol (IP)

The Internet Protocol (IP) is a network layer (layer 3) protocol that contains addressing information and some control information that enables packets to be routed through a network. IP is part of a suite of communications protocols better known as TCP/IP. This suite of protocols, which includes IP, was originally developed by the Department of Defense to enable dissimilar computers to communicate over a distance.

IP provides a connectionless, best-effort delivery service. When datagrams are transmitted from the source to the destination, it is possible that the datagrams could arrive at the destination in a different sequence from that in which they were sent. The IP layer does not ensure that the datagrams are delivered to the application in the destination host in the correct order. Nor does it make any attempt to ensure that the datagrams are delivered reliably to the destination. This form of delivering datagrams in the correct order is sequencing. Sequencing and reliability are functions of upper-layer protocols such as TCP. This makes IP more versatile to integrate onto a variety of hardware. Upper-layer protocols can add levels of reliability as needed by applications.

IP is used mostly in conjunction with upper-layer protocols, which provide additional upper-layer functions like guaranteed delivery of datagrams. IP uses best effort to deliver datagrams to the destination and is inherently unreliable. IP attempts to deliver the packet and does not make up for the faults encountered in its attempts. Any failure in the delivery of the datagram and the IP layer will not inform anyone. The upper-layer protocols must provide error discovery and recovery.

The IP protocol is not concerned with the type of data in the packet. All IP is concerned about is applying its control information to the segment received from the upper-layer protocol (presumably TCP or User Datagram Protocol [UDP]). This control information is called an IP header, which is used to deliver the datagram to some station on the network or Internet. The IP protocol does provide some means of control on how the hosts and routers should process transmitted or received packets or when an error should be generated and when an IP packet should be discarded. The IP datagram format contains an IP header and the IP data from upper-layer protocols (see Figure 2-3). The IP header is designed to accommodate the features of the IP layers.

An IP datagram is the unit of data exchanged between IP modules. In addition to data, a datagram includes a header with fields that provide the information used by IP routers to forward the packet through the network. The following is the format of the IP header.

The fields in Figure 2-3 can be described as follows:

- **Version**   This field specifies the IP protocol version and is used to verify that the sender, receiver, and gateways in between agree on the format of the datagram. The

32 bits

Version	IHL	TOS	Total Length	
Identification			Flags	Fragoffset
TTL		Protocol	HeaderChecksum	
Source Address				
Destination Address				
Options (+padding)				
Data (variable)				

Figure 2-3   Fourteen fields comprise an IP packet.

current version is 4 (IPv4). This field is 4 bits long. IP software is required to check the version field to ensure that the IP header format is the one it expects. If the software can process only version 4 datagrams, it rejects datagrams with a different value in the version field.

- **IHL**   This field specifies the length of the header (all fields but the IP data field). This field is also 4 bits long and is measured in 32-bit words, which is required because the IP header contains a variable-length options field. All other fields have a fixed length. If necessary, the options field is padded to accommodate a multiple of 32-bit words. The shortest IP header is 20 bytes. In this case, this field contains a 5 (20 bytes = 160 bits; 160 bits / 32 bits = 5).

- **Type of service (TOS)**   This field specifies how the datagram should be handled and informs the network of the QoS desired.

- **Total length**   This field specifies the length of the IP header and data in bytes. Because this field is 16 bits long, the data area of the IP datagram is a maximum of 65,535 bytes.

- **Identification, flags, and fragment offset**   Because packets transmitting from one network may be too large to transmit on another network, a TCP/IP router must be able to fragment the larger packet into smaller packets. For example, the IP layer has the functionality to transmit a packet from an FDDI network that supports a maximum size of 4,472 bytes to an Ethernet network that supports a maximum packet size of 1,518. These fields indicate how to fragment a forwarded datagram that is too large for the attached network. They control the fragmentation and reassembly of datagrams. The identification field contains a unique integer that identifies the datagram. Its primary purpose is to enable the destination to collect all fragments from a datagram. As a fragment arrives, the destination uses the identification field along with the source address to identify the datagram to which the fragment belongs. The host usually generates a unique value for identification by incrementing a global counter each time it creates a datagram. The host assigns the new counter value to the datagram's identification field. Any gateway that fragments the datagram copies the identification field into every fragment. The flags field controls fragmentation. It specifies whether the datagram may be fragmented (it is called the "do not fragment bit" because setting this bit to 1 specifies that the datagram should not be fragmented). The low-order flags bit specifies whether this is the last fragment (the fragment with the highest offset) and is referred to as the more fragment (MF) field. The fragment offset specifies the offset of this fragment in the original datagram, measured in units of 8 octets, starting at offset 0. To reassemble the datagram, the destination must obtain all fragments starting with offset 0 through the fragment with the highest offset. Fragments do not necessarily arrive in order, and there is no communication between the destination that receives fragments and the router that fragmented the datagram. If one or more fragments are lost, the entire datagram must be discarded.

- **Time to Live (TTL)**   The TTL field specifies how long in seconds the datagram is allowed to remain in the network. TTL should be decremented at each router by one. When the TTL field becomes 0, the TTL timer expires. The intent is that TTL expiration causes a datagram to be discarded by the router, but not by the destination host. Hosts acting as routers by forwarding datagrams must follow the same rules as native routers. TTL should not be confused with hop count but should be considered a countdown field.

- **Protocol**   This field is used to indicate the upper-layer protocol to receive the data. The protocol field is used for multiplexing/demultiplexing of data to upper-layer protocols. For example, when IP sees a value of 6, it knows that the IP header encapsulates TCP data and delivers the data to the TCP module. If IP sees a value of 17, it knows that this must be delivered to the UDP module. If IP sees a value of 89, it knows it must be delivered to Open Shortest Path First (OSPF).

- **Header checksum**   This field ensures the integrity of header values. Treating the header as a sequence of 16-bit integers (in network byte order), adding them together forms the IP checksum, which uses the one's complement arithmetic and then takes the one's complement result. This result is recomputed at each router because the TTL field is decremented at the router, and this results in the modification of the IP header.

- **Source and destination address**   The source and destination address fields contain the 32-bit addresses of the source and destination nodes. These addresses are sent in every IP datagram because the IP network is a connectionless network, and each IP datagram must include the sender and destination IP addresses. The routers use the destination IP address value to perform the routing for each IP datagram.

- **Options**   The options field indicates the security of a datagram, source routing information, and timestamp information. This field may or may not be present in a datagram; therefore, IP datagrams vary in length. The three classes of options are as follows:

  - Security, which specifies security level and distribution restrictions
  - Timestamp, which is a 32-bit value measured in milliseconds since midnight universal time or any other value if the high-order bit is set to 1
  - Special routing, which specifies host-discovered paths to other hosts or a specific path for the datagram to take

  The IP options must be handled by all IP nodes and optionally appear in IP datagrams near the IP header. Depending on the environment, the security option may be required in all datagrams.

- **Padding**   Padding is the last field in the IP header that represents octets containing 0, which may be needed to ensure that the Internet header extends to an exact multiple of 32 bits (recall that the header length field is specified in units of 32-bit words).

IP Addressing

One of the most important design decisions of an Internet engineer is the assignment of IP addresses: 32-bit numbers that identify Internet hosts. These numbers are placed in the IP packet header and are used to route packets to their destination.

IP Address Classes

In the original Internet routing scheme developed in the 1970s, sites were assigned addresses from one of these classes: A, B, or C (Figure 2-4). The address classes differ in size and number. Class A addresses are the largest, but few of them exist. Class C addresses are the smallest, but they are numerous. Classes D and E also are defined, but are used in protocols such as OSPF, Routing Information Protocol version 2 (RIPv2),

Summary of IP Address Classes

IP address Class	Format	High Order Bits	Address Range	Number of Hosts
A	N.H.H.H	0	1.0.0.0 to 126.0.0.0	16,777,214
B	N.N.H.H	1,0	128.1.0.0 to 191.254.0.0	65,543
C	N.N.N.H	1,1,0	192.0.1.0 to 223.255.254.0	254
D	N/A	1,1,1,0	224.0.0.0 to 239.255.255.255	
E	N/A	1,1,1,1	240.0.0.0 to 254.255.255.255	

Figure 2-4   IP address classes

and Enhanced Interior Gateway Routing Protocol (EIGRP) for multicast operation. Therefore, Classes D and E are not used in normal operation. To say that class-based IP addressing is still used would be true only in the loosest sense. Many addressing designs are still class based, but an increasing number can be explained using only the more general concept of classless interdomain routing (CIDR), which is backwards compatible with address classes.

The position of the first bit set to 0 (whether it is the first, second, third, or fourth bit) in the first octet of an IP address indicates the network class (A, B, C, or D). If no bit is set to 0, it is a Class E network. You specify IP addresses in dotted decimal notation. To express an IP address in dotted decimal notation, you convert each 8-bit octet of the IP address to a decimal number and separate the numbers by decimal points.

Internet routing used to work like this: A router receiving an IP packet extracted its destination address, which was classified (literally) by examining its first one to four bits. When the address' class had been determined, it was broken down into network and host bits. Routers ignored the host bits and only needed to match the network bits to find a route to the network. When a packet reached its target network, its host field was examined for final delivery.

IP Subnet Addressing

IP networks can be divided into smaller networks called subnetworks. Subnetting provides flexibility and more efficient use of network addresses. Subnetting, documented in RFC 950, originally referred to the subdivision of a class-based network into subnetworks, but now refers more generally to the subdivision of a CIDR block into smaller CIDR blocks. Subnetting enables single-routing entries to refer either to the larger block or to its individual constituents. This permits a single, general routing entry to be used through most of the Internet; more specific routes are required only for routers in the subnetted block.

IP Subnet Mask

A subnet address is created by taking bits from the host field and designating them as the subnet field. The number of bits used for the subnet field varies and is specified by the subnet mask. A subnet mask is a 32-bit number that determines how an IP address is split into network and host portions on a bitwise basis.

Fors example, 255.255.0.0 is a standard Class B mask because the first two bytes are all 1's (network) and the last two bytes are all 0's (host). In a subnetted network, the network portion is extended. For example, a subnet mask of 255.255.255.0 would subnet a Class B address space using its third byte. Using this scheme, the first two bytes of an IP address would identify the Class B network; the next byte would identify the subnet within that network; and the final byte would identify the individual host. Because subnet masks are used on a bit-by-bit basis, masks like 255.255.240.0 (4 bits of subnet, 12 bits of host) are perfectly normal.

Classless Interdomain Routing (CIDR)

Faced with the exhaustion of Class B address space and the explosion of routing table growth triggered by a flood of new Class Cs, IETF began implementing classless interdomain routing (CIDR) in the early 1990s. CIDR is documented in RFC 1518 and RFC 1519. The primary requirement for CIDR is the use of routing protocols that support it, such as RIPv2, OSPF version 2, and BGP version 4.

CIDR can be thought of as "subnetting on steroids." The subnetting mask, previously a magic number set in a computer's boot sequence, becomes an integral part of routing tables and protocols. A route is no longer an IP address broken down into network and host bits according to its class. A route is now a combination of address and mask. Not only can we break networks into subnets, but we can also combine networks into supernets, so long as they have a common network prefix. CIDR defines address assignment and aggregation strategies designed to minimize the size of top-level Internet routing tables.

Subnetting

In a traditional subnetted network, several restrictions apply, which have been lifted by CIDR. However, if older, non-CIDR routing protocols (such as RIPv1) are in use, these restrictions must still be observed.

- **Identical subnet masks**   Because non-CIDR routing updates do not include subnet masks, a router must assume that the subnet mask it has been configured with is valid for all subnets. Therefore, a single mask must be used for all subnets with a network. Different masks can be used for different networks. Based on this assumption, a router can exchange subnet routes with other routers within the network. Because the subnet masks are identical across the network, the routers interpret these routes in the same manner. However, routers not attached to the subnetted network cannot interpret these subnet routes because they lack the subnet mask. Therefore, subnet routes are not relayed to routers on other networks.

- **Contiguous subnets**   A subnetted network cannot be split into isolated portions. All the subnets must be contiguous, because routing information cannot be passed to nonmembers. Within a network, all subnets must be able to reach all other subnets without passing traffic through other networks.

Address Resolution Protocol (ARP) Architecture

Address Resolution Protocol (ARP) is used to resolve a layer 3 address to a layer 2 MAC address. It works by broadcasting a packet to all hosts attached to a LAN. The packet contains the IP address with which the sender is interested in communicating. Most hosts ignore the packet. The target machine, recognizing that the IP address in the packet matches its own, returns an answer. Hosts typically keep a cache of ARP responses based on the assumption that IP-to-hardware address mapping rarely changes.

ARP is transparent to bridging but not to routers. Bridges propagate ARP broadcasts like any other Ethernet broadcast and transparently bridge the replies. A router does not propagate ARP broadcasts because the router is a network level device, and Ethernet, Token Ring, FDDI, and ATM are data link protocols.

ARP: Frame Encapsulation

ARP is not an IP protocol in the sense that the ARP datagrams do not have IP headers. ARP does not use the services of IP because ARP messages do not leave the logical network and never need to be routed. ARP requests must be sent as broadcasts. An ARP request cannot be sent directly to the correct host. After all, the whole reason for sending an ARP request is that the source host does not know the destination host Ethernet address.

An Ethernet address of all 1's is used (FF.FF.FF.FF.FF.FF) as the broadcast address. By convention, every machine on Ethernet is required to pay attention to packets with this as a destination address. Every host listens to the broadcast ARP requests. When a machine sees an ARP request for itself, it is required to respond.

ARP: Header Format

ARP packets do not have a fixed-format header (Figure 2-5). To enable ARP to work with many different types of network technologies, the early header fields contain values that specify the lengths of succeeding fields. Therefore, ARP can be used with technologies that implement arbitrary physical addresses and arbitrary protocol addresses.

The following fields appear in the ARP packet format:

- **Hardware type** This field indicates the type of hardware used at the network level. For Ethernet, this value is 1.

- **Protocol type** This field indicates the protocol used at the network level.

- **Hardware address length** This field indicates the length of the hardware address in bytes. For Ethernet, this value is 6.

- **Protocol address space** This field indicates the length of the protocol address in bytes. For TCP/IP protocols, this value is 4.

- **Operation code** This field describes the function of this packet: ARP request or ARP response.

- **Sender's hardware address** This field is the hardware address of the sending station.

- **Sender's protocol address** This field is the Internet address of the sending station.

0	8	15 16	31
Hardware Type		Protocol Type	
HLEN	PLEN	Operation	
Sender HA (octets 0-3)			
Sender HA (octets 4-5)		Sender IP (octets 0-1)	
Sender IP (octets 2-3)		Target HA (octets 0-1)	
Target HA (octets 2-5)			
Target IP (octets 0-3)			

Figure 2-5 ARP packet format

- **Target hardware address**   When making an ARP request, this field is the destination hardware address. The response carries both the destination machine's hardware and Internet address.

- **Target protocol address**   When making an ARP request, this field is the destination Internet address. The response carries both the destination machine's hardware and Internet address.

Reverse ARP

Reverse ARP (RARP) is a fairly simple bootstrapping protocol that enables a workstation to broadcast using its Ethernet address and expects a server to reply, telling it its IP address. A machine's Internet address is usually kept on its secondary storage where the operating system can find it at startup. How does a diskless workstation determine its Internet address? The diskless machine must resort to using physical addressing to broadcast a request to a server on the local network. The diskless machine uniquely identifies itself to the server by using its physical address (Ethernet address). We make the assumption that the server has secondary storage that contains a database of Internet addresses. The requesting machine waits until it receives responses from one or more servers. After the machine learns its Internet address, it can communicate across the Internet.

Diskless machines use RARP to request a server to supply its Internet address. This protocol is adapted from the ARP protocol and uses the same message format. Like an ARP message, an RARP message is sent from one machine to another encapsulated in the data portion of an Ethernet frame.

Proxy ARP

Proxy ARP can assist machines on a subnet to reach remote subnets without having either routing or default gateways configured. Proxy ARP is a technique that can be used by routers to handle traffic between hosts that don't expect to use a router. Probably the most common case of its use would be the gradual subnetting of a larger network. Those hosts not yet converted to the new system expect to transmit directly to hosts now placed behind a router.

A router using proxy ARP recognizes ARP requests for hosts on the other side of the router that cannot reply for themselves. The router answers for those addresses with an ARP reply that matches the remote IP address with the router's Ethernet address.

Inverse ARP

Inverse ARP provides dynamic address mapping between a protocol address and a specific DLCI. Frame relay inverse ARP is used to request the next-hop protocol address for a specific connection, given its known DLCI. When a frame relay circuit is initialized, the router attached does not have any address information except its own IP address. The router needs a way to determine the IP address of the far-end router on the particular DLCI.

The router accomplishes this by sending an inverse ARP request out of each local DLCI that is defined on the circuit. The inverse ARP request travels to the far-end router where it is received and replied to. The router that initiated the inverse ARP request receives the reply. This reply contains the IP address of the far-end router. Inverse ARP responses are stored as an address-to-DLCI mapping table on the router. This table is used to supply the next-hop protocol address or the DLCI for outgoing traffic. This is similar to how ARP is used to map a MAC address to the known IP address.

Internet Control Message Protocol (ICMP)

Internet Control Message Protocol (ICMP) is used to provide feedback about problems that occur in the network. In a connectionless environment, each host and router operates independently in the routing and delivery of IP datagrams. Because problems can arise in the transmission of datagrams, a way is needed to provide feedback. ICMP provides this mechanism. ICMP uses the IP protocol for delivery across the network. Datagrams carrying ICMP messages are routed exactly like datagrams carrying information for users. No additional reliability is provided for these error messages. As a result, error messages themselves may be lost or discarded. To avoid the infinite regress of messages about messages, no ICMP messages are sent about ICMP messages. Thus, ICMP messages are not generated for errors that result from the loss or discarding of datagrams carrying ICMP messages.

ICMP Encapsulation

Although ICMP is, in effect, at the same level as IP, it is a user of IP. Each ICMP message travels across the Internet in the data portion of an IP datagram.

An ICMP message is constructed and then passed onto IP. IP encapsulates the message with an IP header and then transmits it over the physical network to the destination host or router. The reason IP is used to deliver the ICMP messages is that the messages may need to travel across several different physical networks to reach their final destination. Therefore, they cannot be delivered by the physical network transport alone.

The ultimate destination of the ICMP message is not a user process on the destination machine but the Internet software on that machine. The IP software module on the destination machine handles the problem itself without passing the message to the application's program whose datagram generated the problem.

Transmission Control Protocol (TCP)
Protocol Overview

The Transmission Control Protocol (TCP) makes up for IP's deficiencies by providing reliable, stream-oriented connections that hide most of IP's shortcomings. With stream data transfer, TCP delivers an unstructured stream of bytes identified by sequence numbers.

TCP offers reliability by providing connection-oriented, end-to-end reliable packet delivery through an internetwork. It does this through sequence numbers that are used to coordinate which data has been transmitted and received. Each TCP packet contains the starting sequence number of the data in that packet, and the sequence number (called the acknowledgment number) of the last byte received from the remote peer. With this information, a sliding-window protocol is implemented. Forward and reverse sequence numbers are completely independent, and each TCP peer must track both its own sequence numbering and the numbering being used by the remote peer. TCP retransmits any bytes that are not acknowledged within a specified time.

The reliability mechanism of TCP enables devices to deal with lost, delayed, duplicate, or misread packets. A time-out mechanism enables devices to detect lost packets and request retransmission. When a host transmits a TCP packet to its peer, it must wait a period of time for an acknowledgment. If the reply does not come within the expected period, the packet is assumed to have been lost, and the data is retransmitted. All modern TCP implementations monitor the normal exchange of data packets and develop an estimate of how long is too long. This process is called round-trip time (RTT) estimation. RTT estimates are one of the most important performance parameters in a TCP exchange, especially when you consider that on an indefinitely large transfer, all TCP implementations eventually drop packets and retransmit them, no matter how good the quality of the link. If the RTT estimate is too low, packets are retransmitted unnecessarily; if the estimate is too high, the connection can sit idle while the host waits to timeout.

TCP offers efficient flow control, which means that when sending acknowledgments back to the source, the receiving TCP process indicates the highest sequence number it can receive without overflowing its internal buffers. TCP uses a number of control flags to manage the connection field in each packet it transmits. This field contains the amount of data that may be transmitted into the buffer. If this number falls to 0, the remote TCP can send no more data. It must wait until buffer space becomes available, and it receives a packet announcing a nonzero window size. Sometimes the buffer space is too small. This happens when the network's bandwidth-delay product exceeds the buffer size. The simplest solution is to increase the buffer, but for extreme cases, the protocol itself becomes the bottleneck (because it doesn't support a large enough window size).

TCP provides full-duplex operation, which means that the TCP processes can both send and receive at the same time. No matter what the particular application, TCP almost always operates full-duplex. The algorithms described operate in both directions in an almost completely independent manner. It's sometimes useful to think of a TCP session as two independent bytestreams traveling in opposite directions. No TCP mechanism exists to associate data in the forward and reverse bytestreams. Only during connection start and close sequences can TCP exhibit asymmetric behavior (that is, data transfer in the forward direction but not in the reverse, or vice versa).

Finally, TCP's multiplexing means that numerous simultaneous upper-layer conversations can be multiplexed over a single connection.

TCP Header Format

TCP segments are sent as IP datagrams. The IP header carries several information fields, including the source and destination host addresses, as seen in the previous section. The TCP header follows the Internet header, supplying information specific to the TCP protocol. This division enables the existence of host-level protocols other than TCP.

The following fields appear in the TCP header (Figure 2-6):

- **Source port and destination port**   A 16-bit field that identifies points at which upper-layer source and destination processes receive TCP services.

- **Sequence number**   A 32-bit field that specifies the number assigned to the first byte of data in the current message. In the connection-establishment phase, this

Source port			Destination port	
Sequence number				
Acknowledgment number				
offset	Res	Flags	Window	
Checksum			Urgent pointer	
Options (+padding)				
Data (variable)				

Figure 2-6   Twelve fields comprise a TCP packet.

field also can be used to identify an initial sequence number to be used in an upcoming transmission.

- **Acknowledgment number**   A 32-bit field that contains the sequence number of the next byte of data the sender of the packet expects to receive.

- **Data offset**   A 4-bit field that indicates the number of 32-bit words in the TCP header. This field indicates where the data begins. The TCP header (even one including options) is an integral number of 32-bits.

- **Reserved**   A 6-bit field that is reserved for future use. This must be zero.

- **Control bits**   A 6-bit field that carries a variety of control information, including the SYN and ACK bits used for connection establishment, and the FIN bit used for connection termination.

  (The following illustration shows the control bits from left to right.)

URG	Urgent Pointer field significant
ACK	Acknowledgment field significant
PSH	Push Function
RST	Reset the connection
SYN	Synchronize sequence numbers
FIN	No more data from sender

- **Window**   A 16-bit field that specifies the size of the sender's receive window (that is, the buffer space available for incoming data). This is the number of data octets beginning with the one indicated in the acknowledgment field, which the sender of this segment is willing to accept.

- **Checksum**   A 16-bit field that indicates whether the header was damaged in transit The checksum field is the 16-bit one's complement of the one's complement sum of all 16-bit words in the header and text. If a segment contains an odd number of header and text octets to be checksummed, the last octet is padded on the right with 0's to form a 16-bit word for checksum purposes. The pad is not transmitted as part of the segment. While computing the checksum, the checksum field itself is replaced with 0's. The checksum also covers a 96-bit pseudoheader conceptually prefixed to the TCP header. This pseudoheader contains the source address, the destination address, the protocol, and TCP length. This gives the TCP protection against misrouted segments. This information is carried in the IP and is transferred across the TCP/network interface in the arguments or results of calls by the TCP on the IP.

- **Urgent pointer** A 16-bit field that indicates the current value of the urgent pointer as a positive offset from the sequence number in this segment. The urgent pointer points to the sequence number of the octet following the urgent data. This field is interpreted only in segments with the URG control bit set.

- **Options** A variable-length field that specifies various TCP options.

- **Padding** A variable-length field that is used to ensure that the TCP header ends and that data begins on a 32-bit boundary. The padding is composed of 0's.

User Datagram Protocol (UDP)

The User Datagram Protocol (UDP) is defined in RFC 768. This protocol makes available a datagram mode of packet-switched computer communication in the environment of an interconnected set of computer networks. UDP is used by applications that need only a connectionless, best-effort transport service. UDP assumes that the IP is used as the underlying protocol. UDP provides a procedure for application programs to send messages to other programs with a minimum of protocol mechanism. UDP is transaction-oriented, and delivery and duplicate protection are not guaranteed. The major uses for this protocol are to support the following application-level protocols: domain name service (DNS), Trivial File Transfer Protocol (TFTP), NetBIOS name and datagram service, and Simple Network Management Protocol (SNMP).

Because UDP uses the services of IP, it provides the same connectionless delivery service as the IP. UDP does not flow control the rate of information exchange between machines; UDP does not use acknowledgements to guarantee the arrival of messages; and UDP does not order incoming messages. It provides a way to send a message with a high probability of arrival, but without a specific guarantee. This service is termed unreliable because the destination host does not acknowledge a receipt of a message.

To use UDP, the application must supply the IP address and port number of the destination application. A port is an abstraction to give transport protocols like UDP and TCP the capability of handling communications between multiple hosts. Ports enable a communication to be uniquely identified by a positive integer.

UDP and the ISO Model

UDP provides one additional capability beyond those provided by IP. Although IP enables communication between two hosts across the Internet, UDP creates a mechanism to distinguish among multiple destinations within a given host, which enables multiple application programs executing on a given host to send and receive datagrams independently. Think of the ultimate destination within a machine as a collection of destination points, or ports. Each port is identified by a positive integer. The protocol software in each destination machine queues the packets arriving for a particular port until an application process extracts them.

To communicate with another machine, the source station must know the Internet address of the destination machine, and the port number of the destination process within that machine. The source station also supplies one of its own port numbers to which replies may be sent. Depending on the application, the destination machine may or may not send a reply.

UDP Header Encapsulation

The complete UDP message, including the header and data, is encapsulated in an IP datagram as it travels across the Internet. The Ethernet layer is responsible for transferring data between two hosts or routers on the same physical network. The IP layer is responsible for transferring data across routers between hosts on the Internet. The following is the format of the UDP header (Figure 2-7).

The following describes the fields of the UDP packet.

- **Source port** This field is optional. When used, it indicates the port of the sending process, as well as the port to which a reply should be addressed. If the transmitting host does not supply a source port, this field should have a value of 0.

- **Destination port** This field is used to demultiplex datagrams among the processes in the destination machine.

- **Length** This field is the combined length of the UDP header and data and is expressed in octets.

32 Bits	
Source port	Destination port
Length	Checksum

Figure 2-7 The UDP packet consists of four fields.

- **Checksum**   The UDP checksum is optional. A value of 0 indicates that the checksum has not been computed. Because IP does not compute a checksum on the data portion of the datagram (the IP checksum is based only on the IP header), the UDP checksum provides the only means to determine whether the data has arrived without errors.

The UDP checksum is calculated from the fields used to create a pseudoheader. This pseudoheader is composed of fields that are part of the actual IP and UDP headers. The pseudoheader contains the source address, destination address, and protocol fields from the IP header. It also contains the UDP length and the UDP data fields. The data field is padded with a 0 octet (if necessary) to ensure the object is an exact multiple of 2 octets. (There must be an exact number of octets in the pseudoheader. For example, if the data field contains 13 octets, it must be padded with one extra octet of 0's to make it even.)

This checksum gives protection against misrouted datagrams. We know that a datagram has reached the proper location if it is delivered to the correct destination machine on the Internet and to the proper port within that machine. The UDP header specifies only the destination port number, but does not specify the destination Internet address. The destination Internet address can be obtained only from the IP header. Thus, to verify datagram arrival, the checksum must span fields in both the IP and the UDP headers.

To verify the checksum, the receiving machine must extract the required fields from the IP header, assemble them into the pseudoheader format, and compute the checksum. If the checksums agree, the datagram has reached the correct port on the destination machine.

Questions

1. The fragmented offset field in an IP header is used to _____.
   a. Identify that the packet is fragmented.
   b. Specify special handling of the packet.
   c. Specify the offset from the beginning of the header to the beginning of the fragment.
   d. Specify the number of fragments in a packet.

2. Which of the following fields in an IP packet are protected by the IP header checksum?

   a. The TTL field

   b. The TCP or UDP payload

   c. The entire IP packet

   d. Only the first 12 octets of the IP header

3. If a single IP fragment is lost during transmission, _____.

   a. Only the lost fragment must be resent.

   b. The entire packet must be resent.

   c. Only the lost fragment and prior fragments must be resent, not the entire packet.

   d. Only the lost fragment and subsequent fragments must be resent, not the entire packet.

4. Cisco's **trace route** command relies on what field in the IP header?

   a. The TOS field

   b. The TTL field

   c. Cisco's **trace route** command does not use any fields in the IP header.

   d. Cisco's **trace route** command relies on the TCP payload.

5. Which of the following is true regarding an IP address? (multiple answers)

   a. An IP address is 32 bits in length.

   b. The network and host portion can vary in size within the 32-bit boundary.

   c. Looking at the first octet, you can determine the class of the network.

   d. Class B addresses always have their two left-most bit set to 1.

   e. All of the above

6. IP is a _____ protocol.

   a. Connection-oriented

   b. Media access

   c. Connectionless

   d. Transport layer

7. _____ provides a reliable delivery service.

   a. UDP

   b. IP

   c. TCP

   d. ICMP

8. _____ provides dynamic address mappings between a protocol address and a specific DLCI.
   a. Frame relay map command
   b. ARP
   c. Reverse ARP
   d. Inverse ARP

9. Each IPv4 datagram includes a _____ source address.
   a. 64-byte
   b. 64-bit
   c. 32-bit
   d. 32-byte

10. IP datagrams are _____ if the receiver does not acknowledge them.
    a. Discarded
    b. Retransmitted
    c. Fragmented
    d. None of the above

11. The _____ field in the TCP header is used to tell the receiver the next byte of data that the sender of the packet expects to receive.
    a. Window
    b. Fragment offset
    c. Options
    d. Acknowledgment number

12. Which of the following fields are used in the TCP handshake process? (multiple answers)
    a. Push
    b. ACK
    c. SYN
    d. Urgent

13. What is the subnet address for the following host address and mask combination of 152.32.1.125 255.255.255.224?
    a. 152.32.1.95
    b. 152.32.1.96
    c. 152.32.1.120
    d. 152.32.1.124

14. What is the directed broadcast address for the host address and mask combination of 172.32.10.120 255.255.255.128?
    a. 172.32.10.127
    b. 172.32.10.255
    c. 255.255.255.255
    d. None of the above

15. A Class B address with a mask of 255.255.248.0 will give how many subnets and how many hosts per subnet (without using subnet zero)?
    a. 30 subnets with 2,046 hosts each
    b. 62 subnets with 1,022 hosts each
    c. 14 subnets with 4,094 hosts each
    d. 2 subnets with 16,382 hosts each

16. Class D IP addresses range from _____.
    a. 224.0.0.1 to 239.255.255.255
    b. 224.0.0.0 to 239.255.255.255
    c. 224.0.0.0 to 255.255.255.255
    d. 224.0.0.1 to 255.255.255.255

17. The multicast group 224.0.0.1 is _____.
    a. A well-known multicast group address, which means all routers on the subnet
    b. A well-known multicast group address, which means all systems on the subnet
    c. A well-known multicast group address used by RIPv2
    d. A well-known multicast group address used by NTP

18. The multicast group 224.0.0.2 is _____.
    a. A well-known multicast group address, which means all routers on the subnet
    b. A well-known multicast group address, which means all systems on the subnet
    c. A well-known multicast group address used by RIPv2
    d. A well-known multicast group address used by NTP

19. Which of the following is not a valid subnet mask?
    a. 255.0.0.0
    b. 255.255.255.254
    c. 255.255.255.255
    d. 255.255.255.252

20. Which of the following is false regarding an IP address?

    a. An IP address is 32 bits long.

    b. The network and host portions of the address may vary in size.

    c. The network and host portions are fixed length.

    d. None of the above

21. Which of the following is not part of the UDP header?

    a. Source address

    b. Length

    c. Urgent pointer

    d. Checksum

22. Which of the following are not valid flags in an IP header? (multiple answers)

    a. DF

    b. MF

    c. URG

    d. PSH

23. The first octet rule _____.

    a. Is a way to determine the class to which an IP address belongs by looking at the first octet of the address

    b. Is used to determine how the IP address should be subnetted

    c. Does not work when VLSM is used

    d. None of the above

24. The options field in an IP header is _____.

    a. A mandatory field

    b. Fixed length

    c. Primarily used for testing

    d. Never used

25. Which of the following are flags in the TCP header? (multiple answers)

    a. PSH

    b. RST

    c. URG

    d. ACK

    e. DF

26. The 16-bit checksum in the TCP header is calculated on _____.

    a. The IP header

    b. The TCP header

c. The TCP header and payload

d. The IP header and payload

27. The checksum in the UDP header is _____.

   a. Optional

   b. Calculated on both the UDP header and payload

   c. Calculated on the UDP header

   d. A and B

   e. A and C

   f. None of the above—there is no checksum in UDP.

28. The _____ field is carried in the IP header and specifies the number of routing hops allowed before a datagram is discarded.

   a. Window

   b. TTL

   c. Checksum

   d. Urgent

29. IP datagrams are _____ in length.

   a. Fixed

   b. Short

   c. Long

   d. Variable

30. ARP uses the _____ protocol.

   a. TCP

   b. UDP

   c. IP

   d. A and C

   e. None of the above

31. ICMP uses the _____ protocol.

   a. IP

   b. TCP

   c. UDP

   d. A and B

   e. None of the above

32. Which of the following is an example of a connection-oriented service?

   a. Telnet and FTP

   b. Telnet and SNMP

    c. FTP and TFTP

    d. None of the above

33. A router sends a _____ ICMP message to the source station if it cannot accept data at that time.

    a. Time exceeded

    b. Host unreachable

    c. Source quench

    d. Buffer overflow

34. A router generates a/an _____ ICMP message if it does not know how to reach a given destination.

    a. Information needed

    b. Source quench

    c. Host unreachable

    d. No route to host

35. With frame relay, the LMI type should agree _____.

    a. Between end devices

    b. Between the end device and the switch

    c. Between switches

    d. It does not need to agree; it is local only.

36. CIR refers to _____.

    a. The minimum bandwidth available on the frame relay link

    b. The maximum bandwidth available on the frame relay link

    c. The guaranteed bandwidth available on the frame relay link

    d. None of the above

37. LMI is the _____.

    a. X.25 signaling format

    b. ISDN signaling format

    c. Signaling interface between the frame relay DTE and DCE

    d. Signaling interface between frame relay switches

38. The 2-byte address field in frame relay is broken into _____.

    a. 10 bits for circuit identification and 6 bits for congestion management

    b. 8 bits for circuit identification and 8 bits for congestion management

    c. 6 bits for circuit identification and 10 bits for congestion management

    d. 12 bits for circuit identification and 4 bits for congestion management

39. Which of the following is not used by frame relay for congestion control?

   a. FECN

   b. BECN

   c. DLCI

   d. DE

40. Frame relay networks are considered to be _____.

   a. Non-broadcast multiple access

   b. Broadcast multiple access

   c. Shared media

   d. None of the above

41. A frame relay switch makes forwarding decisions based on the _____.

   a. Network layer address

   b. Data link address

   c. Physical address

   d. Application layer address

42. The end node addressing for frame relay is a/an _____.

   a. BECN

   b. FECN

   c. IP address

   d. DLCI

43. The primary differences between frame relay and X.25 are _____. (multiple answers)

   a. Media types

   b. Supported speeds

   c. Error correction and flow control

   d. Network protocols supported

44. Which of the following is false?

   a. The frame relay DTE regularly transmits status inquiries and the network answers with status report messages.

   b. The network regularly transmits status inquiries and the DTE answers with status report messages.

   c. LMI enables the end station to learn about the deletion of a PVC.

   d. LMI enables the end station to learn about the availability of a PVC.

45. The frame relay data link provides for all of the following except _____.

    a. Addressing

    b. Flow control

    c. Sequencing and acknowledgements

    d. Error detection

46. Which of the following is false?

    a. The DLCI addressing space allows for 1,024 addresses for virtual circuit addressing.

    b. Because of signaling and management, only 992 addresses are available for virtual circuit addressing.

    c. DLCI 0 is reserved for LMI.

    d. EA enables the DLCI header to be extended, creating more address space.

47. The valid fields in a frame relay header are _____.

    a. Flag, address, data, and FCS

    b. Flag, control, address, data, and FCS

    c. Flag, address, control, management, data, and FCS

    d. Flag, data, address, and control

48. Which of the following addresses is not an RFC 1918 reserved address?

    a. 10.1.1.1

    b. 192.168.1.1

    c. 172.32.1.1

    d. 172.16.1.1

49. Which of the following subnet masks gives you two usable host addresses?

    a. 255.255.255.248

    b. 255.255.255.250

    c. 255.255.255.252

    d. 255.255.255.255

50. How many subnets are available (without using the subnet zero command) if a Class C address has 6 bits of subnetting?

    a. 62

    b. 63

    c. 2

    d. 3

51. Which of the following is/are true about ARP?
    a. In an ARP request packet, the destination address is set to all 1's.
    b. In an ARP request packet, the destination address is the MAC address of the default gateway.
    c. The target IP address is set to all 1's.
    d. The target IP address is the address of the device that the stations want to receive a MAC address for.
    e. None of the above

52. Which of the following is true regarding gratuitous ARP? (multiple answers)
    a. A gratuitous ARP is when a host issues an ARP request with its own IP address as the target address.
    b. A gratuitous ARP may be used for duplicate address checks.
    c. A gratuitous ARP may be used to advertise a new data link identifier.
    d. A gratuitous ARP is the same as reverse ARP.
    e. All of the above

53. Which of the following is false regarding proxy ARP?
    a. The router responds with the MAC address of the destination station.
    b. The router responds with its own MAC address.
    c. Proxy ARP is when an intermediate device such as a router sends an ARP response on behalf of an end node to the requesting host.
    d. Proxy ARP is not needed if the host is configured with a default gateway.

54. The primary disadvantage of using proxy ARP is what?
    a. It is difficult to configure and troubleshoot.
    b. Proxy ARP results in more ARP traffic on the LAN.
    c. Proxy ARP can cause black-hole routing.
    d. None of the above

55. The port number of an application coupled with the IP address of the host that the application resides on is called what?
    a. Header
    b. SP pair
    c. Socket
    d. Window

56. Which of the following is false regarding reverse ARP?
    a. It is used for hosts that do not know their IP address at startup.
    b. It is being replaced by DHCP.

    c. It is used to map a MAC address to a known IP address.

    d. It cannot be routed off the local data link.

57. RouterA and RouterB are connected to the same Ethernet. HostA also on the same Ethernet is configured to use RouterA as its default gateway. HostA sends a packet to RouterA, which sees that the destination is reachable through RouterB via the Ethernet interface. What does RouterA do?

    a. It drops the packet and sends an ICMP redirect to HostA informing it to use RouterB in the future to reach the particular destination.

    b. It forwards the packet to RouterB.

    c. It forwards the packet to RouterB and sends an ICMP redirect to HostA informing it to use RouterB in the future to reach the particular destination.

    d. It drops the packet and sends an ICMP host unreachable message to HostA.

58. Which of the following is false?

    a. TCP is a connection-oriented service.

    b. TCP uses windowing to regulate the flow of packets.

    c. The 16-bit TCP checksum is calculated on the header and payload.

    d. The urgent pointer is used only when the URG flag is set and is added to the sequence number to indicate the beginning of the urgent data.

59. Which of the following is false?

    a. A UDP header is smaller than a TCP header.

    b. Applications that send short bursts of data can get better performance with UDP because no time is spent setting up a connection.

    c. Unlike TCP, UDP does not have a checksum.

    d. UDP provides connectionless best-effort packet delivery.

60. The OSI reference model divides networking activity into how many layers?

    a. Four

    b. Five

    c. Three

    d. Seven

61. Which layer handles general network access, flow control, and recovery from network failures?

    a. Network

    b. Physical

    c. Data link

    d. Transport

62. Which layer determines the route that a packet will take from sender to receiver?
  a. Network
  b. Physical
  c. Data link
  d. Transport

63. The subnet mask of an IP address _____.
  a. Enables automated IP address configuration
  b. Enables duplicate IP address to be used in different domains
  c. Defines which part of the address specifies the network and which part address specifies the host portion
  d. Is carried in all distance vector routing updates

64. Which is true about CSMA/CD?
  a. It is used by Token Ring as a media access scheme.
  b. Network devices access the physical medium based on possession of a token.
  c. With CSMA/CD, it is impossible to have a collision on the LAN.
  d. CSMA/CD stations can detect collisions, so they know when they must retransmit.

65. Which of the following is false?
  a. Token Ring is deterministic.
  b. Collisions cannot occur in Token Ring networks.
  c. The receiving station removes the frame from the ring.
  d. If early token release is supported, a new token can be released when frame transmission is complete.

66. The active monitor on a Token Ring _____.
  a. Acts as a centralized source of timing information for other ring stations
  b. Removes continuously circulating frames from the ring
  c. Is selected based on the MAC address
  d. All of the above
  e. None of the above

67. The three-way handshake in TCP is not used to _____.
  a. Synchronize both ends of a connection.
  b. Enable both sides to agree upon initial sequence numbers.
  c. Ensure that both sides are ready to transmit and receive data.
  d. Ensure that both sides have the same window.

68. TCP sliding window _____. (multiple answers)
  a. Only permits one packet to be sent at a time
  b. Provides flow control
  c. Is established during connection setup and cannot change for the life of the connection
  d. Enables hosts to send multiple bytes or packets before waiting for an acknowledgment

69. Which of the following is not an ICMP error message?
  a. Destination unreachable
  b. Time exceeded
  c. Source quench
  d. Keepalive

70. A type 2 beacon in Token Ring indicates that _____.
  a. A station is sending claim tokens, but is not seeing them come back around the ring.
  b. A station is seeing an upstream neighbor transmitting all of the time.
  c. There is a physical break in the ring topology.
  d. None of the above
  e. All of the above

71. A router is being used as a translation bridge between a Token Ring network and an Ethernet network. Host X on the Token Ring sends a packet to Host Y on the Ethernet. The source MAC address of the packet is 4000.A089.0002. How would the MAC address be interpreted in an Ethernet environment?
  a. 2000.980A.0004
  b. 0040.89A0.2000
  c. 0200.0591.0040
  d. 4000.A089.0002

72. Which of the following is false?
  a. Frame relay is a packet-switched technology.
  b. Frame relay uses fixed-length packets.
  c. Frame relay uses BECN and FECN for flow control.
  d. Virtual circuits provide a bidirectional communications path from one DTE device to another.

73. If the FECN bit is set in the frame relay header, which of the following can be said?

   a. The frame experienced congestion in the path opposite of the frame transmission.

   b. The frame experienced congestion in the path and was discarded.

   c. The frame experienced congestion in the path from the source to the destination.

   d. The frame has lower importance than other frames.

74. Which of the following is false?

   a. Frame relay inverse ARP is used to map between a specific protocol address and a specific DLCI.

   b. Inverse ARP is enabled by default on Cisco routers.

   c. Inverse ARP is not required on point-to-point interfaces.

   d. When running DECnet over frame relay, inverse ARP is not used.

75. In the following illustration, PC A transmits a packet to PC B. The packet is errored in transit from R1 to R2. Who retransmits the packet?

   a. PC A

   b. R2

   c. R1

   d. None of the above

76. In the following illustration, PC A transmits a packet to PC B. The packet is errored when it arrives at R2. Who retransmits the packet?

   a. PC A

   b. R1

   c. R2

   d. None of the above—R2 cannot detect if the packet is errored.

77. Which of the following is/are true about X.25?
    a. The X.25 protocol suite maps to the lowest three layers of the OSI reference model.
    b. X.25 supports both switched and permanent virtual circuits.
    c. X.25 provides windowing and retransmission of lost data.
    d. All of the above
    e. None of the above

78. Which of the following is not a circuit-switched technology?
    a. ISDN
    b. DSL
    c. Analog dial
    d. None of the above

79. Which of the following is not a packet-switched technology?
    a. Frame relay
    b. X.25
    c. HDLC
    d. None of the above

80. Which of the following is/are true about ISDN BRI?
    a. BRI B channels are used only for voice; data is carried on the D channel only.
    b. The D channel is used for control and signaling data and cannot support user data.
    c. With framing control and other overhead, the total bit rate is 192 Kbps.
    d. The service offers 23 B channels and 1 D channel.
    e. None of the above

81. The primary difference between ISDN BRI-U and an analog line is what?
    a. ISDN BRI-U requires a four-wire local loop, whereas analog requires only a two-wire local loop.
    b. ISDN is digital.
    c. ISDN cannot support voice.
    d. None of the above

82. Which of the following is not true about virtual circuits?
    a. A virtual circuit is a logical circuit.
    b. Virtual circuits can be permanent or switched.
    c. A dedicated physical circuit is established.
    d. Virtual circuits are used in X.25.

83. The transport layer is responsible for _____.
    a. Routing datagrams between hosts
    b. Encapsulating the IP datagrams into frames
    c. End-to-end data integrity
    d. None of the above
    e. All of the above

84. Which ATM layer is responsible for multiplexing and demultiplexing cells of different virtual connections?
    a. ATM physical layer
    b. ATM layer
    c. ATM Adaptation Layer
    d. Both A and C

85. The ATM protocol consists of which of the following functional layers?
    a. ATM physical layer
    b. ATM layer
    c. ATM Adaptation Layer
    d. Data link layer
    e. All of the above except D
    f. A and C

86. Which ATM layer is responsible for keeping track of ATM cell boundaries and packaging cells into the appropriate type of frame for the physical medium transport?
    a. ATM physical layer
    b. ATM layer
    c. ATM Adaptation Layer
    d. Data link layer

87. Which ATM Adaptation Layer is best suited for transporting voice and video?
    a. AAL 5
    b. AAL 4
    c. AAL 1
    d. AAL 3 and 4

88. Which ATM layer is responsible for segmentation and reassembly?
    a. ATM physical layer
    b. ATM layer
    c. ATM Adaptation Layer
    d. All of the above

89. Which ATM layer is responsible for cell delineation?

   a. ATM physical layer

   b. ATM layer

   c. ATM Adaptation Layer

   d. All of the above

90. ATM UNI is between _____.

   a. Two end stations

   b. The end station and the ATM switch

   c. Two ATM switches

   d. None of the above

91. Which of the following is true?

   a. A virtual path is a logical grouping of virtual circuits.

   b. ATM cells consist of 5 bytes of header information and 48 bytes of payload data.

   c. The VPI and VCI fields of the cell header identify the next network segment that a cell needs to transmit on its way to its final destination.

   d. B and C

   e. All of the above

92. On a PPP link, what is the order of operation?

   a. NCP negotiation, LCP negotiation, and authentication

   b. LCP negotiation, NCP negotiation, and authentication

   c. LCP negotiation, authentication, and NCP negotiation

   d. NCP negotiation, authentication, and LCP negotiation

93. Which of the following is/are not the responsibility of the LCP in PPP?

   a. Detection of looped-back links

   b. Assignment and management of IP addresses

   c. Termination of the link

   d. Authentication

94. In a MAC address, the first _____ bits identify the vendor.

   a. 8

   b. 12

   c. 24

   d. 48

95. TCP slow start provides _____.

    a. Flow control by increasing the TCP window size only after an ACK is received

    b. Error detection and correction

    c. Flow control by increasing the TCP window size only after two consecutive ACKs are received

    d. Better performance by enabling TCP at the start of the connection to send multiple segments up to the window size of the receiver

96. Global synchronization in an IP network refers to _____.

    a. The convergence of the routing protocol

    b. When the TCP three-way handshake is complete

    c. The event when multiple TCP hosts reduce their transmission rate rates in response to packet dropping, and then increase their transmission rates once again when the congestion is reduced

    d. When multiple TCP streams transverse the same link

97. The capability to transmit data in only one direction at a time between a sending and a receiving station is called _____.

    a. Simplex

    b. Full-duplex

    c. Duplex

    d. Unicast

98. Which of the following is an example of a simplex technology?

    a. Ethernet

    b. Token Ring

    c. Broadcast TV

    d. T1

99. Which of the following authentication protocols are used by PPP?

    a. PPPA and DHCP

    b. DHCP and PAP

    c. CHAP and PAP

    d. None of the above

100. Which of the following is false?

    a. With CHAP, the remote device's password is never sent in the clear.

    b. With PAP, the password is encrypted.

    c. CHAP is considered more secure than PAP.

    d. To use PAP or CHAP, you must be running PPP.

Answer Key

1. C
2. A
3. B
4. B
5. A, B, C
6. C
7. C
8. D
9. C
10. B
11. D
12. B and C
13. B
14. A
15. A
16. B
17. B
18. A
19. B
20. C
21. C
22. C and D
23. A
24. C
25. A, B, C, and D
26. C
27. D
28. B
29. D
30. E
31. A
32. A
33. C
34. C
35. B
36. C
37. C

38. A
39. C
40. A
41. B
42. D
43. B and C
44. A
45. C
46. A
47. A
48. C
49. C
50. A
51. A and D
52. A, B, and C
53. A
54. B
55. C
56. C
57. C
58. D
59. C
60. D
61. C
62. A
63. C
64. D
65. C
66. D
67. D
68. B and D
69. D
70. C
71. C
72. B
73. C
74. D
75. C

76. A
77. D
78. B
79. C
80. C
81. B
82. C
83. C
84. B
85. E
86. A
87. C
88. C
89. A
90. B
91. E
92. C
93. B
94. C
95. A
96. C
97. A
98. C
99. C
100. B

Answer Guide

1. The fragmented offset field in an IP header is used to _____.
   a. Identify that the packet is fragmented.
   b. Specify special handling of the packet.
   c. Specify the offset from the beginning of the header to the beginning of the fragment.
   d. Specify the number of fragments in a packet.

The correct answer is C. The fragment offset is a 13-bit field that specifies the offset in units of 8 octets from the beginning of the header to the beginning of the fragment.

Because fragments can arrive out of sequence, the fragment offset field enables the pieces to be reassembled in the correct order.

Answer A is incorrect. The more fragment (MF) field is used to indicate that the packet is fragmented and more fragments follow. When a router fragments a packet, it sets the more fragments bit to 1 in all but the last fragment so the receiver knows to keep expecting fragments until it receives a fragment with an MF equal to 0. The MF flag is the third bit in the flag field of the IP header.

Answer B is incorrect. The type of service (TOS) field in the IP header is used to specify how the packet should be handled as it's routed through the network. The TOS field is an 8-bit field that is used to specify special handling of the IP packet. The field is broken into precedence and TOS subfields. The precedence field indicates the priority of the packet (routine, immediate, network control, and so on). The TOS subfield indicates the delivery service in terms of throughput, delay, reliability, and monetary cost.

Answer D is incorrect. There is no field in the IP header that specifies the number of fragments in a packet.

2. Which of the following fields in an IP packet are protected by the IP header checksum?
    a. The TTL field
    b. The TCP or UDP payload
    c. The entire IP packet
    d. Only the first 12 octets of the IP header

The correct answer is A. The IP header checksum is calculated on the IP header only; the encapsulated data is not protected by the checksum. The Time to Live (TTL) field is part of the IP header and is protected by the checksum. Because each router decrements the TTL, the checksum has to be recalculated at each router.

Answer B is incorrect. The IP header checksum is not calculated for the encapsulated data; UDP and TCP have their own checksums to do this.

Answer C is incorrect. The IP header checksum is only calculated on the IP header, not the entire packet.

Answer D is incorrect. The shortest IP header allowed is 20 bytes, so 12 bytes would only cover approximately half of the header.

3. If a single IP fragment is lost during transmission, _____.
    a. Only the lost fragment must be resent.
    b. The entire packet must be resent.
    c. Only the lost fragment and prior fragments must be resent, not the entire packet.
    d. Only the lost fragment and subsequent fragments must be resent, not the entire packet.

The correct answer is B. If a single IP fragment is lost during transmission, the entire packet (all of the fragments) must be resent.

4. Cisco's **trace route** command relies on what field in the IP header?
    a. The TOS field
    b. The TTL field
    c. Cisco's **trace route** command does not use any fields in the IP header.
    d. Cisco's **trace route** command relies on the TCP payload.

The correct answer is B. The TTL field is an 8-bit field in the IP header. It specifies how long a datagram is allowed to remain in the network. The TTL field is used to prevent datagrams from endlessly traveling through the network. As an IP packet passes through the network, each router will decrement the TTL by 1. If the TTL reaches 0, the packet is discarded and an error message is sent to the source.

When the router traces a route to a destination, it does so by manipulating the TTL field. Say, for example, you were tracing a route to a network that is three router hops away. The first trace packet the router sends out has its TTL set to 1. When the first router in the path receives the packet, it decrements the TTL to 0, drops the packet, and sends an error message back to the source. By looking at the source address of this error message, you now know the first router in the path to the destination. The next trace packet is sent out with a TTL of 2, so the second router in the path decrements the TTL to 0 and sends an error message back. Again, by looking at the source address of the packet, you can determine the second router is the path. This process continues until the packet reaches the final destination, providing a complete picture of which routers the packet passed through from source to destination.

5. Which of the following is true regarding an IP address? (multiple answers)
    a. An IP address is 32 bits in length.
    b. The network and host portion can vary in size within the 32-bit boundary.
    c. Looking at the first octet, you can determine the class of the network.
    d. Class B addresses always have their two left-most bit set to 1.
    e. All of the above

The correct answers are A, B, and C. An IP address is 32 bits in length and is broken into a network portion and host portion. The network and host portion of the address can vary in size within the 32- bit boundary. The network portion of the address may use the majority of the 32 bits or the host portion might or the bits could be divided equally among the two. With other protocols such as IPX and AppleTalk, the network and host portions of the address are fixed in size.

In the original Internet routing scheme, sites were assigned addresses from one of three classes: A, B, or C. The address classes differ in size by the number of networks and the number of hosts. For example, Class A networks have a huge number of hosts, but there is a relatively small number of them. Class C networks provide a large number of networks, each with a small number of hosts. Class B networks provide a medium number of networks, each with a medium number of hosts.

The first octet rule can be used to quickly determine the class of a network based (as the name implies) on the first octet of the IP address. For a Class A network, the first bit of the first octet is always set to 0. For a Class B network, the first bit of the first octet is always set to 1 and the second bit is always set to 0. For a Class C network, the first two bits are always set to 1 and the third bit is always set to 0. See the following illustration.

Class	First Octet Rule	Range
A	00000000 to 01111111	1 – 126 (0 and 127 are reserved)
B	10000000 to 10111111	128 – 191
C	11000000 to 11011111	192 – 223

Answer D is incorrect. A Class B address always has its left-most bit of the first octet set to 1 and the second bit set to 0.

6. IP is a _____ protocol.
   a. Connection-oriented
   b. Media access
   c. Connectionless
   d. Transport layer

The correct answer is C. IP is a connectionless protocol. IP is responsible for transmitting blocks of datagrams received from its upper-layer protocols. The IP layer does not guarantee that all packets will take the same path through the network or that they will even arrive at the destination. It is a best-effort packet delivery system. IP does not establish a session with the destination before transmitting its data; therefore, it is classified as a connectionless protocol.

7. _____ provides a reliable delivery service.
   a. UDP
   b. IP
   c. TCP
   d. ICMP

The correct answer is C. TCP makes up for IP's deficiencies by providing a reliable delivery service. It does this through the use of sequence numbers, acknowledgements, checksum, timers, and windowing. These are described as follows:

- **Sequence numbers**   Sequence numbers are used to coordinate which data has been transmitted and received. They also enable the receiving TCP service to put out-of-sequence packets into the correct order before delivering them to the application layer.

- **Acknowledgments**   The acknowledgement number identifies the next sequence number that the source expects to receive from the destination. This enables the sender to determine which packets the destination has received. If the acknowledgement number does not match the next sequence number, the sender knows not only that a packet was lost, but also which packet was lost.

- **Checksum**   The TCP checksum covers not only the header, but the payload as well, enabling TCP to detected any errors.

- **Timers**   When a host transmits a TCP packet to its peer, it waits for an acknowledgement. If the acknowledgement does not come within the expected time, the packet is assumed to be lost and the packet is retransmitted. The amount of time that the host waits is determined by round-trip time (RTT) estimation. TCP monitors the normal data transfer between two hosts and determines the average round-trip delay. The actual time that the host waits is based on the TCP implementation. The original RFC793 TCP sets the time out to twice the RTT.

- **Windowing**   Each endpoint of a TCP connection has buffers that are used to store data received until the application layer is ready to process it. To avoid overflowing the buffer, TCP uses the window field in the TCP packet to signal the sender on how much data it can receive. If the window size falls to 0, the sender cannot transmit any data to the receiver. The windowing mechanism provides flow control and decreases the chance of packets being dropped due to buffer overflow on the receiving end.

8. _____ provides dynamic address mapping between a protocol address and a specific DLCI.
   a. Frame relay map command
   b. ARP
   c. Reverse ARP
   d. Inverse ARP

The correct answer is D. Inverse ARP provides dynamic address mapping between a protocol address and a specific DLCI. Frame relay inverse ARP is used to request the next-hop protocol address for a specific connection, given its known DLCI. When a frame relay circuit is initialized, the router attached does not have any address information except its own IP address. The router needs a way to determine the IP address of the far-end router on the particular DLCI.

The router accomplishes this by sending an inverse ARP request out of each local DLCI that is defined on the circuit. The inverse ARP request travels to the far-end router where it is received and replied to. The router that initiated the inverse ARP request receives the reply. This reply contains the IP address of the far-end router. Inverse ARP responses are stored as an address-to-DLCI mapping table on the router. This table is used to supply the next-hop protocol address or the DLCI for outgoing traffic. This is similar to how ARP is used to map a MAC address to the known IP address.

Answer A is incorrect. The frame relay map command provides a static address mapping between a protocol address and a specific DLCI.

Answer B is incorrect. ARP is used to resolve a layer 3 network address to a layer 2 MAC address. It works by broadcasting a packet to all hosts attached to a LAN or virtual LAN (VLAN). The packet contains the IP address with which the sender wants to communicate. The target machine recognizes that the IP address in the packet matches its own and returns its MAC address in the reply. The MAC-to-IP address binding is kept in a cache on the router. The next time the source wants to send a packet to the destination, it will not need to send an ARP request out because it already has one in its ARP cache.

Answer C is incorrect. Reverse ARP (RARP) is used to map a MAC address to a given IP address. Some devices may not know their IP address at startup. One way for them to discover this is through the use of RARP. RARP has been largely replaced with BOOTP and DHCP, both of which provide more information than just the IP address of the host.

9. Each IPv4 datagram includes a _____ source address.
   a. 64-byte
   b. 64-bit
   c. 32-bit
   d. 32-byte

The correct answer is C. An IP address is 32 bits in length and is broken into a network portion and host portion. An IP datagram includes a 32-bit source and destination address.

10. TCP datagrams are _____ if the receiver does not acknowledge them.
    a. Discarded
    b. Retransmitted
    c. Fragmented
    d. None of the above

The correct answer is B. TCP datagrams are retransmitted if the receiver does not acknowledge them. The acknowledgement number in the TCP header identifies the next sequence number that the source expects to receive from the destination. This enables the sender to determine which packets the destination has received. If the acknowledgement number does not match the next sequence number, the sender knows not only that a packet was lost, but also which packet was lost. If no acknowledgement is received, the packet is retransmitted.

11. The _____ field in the TCP header is used to tell the receiver the next byte of data that the sender of the packet expects to receive.

   a. Window
   b. Fragment offset
   c. Options
   d. Acknowledgment number

The correct answer is D. The acknowledgement number field in the TCP header is used to tell the receiver the next byte of data that the sender of the packet expects to receive.

Answer A is incorrect. The TCP window is used for flow control. Each endpoint of a TCP connection has buffers that are used to store data received until the application layer is ready to process it. To avoid overflowing, the buffer TCP uses the window field in the TCP packet to signal the sender on how much data it can receive. If the window size falls to 0, the sender cannot transmit any data to the receiver. The windowing mechanism provides flow control and decreases the chance of packets being dropped due to buffer overflow on the receiving end.

Answer B is incorrect. The fragment offset field is not part of the TCP header; it is part of the IP header. It is used to specify the offset from the beginning of the header to the beginning of the fragment.

Answer C is incorrect. The options field in the TCP header specifies the options required by the sender's TCP process. A commonly used option is maximum segment size, which informs the receiver of the largest segment that the sender is willing to accept.

12. Which of the following fields are used in the TCP handshake process? (multiple answers)

   a. Push
   b. ACK
   c. SYN
   d. Urgent

The correct answers are B and C. Because TCP is connection-oriented, hosts must establish a session before data transfer can occur. The TCP three-way handshake is used to establish this connection. The three-way handshake enables both sides to agree upon initial sequence numbers and guarantees that both sides are ready to receive and transmit data.

This is how it works:

1. Each host randomly chooses a sequence number, which is used to track bytes within the stream it is sending and receiving.

2. The first host initiates a connection by sending a packet with the SYN bit set in the TCP header. The random sequence number generated in step 1 is placed in the TCP header.

3. When the second host receives the packet, it records the sequence number and replies with an acknowledgement number equal to the first host's sequence number plus 1. The host also includes its own randomly generated sequence number in the TCP header.

4. When the first host receives the packet, it records the sequence number and replies with an acknowledgement number equal to the second host's sequence number plus 1.

5. At this point, both have agreed upon initial sequence numbers and data transfer can begin.

Answer A is incorrect. Sometimes users need to be sure that all the data they have submitted to the TCP has been transmitted. For this purpose, a push function is defined. To ensure that data submitted to TCP is actually transmitted, the sending user indicates that it should be pushed through to the receiving user. A push causes TCP to promptly forward and deliver data up to that point to the receiver.

A sending TCP session is allowed to collect data from the sending user and to send that data in segments at its own convenience until the push function is signaled, and then it must send all unsent data. When a receiving TCP session sees the PSH flag, it must not wait for more data from the sending TCP before passing the data to the receiving process.

Answer D is incorrect. The urgent pointer is used to communicate to the receiver of data that at some point farther along in the data stream than the receiver is currently reading, there is urgent data. The urgent pointer indicates that the receiving process should take action to process the urgent data quickly.

13. What is the subnet address for the following host address and mask combination of 152.32.1.125 255.255.255.224?
   a. 152.32.1.95
   b. 152.32.1.96

    c. 152.32.1.120

    d. 152.32.1.124

The correct answer is B. The subnet address can be found by performing a Boolean logical AND function on the IP address and the mask for every bit position. With a logical AND function, the result is 1 if and only if both bits are 1. If either or both bits are 0, the result will be 0.

1. The first step is to convert the dotted decimal address and mask to binary.

```
152.32.1.125      = 1001100 000100000 00000001 01111101
255.255.255.224 = 11111111 11111111 11111111 11100000
```

2. For each bit in the IP address, perform a Boolean logical AND function with the corresponding bit in the address mask.

```
10011000 00100000 00000001 01111101
11111111 11111111 11111111 11100000
10011000 00100000 00000001 01100000
```

3. Convert the binary address back to dotted decimal format. This gives you the address of the subnetwork.

```
10011000 00100000 00000001 01100000 = 152.32.1.96
```

14. What is the directed broadcast address for the host address and mask combination of 172.32.10.120 255.255.255.128?

    a. 172.32.10.127

    b. 172.32.10.255

    c. 255.255.255.255

    d. None of the above

The correct answer is A. All that you need to do to find the directed broadcast address is change the host's bits in the IP address to 1's and convert them back to decimal.

1. The first step is to convert the dotted decimal address and mask to binary. Remember a 1 in the mask identifies the corresponding bit in the IP address as a network bit, and a 0 in the mask identifies the corresponding bit in the IP address as a host bit. As you can see, the first 25 bits of the IP address represent the network portion of the address; the last seven bits represent the host portion.

```
172.32.10.120      = 10101100 00100000 00001010 01111000
255.255.255.128 = 11111111 11111111 11111111 10000000
```

2. Change the host bits in the IP address to all 1's.

```
10101100 00100000 00001010 01111111
```

3. Convert the binary address back to decimal format. This gives you the directed broadcast address.

10101100 00100000 00001010 01111111 = **172.32.10.127**

15. A Class B address with a mask of 255.255.248.0 will give how many subnets and how many hosts per subnet (without using subnet zero)?
   a. 30 subnets with 2,046 hosts each
   b. 62 subnets with 1,022 hosts each
   c. 14 subnets with 4,094 hosts each
   d. 2 subnets with 16,382 hosts each

The correct answer is A. A Class B address with a 21-bit mask will give you 30 subnets with 2,046 hosts each (not counting subnet zero). The following is a simplified method that can be used to calculate the number of subnets and hosts for a given address mask combination.

1. Convert the dotted decimal mask to binary:

255.255.248.0 = 11111111 11111111 11111000 00000000

2. Count the number of 1's in the mask.
21 bits are set to 1.

3. Subtract from that the number of bits used for the network portion of the address (8 for a Class A, 16 for a Class B, or 24 for a Class C. This will give you the number of bits being used for the subnet portion of the address.
21 - 16 = 5 (Five bits are being used for the subnet portion of the address.)

4. Count the number of 0's in the mask. This is the number of bits that are being used for the host portion of the address.
11 (11 bits are being used for the host portion of the address.)

5. You can now calculate the number of subnets and hosts per subnet using the formula 2^n - 2 where n is the number of bits.

Subnets = $2^5 - 2$ = **30**

Hosts = $2^{11} - 2$ = **2,046**

16. Class D IP addresses range from _____.
   a. 224.0.0.1 to 239.255.255.255
   b. 224.0.0.0 to 239.255.255.255
   c. 224.0.0.0 to 255.255.255.255
   d. 224.0.0.1 to 255.255.255.255

The correct answer is B. The address range for a Class D address is 224.0.0.0 to 239.255.255.255.

The Class D Internet address format is reserved for multicast groups, as discussed in RFC 988. In Class D addresses, the four highest-order bits are set to 1, 1, 1, and 0. The range is from 224.0.0.0 to 239.255.255.255. The Class E Internet address format is reserved for future use. In Class E addresses, the four highest-order bits are set to 1, 1, 1, and 1. The range is from 240.0.0.0 to 255.255.255.254.

17. The multicast group 224.0.0.1 is _____.
   a. A well-known multicast group address, which means all routers on the subnet
   b. A well-known multicast group address, which means all systems on the subnet
   c. A well-known multicast group address used by RIPv2
   d. A well-known multicast group address used by NTP

The correct answer is B. The address 224.0.0.1 is assigned to all systems on a subnet. Answer A is incorrect. The address 224.0.0.2 is assigned to all routers on a subnet. Answer C is incorrect. RIPv2 uses multicast address 224.0.0.9

Answer D is also incorrect. NTP uses multicast address 224.0.1.1.

18. The multicast group 224.0.0.2 is _____.
   a. A well-known multicast group address, which means all routers on the subnet
   b. A well-known multicast group address, which means all systems on the subnet
   c. A well-known multicast group address used by RIPv2
   d. A well-known multicast group address used by NTP

The correct answer is A. The well-known multicast group address 224.0.0.2 means all hosts on the subnet.

19. Which of the following is not a valid subnet mask?
   a. 255.0.0.0
   b. 255.255.255.254
   c. 255.255.255.255
   d. 255.255.255.252

The correct answer is B. A mask of 255.255.255.254 is invalid because it provides only one bit for host addressing, providing only two possible hosts. Out of the two hosts possible, one is the subnet address and the other is broadcast address for that subnet.

20. Which of the following is false regarding an IP address?
   a. An IP address is 32 bits long.
   b. The network and host portions of the address may vary in size.

    c. The network and host portions are fixed length.

    d. None of the above

The correct answer is C. An IP address is 32 bits in length and is broken into a network portion and host portion. The network and host portion of the address are not fixed length and can vary in size within the 32-bit boundary. The network portion of the address may use the majority of the 32 bits or the host portion might. The bits could also be divided equally among the two. With other protocols such as IPX and AppleTalk, the network and host portions of the address are fixed in size.

21. Which of the following is not part of the UDP header?

    a. Source address

    b. Length

    c. Urgent pointer

    d. Checksum

The correct answer is C. The urgent pointer is not part of the UDP header. It is part of the TCP header and is used only when the URG flag is set. One advantage of UDP over TCP is that UDP has a much smaller header. The UDP header has four fields:

- **Source port** This field indicates the port of the sending process, as well as the port to which a reply should be addressed. If the transmitting host does not supply a source port, this field will have a value of 0.

- **Destination port** This field is used to demultiplex datagrams among the processes in the destination machine.

- **Length** This field is the combination length of the UDP header and the data, and is expressed in octets.

- **Checksum** The UDP checksum is optional. A value of 0 indicates that the checksum has not been computed. Because IP does not compute a checksum on the data portion of the datagram, the UDP checksum provides the only means to determine whether the data has arrived without errors.

22. Which of the following are not valid flags in an IP header? (multiple answers)

    a. DF

    b. MF

    c. URG

    d. PSH

The correct answers are C and D. The URG and PSH flags are two of the six 1-bit flags used in the TCP header for flow and connection control. The other four are ACK, RST, SYN, and FIN.

An IP header has a three-bit field for flags. The first bit is not used. The second bit is the don't fragment (DF) bit. The third bit is the more fragments (MF) bit, which is used to indicate whether this is the last fragment.

23. The first octet rule _____.

    a. Is a way to determine the class to which an IP address belongs by looking at the first octet of the address

    b. Is used to determine now the IP address should be subnetted

    c. Does not work when VLSM is used

    d. None of the above

The correct answer is A. The first octet rule can be used to quickly determine the class of a network based (as the name implies) on the first octet of the IP address. For a Class A network, the first bit of the first octet is always set to 0. For a Class B network, the first bit of the first octet is always set to 1 and the second bit is always set to 0. For a Class C network, the first two bits are always set to 1 and the third bit is always set to 0. See the following illustration, which was also shown earlier in this chapter.

Class	First Octet Rule	Range
A	00000000 to 01111111	1 – 126 (0 and 127 are reserved)
B	10000000 to 10111111	128 – 191
C	11000000 to 11011111	192 – 223

24. The options field in an IP header is _____.

    a. A mandatory field

    b. Fixed length

    c. Primarily used for testing

    d. Never used

The correct answer is C. The options field in the IP header is a variable-length field, and as the name implies, it is optional. The options field is primarily used for testing and includes options for loose source routing, strict source routing, record route, and timestamp.

25. Which of the following are flags in the TCP header? (multiple answers)

    a. PSH

    b. RST

    c. URG

    d. ACK

    e. DF

The correct answers are A, B, C, and D. The TCP header contains a flags field that is 6 bits long and is used for data flow and connection control. The six bits from left to right are shown in the followng illustration, which also appeared earlier in the chapter.

URG	Urgent Pointer field significant
ACK	Acknowledgment field significant
PSH	Push Function
RST	Reset the connection
SYN	Synchronize sequence numbers
FIN	No more data from sender

Answer E is incorrect. The DF flag is part of the IP header.

26. The 16-bit checksum in the TCP header is calculated on _____.
   a. The IP header
   b. The TCP header
   c. The TCP header and payload
   d. The IP header and payload

The correct answer is C. The TCP header checksum covers both the header and the payload. This is unlike the checksum in the IP header, which only covers the IP header and no data in the IP datagram.

The checksum in the TCP header is the one's complement sum of 16-bit words in the header and the text. If the segment contains an odd number of header and text octets to be checksummed, the last octet is padded on the right with 0 to form a 16-bit word.

27. The checksum in the UDP header is _____.
   a. Optional
   b. Calculated on both the UDP header and payload
   c. Calculated on the UDP header
   d. A and B
   e. A and C
   f. None of the above—there is no checksum in UDP.

The correct answer is D. Like the TCP checksum, the UDP checksum covers both the header and the data. With UDP, the checksum is optional, whereas with TCP, it is mandatory.

28. The _____ field is carried in the IP header and specifies the number of routing hops allowed before a datagram is discarded.

   a. Window

   b. TTL

   c. Checksum

   d. Urgent

The correct answer is B. The TTL field is carried in the IP header and specifies the number of routing hops allowed before a datagram is discarded. The TTL field is an 8-bit field in the IP header. It specifies how long a datagram is allowed to remain in the network. The TTL field is used to prevent datagrams from endlessly traveling through the network. As an IP packet passes through the network, each router will decrement the TTL by 1. If the TTL reaches 0, the packet is discarded and an error message is sent to the source.

29. IP datagrams are _____ in length.

   a. Fixed

   b. Short

   c. Long

   d. Variable

The correct answer is D. IP datagrams are variable in length. An IP datagram can vary in length up to 65,535 octets.

30. ARP uses the _____ protocol.

   a. TCP

   b. UDP

   c. IP

   d. A and C

   e. None of the above

The correct answer is E. In order for two machines on an Ethernet to communicate, they must know the other's physical address or MAC address. ARP is a layer 2 protocol that is used dynamically to discover the MAC-layer address corresponding to a particular IP network layer address. It operates between the IP layer and the data link layer.

31. ICMP uses the _____ protocol.

   a. IP

   b. TCP

   c. UDP

   d. A and B

   e. None of the above

The correct answer is A. Internet Control Message Protocol (ICMP) is used to provide feedback about problems that occur in the network. In a connectionless environment, each host and router operates independently in the routing and delivery of IP datagrams. Because problems can arise in the transmission of datagrams, a way is needed to provide feedback. ICMP provides this mechanism. ICMP uses the IP protocol for delivery across the network.

32. Which of the following is an example of a connection-oriented service?
   a. Telnet and FTP
   b. Telnet and SNMP
   c. FTP and TFTP
   d. None of the above

The correct answer is A. Telnet and FTP are examples of applications that use TCP as their transport layer. TCP provides a reliable connection-oriented service.

Answers B and C are incorrect. Both SNMP and TFTP use UDP as their transport layer, which provides a connectionless best-effort packet delivery service.

33. A router sends a _____ ICMP message to the source station if it cannot accept data at that time.
   a. Time exceeded
   b. Host unreachable
   c. Source quench
   d. Buffer overflow

The correct answer is C. A router sends a source quench ICMP message to the source station if it cannot accept data at that time.

Source quench messages provide a basic form of flow control. When datagrams arrive too quickly for a router or host to process them, the receiving device's buffers quickly fill, causing additional datagrams to be discarded. At this point, the receiving device begins sending source quench messages to the transmitting device at the rate of one message for each packet dropped. The source device receives the source quench messages and lowers the transmission data rate until it stops receiving the messages. The sender will then gradually increase its transmission rate as long as it does not receive any more source quench requests.

34. A router generates a/an _____ ICMP message if it does not know how to reach a given destination.
   a. Information needed
   b. Source quench
   c. Host unreachable
   d. No route to host

The correct answer is C. If the router receives a datagram that it is unable to deliver to its ultimate destination, it sends an ICMP host unreachable message to the source. This occurs if there is no match in the routing table for the particular destination network or if the distance to reach that network is infinity.

Answer B is incorrect. A source quench message is sent by the receiver to request the original source to slow down its transmission rate.

Answers A and D are not valid ICMP messages.

35. With frame relay, the LMI type should agree _____.
   a. Between end devices
   b. Between the end device and the switch
   c. Between switches
   d. It does not need to agree; it is local only.

The correct answer is B. With frame relay, the LMI type should agree between the end device and the switch.

Frame relay provides a simple signaling protocol between the frame relay switch and the DTE or end device. The signaling protocol called local management interface (LMI).

LMI is used to monitor the status of DLCIs and to provide communication and synchronization between frame relay DTE and DCE devices. The LMI must be set on the same on the frame relay switch and frame relay DTE.

When a DTE connected to a frame relay network becomes active, LMI is used to determine what DLCIs are available to the DTE. The DTE also periodically polls the switch to determine that the DLCI is still active, preventing data from being sent into black hole. Cisco's implementation of frame relay supports three LMI types: Cisco, ANSI Annex D, and ITU-T (formally the CCITT) Q.933 Annex A.

- **Cisco LMI**   Cisco LMI uses DLCI 1,023 to pass status information between the frame relay switch and the frame relay DTE.

- **ANSI Annex D**   Annex D uses DLCI 0 to pass status information between the frame relay switch and the frame relay DTE.

- **ITU-T Annex A**   Annex A also uses DLCI 0 to pass status information between the frame relay switch and the frame relay DTE. Annex A also provides the CIR value of each PVC that is provisioned on the frame relay switch.

36. CIR refers to _____.
   a. The minimum bandwidth available on the frame relay link
   b. The maximum bandwidth available on the frame relay link
   c. The guaranteed bandwidth available on the frame relay link
   d. None of the above

The correct answer is C. The committed information rate (CIR) of a PVC is a measurement in bits per second of the maximum amount of traffic that the frame relay service provider agrees to carry through the network. The CIR value will usually be less than the access rate of the line. Keep in mind that several PVCs will be sharing the same physical link between the user's equipment and the frame relay switch.

37. LMI is the _____.
  a. X.25 signaling format
  b. ISDN signaling format
  c. Signaling interface between the frame relay DTE and DCE
  d. Signaling interface between frame relay switches

The correct answer is C. LMI is the signaling interface between the frame relay DTE and DCE.

Frame relay provides a simple signaling protocol between the frame relay switch and the frame relay DTE (router). This signaling protocol is known as the LMI.

The LMI signaling protocol provides for notification of the addition and deletion of PVCs as well as the periodic keepalive messages between the frame relay switch and frame relay DTE.

LMI works in the following manner:

1. Every ten seconds the DTE requests status from the frame relay switch. This status request will be sent to the switch over one of two reserved DLCIs: 0 or 1,023 depending on which of the three LMI signaling protocols has been chosen.

2. The frame relay switch will respond to the status request with a status response. This exchange is referred to as a keepalive or aliveness check because its function is to tell both the DTE and the frame relay switch that there is still a communication path between them.

3. Every sixth status request from the DTE is sent as a full status request. A full status request is not only an aliveness check, but it also requests the frame relay switch to respond with a list of all DLCIs that have been defined on the port of the frame relay switch.

4. The frame relay switch responds with a list of all defined DLCIs on the particular frame relay switch port.

Both the DTE and the frame relay switch maintain individual sequence numbers during their exchanges. These sequence numbers can be used to determine if an LMI sequence has been lost.

38. The 2-byte address field in a frame relay header is broken into _____.

    a. 10 bits for circuit identification and 6 bits for congestion management

    b. 8 bits for circuit identification and 8 bits for congestion management

    c. 6 bits for circuit identification and 10 bits for congestion management

    d. 12 bits for circuit identification and 4 bits for congestion management

The correct answer is A. The frame relay address field can be 2, 3, or 4 bytes long. A 2-byte address field is almost always used. The 2-byte address field is broken into 10 bits for circuit identification and 6 bits for congestion management.

39. Which of the following is not used by frame relay for congestion control?

    a. FECN

    b. BECN

    c. DLCI

    d. DE

The correct answer is C. The DLCI is a 10-bit field that contains the DLCI value that identifies a virtual circuit. For a typical 2-byte frame relay header, this field can take on a value between 0 and 1,023. Some DLCI values such as 0 and 1,023 are reserved for frame relay management. Valid user DLCI values range from 16 through 991. Recall that the DLCI value tells the frame relay switch the proper destination of traffic sent into the frame relay network.

Answer A is incorrect. The forward explicit congestion notification (FECN) bit is used for congestion control. When the FECN bit is set, it tells the user receiving frame relay frames that congestion exists in the direction that the frame was sent.

Answer B is incorrect. The backward explicit congestion notification (BECN) bit is used for congestion control. When the BECN bit is set, it tells the user receiving frame relay frames that congestion exists in the reverse direction that the frame was sent.

Answer D is incorrect. The discard eligible (DE) bit is used for congestion control. This bit can be set by either the frame relay DTE equipment (such as a router) or by the frame relay switch network. A frame with the DE bit set indicates that the frame can be discarded when the frame relay network becomes congested. Whether or not DE-flagged frames are discarded depends on how the frame relay network has been provisioned.

40. Frame relay networks are considered to be _____.

    a. Non-broadcast multiple access

    b. Broadcast multiple access

    c. Shared media

    d. None of the above

The correct answer is A. A frame relay network is considered to be non-broadcast multiple access. A non-broadcast multiple access (NBM) network is defined as a network that supports two or more routers, but does not have broadcast capabilities. Frame relay and ATM are two examples of NBMA networks.

41. A frame relay switch makes forwarding decisions based on the _____.

    a. Network layer address

    b. Data link address

    c. Physical address

    d. Application layer address

The correct answer is B. When a frame relay switch receives a frame, it makes its forwarding decision based on the data link address.

42. The end node addressing for frame relay is a/an _____.

    a. BECN

    b. FECN

    c. IP address

    d. DLCI

The correct answer is D. The end node addressing for frame relay is a DLCI. The DLCI is a 10-bit field that contains the DLCI value that identifies a virtual circuit. For a typical 2-byte frame relay header, this field can take on a value between 0 and 1,023. Some DLCI values such as 0 and 1,023 are reserved for frame relay management. Valid user DLCI values range from 16 through 991.

Answer A is incorrect. The BECN bit is used to tell the user receiving frame relay frames that congestion exists in the reverse direction that the frame was sent.

Answer B is incorrect. The FECN bit is used to tell the user receiving frame relay frames that congestion exists in the direction that the frame was sent.

Answer C is incorrect. The IP address is the network layer address of the end node.

43. The primary differences between frame relay and X.25 are _____. (multiple answers)

    a. Media types

    b. Supported speeds

    c. Error correction

    d. Network protocols supported

The correct answers are B and C. X.25 was designed to provide error-free delivery using high error-rate links. Frame relay assumes clean digital lines that enable it to eliminate many of the services provided by X.25. The elimination of functions and fields, combined with digital links, enables frame relay to operate at speeds 20 times greater than X.25.

X.25 is defined for layers 1, 2, and 3 of the ISO model, whereas frame relay is defined for layers 1 and 2 only. This means that frame relay has significantly less processing to do at each node, which improves throughput by an order of magnitude.

X.25 packets contain several fields used for error and flow control, none of which is needed by frame relay. The frames in frame relay contain an expanded address field that enables frame relay nodes to direct frames to their destinations with minimal processing.

44. Which of the following is false?

    a. The frame relay DTE regularly transmits status inquiries and the network answers with status report messages.

    b. The network regularly transmits status inquiries and the DTE answers with status report messages.

    c. LMI enables the end station to learn about the deletion of a PVC.

    d. LMI enables the end station to learn about the availability of a PVC.

Answer A is false. The network regularly transmits status inquiries and the DTE answers with status report messages.

The frame relay DTE regularly requests status from the frame relay switch. This status request will be sent to the switch over one of two reserved DLCIs: 0 or 1,023 depending on which of the three LMI signaling protocols has been chosen. The frame relay switch responds to the status request with a status response. This exchange is referred to as a keepalive or aliveness check because its function is to tell both the DTE and the frame relay switch that there is still a communication path between them.

45. The frame relay data link provides for all of the following except _____.

    a. Addressing

    b. Flow control

    c. Sequencing and acknowledgements

    d. Error detection

The correct answer is C. The frame relay data link does not provide any sequencing or acknowledgements for frames. Frame relay relies on the higher-layer protocols to ensure packet delivery.

Addressing, flow control, and error detection are all provided by frame relay.

46. Which of the following is false?

    a. The DLCI addressing space allows for 1,024 addresses for virtual circuit addressing.

    b. Because of signaling and management, only 992 addresses are available for virtual circuit addressing.

    c. DLCI 0 is reserved for LMI.

    d. EA enables the DLCI header to be extended, creating more address space.

Answer A is false. The DLCI addressing space allows for 1,024 addresses for virtual circuit addressing. For a typical 2-byte frame relay header, this field can take on a value between 0 and 1,023. However, not all values can be used for virtual circuit addressing. Some DLCI values such as 0 and 1,023 are reserved for frame relay management.

47. The valid fields in a frame relay header are _____.

    a. Flag, address, data, and FCS

    b. Flag, control, address, data, and FCS

    c. Flag, address, control, management, data, and FCS,

    d. Flag, data, address, and control

The correct answer is A. One of frame relay's attractions is the fact that it is very efficient. With only 2 bytes of address overhead, you can transmit up to 8KB of data. The following illustration, which appeared earlier in the chapter, shows the format of the frame relay frame.

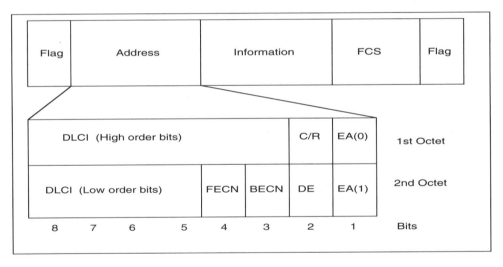

The fields in the preceding illustration can be explained as follows:

- **Flag** Each frame relay frame starts and ends with at least one delimiter character of 0x7E. This bit sequence enables the receiver to synchronize on the start and end of a frame. A special bit-stuffing algorithm exists that ensures that this 0x7E character cannot appear in the user traffic.

- **Address** The address field is either 2, 3, or 4 bytes long. A 2-byte address field is almost always used. The following fields are contained in a 2-byte address field:

    - **DLCI** This is a 10-bit field that contains the DLCI value that identifies a virtual circuit. For a typical 2-byte frame relay header, this field can take on a value between 0 and 1,023. Some DLCI values such as 0 and 1,023 are reserved for frame relay management.

- **Command response (CR)** This bit is not used in most frame relay implementations.

- **Extended address (EA)** This bit is used to indicate whether a 2-, 3-, or 4-byte header is being used. This bit is set to a 1 in the last byte of the header.

- **Forward explicit congestion notification (FECN)** This bit is used to tell the user receiving frame relay frames that congestion exists in the direction that the frame was sent.

- **Backward explicit congestion notification (BECN)** This bit is used to tell the user receiving frame relay frames that congestion exists in the reverse direction that the frame was sent.

- **Discard eligible (DE)** This bit can be set by either the frame relay DTE equipment (such as a router) or by the frame relay switch network. A frame with the DE bit set indicates that the frame can be discarded when the frame relay network becomes congested. Whether or not DE-flagged frames are discarded depends on how the frame relay network has been provisioned.

- **User data** This field contains the actual user payload. The default Cisco frame relay frame size is 1,500 bytes for a synchronous serial interface. Most frame relay equipment can pass larger frames. The largest frame size is 8,192 bytes, although many frame relay devices cannot pass a frame that large. The main disadvantage of using frames larger than 4KB is that the frame check sequence can no longer detect many types of data errors.

- **Frame check sequence (FCS)** This is a 2-byte CRC that is calculated on the entire frame except the flags and the 2 bytes of FCS. A frame relay network will discard any frames that have a bad FCS. The FCS is only guaranteed for frame relay frames of 4KB or less; larger frames may not have their errors detected with the 2-byte CRC check that frame relay provides.

48. Which of the following address is not an RFC 1918 reserved address?
   a. 10.1.1.1
   b. 192.168.1.1
   c. 172.32.1.1
   d. 172.16.1.1

The correct answer is C. The Internet Assigned Numbers Authority (IANA) has reserved three blocks of the IP addressing space for private intranets. The first block is a single Class A network number, whereas the second block is a set of 16 contiguous Class B network numbers. The third block is a set of 256 contiguous Class C network numbers. The following illustration shows the three reserved blocks:

Class	Range	Prefix
A	10.0.0.0 to 10.255.255.255	10/8 prefix
B	172.16.0.0 to 172.31.255.255	172.16/12 prefix
C	192.168.0.0 to 192.168.255.255	192.168/16 prefix

49. Which of the following subnet masks gives you two usable host addresses?

   a. 255.255.255.248
   b. 255.255.255.250
   c. 255.255.255.252
   d. 255.255.255.255

The correct answer is C. A 30-bit mask gives you four host addresses of which two are useable.

Answer A is incorrect. A 29-bit mask gives you eight host addresses of which six are useable.

Answer B is incorrect. This is not a valid mask.

Answer D is incorrect. A 32-bit mask only provides one host address.

50. How many subnets are available (without using the subnet zero command) if a Class C address has 6 bits of subnetting?

   a. 62
   b. 63
   c. 2
   d. 3

The correct answer is A. The number of subnets can be calculate using the formula $2^n - 2$ where n is the number of bits used for subnetting.

Subnets = $2^6 - 2 = $ **62**

51. Which of the following is/are true about ARP?

   a. In an ARP request packet, the destination address is set to all 1's.
   b. In an ARP request packet, the destination address is the MAC address of the default gateway.
   c. The target IP address is set to all 1's.
   d. The target IP address is the address of the device that the stations want to receive a MAC address for.
   e. None of the above

The correct answers are A and D. ARP is used to resolve a layer 3 network address to a layer 2 MAC address. It works by broadcasting a packet to all hosts attached to a LAN. The packet contains the IP address with which the sender wants to communicate—the target address. The target machine recognizes that the IP address in the packet matches its own and returns its MAC address in the reply. The MAC IP address binding is kept in a cache on the router. The next time the source wants to send a packet to the destination, it will not need to send an ARP request out because it already has one in its ARP cache. Figure 2-8, which appeared earlier in this chapter, shows the format of an ARP packet.

52. Which of the following is true regarding gratuitous ARP? (multiple answers)

    a. A gratuitous ARP is when a host issues an ARP request with its own IP address as the target address.

    b. A gratuitous ARP may be used for duplicate address checks.

    c. A gratuitous ARP may be used to advertise a new data link identifier.

    d. A gratuitous ARP is the same as reverse ARP.

    e. All of the above

The correct answers are A, B, and C. A gratuitous ARP is when a host or router issues an ARP request using its own IP address as the target. A gratuitous ARP is often used by a host for duplicate IP address checks. If a host or router issues an ARP request with its own IP address as the target and another host responds, the host will know that the address is a duplicate. The other use of a gratuitous ARP is to advertise a new data link identifier. When a device receives an ARP request for an IP address that is already in its ARP cache, the cache will be updated with the sender's new MAC address. An example of when this would be used on a router is when HSRP is configured to use the burned-in MAC address of the interface instead of the virtual MAC address. In order to let hosts know that the MAC address associated with the virtual IP address has changed, the active router sends a number of unsolicited or gratuitous ARP responses. This lets host implementations update their ARP tables.

0 8 15 16 31	
Hardware Type	Protocol Type
HLEN PLEN	Operation
Sender HA (octets 0-3)	
Sender HA (octets 4-5)	Sender IP (octets 0-1)
Sender IP (octets 2-3)	Target HA (octets 0-1)
Target HA (octets 2-5)	
Target IP (octets 0-3)	

Figure 2-8   ARP packet format

53. Which of the following is false regarding proxy ARP?

    a. The router responds with the MAC address of the destination station.

    b. The router responds with its own MAC address.

    c. Proxy ARP is when an intermediate device such as a router sends an ARP response on behalf of an end node to the requesting host.

    d. Proxy ARP is not needed if the host is configured with a default gateway.

Answer A is false. Proxy ARP is a technique used by a router to enable hosts with no knowledge of routing to determine the hardware addresses of hosts on other networks or subnets. A router using proxy ARP recognizes ARP requests for hosts on the other side of the router that cannot reply for themselves. The router answers for those addresses with an ARP reply that matches the remote IP address with the router's Ethernet address.

For example, the host 10.1.1.1/24 wants to send a packet to 10.1.2.1/24 , which is a different subnet attached to the router. The host is not configured with a default gateway so it does not know how to reach the router. The host will issue an ARP request for 10.1.2.1; the local router will receive the request and because it knows how to reach the host, it will issue an ARP reply with is own MAC address. The host will now send all packets destined for 10.1.2.1 to the router, which will forward them onto the other subnet.

54. The primary disadvantage of using proxy ARP is what?

    a. It is difficult to configure and troubleshoot.

    b. Proxy ARP results in more ARP traffic on the LAN.

    c. Proxy ARP can cause black-hole routing.

    d. None of the above

The correct answer is B. One of the major disadvantages of using proxy ARP is that it results in more ARP traffic on the LAN. The reason being is that hosts will now ARP for all hosts, not just those on their local subnet. Because ARP requests are sent out as broadcasts, this will also cause additional loading on every host on your network; they all have to process the ARP enough to determine that it is not for them.

The other disadvantage is that the host's ARP tables will be larger, because they will include entries for remote hosts as well as local hosts. On systems with limited-sized ARP tables, this may result in more entries being dropped, resulting in more ARP traffic.

55. The port number of an application coupled with the IP address of the host that the application resides on is called what?

    a. Header

    b. SP pair

c. Socket

d. Window

The correct answer is C. An application port number coupled with the IP address of the host the application resides on is called a socket. A socket is used to uniquely identify every application in a network.

56. Which of the following is false regarding reverse ARP?

a. It is used for hosts that do not know their IP address at startup.

b. It is being replaced by DHCP.

c. It is used to map a MAC address to a know IP address.

d. It cannot be routed off the local data link.

Answer C is false. ARP is used to resolve a layer 3 network address to a layer 2 MAC address. It works by broadcasting a packet to all hosts attached to a LAN. The packet contains the IP address with which the sender wants to communicate. The target machine recognizes that the IP address in the packet matches its own and returns an its MAC address in the reply. Reverse ARP (RARP) is used to map a MAC address to a given IP address. Some devices may not know their IP address at startup. One way for them to discover this is through the use of RARP. RARP has been largely replaced with BOOTP and DHCP, both of which provide more information than just the IP address of the host.

57. RouterA and RouterB are connected to the same Ethernet. HostA also on the same Ethernet is configured to use RouterA as its default gateway. HostA sends a packet to RouterA, which sees that the destination is reachable through RouterB via the Ethernet interface. What does RouterA do?

a. It drops the packet and sends an ICMP redirect to HostA informing it to use RouterB in the future to reach the particular destination.

b. It forwards the packet to RouterB.

c. It forwards the packet to RouterB and sends an ICMP redirect to HostA informing it to use RouterB in the future to reach the particular destination.

d. It drops the packet and sends an ICMP host unreachable message to HostA.

The correct answer is C. Routers use an ICMP redirect to notify hosts that another router on the same data link should be used instead of itself to forward packets to the particular destination. If a router receives a packet and determines that the destination is reachable through the other router on the data link (that is, the router must forward the packet over the same interface it was received onto the reach the destination). It will forward the packet and issue an ICMP redirect to host, informing it that in the future, in order to reach the particular destination, it should forward the packet to the other router on the data link.

58. Which of the following is false?

    a. TCP is a connection-oriented service.

    b. TCP uses windowing to regulate the flow of packets.

    c. The 16-bit TCP checksum is calculated on the header and payload.

    d. The urgent pointer is used only when the URG flag is set and is added to the sequence number to indicate the beginning of the urgent data.

Answer D is false. The first part of answer D is correct; the urgent pointer is used only when the URG flag is set. However, the 16-bit number that is added to the sequence number indicates the end of the urgent data, not the beginning.

59. Which of the following is false?

    a. A UDP header is smaller than a TCP header.

    b. Applications that send short bursts of data can get better performance with UDP because no time is spent setting up a connection.

    c. Unlike TCP, UDP does not have a checksum.

    d. UDP provides connectionless best-effort packet delivery.

Answer C is false. UDP does have a checksum; however, unlike TCP, it is optional.

60. The OSI reference model divides networking activity into how many layers?

    a. Four

    b. Five

    c. Three

    d. Seven

Answer D is correct. The OSI reference model is divided into seven layers: application, presentation, session, transport, network, data link, and physical.

The application layer plays the same role as the application interface in operating systems. It provides network services to users of the network. Application level protocols include Telnet, File Transfer Protocol (FTP), and Simple Mail Transfer Protocol (SMTP).

The presentation layer is responsible for translating text and data syntax, such as Extended Binary-Coded Decimal Interchange Code (EBCDIC) used by IBM systems and American Standard Code for Information Interchange (ASCII) used in most computer systems.

The session layer assumes that a reliable virtual point-to-point connection has been made and contains specifications for the dialog between the two end systems such as dialog discipline, data grouping, and recovery of an interrupted session. The session layer is responsible for creating, maintaining, and ending a communication session.

The primary function of the transport layer is to provide reliable end-to-end communication. The transport layer provides error detection and control at the message level across a network. The transport layer handles sequencing, multiplexing, flow control, flow control as well as retransmissions for bad or lost packets.

The network layer makes routing decisions across the network selecting the appropriate path a packet should take to reach its final destination. This layer contains all the specifications for the transmission and switching technologies needed to build circuits through a network of nodes.

The data link layer contains specifications for frames, synchronization, and error control. These specifications change the raw bit stream supplied by layer 1 into data and converts data into bits for transmitting by the physical layer. The data link layer also addresses reliability and integrity issues because the data link handles error control within each packet using CRC checks. The data link layer is broken into two sublayers: Media Access Control (MAC) and Logical Link Control (LLC).

The physical layer is lowest layer in the OSI model. The physical layer is concerned with the transmission of a bit stream over a communication channel. Specifications that define the signal voltages, bit duration, and channel definition are at this layer. The physical layer deals with mechanical and electrical characteristics needed to activate, maintain, and de-activate the physical connections. Examples include RS232C, Token Ring, and Ethernet.

61. Which layer handles general network access, flow control, and recovery from network failures?

   a. Network

   b. Physical

   c. Data link

   d. Transport

The correct answer is C. The data link layer is responsible for network access and recovery from network failures.

62. Which layer determines the route a packet will take from sender to receiver?

   a. Network

   b. Physical

   c. Data link

   d. Transport

The correct answer is A. The network layer makes routing decisions across the network selecting the appropriate path a packet should take to reach its final destination.

63. The subnet mask of an IP address _____.

   a. Enables automated IP address configuration

   b. Enables duplicate IP address to be used in different domains

    c. Defines which part of the address specifies the network and which part address specifies the host portion

    d. Is carried in all distance vector routing updates

The correct answer is C. The subnet mask is a 32-bit number that determines how an IP address is split into network and host portions on a bitwise basis.

64. Which is true about CSMA/CD?

    a. It is used by Token Ring as a media access scheme.

    b. Network devices access the physical medium based on possession of a token.

    c. With CSMA/CD, it is impossible to have a collision on the LAN.

    d. CSMA/CD stations can detect collisions, so they know when they must retransmit.

Answer D is true. Carrier sense multiple access with collision detection (CSMA/CD) is a control mechanism for Ethernet. This is how it works. An Ethernet station wanting to transmit first checks to see if the channel is busy (the station uses the carrier sense capability). It does this by looking for any signals on the medium. If none are present, the station can transmit. If others are transmitting, the station must wait. During the transmission, the station monitors the channel to ensure that no other stations are transmitting during its transmission. If no other stations are transmitting during this time and the station transmits all of its data, the transmission is successful.

If, however, any other station transmitted during this time, a collision would occur. The transmitting station would recognize this because the strength of the signal would double; this is the collision detection mechanism. When a collision occurs, each of the stations involved in the collision continue to transmit for a small length of time. This delay is to ensure that all stations have seen the collision. The stations involved in the collision then invoke a collision backoff algorithm. The algorithm generates a random number, which is used as the amount of time before each host can transmit again.

Answer A is false. CSMA/CD is used by Ethernet, not Token Ring, as a media access scheme.

Answer B is false. With CSMA/CD, network devices access the physical media only if no other stations are transmitting. The station uses the carrier sense capability to determine if the media is being used by another station.

Answer C is false. It is still possible to have a collision on an Ethernet LAN.

65. Which of the following is false?

    a. Token Ring is deterministic.

    b. Collisions cannot occur in Token Ring networks.

    c. The receiving station removes the frame from the ring.

    d. If early token release is supported, a new token can be released when frame transmission is complete.

Answer D is false. In Token Ring, the sending station removes the token from the ring. The information frame circulates the ring until it reaches the intended destination station, which copies the information for further processing. The information frame continues to circle the ring and is finally removed when it reaches the sending station.

Answer A is true because only a station in possession of a token can transmit onto the ring. Token Ring is deterministic in that you can determine the throughput that each station will have depending on the number of stations on the ring.

Answer B is true. Because only a station in possession of a token can transmit onto the ring, no collision can occur.

Answer C is true. Each station repeats the data, removes the jitter, checks for errors, and copies the data if appropriate. When the data is returned to the sending station, it removes the data from the ring.

66. The active monitor on a Token Ring _____.
   a. Acts as a centralized source of timing information for other ring stations
   b. Removes continuously circulating frames from the ring
   c. Is selected based on MAC address
   d. All of the above
   e. None of the above

The correct answer is D. The active monitor in Token Ring resolves certain error conditions that may occur on the ring, such as lost tokens and frames, priority tokens that circle the ring more than once, two active monitors present on the same ring, and clocking errors. The active monitor provides the ring's master clock, which ensures that all stations on the ring are synchronized.

67. The three-way handshake in TCP is not used to _____.
   a. Synchronize both ends of a connection.
   b. Enable both sides to agree upon initial sequence numbers.
   c. Ensure that both sides are ready to transmit and receive data.
   d. Ensure that both sides have the same window.

The correct answer is D. The three-way handshake in TCP is not used to ensure that both sides have the same window value. The three-way handshake is used to synchronize both ends of the connections, ensuring that they are ready to transmit and receive data. The three-way handshake enables both sides to agree upon initial sequence numbers and guarantees that both sides are ready to receive and transmit data.

This is how it works:

   1. Each host randomly chooses a sequence number, which is used to track bytes within the stream it is sending and receiving.

2. The first host initiates a connection by sending a packet with the SYN bit set in the TCP header. The random sequence number generated in step 1 is placed in the TCP header.

3. When the second host receives the packet, it records the sequence number and replies with an acknowledgement number equal to the first host's sequence number plus 1. The host also includes its own randomly generated sequence number in the TCP header.

4. When the first host receives the packet, it records the sequence number and replies with an acknowledgement number equal to the second host's sequence number plus 1.

5. At this point, both have agreed upon initial sequence numbers and data transfer can begin.

68. TCP sliding window _____. (multiple answers)
    a. Only permits one packet to be sent at a time
    b. Provides flow control
    c. Is established during connection setup and cannot change for the life of the connection
    d. Enables hosts to send multiple bytes or packets before waiting for an acknowledgment

The correct answers are B and D. The TCP sliding window provides flow control and enables hosts to send multiple bytes or packets before waiting for an acknowledgement.

69. Which of the following is not an ICMP error message?
    a. Destination unreachable
    b. Time exceeded
    c. Source quench
    d. Keepalive

The correct answer is D. ICMP messages are classified as either error messages or queries and responses; keepalive is not an ICMP message.

Answer A is incorrect. Destination unreachable is an ICMP message. It is sent to the source address if the router does not know how to reach the destination network.

Answer B is incorrect. Time exceeded is an ICMP message. A router returns a time exceeded message if it is forced to discard a datagram because the TTL field is 0. If a router processing a datagram finds that the TTL field is zero, it must discard the datagram and notify the source via the time exceeded ICMP message.

Answer C is incorrect. Source quench is an ICMP message. The source quench messages provide a basic from of flow control. When datagrams arrive too quickly for a router or host to process them, the receiving device's buffers quickly fill, causing additional datagrams to be discarded. At this point, the receiving device begins sending source quench messages to the transmitting device at the rate of one message for each packet dropped. The source device receives the source quench messages and lowers the transmission data rate until it stops receiving the messages. The sender will then gradually increase its transmission rate as long as it does not receive any more source quench requests.

70. A type 2 beacon in Token Ring indicates that _____.
   a. A station is sending claim tokens, but is not seeing them come back around the ring.
   b. A station is seeing an upstream neighbor transmitting all of the time.
   c. There is a physical break in the ring topology.
   d. None of the above
   e. All of the above

The correct answer is C. In the IBM Token Ring architecture, there are four types of beacons. A beacon type 1 is used for recovery purposes. A beacon type 2 is the most common beacon and indicates a physical break in the ring topology. A beacon type 3 is a claim token beacon and is sent by a station when it is sending claim tokens, but is not seeing them come back around the ring. A beacon type 4 is a streaming beacon and is sent by a station that is seeing an upstream neighbor transmitting all of the time.

71. A router is being used as a translation bridge between a Token ring network and an Ethernet network. Host X on the Token Ring sends a packet to Host Y on the Ethernet. The source MAC address of the packet is 4000.A089.0002. How would the MAC address be interpreted in an Ethernet environment?
   a. 2000.980A.0004
   b. 0040.89A0.2000
   c. 0200.0591.0040
   d. 4000.A089.0002

The correct answer is C. Ethernet uses canonical bit ordering. This means that the least significant bit in a byte is translated or read first. Non-canonical bit ordering is used by Token Ring, which means the most significant bit in a byte is translated first. It is important to understand that the concepts of canonical and non-canonical do not refer to the 0's and 1's in a MAC address being in different order on the wire itself. It is how the network interface cards (NICs) read the 0's and 1's that are different.

Based on this, to find the conical address, break down the packet in hexadecimal, take groupings of two hex digits (8 bits), look up their opposite in Table 2-1, and then swap them.

It is a good idea to create a table like Table 2-1 before you begin converting the address. The table is created by taking the nibble, which is half a byte, and reversing the order of the bits. For example, decimal value 1 is written as binary 0001. This becomes 1000 or decimal 8.

1. Break down the packet into hexadecimal.
4000.A089.0002 = **40 00 A0 89 00 02**

2. Take the hexadecimal values and covert them to the opposite value using Table 2-1. So for the first hexadecimal value, 4 becomes 2 and 0 remains 0.
40 00 A0 89 00 02 becomes 20 00 50 19 00 04.

3. Now swap the two numbers in each hexadecimal grouping. For example, 20 becomes 02. Do this for all of the hexadecimal groupings. The result is the conical address.
20 00 50 19 00 04 becomes **02 00 05 91 00 40**.

72. Which of the following is false?
    a. Frame relay is a packet-switched technology.
    b. Frame relay uses fixed-length packets.
    c. Frame relay uses BECN and FECN for flow control.
    d. Virtual circuits provide a bidirectional communications path from one DTE

Table 2-1   Conical Addresses

0=0	8=1
1=8	9=9
2=4	A=5
3=C	B=D
4=2	C=3
5=A	D=B
6=6	E=7
7=E	F=F

device to another.

Answer B is false. Frame relay packets are variable length. One of frame relays attractions is the fact that it is very efficient. With only 2 bytes of address overhead, you can transmit up to 8KB of data.

73. If the FECN bit is set in the frame relay header, which of the following can be said?
   a. The frame experienced congestion in the path opposite of the frame transmission.
   b. The frame experienced congestion in the path and was discarded.
   c. The frame experienced congestion in the path from the source to the destination.
   d. The frame has lower importance than other frames.

The correct answer is C. If the FECN bit is set in the frame relay header, the frame experienced congestion in the path from the source to the destination. If the BECN bit is set, congestion exists in the reverse direction that the frame was sent.

74. Which of the following is false?
   a. Frame relay inverse ARP is used to map between a specific protocol address and a specific DLCI.
   b. Inverse ARP is enabled by default on Cisco routers.
   c. Inverse ARP is not required on point-to-point interfaces.
   d. When running DECnet over frame relay, inverse ARP is not used.

Answer D is false. Frame relay inverse ARP is used to request the next-hop protocol address for a specific connection, given its known DLCI. When a frame relay circuit is initialized, the router attached does not have any address information except its own IP address. The router needs a way to determine the IP address of the far-end router on the particular DLCI. Inverse ARP is supported for IP, DECnet, AppleTalk, XNS, Novell, Vines, and ISO CLNS.

75. In Figure 2-9, PC A transmits a packet to PC B. The IP packet is errored in transit from R1 to R2. Who retransmits the packet?

Figure 2-9 X.25 network scenario

    a. PC A

    b. R2

    c. R1

    d. None of the above

The correct answer is C. X.25 was designed to provide error-free delivery using high error-rate links. X.25 provides windowing and retransmission of lost data. Because the packet was errored in transmission from R1 to R2, R1 will retransmit the packet.

76. In Figure 2-10, PC A transmits a packet to PC B. The packet is errored when it arrives at R2. Who retransmits the packet?

    a. PC A

    b. R1

    c. R2

    d. None of the above—R2 cannot detect if the packet is errored.

The correct answer is A. Frame relay can only detect errors, not correct them. It is up to the higher-layer protocols (in this case, TCP) to retransmit the packet. PCA resends the error packet.

77. Which of the following is true about X.25?

    a. The X.25 protocol suite maps to the lowest three layers of the OSI reference model.

    b. X.25 supports both switched and permanent virtual circuits.

    c. X.25 provides windowing and retransmission of lost data.

    d. All of the above

    e. None of the above

The correct answer is D. The X.25 protocol suite maps to the lowest three layers of the OSI reference model. It provides support for both switched virtual circuits (SVCs) and permanent virtual circuits (PVCs). X.25 provides windowing and retransmission of lost data.

78. Which of the following is not a circuit-switched technology?

    a. ISDN

    b. DSL

A   B

Figure 2-10   Frame relay network scenario

c. Analog dial

d. None of the above

The correct answer is B. Both ISDN and analog dial are examples of circuit-switched technologies. Digital subscriber line (DSL) is a dedicated, point-to-point, public network access over twisted-pair copper wire on the local loop (last mile) between a network service provider's (NSP's) central office and the customer site.

79. Which of the following is not a packet-switched technology?

a. Frame relay

b. X.25

c. HDLC

d. None of the above

The correct answer is C. ATM, frame relay, and X.25 are all examples of packet-switched technologies. HDLC is not a packet-switching technology; it is a link layer protocol.

80. Which of the following is/are true about ISDN BRI?

a. BRI B channels are used only for voice; data is carried on the D channel only.

b. The D channel is used for control and signaling data and cannot support user data.

c. With framing control and other overhead, the total bit rate is 192 Kbps.

d. The service offers 23 B channels and 1 D channel.

e. None of the above

The correct answer is C. The ISDN Basic Rate Interface (BRI) service offers two B channels and one D channel (2B + D). BRI B channel service operates at 64 Kbps and is can carry user data or voice; BRI D channel service operates at 16 Kbps and is meant to carry control and signaling information, although it can support user data transmission. The D channel signaling protocol comprises layers 1 through 3 of the OSI reference model. BRI also provides for framing control and other overhead, bringing its total bit rate to 192 Kbps.

81. The primary difference between ISDN BRI-U and an analog line is what?

a. ISDN BRI-U requires a four-wire local loop, whereas analog requires only a two-wire local loop.

b. ISDN is digital.

c. ISDN cannot support voice.

d. None of the above

The correct answer is B. The primary difference between ISDN and an analog line is ISDN is digital. ISDN can support both voice and data and is delivered over an existing two-wire local loop.

82. Which of the following is not true about virtual circuits?
    a. A virtual circuit is a logical circuit.
    b. Virtual circuits can be permanent or switched.
    c. A dedicated physical circuit is established.
    d. Virtual circuits are used in X.25.

The correct answer is C. A virtual circuit is a logical not a physical circuit and can be either switched (SVC) or permanent (PVC).

83. The transport layer is responsible for _____.
    a. Routing datagrams between hosts
    b. Encapsulating the IP datagrams into frames
    c. End-to-end data integrity
    d. None of the above
    e. All of the above

The correct answer is C. The transport layer provides reliable end-to-end communication, ensuring data integrity. The transport layer provides error detection and control at the message level across a network. The transport layer handles sequencing, multiplexing, flow control, as well as retransmissions for bad or lost packets. The network layer is responsible for routing datagrams between hosts. The data link layer is responsible for encapsulating IP datagrams into frames.

84. Which ATM layer is responsible for multiplexing and demultiplexing cells of different virtual connections?
    a. ATM physical layer
    b. ATM layer
    c. ATM Adaptation Layer
    d. Both A and C

The correct answer is B. Among other things, the ATM layer is responsible for multiplexing and demultiplexing cells of different virtual connections.

85. The ATM protocol consists of which of the following functional layers?
    a. ATM physical layer
    b. ATM layer
    c. ATM Adaptation Layer
    d. Data link layer
    e. All of the above except D
    f. A and C

The correct answer is E. The ATM protocol stack is composed of the following components:

- **Physical layer**   The ATM physical layer manages the medium-dependent transmission. It performs tasks such as

  - Converting the 53-byte ATM cell into an outgoing bit stream and converting an incoming bit stream to a 53-byte ATM cell

  - Keeping track of the ATM cell boundaries

  - Electrical and physical specifications

- **ATM layer**   The ATM layer is responsible for establishing connections and passing cells through the ATM network. To do this, it uses information in the header of each ATM cell. It performs tasks such as

  - VPI and VCI switching

  - Cell multiplexing and demultiplexing

  - Flow control

  - Header error control

  - CLP processing

  - QoS support

- **ATM Adaptation Layer (AAL)**   The AAL is responsible for isolating higher-layer protocols from the details of the ATM processes. It performs tasks such as

  - Segmentation and reassembly of the data

  - Payload error control

  - End-to-end timing

86. Which ATM layer is responsible for keeping track of ATM cell boundaries and packaging cells into the appropriate type of frame for the physical medium transport?

    a. ATM physical layer
    b. ATM layer
    c. ATM Adaptation Layer
    d. Data link layer

The correct answer is A. The ATM physical layer is responsible for keeping track of ATM cell boundaries and packaging cells into the appropriate type of frame for the physical medium transport.

87. Which ATM Adaptation Layer is best suited for transporting voice and video?

    a. AAL 5
    b. AAL 4

    c. AAL 1

    d. AAL 3 and 4

The correct answer is C. Because AAL 1 is a connection-oriented service, it is most suitable for handling circuit-emulation applications, such as voice and video conferencing.

88. Which ATM layer is responsible for segmentation and reassembly?

    a. ATM physical layer

    b. ATM layer

    c. ATM Adaptation Layer

    d. All of the above

The correct answer is C. The ATM Adaptation Layer is responsible for isolating higher-layer protocols from the details of the ATM processes. It performs segmentation and reassembly of the data, payload error control, and end-to-end timing.

89. Which ATM layer is responsible for cell delineation?

    a. ATM physical layer

    b. ATM layer

    c. ATM Adaptation Layer

    d. All of the above

The correct answer is A. The ATM physical layer manages the medium-dependent transmission. It is responsible for converting the 53-byte ATM cell into an outgoing bit stream and converting an incoming bit stream to a 53-byte ATM cell, keeping track of the ATM cell boundaries (cell delineation), and electrical and physical specifications.

90. ATM UNI is between _____.

    a. Two end stations

    b. The end station and the ATM switch

    c. Two ATM switches

    d. None of the above

The correct answer is B. ATM networks are made up of ATM switches and ATM end-user equipment.

An ATM switch is responsible for transmitting ATM cells through an ATM network. The ATM switch takes an incoming cell and reads and updates the cell-header information; for example, the VPI and VCI values may change. It then switches the cell towards its final destination.

An ATM end-user device connects to an ATM switch and is responsible for generating and sending ATM traffic into the network.

As shown in Figure 2-11, an ATM network consists of a set of ATM switches interconnected by point-to-point ATM links, which are often referred to as trunks. ATM switches support two primary types of interfaces: user-network interface (UNI) and network-

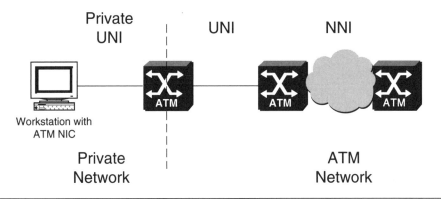

Figure 2-11   ATM UNI and NNI interfaces

network interface (NNI). The UNI connects ATM end systems (such as hosts and routers) to an ATM switch. The NNI connects two ATM switches.

91. Which of the following is true?
    a. A virtual path is a logical grouping of virtual circuits.
    b. ATM cells consist of 5 bytes of header information and 48 bytes of pay-load data.
    c. The VPI and VCI fields of the cell header identify the next network segment that a cell needs to transmit on its way to its final destination.
    d. B and C
    e. All of the above

The correct answer is E. An ATM circuit is based on a connection-oriented, end-to-end link. Addressing information is contained in the ATM cell header in the form of a VPI and a VCI. A virtual channel can be thought of as a transport of cells. A virtual path is a logical grouping of virtual circuits.

ATM cells consist of a 5-byte header and 48-byte payload. The 5-byte ATM cell header contains information needed to switch the ATM cell to its next destination. The ATM cell header is examined and updated on a switch-by-switch basis.

The VPI is an 8-bit field that along with the VCI identifies the next destination of a cell as it passes through an ATM network towards its final destination.

92. On a PPP link, what is the order of operation?
    a. NCP negotiation, LCP negotiation, and authentication
    b. LCP negotiation, NCP negotiation, and authentication
    c. LCP negotiation, authentication, and NCP negotiation
    d. NCP negotiation, authentication, and LCP negotiation

The correct answer is C. The first phase of negotiation on a PPP link is LCP. LCP is used to establish the connection through an exchange of configure packets. LCP is used to automatically agree upon the encapsulation format options, handle varying limits on sizes of packets, detect a looped-back link and other common misconfiguration errors, and terminate the link. This exchange is complete and the LCP opened state is entered once a configure-ACK packet has been both sent and received.

The next phase is authentication, although authentication is not mandatory. Two common authentication protocols are Password Authentication Protocol (PAP) and Challenge Handshake Authentication Protocol (CHAP).

If PAP is used for authentication, the dialing router sends an authentication request to the server containing a username and password. This information is passed in the clear. The server compares this username and password to the list of defined users; if it matches the authentication request is accepted, the Cisco IOS software sends an authentication acknowledgment.

If CHAP is used the server sends a request or challenges the remote device to respond. The challenge packet consists of an ID, a random number, and the hostname of the local router. When the remote device receives the challenge packet, it concatenates the ID, the remote device's password, and the random number, and then encrypts all of it using the remote device's password. The remote device sends the results back to the server, along with the name associated with the password used in the encryption process. When the server receives the response, it uses the name it received to retrieve a password in its list of defined users. The retrieved password is the same password the remote device used in its encryption process. The access server then encrypts the concatenated information with the newly retrieved password—if the result matches the result sent in the response packet, authentication succeeds.

The benefit of using CHAP authentication is that the remote device's password is never transmitted in clear text. This prevents other devices from stealing the password and gaining illegal access to the network.

At this point, network layer protocol configuration negotiation occurs. After LCP has finished the link-quality determination phase and authentication has occurred, network layer protocols can be configured separately by the appropriate Network Control Protocol (NCP) and can be brought up and taken down at any time.

93. Which of the following is/are not the responsibility of the LCP in PPP?
   a. Detection of looped-back links
   b. Assignment and management of IP addresses
   c. Termination of the link
   d. Authentication

The correct answer is B. NCP is responsible for the assignment and management of IP addresses. LCP is responsible for detecting loopback links and terminating the link.

94. In a MAC address, the first _____ bits identify the vendor.

    a. 8

    b. 12

    c. 24

    d. 48

The correct answer is C. A MAC addresses is 48 bits in length and is expressed as 12 hexadecimal digits. The first six hexadecimal digits (24 bits), which are administered by the IEEE, identify the manufacturer or vendor and thus comprise the Organizational Unique Identifier (OUI). The last six hexadecimal digits (24 bits) comprise the interface serial number, or another value administered by the specific vendor.

95. TCP slow start provides _____.

    a. Flow control by increasing the TCP window size only after an ACK is received

    b. Error detection and correction

    c. Flow control by increasing the TCP window size only after two consecutive ACKs are received

    d. Better performance by enabling TCP at the start of the connection to send multiple segments up to the window size of the receiver

The correct answer is A. TCP slow start provides flow control by only increasing the TCP window size after an ACK is received. The sender starts by transmitting one segment and waiting for an ACK. When that ACK is received, the TCP congestion window is incremented from one to two, and two segments can be sent. When each of those two segments is acknowledged, the congestion window is increased to four.

96. Global synchronization in an IP network refers to _____.

    a. The convergence of the routing protocol

    b. When the TCP three-way handshake is complete

    c. The event when multiple TCP hosts reduce their transmission rate rates in response to packet dropping, and then increase their transmission rates once again when the congestion is reduced

    d. When multiple TCP streams transverse the same link

The correct answer is C. Global synchronization is the event when congestion occurs in the network and multiple TCP streams reduce their transmission rates in response. As congestion is reduced, the TCP hosts increase their transmission rates until congestion is reach. When congestion occurs, the TCP hosts reduce their transmission rate again. This synchronization causes waves of congestion followed by periods during which the transmission link is not fully utilized.

97. The capability to transmit data in only one direction between a sending and a receiving station is called _____.

    a. Simplex

    b. Full-duplex

    c. Half-duplex

    d. Unicast

The correct answer is A. Simplex transmission is the capability to transmit data in only one direction at a time. A good example of simplex technology is broadcast TV. Full-duplex transmission is the capability to have simultaneous data transmission between a sending station and a receiving station. A good example of a full-duplex technology is FDDI. Half-duplex transmission is the capability to transmit data in only one direction at a time between the sending and receiving station.

98. Which of the following is an example of a simplex technology?

    a. Ethernet

    b. Token Ring

    c. Broadcast TV

    d. T1

The correct answer is C. Broadcast TV is an example of a one-way or simplex technology.

99. Which of the following authentication protocols are used by PPP?

    a. PPPA and DHCP

    b. DHCP and PAP

    c. CHAP and PAP

    d. None of the above

The correct answer is C. Two common authentication protocols used by PPP PAP and the CHAP. One of the key differences between the two is that with CHAP authentication, the remote device's password is never transmitted in clear text. This prevents other devices from stealing the password and gaining illegal access to the network.

100. Which of the following is false?

    a. With CHAP, the remote device's password is never sent in the clear.

    b. With PAP, the password is encrypted.

    c. CHAP is considered more secure than PAP.

    d. To use PAP or CHAP, you must be running PPP.

The correct answer is B. If PAP is used for authentication, the dialing router sends an authentication request to the server containing a username and password. This information is passed in the clear. The server compares this username and password to the list of defined users, if it matches the authentication request is accepted, the Cisco IOS software sends an authentication acknowledgment.

If CHAP is used, the server sends a request or challenges the remote device to respond. The challenge packet consists of an ID, a random number, and the hostname of the local router. When the remote device receives the challenge packet, it concatenates the ID, the remote device's password, and the random number, and then encrypts all of it using the remote device's password. The remote device sends the results back to the server, along with the name associated with the password used in the encryption process. When server receives the response, it uses the name it received to retrieve a password in its list of defined users. The retrieved password is the same password that the remote device used in its encryption process. The access server then encrypts the concatenated information with the newly retrieved password—if the result matches the result sent in the response packet, authentication succeeds.

CCIE Qualification Exam 2 (Routing Fundamentals)

This chapter will cover:

- Routing fundamentals
- RIP
- OSPF
- IS-IS
- EIGRP
- BGP

Introduction

This chapter focuses on routing fundamentals and routing protocols. The goal of this practice exam is to test the user's aptitude on the design fundamentals and operation of today's most popular routing protocol. The exam includes questions on Open Shortest Path First (OSPF), Integrated Intermediate System to Intermediate System (IS-IS), Enhanced Interior Gateway Routing Protocol (EIGRP), Interior Gateway Routing Protocol (IGRP), and Border Gateway Protocol (BGP).

Technology Overview

A router operates at the network layer or layer 3 of the OSI model. Its primary job is to forward packets of data between nodes that are not connected to same network. In order to correctly route packets to their respective destinations, a router must acquire and store routing information for each destination network.

In order to understand what information is required to route a packet, it useful to examine what happens when a framed packet arrives on one of the router's interfaces (see Figure 3-1). When an Ethernet frame arrives at a router, the destination Media Access Control (MAC) address is examined. If the MAC address is that of the router's interfaces or the broadcast address, the router strips off the layer 2 frame and passes the packet to the indicated network layer protocol in the Ethernet header. In the case of our scenario, the layer 3 protocol is IP; it could have been Internetwork Packet Exchange (IPX), AppleTalk, or any other routable protocol.

Once the packet is passed to the network layer, the router examines the destination address of the packet. If the destination address is either the IP address of one of the interfaces on the router or set to the broadcast address, the protocol field of the IP packet is examined and the packet is sent the appropriate internal process. If the destination address is any other, the packet must be routed.

In order to route the packet, the router queries its routing table in order to determine the appropriate interface to forward the packet. The routing table contains the destination address of all of the networks that the router can reach. The table also contains a pointer that indicates the interface to forward the packet out and if the network is not directly connected the IP address of another router on a directly connected interface. This router is called the next-hop router and is one router hop closer to the destination.

The routing table is searched for a routing entry that contains the most specific match to the destination network; this is referred to as longest match routing. The routing table can contain host-specific addresses, subnets, summary routes, major network numbers, supernets, or default addresses (see Table 3-1). If the router cannot match the destination address to any entry in the routing table the packet is dropped and an Internet Control Message Protocol (ICMP) host unreachable message is sent to the source address.

Table 3-1 Longest Match Routing

192.1.1.1 /32	Host-specific route
192.1.1.0 /30	Subnet
192.1.1.0 /25	Summary
192.1.1.0/24	Major network
192.1.0.0/16	Supernet
0.0.0.0	Default network

The routing table can be populated in multiple ways. The first is if the destination network is directly connected to the router. In this case, the destination network is automatically placed in the routing table, along with the interface of the router that connects to that network.

The other two ways that the router acquires information is through manual configuration (static routes) or dynamic routing protocols. This case study is focused on dynamic IP routing protocols, which can be further broken into two groups: distance vector and link state protocols.

Static Routes

Although static routes require manual configuration, they are very useful in certain situations. Static routes provide precise control over routing behavior, which often cannot be obtained through dynamic protocols. The drawback, of course, is that these routes must be reconfigured any time a topology change occurs.

Static routes are often used in hub-and-spoke situations where the spoke is singly homed, to reduce routing overhead. In Figure 3-1 the spoke router only has one connection to the network; if that link were to go down, no alternative path would be available. Static routes are also useful in dial backup scenarios, where a floating static route is configured. A floating static route is similar to a regular static route in that it is not

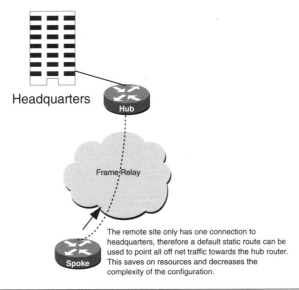

Figure 3-1 Static route in single homed environment

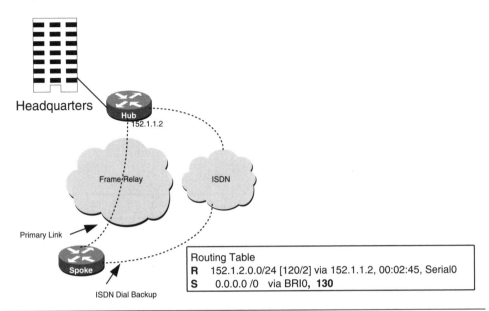

Figure 3-2 Using floating static routes for dial backup

permanently entered in the routing table. It appears only after the failure of a more pre-ferred route.

In Figure 3-2 the spoke router is learning its routes via the Routing Information Pro-tocol (RIP) over its primary link from the hub. It also has a floating static route that points all traffic out of the Integrated Services Digital Network (ISDN) interface. This route has a higher administrative distance (admin distance of 130) than RIP (admin distance of 120). Administrative distance is the measure of preference that the router gives to all of its routing protocols. The lower the administrative distance, the more pre-ferred the route. A static route that is configured with a higher admin distance is said to be floating because the only time that it will be invoked is if the more-preferred route, which in this case is the one learned by RIP, was to go away.

Dynamic Routing Protocols

Dynamic routing protocols allow routers to discover and share information automati-cally with other routers. A routing protocol can be thought of as a language that routers use to communicate reachability information and status of networks. Routing proto-cols not only share information between routers, but they also calculate the best paths to a destination. This capability to determine the best path to the destination during topology changes is the most important advantage dynamic protocols have over static routing.

Eight major IP routing protocols can be used to calculate and exchange routing information. Each have major advantages and disadvantages, which will be explored throughout this case study. Table 3-2 lists all eight protocols along with their administrative distance.

The router uses the administrative distance to select the most preferred source of routing updates. For example, if a router is running multiple protocols and learns a route to the same destination from each protocol, it needs a way to determine which one to use. This can be thought of as the measure of believability. The lower the administrative distance, the more believable the routing protocol. Admin distances are assigned based on the routing protocol's capability to select the best path. For example, suppose that a router running RIP and EIGRP learns of the same network from both protocols. Because RIP calculates the route based on hop count and EIGRP uses a composite metric, EIGRP is most likely to have calculated the best path. As we explore each protocol in depth, the reasons that one protocol is preferred over another will become clear.

Table 3-2 Administrative Distance

Routing Protocol	Administrative Distance
Static route	1
EIGRP summary	
BGP	20
EIGRP	90
IGRP	100
OSPF	110
IS-IS	115
RIP	120
EGP	140
External EIGRP	170
IBGP	200
Unknown	255

Dynamic routing protocols are broken into two classes: distance vector and link state protocols.

Distance Vector Protocols

The name distance vector is derived from the fact that routes are advertised as vectors of distance and direction. Distance is defined in terms of a metric (hop count, in the case of RIP), and direction in terms of next-hop router. For example, destination X is a distance of three hops away in the direction of next–hop router Y. Each router learns routes from its neighboring router perspective, adds a distance vector—its own distance value —to the route, adds the route to its routing table, and advertises it on to its immediate neighbors.

This type of routing is often referred to as routing by rumor, because each router depends on its neighbor for routing information, which in turn may have been received from that router's neighbor. Most distance vector routing algorithms are based on the work done by Bellman, Ford, and Fulkerson; therefore, they are often referred to as Bellman-Ford algorithms.

For the most part, all distance vector protocols share the same characteristics and limitations. They exchange reachability information by sending periodic updates to all neighbors by broadcasting their entire routing table. In large networks, the routing table exchanged between routers becomes very large and hard to maintain, which leads to slow convergence. Convergence is the point in time when the entire network becomes updated to the fact that a route has appeared or disappeared.

Distance vector routers work on the basis of periodic updates and holddown timers. If an update is not received in a given interval, the route goes into holddown state and is aged from the routing table. The holddown aging process translates into minutes in convergence time before the whole network detects that a route has disappeared. This slow convergence problem creates inconsistencies, because routing Update messages propagate slowly across the network. The larger the network, the greater the convergence time.

The other major drawback of distance vector protocols is their classful nature. They do not support Classless Interdomain Routing (CIDR) or Variable Length Subnet Masks (VLSM) because no mask information is exchanged in their routing updates.

Finally, distance vector protocols are considered to be non-hierarchical or flat, which makes them incapable of scaling in large enterprise networks.

This case study will explore the three most popular distance vector algorithms: RIP, IGRP, and EIGRP. Although EIGRP is occasionally described as a distance vector protocol that acts like a link state protocol (a hybrid), it still retains the routing characteristics of a distance vector protocol.

Routing Information Protocol (RIP)

Routing Information Protocol (RIP) is a distance vector protocol used to exchange routing information among gateways (routers) and hosts. RIP is based on the Bellman-Ford (distance vector) algorithm, which was originally used in computer routing in 1969 by ARPANET. However, Xerox originally developed the protocol RIP as we know it today in the late 1970s as part of their Xerox Networking Services (NXS) protocol suite.

Despite its technical limitations, RIP is one of the most widely used Interior Gateway Protocols (IGPs) designed for medium-sized homogeneous networks. RIP owes its widespread installed base to the fact that Berkley distributed routed software along with their popular 4BSD UNIX. Routed software used RIP to provide consistent routing and reachability information for machines on local networks. TCP/IP sites started using RIP to provide local area routing and eventually began using it in the wide area.

How It Works

RIP uses two packet types to convey information: updates and requests. Each RIP-enabled router on the network broadcasts Update messages every 30 seconds using UDP port 520 to all directly connected neighbors. Update messages reflect the complete routing database, which currently exits in the router. Each entry in the database consists of two elements: the IP address of the network that can be reached and the distance to that network. The router uses request messages to discover other RIP-speaking devices on the network.

RIP uses hop count as the metric to measure the distance to a network. Each router adds its internal distance (1) to the route before advertising the route to its neighbors. In Figure 3-3, R3 is directly connected to Network C. When it advertises its route to R2, it increments the metric by one; likewise, R2 increases the metric to two and advertises the route to R1. R2 and R1 are said to be one and two hops, respectively, from Network C.

As per Figure 3-3, the number of hops to get to a given destination is the number of routers that a datagram must pass through to get to that destination network. Using hop count for path determination will not always provide the best path. For example, in Figure 3-4, to get from R1 to Network B, RIP will prefer the shorter path via the 56-Kbps link over the longer path via the 1.5-Mbps link. Even though the delay across a 56-Kbps serial circuit will be substantially longer than a path with a hop count of two that crosses two 1.5-Mbps serial circuits, RIP cannot make the distinction.

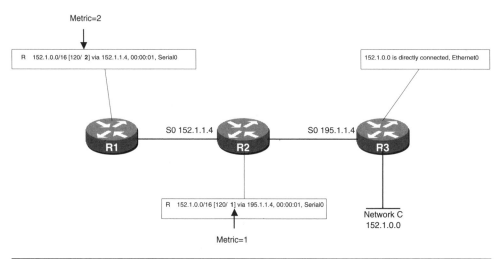

Figure 3-3 RIP metrics

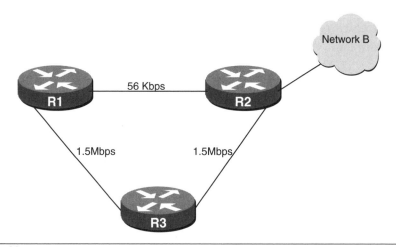

Figure 3-4 Hop count

Routing Loops

The problem with any distance vector routing protocol like RIP is that each router does not have a complete view of the network. Routers must rely on the neighboring routers for network reachablity information. The distance vector routing algorithm creates a slow convergence problem in which inconsistencies arise, because routing Update messages propagate slowly across the network. To reduce the likelihood of routing loops caused by inconsistencies across the network, RIP uses the following mechanisms: count-to-infinity, split horizons, poison reverse updates, holddown counters, and triggered updates.

Count-to-Infinity Problem   RIP permits a maximum hop count of 15. Any destination that is more than 15 hops away is considered unreachable. This number, although severely limiting the size of a network, prevents a problem called count-to-infinity (see Figure 3-5).

1. Count-to-infinity works like this: R1 loses its Ethernet interface and generates a triggered update, which is sent to R2 and R3. The triggered update tells R2 and R3 that R3 no longer can reach Network A. The update is delayed during transmission to R2 (busy CPU, congested link, and so on) but arrives at R3. R3 removes the route to Network A from its routing table.

2. R2 still has not received the triggered update from R1 and sends its regular routing update advertising Network A as reachable with a hop count of two. R3 receives the update and thinks a new route exits to Network A.

3. R3 then advertises to R1 that it can reach Network A with a hop count of three.

4. R1 then advertises to R2 that that it can reach Network A with a hop count of four.

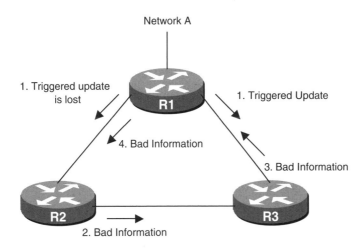

Figure 3-5   Count-to-infinity problem

5. This loop will continue until the hop count reaches infinity, which is defined by RIP as 16. Once a route reaches infinity (16), it is declared unusable and deleted from the routing table.

With the count-to-infinity problem, the routing information will continue to pass from router to router incrementing the hop count by one. This problem, and the routing loop, will continue indefinitely, or until some limit is reached. That limit is RIP's maximum hop count. When the hop count of a route exceeds 15, the route is marked unreachable, and over time, eventually removed from the routing table.

Split Horizons   The rule of split horizon states that it is never useful for a router to advertise a route back in the direction from which it came. When split horizons is enabled on a router's interface, the router records the interface over which a route was received and does not propagate information about that route back out that interface.

The Cisco router enables you to disable split horizons on a per-interface basis. This is sometimes necessary in Non-Broadcast Multiple Access (NBMA) hub-and-spoke environments. In Figure 3-6, R2 is connected to R3 and R1 via Frame Relay; both Permanent Virtual Circuits (PVCs) are terminating on one physical interface on R2.

In Figure 3-6 if split horizon is not disabled on R2's serial interface, then R3 will not receive R1's routing advertisements and vise versa. Use the **no ip split-horizon** interface subcommand to disable split horizons.

Poison Reverse   Split horizon is a scheme used by the router to avoid problems caused by advertising routes back to the router from which they were learned. The split horizon scheme omits routes learned from one neighbor in updates sent to that neighbor. Split horizon with poisoned reverse includes the routes in updates, but sets their metrics to 16 (infinity).

By setting the hop count to infinity and advertising the route back to its source, it is possible to immediately break a routing loop. Otherwise, the inaccurate route will stay in the routing table until it times out. The disadvantage to poison reverse is that it increases the size of the routing table.

Holddown   Holddown timers prevent the router from accepting routing information about a network for a fixed period of time after the route has been removed from the routing table. The idea is to make sure all routers have received the information, and no router sends out an invalid route. For example, in Figure 3-5, R2 advertised bad information to R3 because of the delay in the routing update. With holddown counters, this would not happen because R3 would not install a new route to Network A for 180 seconds. By then, R2 would have converged with the proper routing information.

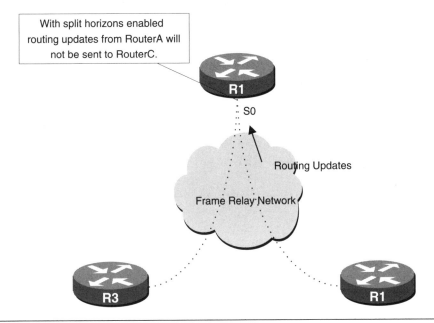

> With split horizons enabled routing updates from RouterA will not be sent to RouterC.

Figure 3-6 Split horizons

Triggered Updates Split horizons with poison reverse breaks any loop between two routers. Loops containing three or more routers can still occur, ending only when infinity (16) is reached. Triggered updates are an attempt to speed up convergence time; whenever the metric of a route changes, the router must send an Update message immediately. A triggered Update message is sent immediately regardless of when the regular Update message is scheduled to be sent.

RIP Message Format

Figure 3-7 shows the format of an RIP message; after the 32-bit header, the message contains a sequence of pairs. The pairs contain the network IP address and an integer distance to that network that can be reached.

The contents of the RIP message format are defined as follows:

- **Commands** The command is generally either an RIP request (1) or an RIP response (2). Commands 3 and 4 are obsolete and command 5 is reserved for Sun Microsystems internal use.

- **Version** This field contains the protocol version number. Two versions of RIP are available.

0		8		16		24		31
COMMAND(1-5)		VERSION (1)			MUST BE ZERO			
FAMILY OF NET1					MUST BE ZERO			
IP ADDRESS OF NET1								
MUST BE ZERO								
MUST BE ZERO								
DISTANCE TO NET1								
FAMILY OF NET2					MUST BE ZERO			
IP ADDRESS OF NET2								
MUST BE ZERO								
MUST BE ZERO								
DISTANCE TO NET2								

Figure 3-7   RIP message format

- **Address family identifier**   RIP was designed to carry routing information for multiple protocols. This field specifies the family of the protocol that is being carried. The address family identifier for IP is 2.

- **IP address**   This field contains the IP address, which is stored as a four-octet number.

- **Must be zero**   RIP can carry network addresses that are up to 12 octets long. Because an IP address only uses 4 of the 32 octets, the remaining 8 octets are padded with zeros.

- **Distance to net**   This field contains an integer count of the distance to the specified network. It contains a value of 16 if the network is unreachable.

RIP is the most widely used IGP in large organizations today, especially in organizations that have a large Unix-based routing environment. However, it is worth noting the limitations that one faces when deploying a large RIP network.

- RIP uses a 4-bit metric to count router hops to destinations. This limits the size of an RIP network, which cannot contain more than 15 hops to a destination. This is a severe limitation when trying to implement a typical modern large-scale network.

- RIP uses hop count as a routing metric, which does not provide the most optimal path selection. More advanced protocols like IGRP use complex metrics to determine the optimal path.

- RIP was deployed prior to subnetting and has no subnet support. RIP assumes that all interfaces on the network have the same mask.

- RIP broadcasts a complete list of networks it can reach every 30 seconds. This can amount to a significant amount of traffic, especially on low-speed links.

- RIP has no security features built in; an RIP-enabled device will accept RIP updates from any other device on the network. More modern routing protocols such as OSPF enable the router to authenticate updates.

Interior Gateway Routing Protocol (IGRP)

Interior Gateway Routing Protocol (IGRP) is a Cisco proprietary distance vector routing protocol developed in 1986 to address the limitations of RIP. Unlike RIP, which uses UDP, IGRP accesses IP directly as protocol 9. IGRP uses a concept of autonomous systems to separate IGRP process domains. These processes are kept completely separate, enabling IGRP to run multiple processes within the same domain. No routes are exchanged between domains unless explicitly defined through the redistribution command. This enables traffic between IGRP processes to be closely regulated by redistribution and route filtering.

Although RIP works quite well in small, homogenous internetworks, its small hop count (16) severely limits the size of the network and its single metric (hop count) does not provide the routing flexibility needed in complex networks. IGRP addresses the shortcomings of RIP by permitting the network to grow up to 255 hops and by providing a wide range of metrics (link reliability, bandwidth, internetwork delay, and load) to provide routing flexibility in today's complex networks.

IGRP's other advantages over RIP are unequal-cost load balancing, an update period that is three times longer than RIP's, and a more efficient update packet format. The key disadvantage is that it is a Cisco proprietary, whereas RIP is open standard.

Routing Loops

The problem with the first- and second-generation distance vector routing protocols like IGRP is that each router does not have a complete view of the network. Routers must rely on the neighboring routers for network reachablity information. This creates a slow convergence problem in which inconsistencies arise because routing Update messages propagate slowly across the network. To reduce the likelihood of routing loops caused by inconsistencies across the network, IGRP uses split horizons, poison reverse updates, holddown counters, and flash updates. In the previous section, we discussed split horizons, poison reverse updates, and holddown counters, so we will only cover flash updates in this section.

Flash Updates   Flash updates are an attempt to speed up convergence time; whenever the metric of a route changes, the router must send an Update message immediately. A flash Update message is sent immediately regardless of when the regular Update message is scheduled to be sent.

IGRP Routes

IGRP advertises three types of routes: interior, system, and exterior. Interior routes are routes between subnets that are attached to the same router interface. System routes are routes to networks that are in the same autonomous system and exterior routes are routes to networks outside the autonomous system (see Figure 3-8).

IGRP Metrics

The IGRP metric is a 32-bit number, which is calculated using bandwidth, delay, reliability, loading, and maximum transmission unit (MTU). By default, the IGRP chooses a route based on bandwidth and delay.

Bandwidth is expressed in units of kilobits per second. It is a static number that may not actual reflect the bandwidth of the link. For example, the default bandwidth of a serial link is 1,544 regardless of the actual bandwidth of the link. The bandwidth command should be used to set the interface to the actual bandwidth of the link.

Delay is expressed in ten-microsecond units and represents the end-to-end travel time. Like bandwidth, delay is also a static figure and may not actually reflect the delay of the link. For example, the default delay for a serial link is 1,000 microseconds regardless of the actual delay of the link. The delay command should be used to match the delay of the interface to the actual delay of the link.

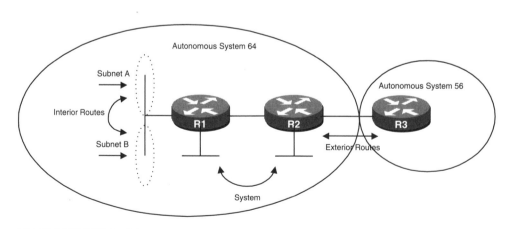

Figure 3-8   IGRP route types

Calculating the metric for a route is a two-step process using the five different characteristics of the link and the K values. The K values are configurable, but this is not recommended. The default K values are K1 = 1, K2 = 0, K3 = 1, K4 = 0, and K5 = 0.

1. Metric = K1×Bandwidth + (K2×Bandwidth) / (256-load) + K3×Delay

2. If K5 is not equal to zero, take the metric from step 1 and multiple it by [K5 / (reliability + K4)]. If K5 is zero, ignore step 2.

Metric = Metric×[K5 / (reliability + K4)]

As shown previously, Cisco sets K2, K4, and K5 to zero. This leaves only two variables to compute the IGRP metric (bandwidth and delay). Because three of the K values are zero, the formula reduces to

Metric = Bandwidth + Delay

Finding the smallest of all bandwidths in path to the destination and dividing 10,000,000 by that number derives the IGRP bandwidth.

Delay is found by adding all of the delays along the paths and dividing that number by 10. The equation is written as the following:

Metric = [(10,000,000 / min bandwidth) + (SUM (interface delay) / 10)]

IGRP Message Format

Figure 3-9 shows the format of an IGRP packet. This figure shows the efficient design in comparison to RIP. IGRP updates provide much more information than RIP, which sends little more than a snapshot of the sender's routing table. Unlike RIP, no field is unused. After the 12-byte header, individual route entries appear one after the other with no padding, like RIP, to force each entry to end on a 32-bit word boundary. Update packets can contain 104 network entries, verses the 25 for RIP. After the 32-bit header, the message contains a sequence of pairs. The pairs contain the network IP address and an integer distance to that network.

The contents of the IGRP packet format are defined as follows:

- **Version**   This will always be set to one.

- **Opcode**   This will be set to one for an IGRP request packet and two for an IGRP update packet. A request packet consists of a header with no entries.

- **Edition**   This is incremented by the sender of an update whenever a change of routing information occurs. The edition number prevents the router from accepting old updates that arrive after newer updates.

0		8		16		24		31
Version	OPCode	Edition		Autonomous System Number				
Number of Interior Routes				Number of System Routes				
Number of Exterior Routes				Checksum				
Destination							Delay	
Delay				Bandwidth				
Bandwidth		MTU				Reliability		
Load		Hop Count		Destination				
Destination		Delay						
Bandwidth						MTU		
MTU		Reliability		Load		Hop Count		

Figure 3-9 IGRP packet format

- **Autonomous system number**   This is the ID number of the IGRP process. This number enables multiple processes to exchange information over a common data link.

- **Number of interior routes**   The number of entries in the update that are subnets of a directly connected network. If none of the entries are subnets of a directly connected network, the field will be zero. This field along with the next two fields tells the router how many 14-octet entries are contained in the packet.

- **Number of system routes**   This represents the number of entries in the update that are not directly connected network. These are networks that have been summarized by a network border router.

- **Number of exterior routes**   This represents the number of routes to networks that have been identified as default networks.

- **Checksum**   A 16-bit ones complement sum of the packet is calculated on the IGRP header and all entries.

- **Destination**   The address of the destination, which is only three octets long. At first this might seem odd because an IP address is four octets long. This is possible because IGRP uses route categorization. If the entry is an interior route, at least the first octet of the IP address will always be known from the address of the interface on which the update was received. So the destination field of an interior route entry will only contain the last three octets of the address. If the entry is a system or an external route, the route will be summarized and at least the last octet will be all zeros. Therefore, the destination fields of system and external routes will contain only the first three octets of the address.

- **Delay**   This is a 24-bit number that is the sum of all of configured delays along the path and is expressed in units of ten microseconds.

- **Bandwidth** This is a 24-bit number that is 10,000,000 divided by the lowest bandwidth along the path.

- **MTU** This is the smallest maximum transmit unit of any link along the route to the destination.

- **Reliability** This is the number between 0x01 and 0xFF that reflects the total outgoing error rate of the interface along the route and is calculated every five minutes.

- **Load** This is a number between 0x01 and 0xff that reflects the total outgoing load of the interface along the route and is calculated every five minutes.

- **Hop count** This is a number between 0x01 and 0xFF indicating the number of hops to the destination.

Because IGRP is a distance vector protocol, its suffers from some of the same limitations as RIP, namely slow convergence. However, unlike RIP, IGRP can scale across large networks. IGRP's maximum hop count of 255 enables the protocol to be run in even the largest networks. Because IGRP uses five metrics to calculate route feasibility, it provides a more intuitive route selection process providing optimal performance in even the most complex networks.

Enhanced Interior Gateway Routing Protocol (EIGRP)

Enhanced Interior Gateway Routing Protocol (EIGRP) is a Cisco proprietary advanced distance vector routing protocol, which was first released in 1994 (IOS 9.21) to address the limitations of first and second-generation distance vector protocols and link state protocols.

Traditional distance vector protocols such as RIP and IGRP forward routing updates to all attached neighbors, which in turn forward the updates to their neighbors. This hop-by-hop propagation of routing information creates large convergence times and looped topology problems.

Link state protocols such as OSPF have been offered as an alternative to the tradition distance vector protocols. The problem with link state protocols is that they solve the convergence problems of traditional distance vector protocols by replicating the topology information across the entire domain. This replication becomes undesirable in large networks and greatly affects CPU utilization due to the number of SPF calculations that need to be run.

EIGRP is different from the protocols discussed so far in that EIGRP uses a system of diffusing computations (route calculations that are performed in a coordinated fashion among multiple routers) to attain fast convergence while remaining loop free at every instant. Unlike the protocols discussed earlier, EIGRP updates are non-periodic, partial, and bounded.

So what does all that mean? Non-periodic means that updates are not sent at regular intervals; EIGRP only sends updates in the event of a metric or topology change. *Partial* means that only the routes that have changed are sent, not all of the routes in the table. *Bounded* means that updates are only sent to the routers that are affected by the change. This means that EIGRP uses much less bandwidth than traditional distance vector protocols.

Some of the other major advantages of EIGRP are

- By default, EIGRP uses no more than 50 percent of the bandwidth of the link. This is major benefit when routing over low-speed or high-cost WAN links.

- EIGRP is a classless protocol; each route entry in an update includes a subnet mask.

- EIGRP supports message digest 5 (MD5) authentication.

- EIGRP can also route IPX and AppleTalk traffic.

EIGRP Terminology

When dealing with EIGRP, it is important to understand the terminology being used.

The *successor* is the directly connected neighboring router that has the best route to reach a particular destination. This is the route that is used by the router to forward packets to a given destination. In order for a neighbor to become the successor for a particular destination, it must first meet the feasibility condition.

The *feasibility condition* states that the route must be advertised from a neighbor that is downstream with respect to the destination and the cost to reach the destination must be less than or equal to the cost of the route that is currently being used by the routing table.

For example, in Figure 3-10, R2's successor to reach Network A is R1, because the cost to reach Network A is two, which is lower than going through R3 which is three. However, if the metric of the link between R1 and R2 changed from 1 to 20, then R3 would meet the feasibility condition and become the successor.

Feasible Successor: The *feasible successor* is a neighboring router that the destination can be reached through, but is not used because the cost to reach the destination is higher than via a different router. The feasible successor can be thought of as having the next best route to a destination.

Feasible successors are kept in the topology table and are used as backup routes. For example, in Figure 3-10, R2's feasible successor to reach Network A is R3. R3

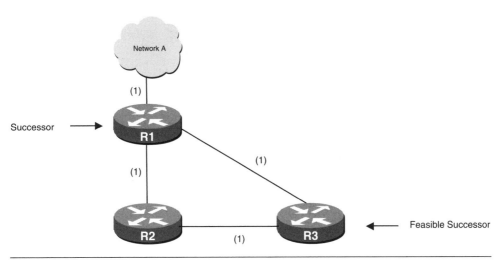

Figure 3-10   EIGRP terminology

has a route to Network A; however, it not the least-cost path and therefore is not used to forward data.

Feasibility Condition: The feasible condition is used to prevent routing loops. In order for the feasibility condition to be met, the route must be advertised from a neighbor that is downstream with respect to the destination. The cost to reach the destination must be less than or equal to the cost of the route that is currently being used in the routing table. If the feasibility condition is met, then the neighbor becomes the successor. For example, in Figure 3-10, if the link between R2 and R1 were to fail, R1 would no longer be the successor. R3 would move from being the feasible successor to the successor. If the link between R1 and R2 became active again, R1 would take over as successor because it meets the feasibility condition. It is downstream from Network A and its cost to reach Network A is less than R3's cost to reach Network A.

Active State: When the router loses its route to a destination and no feasible successor is available, the router goes into *active state*. While in active state, the router sends out queries to all neighbors in order to find a route to the destination. At this time the router must run the routing algorithm to recompute a new route to the destination.

Passive State: When the router loses its successor but has a feasible successor, it goes into *passive state*.

Hello: *Hello* packets are exchanged between neighboring routers. As long as hello packets are received, the router can determine that the neighbor is alive and functioning.

ACKs: *Acknowledgement* packets (ACKs) are sent by the router to acknowledge the receipt of update packets.

Update: *Update* packets are used by the router to send routing information between neighbors. Update messages are sent if the metric of a route changes or when a router first comes up.

Query: When the router loses its route to a destination and no feasible successor is available, the router goes into active state. While in this active state, the router sends out *query* packets to all neighbors for a particular destination. The router waits for a response back from all neighbors before starting the computation for a new successor.

Replies: *Replies* are sent in response to queries. The reply contains information on how to reach a destination. If the queried neighbor does not have the information requested, it sends queries to all its neighbors.

Technology Overview

When an EIGRP-enabled router first comes online, it sends hello packets out all EIGRP-enabled interfaces using multicast address 224.0.0.10. The hello packets are used for two things: discovering neighboring routers and after the neighbor are discovered, determining if a neighbor has become unreachable or inoperative.

Once a new neighbor is discovered via a hello packet, the router records the IP address and interface that the neighbor was discovered on. The router then sends an update to the neighbor containing all of the routes that it knows about and the neighbor does the same.

This information is stored in the EIGRP topology table.

Subsequently, hello packets are sent out every 5 seconds or every 60 seconds on low-speed NBMA networks. The hello packets enable the router to discover loss of its neighbor dynamically and quickly. If a hello packet is not received from the neighbor router before the expiration of the hold timer, then the neighbor is declared down. At this point, the neighbor adjacency is deleted and all routes associated with that neighbor are removed.

The topology table includes the router's metric to reach the destination as well as the neighbor's metric to reach the destination. The DUAL algorithm uses the topology table to find the lowest metric loop-free path to each destination. The next-hop router for the lowest-cost path is referred to as the successor and is the next-hop IP address that is loaded in the routing table. The DUAL algorithm also tries to find a feasible successor, or the next best route, which is kept in the topology database.

If the router loses its successor and a feasible successor is available, no route recomputation is necessary. The router simply makes the feasible successor the successor and adds the new route to the routing table remaining in a passive state. However, if no feasible successor is available, then the router goes into active state for the destination network and recomputation for the route is necessary.

While the router is in active state, it sends a query packet out all EIGRP-enabled interfaces, except the interface that the successor is on, inquiring if the neighbor has a route to the given destination. The neighbors respond and notify the sender if it has a route to the destination or not. Once all replies are received, the router can then calculate a new successor. If the neighbor receiving the query packet was using the sender to reach the destination network (as its successor), it will query all of its neighbors for a route to the destination. The queried neighbors go through the same process; this creates a cascading of queries through the network, searching the network for a path to the destination.

As long as EIGRP has a feasible successor, no recomputation is necessary; this prevents the router from having to use CPU cycles and also speeds up convergence. Routers that are not affected by topology changes are not involved in recomputations.

EIGRP Metrics

The EIGRP metric is a 32-bit number, which is calculated using bandwidth, delay, reliability, loading, and MTU. Calculating the metric for a route is a two-step process using the five different characteristics of the link and the K values. The K values are configurable, but this is not recommended. The default K values are K1 = 1, K2 = 0, K3 = 1, K4 = 0, and K5 = 0.

1. Metric = K1×Bandwidth + (K2×Bandwidth) / (256-load) + K3×Delay

2. If K5 is not equal to zero, take the metric from step 1 and multiple it by [K5 / (reliability + K4)]. If K5 is zero, ignore step 2.

Metric = Metric×[K5 / (reliability + K4)]

As shown previously, Cisco sets K2, K4, and K5 to zero. This leaves only two variables to compute the EIGRP metric (bandwidth and delay). Because three of the K values are zero, the formula reduces to

Metric = Bandwidth + Delay

The bandwidth is derived by finding the smallest of all bandwidths in path to the destination and dividing 10,000,000 by that number.

Delay is found by adding all of the delays along the paths and dividing that number by ten. The sum of the two numbers is then multiplied by 256. This equation can be written as the following:

$$\text{Metric} = [(10,000,000 / \text{min bandwidth}) + (\text{SUM (interface delay)} / 10)] \times 256$$

Let's look at Figure 3-11 and determine what the metric is to reach network 1.0.0.0 from R2.

Use the **show interface** command on each router to determine what the bandwidth and delay is for each interface. The following shows the output from the command:

```
R2#show interfaces S0/0
Serial0/0 is up, line protocol is up
 Hardware is QUICC Serial
 Internet address is 192.1.1.1/24
 MTU 1500 bytes, BW 1544 Kbit, DLY 20000 usec, rely 255/255, load 1/255
 Encapsulation HDLC, loopback not set, keepalive set (10 sec)
 Last input 00:00:02, output 00:00:02, output hang never
 Last clearing of "show interface" counters never
 Input queue: 0/75/0 (size/max/drops); Total output drops: 0
 Queueing strategy: weighted fair
 Output queue: 0/64/0 (size/threshold/drops)
  Conversations 0/3 (active/max active)
  Reserved Conversations 0/0 (allocated/max allocated)
 5 minute input rate 0 bits/sec, 1 packets/sec
 5 minute output rate 0 bits/sec, 1 packets/sec
  155 packets input, 10368 bytes, 0 no buffer
  Received 80 broadcasts, 0 runts, 1 giants, 0 throttles
  5 input errors, 1 CRC, 2 frame, 0 overrun, 0 ignored, 1 abort
  246 packets output, 13455 bytes, 0 underruns
```

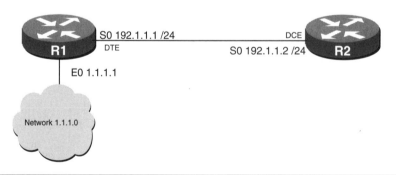

Figure 3-11 EIGRP metric

```
 0 output errors, 0 collisions, 910 interface resets
 0 output buffer failures, 0 output buffers swapped out
 154 carrier transitions
 DCD=up DSR=up DTR=up RTS=up CTS=up

R1#show interfaces e0/0
Ethernet0/0 is up, line protocol is up
 Hardware is AmdP2, address is 00e0.1e5b.25a1 (bia 00e0.1e5b.25a1)
 MTU 1500 bytes, BW 10000 Kbit, DLY 1000 usec, rely 243/255, load 1/255
 Encapsulation ARPA, loopback not set, keepalive not set
 ARP type: ARPA, ARP Timeout 04:00:00
 Last input never, output 00:00:08, output hang never
 Last clearing of "show interface" counters never
 Queueing strategy: fifo
 Output queue 0/40, 0 drops; input queue 0/75, 0 drops
 5 minute input rate 0 bits/sec, 0 packets/sec
 5 minute output rate 0 bits/sec, 0 packets/sec
  0 packets input, 0 bytes, 0 no buffer
  Received 0 broadcasts, 0 runts, 0 giants, 0 throttles
  0 input errors, 0 CRC, 0 frame, 0 overrun, 0 ignored, 0 abort
  0 input packets with dribble condition detected
  6 packets output, 1071 bytes, 0 underruns
  6 output errors, 0 collisions, 2 interface resets
  0 babbles, 0 late collision, 0 deferred
  6 lost carrier, 0 no carrier
  0 output buffer failures, 0 output buffers swapped out
```

To reach network 1.1.1.0 from R2, a packet must cross the serial interface between R1 and R2 and the Ethernet interface on R1. Because the lowest bandwidth is used for the calculation, the bandwidth of the serial interface is used.

Metric = [(10,000,000 / BW Serial link) + ((delay on serial link + delay on the Ethernet link) / 10)]×256

Metric = [(10,000,000 / 1,544) + ((20,000 + 1,000) / 10)]×256

Metric = 2,195,456

Let's take a look at the routing table on R2 and see if our calculations are correct:

```
R2#show ip route
Codes: C - connected, S - static, I - IGRP, R - RIP, M - mobile, B - BGP
 D - EIGRP, EX - EIGRP external, O - OSPF, IA - OSPF inter area
 N1 - OSPF NSSA external type 1, N2 - OSPF NSSA external type 2
 E1 - OSPF external type 1, E2 - OSPF external type 2, E - EGP
 i - IS-IS, L1 - IS-IS level-1, L2 - IS-IS level-2, * - candidate default
 U - per-user static route, o - ODR
Gateway of last resort is not set
D 1.0.0.0/8 [90/2195456] via 192.1.1.1, 00:21:50, Serial0/0
C 192.1.1.0/24 is directly connected, Serial0/0
```

EIGRP Packet Format

EIGRP accesses IP directly using protocol number 88. Figure 3-12 shows the EIGRP header.

The contents of the EIGRP packet format are defined as follows:

- **Version**   This specifies the version of the originating EIGRP process. Two releases of EIGRP software are available, but they both use the same version number.

- **Opcode**   This specifies the EIGRP packet type. Table 3-3 lists five possible opcodes.

- **Checksum**   This is calculated for the entire EIGRP packet.

- **Flags**   Only two possible flags can be set. The right-most bit is the Init bit, which when set, indicates that the enclosed route entries are the first new neighbor rela-

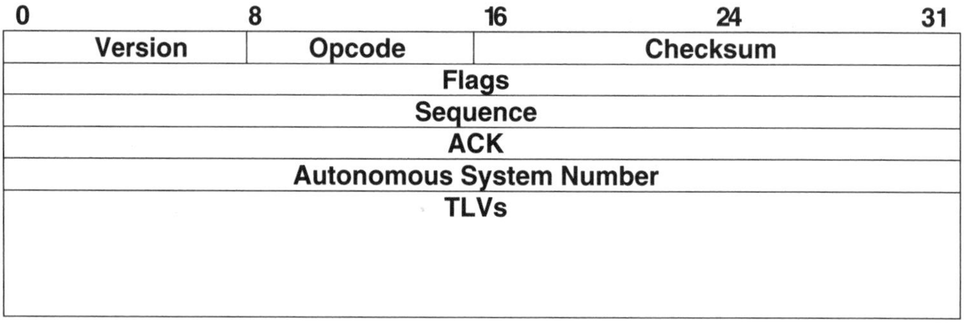

0	8	16	24	31
Version	Opcode		Checksum	
Flags				
Sequence				
ACK				
Autonomous System Number				
TLVs				

Figure 3-12   EIGRP packet format

Table 3-3   EIGRP Opcodes

Opcode	Type
1	Update
3	Query
4	Reply
5	Hello
6	IPX, SAP

tionship. The send bit is the Conditional Receive bit, which is used in the proprietary Reliable Multicast algorithm.

- **Sequence**   This is a 32-bit sequence number used by RTP.

- **ACK**   This is the 32-bit sequence number last heard for the neighbor the packet is being sent to. A hello packet with a nonzero sequence number will be treated as a ACK packet rather than a hello packet.

- **Autonomous system number**   **This is** the number of the EIGRP domain.

- **TLV**   Each TLV contains a 2-byte type number. (The IP types are listed in Table 3-4; AppleTalk and IPX have specific TLV types not covered.) The next 2-byte field specifies the length of the TLV and the final field is variable length and is determined by the type field.

Figure 3-13 shows the format of the IP internal routes and external routes TLV.

EIGRP is an enhanced version of IGRP, which uses the same distance vector algorithm and distance information as IGRP. EIGRP has been enhanced, making it converge faster and operate more efficiently than IGRP.

EIGRP also provides the following benefits:

- EIGRP provides fast convergence through use of the Diffusing Update Algorithm (DUAL).

- EIGRP only sends partial updates for routes that have changed instead of sending the entire routing table.

- EIGRP supports Variable Length Subnet Masking (VLSM).

- The EIGRP metric is large enough to support thousands of hops.

Table 3-4   EIGRP TLV Types

Number	TLV Type
0x0001	EIGRP parameters that are used to convey metric weights and hold time
0x0003	Sequence number used by Reliable Multicast algorithm
0x004	Software version used by Reliable Multicast algorithm
0x005	Next multicast sequence used by Reliable Multicast algorithm
0x0102	IP internal routes
0x0103	IP external routes

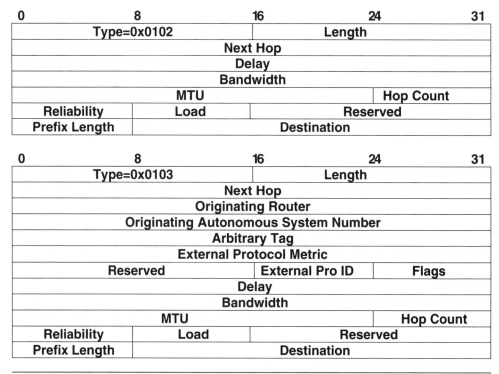

Figure 3-13 EIGRP IP internal route and external routes TLV

Link State Protocols

Link state protocols derive their name from the fact that each router originates information about itself, its links, and the state of the links (hence link state). This information is flooded (passed) by each router throughout the network. Link state protocols are often referred to as Shortest Path First (SPF) protocols because they are built around the graph theory work done by E. W. Dijkstra on the shortest path algorithm.

Each router running a link state algorithm establishes a relationship called an *adjacency* with each neighbor (a router connected to the same network). Each router describes its local environment (its interfaces, cost to send data over the interface, and what the interfaces connect to) in link state advertisements (LSAs). These LSAs are distributed to all routers within a domain by a procedure called flooding. When a router receives a link state update packet, it makes a copy of it and forwards it unchanged to its neighbor. The objective is for each router in the domain to have an identical view of the network, enabling each router to independently calculate its own best path.

The LSAs are stored forming a topological database, also called a link state database. Using the Dijkstra algorithm, each router calculates the shortest path to each network; this information is stored in the routing table used to route packets.

The two popular link state algorithms used today are OSPF and IS-IS.

OSPF

Open Shortest Path First (OSPF) is the most widely deployed link state routing protocol developed for IP networks. It was developed for use within a single autonomous system to distribute routing information. The following section discusses terminology and key concepts of OSPF.

OSPF Terminology

When dealing with OSPF, it is important to understand the terminology being used.

Autonomous system (AS): This is a group of routers that are under the control of a single administrative entity: for example, all of the routers belonging to a particular corporation.

LSA: Link state advertisement (LSA) is used to describe the local state of the router. The LSAs contain information about the state of the router's interfaces and the state of any adjacencies that are formed. The LSAs are flooded through the network.

The information contained in the LSA sent by each router in the domain is used to form the router's topological database. From this information, a shortest path is calculated to each destination.

Area: An *area* is a collection of routers that have an identical topological database. OSPF uses areas to break an AS into multiple link-state domains. Because the topology of an area is invisible to another area, no flooding leaves an area. This greatly reduces the amount of routing traffic within an AS. Areas are used to contain link state updates and enable administrators to build hierarchical networks.

Cost: This is the metric that the router uses to compare routes to the same destination. The lower the cost, the more preferred the route. OSPF calculates the cost of using a link based on bandwidth. The higher the bandwidth, the lower the cost, and the more preferable the route.

Router ID: The *router ID* is a 32-bit number assigned to each OSPF-enabled router, which is used to uniquely identify the router within an autonomous system. The router ID calculated at boot time is the highest loopback address on the router. If no loopback interfaces are configured, the highest IP address on the router is used.

Adjacency: OSPF forms *adjacencies* between neighboring routers in order to exchange routing information. On a multi-access network, each router forms an adjacency with the Designated Router.

Designated Router (DR): This is used to reduce the number of adjacencies that need to be formed on a multi-access network such as Ethernet, Token Ring, or Frame Relay. The reduction in the amount of adjacencies formed greatly reduces the size of the topological database.

The DR becomes adjacent with all other routers on the multi-access network. The routers send their LSAs to the DR and the DR is responsible for forwarding them throughout the network. The idea behind a DR is that routers have a central point to send information to, versus every router exchanging information with every other router on the network.

Backup Designated Router (BDR): This is formed on a multi-access network and is responsible for taking over for the DR if it should fail.

Inter-Area Route: This is a route that is generated in an area other than the local one, inside the current OSPF routing domain.

Intra-Area Route: This is a route that is within one area.

Neighbors: These are routers that share a common network. For example, two routers on an Ethernet interface are said to be neighbors.

Flooding: This is a technique used to distribute LSAs between routers.

Hello: A *hello* packet is used to establish and maintain neighbor relationships. The hello packet is also used to elect a DR for the network.

Technology Overview

Let's start with a brief introduction to OSPF before going into more detail. OSPF uses a link state algorithm to calculate the shortest path to all destinations in each area. When a router is first enabled or if any routing changes occur, the router configured for OSPF floods LSAs to all routers in the same hierarchical area. The LSAs contain information on the state of the router's links and the router's relationship to its neighboring routers. From the collection of LSAs, the router forms what is called a link state database. All routers in an area have an identical database describing the area's topology.

The router then runs the Dijkstra algorithm using the link state database to form a shortest path tree to all destinations inside the area. From this shortest path tree, the IP routing table is formed. Any changes that occur on the network are flooded via packets and will cause the router to recalculate the shortest path tree using the new information.

Link State Routing Protocol

OSPF uses a link state algorithm to calculate the shortest path to all known destinations. Link state refers to the state of a router's interface (up, down, IP address, type of network, and so on) and the router's relationship to its neighbors (how the routers are connected on the network). The link state advertisements are flooded to each router and are used to create a topological database.

The Dijkstra algorithm is run on each router using the topological database, which is created by all LSAs received from all of the routers in the area. The algorithm places each router at the root of the tree and calculates the shortest path to each destination based on the cost to reach that network.

Flooding

Flooding is the process of distributing link state advertisements between adjacent routers. The flooding procedure carries the LSA one hop farther from its point of origin.

Because all routers in an OSPF domain are interconnected via adjacencies, the information disseminates throughout the network. To make this process reliable, each link state advertisement must be acknowledged.

Dijkstra Algorithm

The Dijkstra algorithm is the heart of OSPF. Once the router receives all link state advertisements, it then uses the Dijkstra algorithm to calculate the shortest path to each destination inside the area based on the cumulative cost to reach that destination. Each router will have a complete view of the network topology inside the area. It builds a tree with itself as the route and has the entire path to any destination network or host.

However, the view of the topology from one router will be different from that of another because each router uses itself as the root of the tree. The Dijkstra algorithm is run any time a router receives a new link state advertisement.

Areas

OSPF uses areas to segment the AS and contain link state updates. LSAs are only flooded within an area, so separating the areas reduces the amount of routing traffic on a network.

Each router within an area has an identical topological database as all other routers in the same area. A router in multiple areas has a separate topological database for each area it is connected to.

Routers that have all of their interfaces within the same area are called internal routers (IR). Routers that connect areas within the same AS are called Area Border Routers (ABRs) and routers that act as gateways redistributing routing information

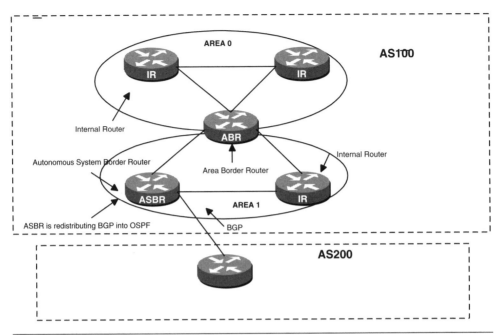

Figure 3-14 OSPF areas

from one AS to another AS are call Autonomous System Border Routers (ASBRs) (see Figure 3-14).

Backbone (Area 0)

OSPF has a concept of a backbone area referred to as area 0. If multiple areas are configured, one of these areas must be configured as area 0. The backbone (area 0) is the center for all areas; that is, all areas must have a connection to the backbone. In cases where an area does not have direct physical connectivity to the backbone, a virtual link must be configured. Virtual links will be discussed later in the chapter.

All areas inject routing information into the backbone area (area 0) and the backbone propagates routing information back to each area.

Designated Router (DR)

All multi-access networks with two or more attached routers elect a Designated Router (DR). The DR concept enables a reduction in the number of adjacencies that need to be formed on a network. In order for OSPF-enabled routers to exchange routing information, they must form an adjacency with one another. If a DR was not used, then each router on a multi-access network would need to form an adjacency with every other router (because link state databases are synchronized across adjacencies). This would result in N-1 adjacencies.

Instead, all routers on a multi-access network form adjacencies only with the DR and BDR. Each router sends the DR and BDR routing information and the DR is responsible for flooding this information to all adjacent routers and originating a network link advertisement on behalf of the network. The BDR is used in case the DR fails.

The reduction in adjacencies reduces the volume of routing protocol traffic as well as the size of the topological database.

The DR is elected using the hello protocol, which was described earlier in this chapter. The election of the DR is determined by the router priority, which is carried in the hello packet. The router with the highest priority will be elected the DR; if a tie occurs, the router with the highest router ID is selected.

The router ID is the IP address of the highest addressed loopback interface. If no loopback is configured, the router ID is the highest IP address on the router. The router priority can be configured on the router interface with the **ip ospf priority** command.

When a router first becomes active on a multi-access network, the router checks to see if a DR is currently present for the network. If a DR is present, the router accepts the DR regardless of priority. Once a DR is elected, no other router can become the DR unless the DR fails. If no DR is present on the network, then the routers negotiate the DR based on router priority.

OSPF Protocol Packets

The OSPF protocol runs directly over IP protocol 89 and begins with the same 24-byte header, as shown in Figure 3-15.

Table 3-5 lists the five OSPF packet types.

0	8	16	24	31
Version Number	OSPF Packet Type		PACKET LENGTH	
ROUTER ID				
AREA ID				
CHECKSUM			AUTHENTICATION TYPE	
AUTHENTICATION				
AUTHENTICATION				

Figure 3-15 OSPF header

Table 3-5 OSPF Packet Types

Type	Packet Name Protocol	Function
1	Hello	Discovers and maintains neighbors
2	Database description	Summarize database contents
3	Link state request	Request for database information
4	Link state update	Database update
5	Link state acknowledgement	Acknowledgement

Hello packets: The *hello* packet protocol is responsible for discovering neighbors and maintaining the neighbor relationship. Hello packets are sent periodically out the router's interface depending on the network type. The hello protocol is also responsible for electing a DR on multi-access networks. The role of the DR is discussed later in the chapter.

Database description packets: *Database description* packets are OSPF type 2 packets. These packets are responsible for describing the contents of the link state database of the router and are one of the first steps to forming an adjacency.

Database descriptor packets are sent in a poll response manner. One router is designated the master and the other the slave. The master sends database polls, which are acknowledged by the database descriptor packets, sent by the slave.

Link state request packets: These are OSPF type 3 packets. Once the complete databases are exchanged between routers using the database description packets, the routers compare the database of their neighbor with their own database. At this point, the router may find that parts of the neighbor's database may be more up-to-date than its own. If so, the router requests these pieces using the link state request packet.

Link state update packets: These are OSPF packet type 4. The router uses a flooding technique to pass LSA. Multiple LSA types are available (router, network, summary, and external), which are described in detail later in this chapter.

Link state acknowledgement packets: These are OSPF type 5 packets, which are used to acknowledge the receipt of LSAs. This acknowledgement makes the OSPF flooding procedure reliable.

Link State Advertisements

All link state advertisements begin with the same 20-byte header as shown in Figure 3-16.

- **LS age**   The time in seconds since the link state advertisement was originated

- **Options**   The optional capabilities supported by the router

- **LS type**   Type of link state advertisement

- **Link state ID**   Identifies the portion of the internet environment that is being described by the advertisement

- **Advertising router**   The router ID of the router that originated the packet

- **LS sequence number**   Used to detect old or duplicate link state advertisements

- **LS checksum**   Checksum of the complete contents of the link state advertisement

- **Length**   The length in bytes of the link state advertisement, including the 20-byte header

Router Link

Each router in the area generates a router LSA (type 1 LSA). This advertisement describes the state and cost of the router's interfaces to that area. All of the router's links to the area must be described in a single router LSA. The router LSAs are only flooded throughout a single area.

Network Link

Network link advertisements are type 2 LSAs. The DR for each multi-access network that has more than one attached router originates a network advertisement. The advertisement describes all of the routers attached to the network as well as the DR itself.

0	8	16	24	31
LS age		Options		LS Type
Link State ID				
Advertising Router				
LS sequence number				
LS checksum		Length		

Figure 3-16   OSPF LSA header

Summary Link

Summary LSAs are type 3 and 4 LSAs. The ABR generates summary LSAs, which describes a route to a single destination. The summary LSA is advertised within the single area and the destination described is external to the area yet part of the same autonomous system. Only intra-area routes are advertised in the backbone.

External Link

The Autonomous System Border Router (ASBR) generates an external type 5 LSA, which advertises each destination known to the router that is external to the AS. AS external type 5 LSAs are used to advertise default routes into the AS.

Two types of external routes are available: external type 1 and external type 2. The difference between the two is the way the cost or metric of the route is calculated. External type 1 routes use the external cost plus the internal cost of reaching a route. External type 2 routes only use the external cost of reaching the route. Type 2 routes are always preferred over type 1 routes, and are the default type for any route that is redistributed into OSPF.

How OSPF Works

When an OSPF-enabled router first comes online, it sends out a hello packet to the multicast address 224.0.0.5. This packet is sent out all OSPF-enabled interfaces periodically depending on the interface type. For broadcast media such as Ethernet or Token Ring or point-to-point interfaces, the hello packet is sent every ten seconds. On an NBMA such as Frame Relay or ATM, the hello packet is sent out every 30 seconds.

The hello packets are not only used to build neighbor relationships and discover what neighbors are on the same wire, but they are also used to describe any optional capabilities of the router, such as whether the router is in a regular or stub area. The hello packet is also used to elect the designated router on multi-access networks.

After the neighbor is discovered, bidirectional communication is ensured and a designated router is elected (on a multi-access media). The router attempts to form an adjacency with the neighboring router.

To form an adjacency, the routers must synchronize their databases. To do this, each router describes its databases to the other by sending a sequence of database description packets. This process is called the database exchange process and will be covered in more detail later in the chapter.

During the database exchange process, the two routers form a master/slave relationship. Each database description packet sent by the master contains a sequence number. The slave acknowledges receipt of the packet by echoing back the sequence number.

During the database exchange process, each router checks its own database to see if any of the Link Sate Advertisements received by its neighbor are more recent than its own database copy. If any are, the router makes note of this and after the database exchange process is over, the router requests updated LSAs using link state request packets. Each router responds to the Link state request using a Link state update. When the requesting router receives the updated LSA, it acknowledges the packet. When the database description process is complete and all link state requests have been updated, the databases are synchronized.

How an Adjacency Is Formed

In order for a router to exchange link state database information with another router, an adjacency must be formed. This is a key part of OSPF and therefore needs to be completely understood.

On a Cisco router you can check the status of the adjacency using the **show ip ospf neighbor** command. The following shows the output from the command. Notice that the state of the adjacency is full, which means that R1's database is synchronized with neighbor 1.1.1.1, which is R2.

```
R1#show ip ospf neighbor

Neighbor ID  Pri  State      Dead Time  Address    Interface
1.1.1.1        1  FULL/BDR   0:00:37    10.10.3.1  Ethernet0
```

Neighbor routers go through five states before fully forming an adjacency or having a full neighbor state. Figure 3-17 shows an example of how an adjacency is formed between two neighboring routers on a broadcast media. R1 and R2 both connect to an Ethernet network and R3 is configured with a higher DR priority.

When R1 and R2 first come online, they both initialize and begin sending hello packets. At this point in time neither router knows of the presence of the other router on the network and no DR is selected. R2 hears the hello from R1 changing the state of the adjacency from down to initializing (Init). This can be seen from the **show ip ospf neighbor** command on R2:

```
R2#show ip ospf neighbor

Neighbor ID  Pri  State        Dead Time  Address    Interface
1.1.1.1        1  INIT/DROTHER 0:00:39    10.10.3.1  Ethernet0
```

At this point the routers have seen themselves in the hello packet from their neighbors and bidirectional communication is established. The adjacency changes from initializing to 2way. This can be seen from the **show ip ospf neighbor** command on R2:

```
R2#show ip ospf neighbor

Neighbor ID  Pri  State        Dead Time  Address    Interface
1.1.1.1        1  2WAY/DROTHER 0:00:36    10.10.3.1  Ethernet0
```

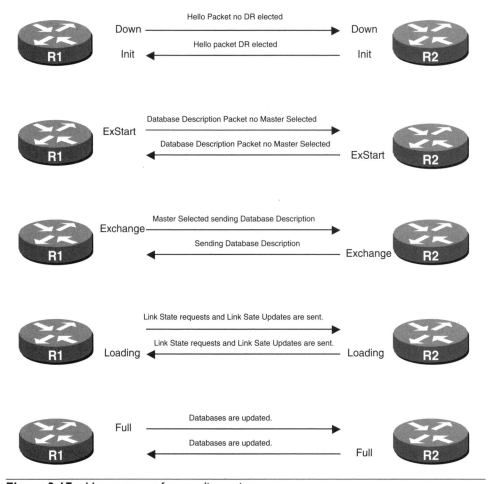

Figure 3-17 How a router forms adjacencies

At the end of this stage, the DR and BDR are elected for the network and the router then decides whether or not to form an adjacency with its neighbor. On a multi-access network, routers will only form adjacencies with the DR and BDR on the network.

R2 in the next hello packet indicates to R1 that it is the DR for the link. At this point the state of the adjacency changes from initializing to exchange (Exstart). This can be seen from the **show ip ospf neighbor** command on R2. During the Exstart state, a master/slave relationship is formed between the two routers and the slave router adopts the master's database description sequence number.

```
R2#show ip ospf neighbor

Neighbor ID  Pri  State       Dead Time  Address     Interface
1.1.1.1       1   EXSTART/BDR 0:00:32    10.10.3.1   Ethernet0
                          ↑ R1 is the Backup DR
```

After the master/slave relationship is formed and the routers agree on a common database description sequence number, the routers begin to exchange database description packets. At this point the state of the adjacency changes from Exstart to exchange. This can be seen from the **show ip ospf neighbor** command on R2:

```
R2#show ip ospf neighbor

Neighbor ID  Pri  State        Dead Time  Address     Interface
1.1.1.1       1   EXCHANGE/DR  0:00:38    10.10.3.1   Ethernet0
```

After the complete databases are exchanged between routers using the database description packets, the routers compare the database of their neighbor with their own database. At this point the router may find that parts of the neighbor's database may be more up-to-date than its own. If so, the router requests these pieces using a link state request packet. At this point the state of the adjacency is loading. This can be seen from the **show ip ospf neighbor** command on R2:

```
R2#show ip ospf neighbor

Neighbor ID  Pri  State       Dead Time  Address     Interface
1.1.1.1       1   LOADING/DR  0:00:38    10.10.3.1   Ethernet0
```

After the link state update requests have all been satisfied R1 and R2 databases are deemed synchronized and the routers are fully adjacent. This can be see from the **show ip ospf neighbor** command on R2:

```
R2#show ip ospf neighbor

Neighbor ID  Pri  State      Dead Time  Address     Interface
1.1.1.1       1   FULL/BDR   0:00:37    10.10.3.1   Ethernet0
```

OSPF Network Types

OSPF has four network types or models: broadcast, non-broadcast, point-to-point, and point-to-multipoint. Depending on the network type, OSPF works differently. Understanding how OSPF works on each network model is essential in designing a stable and robust OSPF network.

Broadcast   The broadcast network type is the default type on LANs (Token Ring, Ethernet, and FDDI).

However, any interface can be configured as broadcast using the **ip ospf network** interface command.

- On a broadcast model, a DR and BDR are elected and all routers form adjacencies with the DR and BDR. This achieves optimal flooding because all LSAs are sent to the DR and the DR floods them to each individual router on the network.

- Neighbors do not need to be defined.

- All routers are on the same subnet.

- Care must be taken if the broadcast model is used on NMBA networks such as Frame Relay or ATM. Because a DR is elected, all routers must have physical connectivity to the DR. A fully meshed environment should be used or the DR should be statically configured using the priority command to ensure physical connectivity.

- The hello timer is 10 seconds, the dead interval is 40 seconds, and the wait interval is 40 seconds.

In Figure 3-18, R1 and R3 are connected via Frame Relay to R2. The network is a hub-and-spoke environment configured as an OSPF network type broadcast.

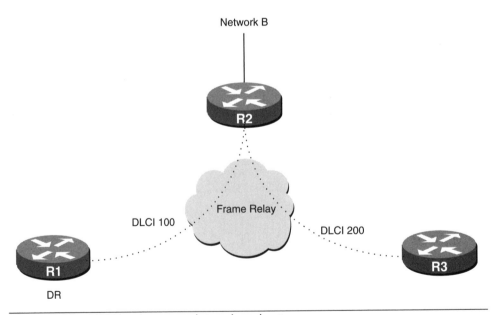

Figure 3-18 NBMA using network type broadcast

Because R2 is the only router that has logical connectivity to each router on the network, it must be elected the DR.

If a broadcast model is used on an NBMA network, all routers should be fully meshed or care should be taken on which router is elected DR. In a hub-and-spoke environment, the hub should be configured as the DR.

The following shows the output from the command **show ip ospf interface ethernet 0**. Note that the command shows the network type along with other key OSPF parameters.

```
R2#show ip ospf interface e0
Ethernet0 is up, line protocol is up
  Internet Address 10.10.3.2 255.255.255.0, Area 0
  Process ID 64, Router ID 2.2.3.2, Network Type BROADCAST, Cost: 10
  Transmit Delay is 1 sec, State BDR, Priority 1
  Designated Router (ID) 9.9.21.9, Interface address 10.10.3.1
  Backup Designated router (ID) 2.2.3.2, Interface address 10.10.3.2
  Timer intervals configured, Hello 10, Dead 40, Wait 40, Retransmit 5
  Hello due in 0:00:07
Neighbor Count is 1, Adjacent neighbor count is 1
  Adjacent with neighbor 9.9.21.9 (Designated Router)
```

Non-Broadcast   The non-broadcast network type is the default type on serial interfaces configured for Frame Relay encapsulation. However, any interface can be configured as non-broadcast using the **ip ospf network** interface command.

- With the non-broadcast model, a DR and BDR are elected and all routers form adjacencies with the DR and BDR. This achieves optimized flooding because all LSAs are sent to the DR and the DR floods them to each individual router on the network.

- Due to the lack of broadcast capabilities, neighbors must be defined using the neighbor command.

- All routers are on the same subnet.

- Similar to the broadcast model, a DR is elected. Care must be taken to ensure that the DR has logical connectivity to all routers on the network.

- The hello timer is 30 seconds, the dead interval is 120 seconds, and the wait interval is 120 seconds.

The following shows the output from the command **show ip ospf interface serial 0**, which is configured for Frame Relay encapsulation. Note that the command shows the network type along with other key OSPF parameters.

```
Serial0.2 is up, line protocol is down
 Internet Address 193.1.1.1 255.255.255.0, Area 0
 Process ID 64, Router ID 2.2.3.2, Network Type NON_BROADCAST, Cost: 64
 Transmit Delay is 1 sec, State DOWN, Priority 1
 No designated router on this network
 No backup designated router on this network
 Timer intervals configured, Hello 30, Dead 120, Wait 120, Retransmit 5
```

Point-to-Point   The network type point-to-point is the default type on serial interfaces that are not using Frame Relay encapsulation or can be selected as a subinterface type point-to-point. A subinterface is a logical way of defining an interface. The same physical interface can be split into multiple logical interfaces. This was originally created to deal with issues caused by split horizons on NBMA networks.

The point-to-point model can be configured on any interface using the **ip ospf network point-to-point** interface command.

- With a point-to-point model, no DR and BDR are elected and directly connected routers form adjacencies.

- Each point-to-point link requires a separate subnet.

- The hello timer is 10 seconds, the dead interval is 40 seconds, and the wait interval is 40 seconds.

The following shows the output from the command **show ip ospf interface serial 0**, which is not configured for Frame Relay encapsulation. Note that the command shows the network type along with other key OSPF parameters:

```
R2#show ip ospf interface s0
Serial0 is up, line protocol is down
 Internet Address 193.1.1.1 255.255.255.0, Area 0
 Process ID 64, Router ID 2.2.3.2, Network Type POINT_TO_POINT, Cost: 64
 Transmit Delay is 1 sec, State DOWN,
 Timer intervals configured, Hello 10, Dead 40, Wait 40, Retransmit 5
```

Point-to-Multipoint   The network type point-to-multipoint can be configured on any interface using the **ip ospf network point-to-multipoint** interface command.

- No DR is elected.

- Neighbors do not need to be defined because additional LSAs are used to convey neighbor router connectivity.

- One subnet is used for the whole network.

- The hello timer is 30 seconds, the dead interval is 120 seconds, and the wait interval is 120 seconds.

The following shows the output from the command **show ip ospf interface serial 0**. Notice that the command shows the network type along with other key OSPF parameters.

```
R2#show ip ospf interface s0
Serial0 is up, line protocol is down
 Internet Address 193.1.1.1 255.255.255.0, Area 0
 Process ID 64, Router ID 2.2.3.2, Network Type POINT_TO_MULTIPOINT, Cost: 64
 Transmit Delay is 1 sec, State DOWN,
 Timer intervals configured, Hello 30, Dead 120, Wait 120, Retransmit 5
```

As you can see from this section, a network that is based on a link state protocol such as OSPF is considerably more complex to configure, design, and troubleshoot than a network based on a distance vector protocol such as RIP. However, OSPF provides the following advantages over RIP version 1:

- Higher limitation on hop count.

- Faster convergence than RIP; this is because routing changes are flooded throughout the network instantly.

- OSPF supports router authentication; RIP does not.

- OSPF has a concept of route tagging of external routes that are injected into the AS. This enables the protocol to keep track of external routes that are injected by other protocols such as BGP.

- OSPF is classless; RIP is classful

- OSPF uses the available bandwidth more effectively by only sending routing updates when a change occurs.

- OSPF uses multicast packets versus broadcast packets to send LSAs. This ensures that routers that are not configured for OSPF do not have to process the packet.

Integrated IS-IS

Integrated Intermediate System to Intermediate System (IS-IS) is an intra-domain routing protocol that supports both IP and CLNS. IS-IS and OSPF have many features in common, which is not surprising since the ISO was working on IS-IS around the same time the Internet Architecture Board was working on OSPF.

Like OSPF, IS-IS is based on two levels of hierarchy: level 1 (L1) and level 2 (L2) routing.

Routing within an area is referred to as level 1 routing, and routing between areas is called level 2 routing. Level 2 routers connect multiple level 1 routers similar to area 0 in OSPF.

Both OSPF and IS-IS use hello packets to form and maintain adjacencies, maintaining a link state database from which a SPF algorithm computes the shortest path. Like OSPF, IS-IS is a classless protocol, which provides address summarization between areas.

IS-IS Terminology

When dealing with IS-IS, it is important to understand the terminology being used.

Intermediate system (IS): A router running IS-IS.

Designated Intermediate System (DIS): This is similar to the DR in OSPF; it is a router on a LAN that is responsible for flooding information for the broadcast network.

End System (ES): This is a host.

Network Service Access Point (NSAP): This is the address used to identify an IS.

Partial Sequence Number Protocol (PSNP): This is used for database synchronization.

Complete Sequence Number Protocol (CSNP): This is used for database synchronization.

IS-IS hello (IIH): This is used to discover other intermediate systems.

For routing IP, the NSAP address is divided into three parts: the area address, the system-ID, and the N-selector (see Figure 3-19).

Area number	System ID	N Sel
← Variable Length →	6 Bytes	1 Byte

Figure 3-19 IS-IS address format

The area address is a variable-length field that identifies the routing domain length of the area field and is associated with a single area within a routing domain. The system-ID is 6 bytes long and defines the ES or IS in an area. The NSAP selector is 1 byte long and identifies a particular network service at the network layer of a node. A network service user can be a transport entity or the IS network itself.

IS-IS Areas

Like OSPF, IS-IS uses areas to create a two-level hierarchical topology; however, a fundamental difference exists in the way that IS-IS defines these areas. With OSPF, area borders are marked by routers, whereas with IS-IS, they are marked by links (see Figures 3-20 and 3-21).

An intermediate system can be a L1 router, L2 router, or a L1/L2 router. Similar to an OSPF non-backbone internal router, a L1 router has no direct connectivity to another area. L2 routers are similar to OSPF backbone routers and L1/L2 routers are analogous to OSPF ABRs. The L1/L2 routers must maintain both a L1 link state database and a L2 link state database, similar to how an OSPF ABR maintains separate databases for each area.

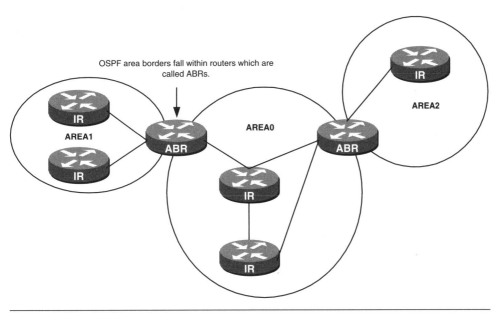

Figure 3-20 OSPF terminology

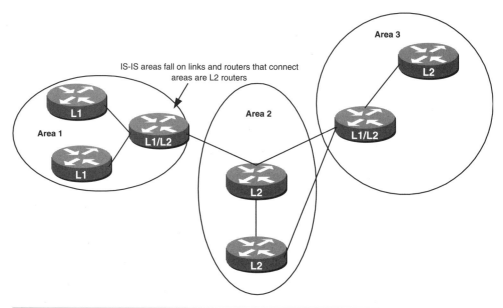

Figure 3-21   IS-IS terminology

How IS-IS Works

IS-IS routers discover and form adjacencies by exchanging IS-IS hello packets, which are transmitted every ten seconds. Like OSPF, an IS-IS hello packet is used to identify its capabilities to a router and describe the interface that it was sent over. If both routers agree on the capabilities and interface parameters, they become adjacent. Once they become adjacent, the hello packets act as keepalives. If the router does not receive a keepalive within the dead interval, the router declares its neighbor dead. The default dead interval is three times the keepalive interval, or 30 seconds.

Once an adjacency is formed, the routers use an update process to construct the L1 and L2 link state databases. L1 LSPs are flooded throughout the area and L2 LSPs are flooded over all L2 adjacencies. Like OSPF, IS-IS ages each LSP in the database, and the LSA must be refreshed every 15 minutes.

On point-to-point networks, routers send LSPs directly to the neighboring router. On broadcast networks, the LSPs are multicast to all neighbors. Unlike OSPF, IS-IS routers on a broadcast network form adjacencies with every router on the broadcast network, not just the DR.

IS-IS uses SNPs to acknowledge the receipt of LSPs and to maintain link state database synchronization. On point-to-point links, if an SNP is not received for a transmitted LSP in five seconds, a new LSP is generated. The IS-IS retransmission interval can be set on a per-interface basis with the command **isis retransmit-interval**. On a broadcast network, LSPs are not acknowledged by each router; instead, the DR periodically multicasts a CSNP that describes every LSP in the link state database. When a router receives a CSNP, it compares it with the LSP in its database. If the routers database does not contain a copy of all of the LSPs listed in the CSNP update, the router multicasts an SNP listing the LSP that it requires. The DR then responds with the appropriate LSP.

Once the update process has built the link state database, it is used to calculate the shortest path tree. From this tree, a forwarding database is constructed and this is what is used to route packets.

IS-IS can use four metrics to calculate the shortest path and each metric can be an integer between 0 to 63. The metrics are **default**, which must be supported and understood by every router, **delay**, which reflects the delay of the transit network, **expense**, which reflects the cost of the link, and **error**, which is similar to IGRP/EIGRP and measures the error probability of the network. For each metric, a separate route is calculated resulting in an SPF calculation. So if a system is using all four metrics to calculate the cost, it will run the SPF algorithm four times for each destination network.

Cisco routers only support the default metric, which as you can see, if all interfaces are left at their default setting, the IS-IS metric becomes a simple measure of hop count. The default metric for every interface is set to ten regardless of the interface type. This can be changed with the interface command **isis metric**.

Similar to OSPF, IS-IS classifies routes as internal and external as well as L1 and L2. Internal routes are routes that originate within the same domain whereas external routes are routes that originate outside of the domain. L2 routes can be internal or external and L1 routes are always internal. L1 routes are always preferred over L2 paths to the same destination. Like OSPF, IS-IS has the capability to load balance over equal cost paths. Cisco's IS-IS implementation supports up to six equal cost paths.

Questions

1. RIP uses what protocol?
   a. UDP port 179
   b. TCP port 179
   c. UDP port 520
   d. TCP port 520

2. Count-to-infinity is the _____.
   a. Problem where the router interfaces counters roll over
   b. Problem where hop count of RIP is limited to 15
   c. Problem where routing loop causes the TTL value to decrement to zero
   d. Problem caused by slow convergence where routing information will continue to pass from router to router incrementing the hop count by one. This problem, and the routing loop, will continue indefinitely, or until some limit is reached

3. What routing protocol rule states that it is never useful for a router to advertise a route back in the direction from which it came?
   a. Split horizon
   b. Poison reverse
   c. Count-to-infinity
   d. None of the above

4. The holddown timer in a distance vector protocol like RIP is used to _____.
   a. Control the rate in seconds at which routing updates are sent.
   b. Prevent the router from accepting routing information about a network for a fixed period of time after the route has been removed from the routing table.
   c. Speed up convergence time; whenever the metric of a route changes, the router must send an Update message immediately.
   d. Set the interval of time in seconds after which a route is declared invalid.

5. Which of the following are true about passive interface command when used in an RIP environment? (multiple answers)
   a. The passive interface command disables the sending of routing updates on a given interface.
   b. If you disable the sending of routing updates on an interface, the particular subnet will continue to be advertised out other RIP-enabled interfaces.
   c. Routes received on a passive will not be processed.
   d. Requests will still be sent out the passive interface.

6. Which of the following are true about RIP? (multiple answers)
   a. RIP is a classful protocol.
   b. RIP does not carry subnet information in its updates.
   c. RIP is based on the Bellman-Ford (distance vector) algorithm.
   d. RIP uses bandwidth as its metric.

7. How many message types does RIP use?
   a. Two (updates and requests)
   b. Three (updates, requests, and keepalives)
   c. One (updates)
   d. None of the above

8. RouterA, RouterB, and RouterC are connected to the same Ethernet LAN. The network administrator has requested that you prevent RouterA from sending routing updates to RouterC. However, RouterA must still send routing updates to RouterB. What should you do to the configuration on RouterA?
   a. Nothing—because RIP is a broadcast protocol, by default it will send updates to all devices on the Ethernet LAN. This cannot be prevented.
   b. Configure the Ethernet interface on RouterA as passive.
   c. Configure the Ethernet interface as passive and define RouterB as a unicast neighbor with the neighbor command.
   d. None of the above

9. RouterA and RouterB in the following illustration are running RIP on all interfaces. RouterB does not have an entry for network 130.1.1.0 in its routing table. What is the problem?

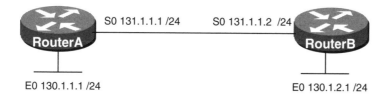

   a. When RouterB receives the update for network 130.1.0.0, it drops it because it has a direct connection to the same network.
   b. The networks are discontiguous.
   c. Both A and B
   d. Not enough information is provided to determine the problem.

10. How can the problem in question 9 be fixed?
    a. A secondary address can be added to the interfaces connecting RouterA to RouterB. The secondary address should be in the same major network as the discontiguous network and use the same subnet mask.
    b. Nothing—RIP does not support this type of configuration.
    c. Add a unicast neighbor on both RouterA and RouterB.
    d. Not enough information is provided to determine the solution to the problem.

11. How do you advertise a default route in RIP? (multiple answers)
   a. Configure a static route to 0.0.0.0 with a mask of 0.0.0.0.
   b. Configure a static route to 0.0.0.0 with a mask of 0.0.0.0 and redistribute the static route into RIP.
   c. Use the IP default-network command.
   d. Configure a static route to 0.0.0.0 and use the IP default-network command.

12. How many IP network entries can be sent in a single RIP Update message?
   a. 20
   b. 15
   c. 25
   d. 100

13. Which of the following are classful protocols? (multiple answers)
   a. RIP
   b. IGRP
   c. EIGRP
   d. OSPF

14. Which of the following is false regarding RIPV2?
   a. RIPV2 multicasts updates.
   b. RIPV2 is classless.
   c. RIPV2 supports authentication.
   d. RIPV2 does not carry subnet mask information with its route entry.

15. What protocol does RIPV2 use?
   a. TCP port 580
   b. UDP port 520
   c. TCP port 520
   d. UDP port 580

16. A router has two RIP learned routes to the same destination. One has a higher cost than the other. When the primary path fails, the users complain about slow convergence time. What can you do to speed up convergence?
   a. Configure the metrics of the routes so they are equal.
   b. Tune the RIP timers.
   c. Nothing—this is the default behavior of RIP.
   d. None of the above

17. What is the hop count limit of IGRP?

    a. 16

    b. 25

    c. 100

    d. 255

18. Which of the following is not a valid IGRP route type?

    a. Interior

    b. Exterior

    c. System

    d. Network

19. Which of the following is not used in calculating the IGRP metric?

    a. Bandwidth

    b. Delay

    c. Reliability

    d. Cost

20. Using the Illustration provided and the output from the **show interface** command on RouterB and RouterA, what is the IGRP metric for RouterB to reach network 1.1.1.0 on RouterA, assuming the K values are set to default?

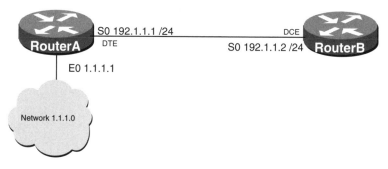

```
RouterB#show interfaces S0/0
Serial0/0 is up, line protocol is up
  Hardware is QUICC Serial
  Internet address is 192.1.1.1/24
  MTU 1500 bytes, BW 1544 Kbit, DLY 20000 usec, rely 255/255, load 1/255
  Encapsulation HDLC, loopback not set, keepalive set (10 sec)
  Last input 00:00:02, output 00:00:02, output hang never
  Last clearing of "show interface" counters never
  Input queue: 0/75/0 (size/max/drops); Total output drops: 0
  Queueing strategy: weighted fair
  Output queue: 0/64/0 (size/threshold/drops)
    Conversations 0/3 (active/max active)
    Reserved Conversations 0/0 (allocated/max allocated)
```

```
    5 minute input rate 0 bits/sec, 1 packets/sec
    5 minute output rate 0 bits/sec, 1 packets/sec
     155 packets input, 10368 bytes, 0 no buffer
     Received 80 broadcasts, 0 runts, 1 giants, 0 throttles
     5 input errors, 1 CRC, 2 frame, 0 overrun, 0 ignored, 1 abort
     246 packets output, 13455 bytes, 0 underruns
     0 output errors, 0 collisions, 910 interface resets
     0 output buffer failures, 0 output buffers swapped out
     154 carrier transitions
     DCD=up DSR=up DTR=up RTS=up CTS=up

RouterA#show interfaces e0/0
Ethernet0/0 is up, line protocol is up
 Hardware is AmdP2, address is 00e0.1e5b.25a1 (bia 00e0.1e5b.25a1)
 MTU 1500 bytes, BW 10000 Kbit, DLY 1000 usec, rely 243/255, load 1/255
 Encapsulation ARPA, loopback not set, keepalive not set
 ARP type: ARPA, ARP Timeout 04:00:00
 Last input never, output 00:00:08, output hang never
 Last clearing of "show interface" counters never
 Queueing strategy: fifo
 Output queue 0/40, 0 drops; input queue 0/75, 0 drops
 5 minute input rate 0 bits/sec, 0 packets/sec
 5 minute output rate 0 bits/sec, 0 packets/sec
  0 packets input, 0 bytes, 0 no buffer
  Received 0 broadcasts, 0 runts, 0 giants, 0 throttles
  0 input errors, 0 CRC, 0 frame, 0 overrun, 0 ignored, 0 abort
  0 input packets with dribble condition detected
  6 packets output, 1071 bytes, 0 underruns
  6 output errors, 0 collisions, 2 interface resets
  0 babbles, 0 late collision, 0 deferred
  6 lost carrier, 0 no carrier
  0 output buffer failures, 0 output buffers swapped out
```

   a. 21,000

   b. 2,195,456

   c. 8,576

   d. 90

21. The variance command in IGRP enables the router to _____.

   a. Redistribute between IGRP and EIGRP.

   b. Allow a configurable variance between timers.

   c. Allow unequal-cost load balancing.

   d. None of the above

22. Which of the following is false regarding IGRP?

   a. IGRP is a distance vector protocol.

   b. IGRP is classful.

   c. IGRP uses UDP as its transport protocol.

   d. IGRP uses a concept of autonomous systems.

23. True or false: The IGRP process number must be consistent across routers that want to share information.

24. Which of the following is false regarding EIGRP?

   a. EIGRP is Cisco proprietary.

   b. EIGRP is classless.

   c. EIGRP is a link state protocol.

   d. EIGRP uses the same composite metrics as IGRP.

25. A successor in EIGRP is _____.

   a. A directly connected neighboring router that has the best route to reach a particular destination

   b. A neighboring router that the destination can be reached through, but is not used because the cost to reach the destination is higher than via a different router

   c. A condition used by EIGRP to prevent routing loops

   d. None of the above

26. An EIGRP router goes into active state if _____.

   a. The router loses its successor but has a feasible successor.

   b. The router loses its route to a destination and no feasible successor is available.

   c. It does not receive a query message.

   d. None of the above

27. EIGRP supports which of the following protocols?

   a. IP

   b. IPX

   c. AppleTalk

   d. All of the above

28. EIGRP acknowledgements are _____.

   a. Unicast

   b. Broadcast

   c. Multicast

29. EIGRP hello packets are _____.

   a. Unicast

   b. Broadcast

   c. Multicast

30. EIGRP queries are _____.
   a. Unicast
   b. Broadcast
   c. Multicast
   d. Both A and C

31. What is the cause of a route being stuck in active state in EIGRP?
   a. The active timer expires before a reply to the query message is received.
   b. No EIGRP neighbor is found.
   c. No feasible successor is available.
   d. An EIGRP route will never be in this state; this is an OSPF concept.

32. Which of the following is true in regards to using the passive interface command for EIGRP?
   a. When an EIGRP-enabled interface is made passive, no EIGRP packets are sent out that interface.
   b. When an EIGRP-enabled interface is made passive, no EIGRP routing updates are received on that interface.
   c. When an EIGRP-enabled interface is made passive, no adjacencies will be formed with the router connected to that interface.
   d. All of the above

33. EIGRP updates are _____. (multiple answers)
   a. Non-periodic
   b. Periodic
   c. Partial
   d. Bounded·

34. What will happen if an EIGRP router loses its successor and a feasible successor is available?
   a. The router makes the feasible successor the successor and adds the new route. The router remains in passive state.
   b. The router goes into active state.
   c. The router makes the feasible successor the successor and adds the new route. The router goes into active state to find a new feasible successor.
   d. None of the above

35. Which of the following routing protocols has the lowest administrative distance?
   a. EBGP
   b. IBGP

    c. IS-IS

    d. EIGRP

36. Which of the following is/are true regarding distance vector protocols?

    a. Distance vector protocols exchange reachability information by sending periodic updates.

    b. Routes are advertised as vectors of distance and direction.

    c. Distance vector routers work on the basis of periodic updates and holddown timers.

    d. One major drawback of distance vector protocols is their classful nature.

    e. All of the above

37. Which of the following is false regarding static routes?

    a. They are more preferred than dynamically learned routes.

    b. Often used in hub-and-spoke situations where the spoke is singly homed to reduce routing overhead.

    c. A floating static route is not permanently entered in the routing table.

    d. Static routes provide precise control over routing behavior, which often cannot be obtained through dynamic protocols.

    e. None of the above

38. Which of the following is false regarding LSAs?

    a. The LSAs contain information on the state of the router's links and the router's relationship to its neighboring routers.

    b. From the collection of LSAs, the router forms what is called a link state database.

    c. Link state advertisement is not acknowledged.

    d. External LSAs are flooded throughout an AS.

39. On OSPF, virtual links updates are _____.

    a. Unicast

    b. Multicast

    c. Broadcast

    d. None of the above

40. Which of the following is true regarding OSPF areas? (multiple answers)

    a. OSPF uses areas to segment the AS and contain link state updates.

    b. A router in multiple areas has a separate topological database for each area it is connected to.

   c. Routers that connect areas within the same AS are called Area Border Routers (ABRs).

   d. If multiple areas are configured, one of these areas must be configured as area 0.

41. Which of the following is false regarding a Designated Router (DR) in OSPF network?

   a. All multi-access networks with two or more attached routers elect a DR.

   b. DR concept enables a reduction in the number of adjacencies that need to be formed on a network.

   c. The DR is elected using the hello protocol.

   d. The router with the lowest priority is elected as the DR.

42. What happens if a router with a higher priority becomes active on a network where a DR is present?

   a. The router with highest priority becomes the DR and the old DR becomes the BDR.

   b. Nothing—if a DR is present, the router accepts the DR regardless of its priority.

   c. They use hello protocol to determine the DR.

   d. The new router takes over as BDR.

43. Which of the following is false regarding the hello protocol used by OSPF?

   a. The hello protocol is responsible for discovering neighbors.

   b. The hello protocol is responsible for maintaining the neighbor relationship.

   c. The hello protocol is responsible for electing the DR.

   d. The hello interval is the same for all network types.

44. Which of the following is not a valid LSA?

   a. Router

   b. Network

   c. Link

   d. Summary

   e. External

45. What is the correct order of the five states that OSPF neighbors go through to form an adjacency?

   a. Init, Exstart, exchange, loading, full

   b. Init, loading, Exstart, exchange, full

   c. Exstart, Init, exchange, loading, full

   d. Init, Exstart, full, exchange, loading

46. Which of the following is not an OSPF network type?

   a. Broadcast

   b. Non-broadcast

   c. Point-to-point

   d. Multiple access

47. The OSPF cost is calculated using which of the following formulas?

   a. cost = (10,000,000 / bandwidth of the interface in bits per second)

   b. cost = (bandwidth of the interface in bits per second)

   c. cost = (100,000,000×bandwidth of the interface in bits per second)

   d. cost = (100,000,000 / bandwidth of the interface in bits per second)

48. You want to make sure that RouterA is always elected the DR for the OSPF network. What should you do?

   a. Reload all of the routers and make sure RouterA is the first to come up.

   b. Set the OSPF priority on RouterA to one and all of the other routers to zero.

   c. Set the OSPF priority on RouterA lower than all of the other routers.

   d. None of the above

49. What is wrong with the network scenario in the following Illustration?

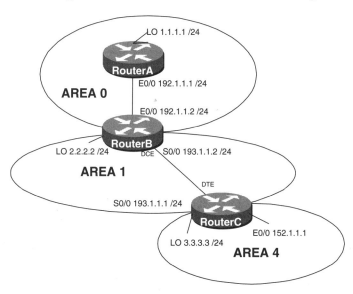

   a. RouterB cannot be in two areas.

   b. The addressing is not valid.

   c. A virtual link needs to be configured between area 1 and area 4.

   d. A virtual link needs to be configured between area 0 and area 4.

50. When you display the routing table on a Cisco router, you see a destination address followed by two numbers (2.2.2.2 [110/120] via 192.1.1.2, 00:02:22, Serial0/0). What does the first number indicate?

a. The cost of the route

b. The administrative distance of the route

c. The local process number

d. None of the above

51. Which of the following is false regarding a point-to-multipoint OSPF interface?

a. A DR and BDR are elected on a point-to-multipoint interface.

b. Neighbors do not need to be defined.

c. Any interface can be configured as a point-to-multipoint interface using the **ip ospf network point-to-multipoint** interface command.

d. The hello timer is 30 seconds and the dead interval is 120 seconds.

52. While debugging on ip ospf events, you received the following message. What is most likely the problem?

```
OSPF: Send with youngest Key 5
OSPF: Rcv pkt from 193.1.1.1, Serial0/0 : Mismatch Authentication
Key - No message digest key 1 on interface
```

a. Only one router is configured for authentication.

b. Message digest is not configured on interface s0/0.

c. One router is configured with a message digest key of 5 the other with a key of 1.

d. None of the above

53. In the following Illustration what command would you use to configure RouterA for ospf process 64 and place interface s0 in area 0?

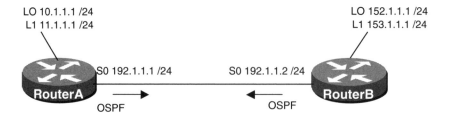

a. `router ospf 64`
   `network 192.1.1.1 255.255.255.255 area 0`

   b. router ospf 64
      network 192.1.1.1 255.255.255.255
      area 0
   c. router ospf 64
      network 192.1.1.0 0.0.0.255 area 0
   d. router ospf 64
      network 192.1.1.0 0.0.0.255
      area 0

54. RouterA is connected serially to RouterB. While debugging on ip ospf events on RouterB, you received the following message. What is most likely the problem?

```
RouterA#
OSPF: Mismatched hello parameters from 192.1.1.2
```

   a. Serial interface on RouterA is configured as OSPF network type point-to-point and RouterB serial interface is configured as OPSF network type broadcast.
   b. Serial interface on RouterA is configured as OSPF network type point-to-multipoint and RouterB serial interface is configured as OPSF network type non-broadcast.
   c. Serial interface on RouterA is configured as OSPF network type point-to-point and RouterB serial interface is configured as OPSF network type non-broadcast.
   d. None of the above

55. An OSPF stub area _____.
   a. Prevents flapping within the domain from affecting the area
   b. Does not permit external LSAs
   c. Does not permit summary LSAs
   d. All of the above

56. Which of the following is false regarding an NSSA area?
   a. An NSSA area can import external routes into the area.
   b. Routes are carried across the area as type 7 LSAs and converted to type 5 LSAs by the ABR.
   c. An NSSA area does not permit summary LSAs.
   d. None of the above

57. Which OSPF command is used to summarize a set of external routes that have been injected into the domain?
   a. Summary address command applied to an ASBR
   b. Area range command applied to an ABR

   c. Summary address command applied to an ABR

   d. Area range command applied to an ASBR

58. Which of the following would cause OSPF neighbors not to form an adjacency? (multiple answers)

   a. The mask on the interface connecting the two routers does not match.

   b. Both of the routers have their OSPF priority set to zero.

   c. The hello interval on the routers does not match.

   d. Both a and b

59. What is the significance of the N-bit in an OSPF hello packet?

   a. The N-bit is used to indicate that the router is capable of supporting OSPF demand circuits.

   b. The N-bit is used to indicate that the router is capable of supporting NSSA external LSAs.

   c. The N-bit is used to indicate that the router is capable of accepting AS external LSAs.

   d. The N-bit is used to indicate that the router is using authentication.

60. Based on the following Illustration (assuming the OSPF priority of each router is set to 1), which router will be elected the DR and which will become the BDR?

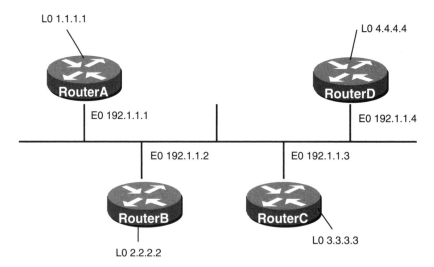

   a. RouterD will become the DR and RouterC will become the BDR.

   b. RouterA will become the DR and RouterB will become the BDR.

   c. RouterC will become the DR and RouterD will become the BDR.

   d. RouterB will become the DR and RouterA will become the BDR.

61. IS-IS is based on _____.

    a. Three levels of hierarchy

    b. Two levels of hierarchy

    c. One level of hierarchy

    d. Four levels of hierarchy

62. For routing IP, the IS-IS NSAP address is divided into which of the following?

    a. The area address, system-ID, and N-selector

    b. The area address and system-ID

    c. The area address and N-selector

    d. The system-ID, area address, and N-selector

63. The metric for Cisco IS-IS is _____.

    a. Dependent on the interface type

    b. Dependent on the delay of the interface

    c. Cisco assigns a metric of ten to every interface, regardless of the interface type.

    d. A composite of four metrics

64. What is the maximum metric that can be assigned to any IS-IS route?

    a. 1,024

    b. 1,023

    c. 63

    d. 256

65. BGP is _____.

    a. An interior gateway protocol

    b. A path vector protocol

    c. A Link state protocol

    d. None of the above

66. CIDR is _____.

    a. A subnetting scheme

    b. An address allocation scheme that eliminates the concept of network class within BGP

    c. A summarization technique

    d. All of the above

67. The BGP rule of synchronization states that _____.

    a. All routers must have their databases synchronized.

    b. Before BGP can announce a route, the route must be present in the IP routing table.

    c. Before BGP can announce a route, the route must be present in the BGP table.

    d. The synchronization rule only applies to OSPF.

68. What protocol does BGP use?

    a. TCP port 83

    b. TCP port 179

    c. UDP port 179

    d. IP protocol number 179

69. What is the correct order of the states of BGP neighbor negotiation?

    a. Idle, Connect, Active State, OpenSent State, OpenConfirm, Established

    b. Idle, Active State, Connect, OpenSent State, OpenConfirm, Established

    c. Idle, Connect, OpenSent State, OpenConfirm, Active State, Established

    d. Idle, Active State, OpenSent State, OpenConfirm, Connect, Established

70. In the following Illustration both RouterB and RouterC are advertising network 1.0.0.0 /8 to RouterA. However, because RouterC is closer to this network, we would like all traffic destined to network 1.0.0.0 /8 from RouterA to be routed through RouterC. What should you do?

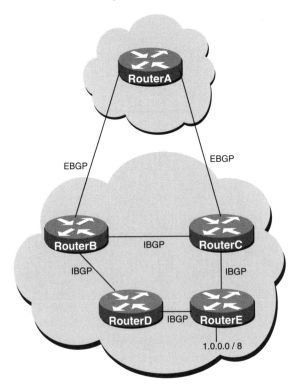

a. Set the Multi Exit Discriminator (MED) on route 1.0.0.0 /8 advertised from RouterC to 200 and the MED on route 1.0.0.0 /8 advertised from RouterB to 100. Because the MED coming from RouterC is higher, RouterA will prefer this route.

b. Set the MED on route 1.0.0.0 /8 advertised from RouterC to 100 and the MED on route 1.0.0.0 /8 advertised from RouterB to 200. Because the MED coming from RouterC is lower, RouterA will prefer this route.

c. Set the local preference on route 1.0.0.0 /8 advertised from RouterC to 200 and the MED on route 1.0.0.0 /8 advertised from RouterB to 100. Because the local preference coming from RouterC is higher, RouterA will prefer this route.

d. Set the local preference on route 1.0.0.0 /8 advertised from RouterC to 100 and the MED on route 1.0.0.0 /8 advertised from RouterB to 200. Because the local preference coming from RouterC is lower, RouterA will prefer this route.

71. What can be used to alleviate the full mesh requirement of IBGP?
    a. Turn off synchronization.
    b. Route reflector.
    c. Use BGP communities.
    d. None of the above

72. BGP uses a set of parameters (attributes) that describe the characteristics of a route. The attributes are sent in the BGP update packets with each route. The router uses these attributes to select the best route to the destination. Which of the following will BGP prefer?
    a. The route with the shortest AS path
    b. The route with the highest local preference
    c. The route with the lowest MED
    d. The route coming from the BGP router with the lowest router ID

73. BGP soft configuration _____.
    a. Enables policies to be configured and activated without resetting the BGP and TCP session
    b. Enables BGP neighbors to be configured but not activated
    c. Automatically disables synchronization
    d. None of the above

74. AS100 peers directly with AS300. AS100 should only accept local routes from AS300. Which regular expression would you use to identify local routes from AS300?
    a. ^300$
    b. ^300*

c. _300_

d. ^300^

75. Which of the following is false regarding BGP confederations?

a. BGP confederations are used to break an AS into multiple sub-ASs.

b. Within a sub-AS, all IBGP rules apply.

c. IBGP is used between sub-ASs.

d. IBGP information such as next hop, MED, and local preference is preserved within the confederation.

76. A BGP community is _____.

a. The same as a confederation

b. A group of routers that share a common property

c. A group of routers within a confederation

d. None of the above

77. What is the concept of BGP backdoor links?

a. A way to force IGP routes to take precedence over EBGP routes

b. A way to configure an alternate path which will only be used if the primary fails

c. An opening in your security policy to all trusted networks direct connectivity

d. None of the above

78. On RouterC network, 1.0.0.0 is loaded in the BGP, but it is not in the IP routing table. The following shows the output from the **show ip bgp** and the **show ip route** commands on RouterC. RouterC has synchronization turned off. Based on the information provided, what is the problem?

```
RouterC#show ip bgp
BGP table version is 1, local router ID is 3.3.3.3
Status codes: s suppressed, d damped, h history, * valid, >
best, i - internal
Origin codes: i - IGP, e - EGP, ? - incomplete

 Network Next-Hop Metric LocPrf Weight Path
* i1.0.0.0 192.1.1.1 0 100 0 100 i

RouterC#show ip route
Codes: C - connected, S - static, I - IGRP, R - RIP, M - mobile,
B - BGP
 D - EIGRP, EX - EIGRP external, O - OSPF, IA - OSPF inter area
 N1 - OSPF NSSA external type 1, N2 - OSPF NSSA external type 2
 E1 - OSPF external type 1, E2 - OSPF external type 2, E - EGP
 i - IS-IS, L1 - IS-IS level-1, L2 - IS-IS level-2, * -
candidate default
```

```
U - per-user static route, o - ODR

Gateway of last resort is not set

 3.0.0.0/24 is subnetted, 1 subnets
C 3.3.3.0 is directly connected, Loopback0
C 193.1.1.0/24 is directly connected, Ethernet0/0
```

   a. Synchronization should be turned on.

   b. The BGP session needs to be restarted.

   c. The next-hop to reach network 1.0.0.0 is via 192.1.1.1 which is not in RouterC's routing table.

   d. None of the above

79. A route received for your peer is frequently going up and down causing BGP UPDATE and WITHDRAWN messages to be repeatedly propagated on the network. What should you do to prevent this?

   a. Stop peering with this provider.

   b. Filter out that particular route.

   c. Apply route dampening.

   d. Configure a static route to that network and redistribute it into BGP.

80. How do you set the default route in OSPF?

   a. Create a static route and redistribute into OSPF.

   b. IP route 0.0.0.0 0.0.0.0

   c. Create a static route and use the default-information originate command to redistribute into OSPF.

   d. Nothing—if a default exists, it will automatically be loaded into OSPF.

81. What command is used to force an OSPF router to advertise a default route regardless whether it actually has a route to 0.0.0.0?

   a. default-information originate

   b. default-network always

   c. default-information always

   d. default-network

82. You want to enable IGRP on a Cisco router. Which of the following are the correct commands to enable IGRP on the router and have network 192.1.1.0 advertised in autonomous system 65.

   a. router IGRP AS 65

      network 192.1.1.0

b. router IGRP 65
network 192.1.1.0 0.0.0.255

c. router IGRP
network 192.1.1.0 65

d. router IGRP 65
network 192.1.1.0

83. Given the following configuration, why aren't the IGRP learned routes being redistributed into EIGRP and vice versa?

```
!
router eigrp 100
 network 194.1.1.0
!
router igrp 200
 network 195.1.1.0
!
```

a. No redistribution command appears under the EIGRP process or the IGRP process.

b. The network numbers are different.

c. No metric is defined, so the router cannot redistribute the routes.

d. The AS numbers are not the same.

84. Given the following configuration, why aren't OSPF learned routes being redistributed into IGRP and vice versa?

```
router ospf 64
redistribute igrp
network 152.1.1.4 0.0.0.3 area 0
!
router igrp 100
 redistribute ospf 64
 network 153.1.0.0
```

a. The network numbers are different.

b. In order to redistribute between OSPF and IGRP, we need to tell the Router what the metric will be used.

c. You cannot redistribute between a classful and a classless protocol.

d. None of the above

85. OSPF has two equal cost paths to the same destination and fast switching is enabled. Which best describes the default behavior of OSPF?

a. By default, OSPF will only use one path.

b. OSPF will load balance across the two paths on a per-destination basis.

c. OSPF will load balance across the two paths on a packet-by-packet basis.

d. None of the above

86. Which of the following is false regarding load balancing?

    a. By default, RIP will load balance across four equal cost paths.

    b. By default, OSPF will load balance across four equal cost paths.

    c. By default, BGP will load balance across four equal cost paths.

    d. The maximum equal paths that a Cisco router can be configured to use is six.

87. Which of following is true regarding policy routing? (multiple answers)

    a. Policy-based routing enables network administrators to select forwarding paths based on source address.

    b. Policy-based routing enables network administrators to select forwarding paths based on protocol type.

    c. Policy-based routing enables network administrators to select forwarding paths based on packet size.

    d. Policy-based routing enables network administrators to select forwarding paths based on application.

88. Which of the following will be used to reach network 192.1.1.1?

    a. A static route to 192.1.1.1

    b. A connected route to 192.1.1.1

    c. A default route to 192.1.1.1

    d. A defined policy route map to 192.1.1.1

89. The Ethernet interface on your router is 152.1.1.1 /24, which is connected to another router that is configured as your gateway of last resort. You are trying to reach two networks, 9.9.9.9 and 152.1.2.1, both of which are directly connected to your gateway of last resort. You are able to reach 9.9.9.9, but not 152.1.2.1. You enable debugging on IP packets and notice that when you ping 9.9.9.9, the router forwards the packet to your gateway of last resort. However, when you ping 152.1.2.1, you get an error message that the packet is unroutable. What is the problem?

    a. The subnet does not exist.

    b. The gateway of last resort is down.

    c. Your router is configured for IP classless.

    d. Your router is configured for no IP classless.

90. When you look at the routing table, you see an * next to one of the routes. What does * mean?

    a. The route best route to the destination

    b. The route has recently been removed from the table and can no longer be used.

    c. The route is candidate default.

    d. All of the above

91. EIGRP uses which of the following algorithms to find the lowest metric loop-free path to each destination?

    a. DUAL

    b. Dijkstra algorithm

    c. Bellman-Ford algorithm

    d. Perlman algorithm

92. Which of the following is not used as part of an IGRP configuration?

    a. Network address

    b. Subnet mask

    c. Autonomous system number

    d. Area number

    e. Both B and D

93. The configuration on your router is growing extremely large and approaching the limitation of NVRAM. Which command can be used to reduce the size of the configuration on the router?

    a. service compress-config

    b. compress-config

    c. no service config

    d. config-size

94. Which of the following routes will be used to reach 192.1.1.1?

    a. An OSPF learned route to 192.1.1.0 /30

    b. A EBGP learned route to 192.1.0.0 /16

    c. A static route to 192.1.1.0 /24

    d. A EIGRP leaned route to 192.1.1.0 /30

95. Which of the following is false regarding IS-IS?

    a. IS-IS routers discover and form adjacencies by exchanging IS-IS hello packets.

    b. Once an adjacency is formed, the routers use an update process to construct the L1 and L2 link state databases.

    c. On broadcast networks, the LSPs are multicast to all neighbors.

    d. Like OSPF, IS-IS routers on a broadcast network form adjacencies with only the DR.

96. Which of the following is true regarding Cisco Discovery Protocol CDP? (multiple answers)

a. CDP runs on all Cisco routers and switches

b. CDP-enabled router will be able to learn directly connected neighbor port and hostname information.

c. CDP-enabled router will be able to learn directly connected neighbor hardware model number and capabilities.

d. CDP cannot be disabled on the router.

97. How can you change the OSPF cost of using an Ethernet interface from 10 to 90 without using the OSPF cost command?

a. Change the bandwidth on the interface.

b. Change the clock rate on the interface.

c. Change the reference bandwidth form 100M to 900M.

d. None of the above

98. A distribute list in OSPF _____.

a. Prevents the filtered routes from being put in the routing table

b. Prevents the filtered routes from being put in the OSPF LSA database

c. Prevents the routes from being flooded to each neighbor

d. All of the above

99. RouterA is not forming an OSPF adjacency with RouterB. The following is the output form the **debug ip ospf** events command on RouterA. What is most likely the problem?

```
03:07:28: OSPF: Hello from 152.1.1.77 with mismatched NSSA option bit
03:07:35: OSPF: service_maxage: Trying to delete MAXAGE LSA
```

a. RouterB is configured as stub area and RouterA is not.

b. The max age timer does not match between the two routers.

c. RouterA and RouterB are not on the same subnet.

d. NSSA bit is set for encryption on RouterB but not RouterA.

100. ISDN is being used for backup between a hub and a spoke. What can be done to prevent OSPF hello messages and LSAs from bringing the link up, while still allowing the benefits of OSPF over the entire domain?

a. Do not define OSPF as interesting traffic.

b. Configure the router for snap shot routing.

c. Make the ISDN interface passive.

d. Use OSPF demand circuits.

Answer Key

1. C

2. D

3. A

4. B

5. A, B, and D

6. A, B, and C

7. A

8. C

9. C

10. A

11. A and C

12. C

13. A and B

14. D

15. B

16. B

17. D

18. D

19. D

20. C

21. C

22. C

23. True

24. C

25. A

26. B

27. D

28. A

29. C

30. D

31. A

32. D

33. A, C, and D

34. A

35. A

36. E

37. E

38. C

39. A

40. A, B, C, and D

41. D

42. B

43. D

44. C

45. A

46. D

47. D

48. B

49. D

50. B

51. A

52. C

53. C

54. C

55. B

56. C

57. A

58. A and C

59. B

60. A

61. B

62. A

63. C

64. B

65. B

66. B

67. B

68. B

69. A

70. B

71. B

72. B

73. A

74. A

75. C

76. B

77. A

78. C

79. C

80. C

81. C

82. D

83. D

84. B

85. B

86. C

87. A, B, C, and D

88. D

89. D

90. C

91. A

92. E

93. A

94. D

95. D

96. A, B, and C

97. C

98. A

99. A

100. D

Answer Guide

1. RIP uses what protocol?
   a. UDP port 179
   b. TCP port 179
   c. UDP port 520
   d. TCP port 520

The correct answer is C. Each RIP-enabled router on the network broadcasts Update messages every 30 seconds using UDP port 520 to all directly connected neighbors.

Answer B is incorrect. BGP uses TCP port 179.

2. Count-to-infinity is the _____.
   a. Problem where the router interfaces counters roll over
   b. Problem where hop count of RIP is limited to 15
   c. Problem where routing loop causes the TTL value to decrement to zero
   d. Problem caused by slow convergence where routing information will continue to pass from router to router incrementing the hop count by one. This problem, and the routing loop, will continue indefinitely, or until some limit is reached.

The correct answer is D. The problem with any distance vector routing protocol is that each router does not have a complete view of the network. Routers must rely on the neighboring routers for network reachablity information. The distance vector routing algorithm creates a slow convergence problem in which inconsistencies arise, because routing Update messages propagate slowly across the network.

Count-to-infinity problem is when routing information continues to pass from router to router incrementing the hop count by one. This problem, and the routing loop, will continue indefinitely, or until some limit is reached. RIP imposes a maximum hop count of 15 to prevent this problem. When the hop count of a route exceeds 15, the route is marked unreachable, and over time, eventually removed from the routing table.

3. What routing protocol rule states that it is never useful for a router to advertise a route back in the direction from which it came?
   a. Split horizon
   b. Poison reverse
   c. Count-to-infinity
   d. None of the above

The correct answer is A. Split horizon is a scheme used by the router to avoid problems caused by advertising routes back to the router from which they were learned. The split horizon scheme omits routes learned from one neighbor in updates sent to that neighbor. When split horizon is enabled on a router's interface, the router records the interface over which a route was received and does not propagate information about that route back out that interface.

Answer B is incorrect. Poisoned reverse includes the routes in updates, but sets their metrics to 16 (infinity). By setting the hop count to infinity and advertising the route back to its source, it is possible to immediately break a routing loop. Otherwise, the inaccurate route will stay in the routing table until it times out. The disadvantage to poison reverse is that it increases the size of the routing table.

4. The holddown timer in a distance vector protocol like RIP is used to _____.
    a. Control the rate in seconds at which routing updates are sent.
    b. Prevent the router from accepting routing information about a network for a fixed period of time after the route has been removed from the routing table.
    c. Speed up convergence time; whenever the metric of a route changes, the router must send an Update message immediately.
    d. Set the interval of time in seconds after which a route is declared invalid.

The correct answer is B. Holddown timers prevent the router from accepting routing information about a network for a fixed period of time after the route has been removed from the routing table. The idea is to make sure all routers have received the information, and no router sends out an invalid route.

Answer A is incorrect. The update timer sets the rate in seconds at which routing updates are sent. The default for RIP is 30 seconds.

Answer C is incorrect. Triggered updates are an attempt to speed up convergence time, by forcing the router to send an Update message immediately whenever the metric of a route changes. A triggered Update message is sent immediately regardless of when the regular Update message is scheduled to be sent.

Answer D is incorrect. The invalid timer sets the interval of time in seconds after which a route is declared invalid. The timer is started if the route is not present in the regular Update message. The default for RIP is 180 seconds.

5. Which of the following is true regarding the passive interface command when used in an RIP environment? (multiple answers)
    a. The passive interface command disables the sending of routing updates on a given interface.
    b. If you disable the sending of routing updates on an interface, the particular subnet will continue to be advertised out other RIP-enabled interfaces.
    c. Routes received on a passive will not be processed.
    d. RIP requests will still be sent out the passive interface.

The correct answers are A, B, and D. The passive interface command disables the sending of routing updates on a given interface. If you disable the sending of routing updates on an interface, the particular subnet will continue to be advertised out other RIP-enabled interfaces and requests will still be sent out the interface.

Answer C is incorrect. Routes received by a passive interface will still be processed.

6. Which of the following are true regarding RIP? (multiple answers)
   a. RIP is a classful protocol.
   b. RIP does not carry subnet information in its updates.
   c. RIP is based on the Bellman-Ford (distance vector) algorithm.
   d. RIP uses bandwidth as its metric.

The correct answers are A, B, and C. Routing Information Protocol (RIP) is a distance vector protocol used to exchange routing information among routers and hosts. RIP is based on the Bellman-Ford (distance vector) algorithm, which was originally used in computer routing in 1969 by ARPANET. However, Xerox originally developed the protocol RIP as we know it today in the late 1970s as part of their Xerox Networking Services (XNS) protocol suite.

RIP is a classful routing protocol that does not carry subnet information. When enabling RIP on a router, you specify which classful network the protocol will be run on.

Answer D is incorrect. RIP uses hop count as the metric to measure the distance to a network. Each router adds its internal distance (1) to the route before advertising the route to its neighbors.

7. How many message types does RIP use?
   a. Two (updates and requests)
   b. Three (updates, requests, and keepalives)
   c. One (updates)
   d. None of the above

The correct answer is A. RIP uses two packet types to convey information, updates, and requests. Each RIP-enabled router on the network broadcasts Update messages every 30 seconds using UDP port 520 to all directly connected neighbors. Update messages reflect the complete routing database, which currently exists in the router. Each entry in the database consists of two elements: the IP address of the network that can be reached and the distance to that network. The router uses request messages to discover other RIP-speaking devices on the network.

8. RouterA, RouterB, and RouterC are connected to the same Ethernet LAN. The network administrator has requested that you prevent RouterA from sending RIP updates to RouterC. However, RouterA must still send routing updates to RouterB.

What should you do to the configuration on RouterA?

a. Nothing—because RIP is a broadcast protocol, by default it will send updates to all devices on the Ethernet LAN. This cannot be prevented.

b. Configure the Ethernet interface on RouterA as passive.

c. Configure the Ethernet interface as passive and define RouterB as a unicast neighbor with the neighbor command.

d. None of the above

The correct answer is C. Because RIP is a broadcast protocol, by default it will send updates to all devices on the Ethernet LAN. To prevent this from happening, RouterA's Ethernet interface is configured as passive. However, in this case a neighbor router configuration command is included. This command permits the sending of routing updates to a specific neighbor. One copy of the routing update is generated per defined neighbor.

The RIP neighbor command permits the point-to-point (non-broadcast) exchange of routing information. This command can be used in combination with the passive-interface router configuration command to exchange information between a subset of routers and access servers all connected to the same LAN.

9. RouterA and RouterB in the Illustration below are running RIP on all interfaces. RouterB does not have an entry for network 130.1.1.0 in its routing table. What is the problem?

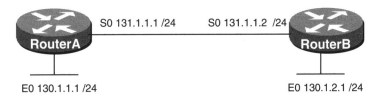

S0 131.1.1.1 /24   S0 131.1.1.2 /24

RouterA   RouterB

E0 130.1.1.1 /24   E0 130.1.2.1 /24

a. When RouterB receives the update for network 130.1.0.0, it drops it because it has a direct connection to the same network.

b. The networks are discontiguous.

c. Both A and B

d. Not enough information is provided to determine the problem.

The correct answer is C. A discontiguous network is a network that has subnets of the same major network separated by another major network. For example, in Figure 3-28, network 130.1.1.0 /24 on RouterA is separated from network 130.1.2.0 /24 on RouterB by the major network 131.1.1.0 /24.

Due to the classful nature of RIP and the fact that no mask information is carried in the routing updates, support for discontiguous networks becomes a problem. For example, in Figure 3-28, when the RouterA sends updates for network 130.1.1.0 to

RouterB, it summarizes the network at the natural class: in this case, class B (130.1.0.0). When RouterB receives an updated advertising network 130.1.0.0, it drops the update because one of its own interfaces is connected to network 130.1.0.0. The router will not accept an update for a network to which its own interface is connected.

10. How can the problem in question 9 be fixed?

    a. A secondary address can be added to the interfaces connecting RouterA to RouterB. The secondary address should be in the same major network as the discontiguous network and use the same subnet mask.

    b. Nothing—RIP does not support this type of configuration.

    c. Add a unicast neighbor on both RouterA and RouterB.

    d. Not enough information is provided to determine the solution to the problem.

The correct answer is A. Due to the classful nature of RIP and the fact that no mask information is carried in the routing updates, support for discontiguous networks becomes a problem. For example, in Figure 3-28, when the RouterA sends updates for network 130.1.1.0 to RouterB, it summarizes the network at the natural class: in this case class B (130.1.0.0). When RouterB receives an updated advertising network 130.1.0.0, it drops the update because one its own interfaces is connected to network 130.1.0.0. The router will not accept an update for a network to which its own interface is connected.

The solution to this problem is to add a secondary address to the interfaces connecting RouterA to RouterB. The secondary address should be in the same major network as the discontiguous network and use the same subnet mask (see Illustration). With the addition of the secondary address, the networks are no longer discontiguous.

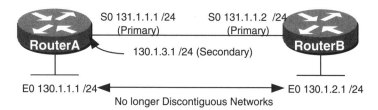

    S0 131.1.1.1 /24 (Primary)   S0 131.1.1.2 /24 (Primary)

    RouterA   130.1.3.1 /24 (Secondary)   **RouterB**

    E0 130.1.1.1 /24   E0 130.1.2.1 /24

No longer Discontiguous Networks

11. How do you advertise a default route in RIP? (multiple answers)

    a. Configure a static route to 0.0.0.0 with a mask of 0.0.0.0.

    b. Configure a static route to 0.0.0.0 with a mask of 0.0.0.0 and redistribute the static route into RIP.

    c. Use the IP default-network command.

    d. Configure a static route to 0.0.0.0 and use the IP default-network command.

The correct answers are A and C. A default route can be injected into an RIP domain either through a static route (IP route 0.0.0.0 0.0.0.0) or through the IP default-network command. No redistribution is needed; if a default route is in the routing table, it will automatically be advertised.

12. How many IP network entries can be sent in a single RIP Update message?

    a. 20

    b. 15

    c. 25

    d. 100

The correct answer is C. Each RIP message can contain up to 25 routes. Each route entry includes an address family identifier, IP address reachable by the route, and next-hop count for the route. If the router has more than 25 entries to send, multiple RIP messages must be sent.

13. Which of the following are classful protocols?

    a. RIP

    b. IGRP

    c. EIGRP

    d. OSPF

The correct answers are A and B. Both RIP and IGRP are classful protocols because they do not carry subnet mask information in their updates. OSPF and EIGRP are both classless protocols.

14. Which of the following is false regarding RIPV2?

    a. RIPV2 multicast updates.

    b. RIPV2 is classless.

    c. RIPV2 supports authentication.

    d. RIPV2 does not carry subnet mask information with its route entry.

Answer D is false. One of the most important advantages of RIPV2 is its capability to carry subnet mask information with its route entries, making it a classless protocol. RIPV2 also multicasts its updates instead of broadcasting them. The advantage of this is that stations on the LAN that are not concerned with RIP routing do not need to waste CPU cycles processing broadcast packets. With multicast updates, only the stations or routers configured for RIPV2 (multicast group 224.0.0.9) will receive the packet.

RIPV2 also supports authentication. This allows RIPV2-enabled routers to authenticate the source of the routing updates received. Without the capability to authenticate the source of routing updates, a router is susceptible to malicious updates.

15. What protocol does RIPV2 use?

   a. TCP port 580
   b. UDP port 520
   c. TCP port 520
   d. UDP port 580

The correct answer is B. Like version one, RIPV2 operates from UDP port 520 and has a maximum datagram size of 512 bytes.

16. A router has two RIP learned routes to the same destination. One has a higher cost than the other. When the primary path fails, the users complain about slow convergence time. What can you do to speed up convergence?

   a. Configure the metrics of the routes so they are equal.
   b. Tune the RIP timers.
   c. Nothing—this is the default behavior of RIP.
   d. None of the above

The correct answer is B. It is possible to tune the timers in RIP to speed up convergence.

Each time a route is updated, which is dependent on the update interval, the invalid timer is reset. If a route is not seen in an update for 180 seconds, the route is put in holddown, which means that the router will use the route to route packets but will not announce the route in its updates. It also means that the router will not install any other route to this destination until the holddown counter expires. This happens after 180 seconds in which case the route is removed from the routing table. As you can see, by default it can take up to 360 seconds before a new route is loaded in the routing table.

The following is a list of configurable timers.

- **update** The update timer sets the rate in seconds at which routing updates are sent. The default is 30 seconds.

- **invalid** The invalid timer sets the interval of time in seconds after which a route is declared invalid. The timer is started if the route is not present in the regular Update message. The default is 180 seconds.

- **holddown** The holddown timer sets the interval in seconds during which routing information regarding better paths is suppressed. The idea is to make sure all routers have received the information, and no router sends out an invalid route. The default is 180 seconds.

- **flush** The flush timer sets in seconds the amount of time that must pass before a route is removed from the routing table. The default is 240 seconds.

The invalid, holddown, and flush RIP timers are all dependent on the value of the update timer. The invalid timer should be at least three times the value of update timer, the holddown timer should be at least three times the value of update timer, and the flush timer must be at least the sum of invalid and holddown timers. So as you can see, if the update timer is changed, then the invalid, holddown, and flush timers must also be changed.

17. What is the hop count limit of IGRP?

    a. 16

    b. 25

    c. 100

    d. 255

The correct answer is D. IGRP addresses the shortcomings of RIP by permitting the network to grow up to 255 hops and by providing a wide range of metrics (link reliability, bandwidth, internetwork delay, and load) to provide routing flexibility in today's complex networks.

18. Which of the following is not a valid IGRP route type?

    a. Interior

    b. Exterior

    c. System

    d. Network

The correct answer is D. IGRP advertises three types of routes: interior, system, and exterior. Interior routes are routes between subnets that are attached to the same router interface (Figure 3-22). System routes are routes to networks that are in the same autonomous system and exterior routes are routes to networks outside the autonomous system.

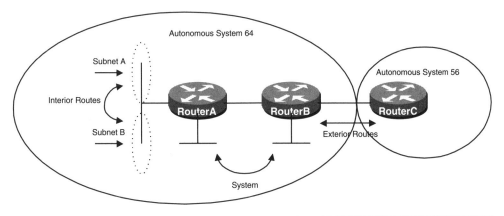

Figure 3-22   IGRP route types

19. Which of the following is not used in calculating the IGRP metric?

    a. Bandwidth

    b. Delay

    c. Reliability

    d. Cost

The answer is D. Cost is not used in calculating the IGRP metric. The IGRP metric is a 32-bit number, which is calculated using bandwidth, delay, reliability, loading, and MTU. The metric of the route is calculated using the five different characteristics of the link and the K values. The K values are configurable, but this is not recommended. The default K values are K1 = 1, K2 = 0, K3 = 1, K4 = 0, and K5 = 0.

20. Use the following illustration and the output from the **show interface** command on RouterB and RouterA. What is the IGRP metric for RouterB to reach network 1.1.1.0 on RouterA, assuming the K values are set to default?

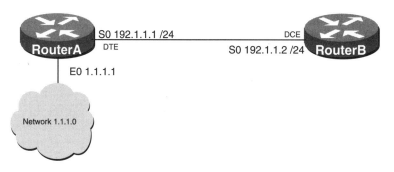

```
RouterB#show interfaces S0/0
Serial0/0 is up, line protocol is up
 Hardware is QUICC Serial
 Internet address is 192.1.1.1/24
 MTU 1500 bytes, BW 1544 Kbit, DLY 20000 usec, rely 255/255, load 1/255
 Encapsulation HDLC, loopback not set, keepalive set (10 sec)
 Last input 00:00:02, output 00:00:02, output hang never
 Last clearing of "show interface" counters never
 Input queue: 0/75/0 (size/max/drops); Total output drops: 0
 Queueing strategy: weighted fair
 Output queue: 0/64/0 (size/threshold/drops)
  Conversations 0/3 (active/max active)
  Reserved Conversations 0/0 (allocated/max allocated)
 5 minute input rate 0 bits/sec, 1 packets/sec
 5 minute output rate 0 bits/sec, 1 packets/sec
  155 packets input, 10368 bytes, 0 no buffer
  Received 80 broadcasts, 0 runts, 1 giants, 0 throttles
  5 input errors, 1 CRC, 2 frame, 0 overrun, 0 ignored, 1 abort
  246 packets output, 13455 bytes, 0 underruns
  0 output errors, 0 collisions, 910 interface resets
  0 output buffer failures, 0 output buffers swapped out
```

```
 154 carrier transitions
 DCD=up DSR=up DTR=up RTS=up CTS=up

RouterA#show interfaces e0/0
Ethernet0/0 is up, line protocol is up
 Hardware is AmdP2, address is 00e0.1e5b.25a1 (bia 00e0.1e5b.25a1)
 MTU 1500 bytes, BW 10000 Kbit, DLY 1000 usec, rely 243/255, load 1/255
 Encapsulation ARPA, loopback not set, keepalive not set
 ARP type: ARPA, ARP Timeout 04:00:00
 Last input never, output 00:00:08, output hang never
 Last clearing of "show interface" counters never
 Queueing strategy: fifo
 Output queue 0/40, 0 drops; input queue 0/75, 0 drops
 5 minute input rate 0 bits/sec, 0 packets/sec
 5 minute output rate 0 bits/sec, 0 packets/sec
 0 packets input, 0 bytes, 0 no buffer
 Received 0 broadcasts, 0 runts, 0 giants, 0 throttles
 0 input errors, 0 CRC, 0 frame, 0 overrun, 0 ignored, 0 abort
 0 input packets with dribble condition detected
 6 packets output, 1071 bytes, 0 underruns
 6 output errors, 0 collisions, 2 interface resets
 0 babbles, 0 late collision, 0 deferred
 6 lost carrier, 0 no carrier
 0 output buffer failures, 0 output buffers swapped out
```

a. 21,000

b. 2,195,456

c. 8,576

d. 90

The correct answer is C. The EIGRP metric is a 32-bit number, which is calculated using bandwidth, delay, reliability, loading, and MTU. Calculating the metric for a route is a two-step process using the five different characteristics of the link and the K values. The K values are configurable, but this is not recommend. The default K values are K1 = 1, K2 = 0, K3 = 1, K4 = 0, and K5 = 0.

1. Metric = K1×Bandwidth + (K2×Bandwidth) / (256-load) + K3×Delay

2. If K5 is not equal to zero, take the metric from step 1 and multiple it by [K5 / (reliability + K4)]. If K5 is zero, ignore step 2.

Metric = Metric×[K5 / (reliability + K4)]

As shown in the previous equation, Cisco sets K2, K4, and K5 to zero. This leaves only two variables to compute the EIGRP metric (bandwidth and delay). Because three of the K values are zero the formula reduces to

Metric = Bandwidth + Delay

The bandwidth is derived by finding the smallest of all bandwidths in path to the destination and dividing 10,000,000 by that number.

Delay is found by adding all of the delays along the paths and dividing that number by 10. This equation can be written as the following:

Metric = [(10,000,000 / min bandwidth) + (SUM (interface delay) / 10)]

The **show interface** command on each router is used to determine what the bandwidth and delay is for each interface. To reach network 1.1.1.0 from RouterB, a packet will cross the serial interface between RouterA and RouterB and the Ethernet interface on RouterA. Because the lowest bandwidth is used for the calculation, the bandwidth of the serial interface is used.

Metric = [(10,000,000 / BW Serial link) + ((delay on serial link + delay on the Ethernet link) / 10)]×256

Metric = [(10,000,000 / 1544) + ((20,000 + 1,000) / 10)]

Metric = 8,576

21. The variance command in IGRP enables the router to _____.
   a. Redistribute between IGRP and EIGRP.
   b. Allow a configurable variance between timers.
   c. Allow unequal-cost load balancing.
   d. None of the above

The correct answer is C. IGRP can be configured to load balance on up to four unequal cost paths to a given destination. This feature is known as unequal-cost load balancing and is set using the variance command. By default, the router will load balance across up to four equal cost paths. The variance command lets you set how much worse an alternate path can be (in terms of metrics) and still be used to load balance across.

For example, if a router has two routes to network 1.1.1.1, one with a cost of four and one with a cost of eight, by default the route will only use the path with a cost of four when sending packets to 1.1.1.1. However, if a variance of two is set, the router will load balance across both paths. This is because the route with the cost of eight is within in the variance, which in this case can be up to two times as bad as the preferred route (4 (preferred route)×2 = 8).

22. Which of the following is false regarding IGRP?
   a. IGRP is a distance vector protocol.
   b. IGRP is classful.

  c. IGRP uses UDP as its transport protocol.

  d. IGRP uses a concept of autonomous systems.

Answer C is false. IGRP does not use TCP or UDP; it accesses IP directly as protocol 9. IGRP is a classful distance vector protocol that uses the concept of autonomous systems. An IGRP AS is an IGRP process domain: a set of routers whose common routing protocol is an IGRP process.

23. True or false: The IGRP process number must be consistent across routers that want to share information.

True. The process ID is carried in the autonomous system field in an IGRP Update message. The IGRP process number must be consistent across routers that want to share information.

24. Which of the following is false regarding EIGRP?

  a. EIGRP is Cisco proprietary.

  b. EIGRP is classless.

  c. EIGRP is a link state protocol.

  d. EIGRP uses the same composite metrics as IGRP.

Answer C is false. Enhanced Interior Gateway Routing Protocol (EIGRP) is a Cisco proprietary advanced classless distance vector routing protocol, which was first released in 1994 (IOS 9.21) to address the limitations of traditional distance vector protocols and link state protocols.

Traditional distance vector protocols such as RIP forward routing updates to all attached neighbors, which in turn forward the updates to their neighbors. This hop-by-hop propagation of routing information creates large convergence times and looped topology problems.

Link state protocols such as OSPF have been offered as an alternative to the tradition distance vector protocols. The problem with link state protocols is that they solve the convergence problems of traditional distance vector protocols by replicating the topology information across the entire domain. This replication becomes undesirable in large networks and greatly affects CPU utilization due to the number of SPF calculations that need to be run. EIGRP uses the same composite metrics as IGRP.

25. A successor in EIGRP is _____.

  a. A directly connected neighboring router that has the best route to reach a particular destination.

  b. A neighboring router that the destination can be reached through, but is not used because the cost to reach the destination is higher than via a different router

    c. A condition used by EIGRP to prevent routing loops

    d. None of the above

The correct answer is A. A successor is the directly connected neighboring router that has the best route to reach a particular destination. This is the route that is used by the router to forward packets to a given destination. In order for a neighbor to become the successor for a particular destination, it must first meet the feasibility condition.

The feasibility condition states that the route must be advertised from a neighbor that is downstream with respect to the destination and the cost to reach the destination must be less than or equal to the cost of the route that is currently being used by the routing table.

Answer B is incorrect. The feasible successor is a neighboring router that the destination can be reached through, but is not used because the cost to reach the destination is higher than via a different router. The feasible successor can be thought of as having the next best route to a destination.

Answer C is also incorrect. The feasible condition is used to prevent routing loops. In order for the feasibility condition to be met, the route must be advertised from a neighbor that is downstream with respect to the destination. The cost to reach the destination must be less than or equal to the cost of the route that is currently being used in the routing table. If the feasibility condition is met, then the neighbor becomes the successor.

26. An EIGRP router goes into active state if _____ .

    a. The router loses its successor but has a feasible successor.

    b. The router losses its route to a destination and no feasible successor is available.

    c. It does not receive a query message.

    d. None of the above

The correct answer is B. When the router loses its route to a destination and no feasible successor is available, the router goes into active state. While in active state, the router sends out queries to all neighbors in order to find a route to the destination. At this time the router must run the routing algorithm to recompute a new route to the destination.

Answer A is incorrect. When the router loses its successor but has a feasible successor, it goes into passive state.

Answer C is also incorrect. When the router loses its route to a destination and no feasible successor is available, the router goes into active state. While in this active state the router sends out query packets to all neighbors for a particular destination. The router waits for a response back from all neighbors before starting the computation for a new successor.

27. EIGRP supports which of the following protocols?

    a. IP

    b. IPX

    c. AppleTalk

    d. All of the above

The correct answer is D. EIGRP implements modules for IP, IPX, and AppleTalk.

28. EIGRP acknowledgements are _____.

    a. Unicast

    b. Broadcast

    c. Multicast

The correct answer is A. EIGRP acknowledgements are hello packets with no data in them. They are always sent as unicast packets.

29. EIGRP hello packets are _____.

    a. Unicast

    b. Broadcast

    c. Multicast

The correct answer is C. Hello packets are exchanged between neighboring routers. As long as hello packets are received, the router can determine that the neighbor is alive and functioning. Hello packets are multicast and use unreliable delivery.

30. EIGRP queries are _____.

    a. Unicast

    b. Broadcast

    c. Multicast

    d. Both A and C

The correct answer is D. EIGRP queries can be multicast or unicast.

31. What is the cause of a route being stuck in active state in EIGRP?

    a. The active timer expires before a reply to the query message is received.

    b. No EIGRP neighbor is found.

    c. No feasible successor is available.

    d. An EIGRP route will never be in this state; this is an OSPF concept.

The correct answer is A. When an EIGRP route goes active, queries are sent to all neighbors. The route will remain in an active state until a reply is received for every query. When the query message is sent, an active timer is sent. If for some reason the timer expires before a reply to the query is received, the route is declared stuck in active.

32. Which of the following is true in regards to using the passive interface command for EIGRP?

    a. When an EIGRP-enabled interface is made passive, no EIGRP packets are sent out that interface.

    b. When an EIGRP-enabled interface is made passive, no EIGRP routing updates are received on that interface.

    c. When an EIGRP-enabled interface is made passive, no adjacencies will be formed with the router connected to that interface.

    d. All of the above

The correct answer is D. Unlike RIP or IGRP (where updates are received but not sent), when the passive interface command is used with EIGRP, routing updates are neither received nor sent because no neighbor relationship is formed. When an EIGRP interface is made passive, no EIGRP packets are sent out that interface, and because EIGRP uses hello packets to form adjacencies with neighbors, no adjacencies will be formed.

33. EIGRP updates are _____. (multiple answers)

    a. Non-periodic

    b. Periodic

    c. Partial

    d. Bounded

The correct answers are A, C, and D. EIGRP updates are non-periodic, partial, and bounded. Non-periodic means that updates are not sent at regular intervals; EIGRP only send updates in the event of a metric or topology change. Partial means that only the routes that have changed are sent, not all of the routes in the table. Bounded means that updates are only sent to the routers that are affected by the change. This means that EIGRP uses much less bandwidth than traditional distance vector protocols.

34. What will happen if an EIGRP router loses its successor and a feasible successor is available?

    a. The router makes the feasible successor the successor and adds the new route. The router remains in passive state.

    b. The router goes into active state.

    c. The router makes the feasible successor the successor and adds the new route. The router goes into active state to find a new feasible successor.

    d. None of the above

The correct answer is A. If the router loses its successor and a feasible successor is available, no route recomputation is necessary. The router simply makes the feasible successor the successor and adds the new route to the routing table and remains in a passive state. However, if no feasible successor is available, then the router goes into active state for the destination network and recomputation for the route is necessary.

35. Which of the following routing protocols has the lowest administrative distance?

    a. EBGP

    b. IBGP

    c. IS-IS

    d. EIGRP

The correct answer is A. The router uses the administrative distance to select the most preferred source of routing updates. For example, if a router is running multiple routing protocols and learns a route to the same destination from each protocol, it needs a way to determine which one to use. This can be thought of as the measure of believability. The lower the administrative distance, the more believable the routing protocol. Admin distances are assigned based on the routing protocol's capability to select the best path. For example, suppose that a router running RIP and EIGRP learns of the same network from both protocols. Because RIP calculates the route based on hop count and EIGRP uses a composite metric, EIGRP is most likely to have calculated the best path. Table 3-6, presented earlier in the chapter and in this section, lists the routing protocols and their administrative distance.

36. Which of the following is/are true regarding distance vector protocols?

    a. Distance vector protocols exchange reachability information by sending periodic updates.

    b. Routes are advertised as vectors of distance and direction.

    c. Distance vector routers work on the basis of periodic updates and holddown timers.

    d. One major drawback of distance vector protocols is their classful nature.

    e. All of the above

The correct answer is E. The name distance vector is derived from the fact that routes are advertised as vectors of distance and direction. Distance is defined in terms of a metric, (hop count, in the case of RIP) and direction in terms of next-hop router. For example, destination X is a distance of three hops away in the direction of next-hop router Y. Each router learns routes from its neighboring router perspective, adds a distance vector —its own distance value—to the route, adds the route to its routing table, and advertises it on to its immediate neighbors.

Table 3-6 Administrative Distance

Routing Protocol	Administrative Distance
Static Route	1
EIGRP Summary	
BGP	20
EIGRP	90
IGRP	100
OSPF	110
IS-IS	115
RIP	120
EGP	140
External EIGRP	170
IBGP	200
Unknown	255

This type of routing is often referred to as routing by rumor, because each router depends on its neighbor for routing information, which in turn may have been received from that routers neighbor. Most distance vector routing algorithms are based on the work done by Bellman, Ford, and Fulkerson; therefore, they are often referred to as Bellman-Ford algorithms.

For the most part, all distance vector protocols share the same characteristics and limitations. They exchange reachability information by sending periodic updates to all neighbors by broadcasting their entire routing table. In large networks, the routing table exchanged between routers becomes very large and hard to maintain, which leads to slow convergence. Convergence is the point in time when the entire network becomes updated to the fact that a route has appeared or disappeared.

Distance vector routers work on the basis of periodic updates and holddown timers. If an update is not received in a given interval, the route goes into holddown state and is aged from the routing table. The holddown aging process translates into minutes in convergence time before the whole network detects that a route has disappeared. This slow convergence problem creates inconsistencies, because routing Update messages propagate slowly across the network. The larger the network, the greater the convergence time.

The other major drawback of distance vector protocols is their classful nature. They do not support Classless Interdomain Routing (CIDR) or Variable Length Subnet Masks (VLSM) because no mask information is exchanged in their routing updates.

Finally, distance vector protocols are considered to be non-hierarchical or flat, which makes them incapable of scaling in large enterprise networks.

Although EIGRP is occasionally described as a distance vector protocol that acts like a link state protocol (a hybrid), it still retains the routing characteristics of a distance vector protocol.

37. Which of the following is false regarding static routes?

  a. They are more preferred than dynamically learned routes.

  b. Often used in hub-and-spoke situations where the spoke is singly homed to reduce routing overhead.

  c. A floating static route is not permanently entered in the routing table.

  d. Static routes provide precise control over routing behavior, which often cannot be obtained through dynamic protocols.

  e. None of the above

The correct answer is E. Although static routes require manual configuration they are very useful in certain situations. Static routes provide precise control over routing behavior, which often cannot be obtained through dynamic protocols. The drawback, of course, is that these routes must be reconfigured any time a topology change occurs.

Static routes are often used in hub-and-spoke situations where the spoke is singly homed to reduce routing overhead. Static routes are also useful in dial backup scenarios, where a floating static route is configured. A floating static route is unlike a regular static route in that it is not permanently entered in the routing table. It appears only after the failure of a more preferred route.

38. Which of the following is false regarding LSAs?

  a. The LSAs contain information on the state of the router's links and the router's relationship to its neighboring routers.

  b. From the collection of LSAs, the router forms what is called a link state database.

  c. Link state advertisement is not acknowledged.

  d. External LSAs are flooded throughout an AS.

Answer C is false. Link state advertisement is used to describe the local state of router. The LSAs contain information about the state of the router's interfaces and the state of any adjacencies that are formed. The LSAs are flooded through the network. This flooding procedure carries the LSA one hop farther from its point of origin. Because all routers in an OSPF domain are interconnected via adjacencies, the information disseminates throughout the network. To make this process reliable, each link state advertisement must be acknowledged.

The information contained in the LSA sent by each router in the domain is used to form the router's topological database. The topological database is used to calculate the shortest path to each destination.

39. On OSPF, virtual links updates are _____.

    a. Unicast

    b. Multicast

    c. Broadcast

    d. None of the above

The correct answer is A. On point-to-point and virtual links networks, updates are unicast to the interface address of the adjacent neighbors. On point-to-multipoint networks, updates are sent to the multicast address 224.0.0.5.

40. Which of the following is true regarding OSPF areas? (multiple answers)

    a. OSPF uses areas to segment the AS and contain link state updates.

    b. A router in multiple areas has a separate topological database for each area it is connected to.

    c. Routers that connect areas within the same AS are called Area Border Routers (ABRs).

    d. If multiple areas are configured one of these areas must be configured as area 0.

The correct answers are A, B, C, and D.

OSPF uses areas to segment the AS and contain link state updates. LSAs are only flooded within an area, so separating the areas reduces the amount of routing traffic on a network.

Each router within an area has an identical topological database as all other routers in the same area. A router in multiple areas has a separate topological database for each area it is connected to.

Routers that have all of their interfaces within the same area are called internal routers (IR). Routers that connect areas within the same AS are called Area Border Routers (ABRs) and routers that act as gateways redistributing routing information from one AS to another AS are call Autonomous System Border Routers (ASBRs).

OSPF has a concept of a backbone area referred to as area 0. If multiple areas are configured one of these areas must be configured as area 0. The backbone (area 0) is the center for all areas; that is, all areas must have a connection to the backbone. In cases where an area does not have direct physical connectivity to the backbone, a virtual link must be configured.

All areas inject routing information into the backbone area (area 0) and the backbone propagates routing information back to each area.

41. Which of the following is false regarding a Designated Router (DR) in OSPF network?

   a. All multi-access networks with two or more attached routers elect a DR.

   b. DR concept enables a reduction in the number of adjacencies that need to be formed on a network.

   c. The DR is elected using the hello protocol.

   d. The router with the lowest priority is elected the DR.

Answer D is false. The router with the highest priority will be elected the DR. If a tie occurs, the router with the highest router ID is selected. The router ID is the IP address of the loopback interface. If no loopback is configured, the router ID is the highest IP address on the router. The router priority can be configured on the router interface with the **ip ospf priority** command.

Answer A is true. All multi-access networks with two or more attached routers elect a DR.

Answer B is true. The DR concept enables a reduction in the number of adjacencies that need to be formed on a network. In order for OSPF-enabled routers to exchange routing information, they must form an adjacency with one another. If a DR was not used, then each router on a multi-access network would need to form an adjacency with every other router (because link State databases are synchronized across adjacencies). This would result in N-1 adjacencies per router. Instead, all routers on a multi-access network form adjacencies only with the DR and Backup Designated Router (BDR). Each router sends the DR and BDR routing information and the DR is responsible for flooding this information to all adjacent routers and originating a network link advertisement on behalf of the network. The BDR is used in case the DR fails.

The reduction in adjacencies reduces the volume of routing protocol traffic as well as the size of the topological database.

Answer C is true. The DR is elected using the hello protocol.

42. What happens if a router with a higher priority becomes active on a network where a DR is present?

   a. The router with highest priority becomes the DR and old DR becomes the BDR.

   b. Nothing—if a DR is present, the router accepts the DR regardless of its priority.

   c. They use hello protocol to determine the DR.

   d. The new router takes over as BDR.

The correct answer is B. When a router first becomes active on a multi-access network, the router checks to see if a DR is currently present for the network. If a DR is present, the router accepts the DR regardless of its priority. Once a DR is elected, no other router can become the DR unless the DR fails. If no DR is present on the network, then the routers negotiate the DR based on router priority.

43. Which of the following is false regarding the hello protocol used by OSPF?

    a. The hello protocol is responsible for discovering neighbors.

    b. The hello protocol is responsible for maintaining the neighbor relationship.

    c. The hello protocol is responsible for electing the DR.

    d. The hello interval is the same for all network types.

Answer D is false. The hello packets are sent periodically out the router's interface depending on the network type. For broadcast networks and point-to-point networks, the default hello interval is ten seconds. For non-broadcast networks and point-to-multipoint networks, it's 30 seconds.

Answer A, B, and C are true. The hello protocol is responsible for discovering neighbors and maintaining the neighbor relationship. Hello packets are sent periodically out the router's interface depending on the network type. The hello protocol is also responsible for electing a DR on multi-access networks.

44. Which of the following is not a valid LSA?

    a. Router

    b. Network

    c. Link

    d. Summary

    e. External

The correct answer is C. Link is not a valid LSA type.

Answer A is a valid LSA. Each router in the area generates a router LSA (type 1 LSA). This advertisement describes the state and cost of the router's interfaces to that area. All of the router's links to the area must be described in a single router LSA. The router LSAs are only flooded throughout a single area.

Answer B is a valid LSA. Network link advertisements are type 2 LSAs. The DR for each multi-access network that has more than one attached router originates a network advertisement. The advertisement describes all of the routers attached to the network as well as the DR itself.

Answer D is a valid LSA. Summary LSAs are type 3 and 4 LSAs. The ABR generates summary LSAs, which describes a route to a single destination. The summary LSA is advertised within the single area and the destination described is external to the area yet part of the same autonomous system. Only intra-area routes are advertised in the backbone.

Answer E is a valid LSA. The Autonomous System Border Router (ASBR) generates an external type 5 LSA, which advertises each destination known to the router that is external to the AS. AS external type 5 LSAs are used to advertise default routes into the AS.

Two types of external routes are available: external type 1 and external type 2. The difference between the two is the way the cost or metric of the route is calculated. External type 1 routes use the external cost plus the internal cost of reaching a route. External type 2 routes only use the external cost of reaching the route. Type 2 routes are always preferred over type 1 routes, and are the default type for any route that is redistributed into OSPF.

45. What is the correct order of the five states that OSPF neighbors go through to form an adjacency?

a. Init, Exstart, exchange, loading, full

b. Init, loading, Exstart, exchange, full

c. Exstart, Init, exchange, loading, full

d. Init, Exstart, full, exchange, loading

The correct answer is A. Neighbor routers go through five states before fully forming an adjacency or having a full neighbor state. Figure 3-23 shows an example of how an adjacency is formed between two neighboring routers on a broadcast media. RouterA and RouterB both connect to an Ethernet network and RouterB is configured with a higher DR priority.

When RouterA and RouterB first come online, they both initialize and begin sending hello packets. At this point in time neither router knows of the presence of the other router on the network and no DR is selected. RouterB hears the hello from RouterA, changing the state of the adjacency from down to initializing (Init).

At this point the routers have seen themselves in the hello packet from their neighbors and bidirectional communication is established. The adjacency changes from initializing to 2way.

At the end of this stage, the DR and BDR is elected for the network and the router then decides whether or not to form an adjacency with its neighbor. On a multi-access network routers will only form adjacencies with the DR and BDR on the network.

RouterB in the next hello packet indicates to RouterA that it is the DR for the link. At this point the state of the adjacency changes from initializing to exchange (Exstart). During the Exstart state, a master/slave relationship is formed between the two routers and the slave router adopts the masters database description sequence number.

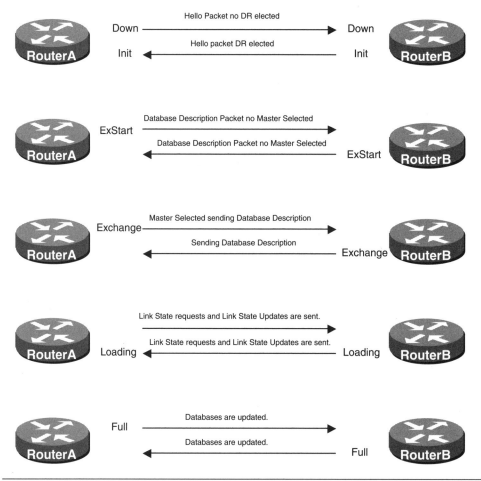

Figure 3-23 How a router forms adjacencies

After the master/slave relationship is formed and the routers agree on common database description sequence number, the routers begin to exchange database description packets. At this point the state of the adjacency changes from Exstart to exchange.

After the complete databases are exchanged between routers using the database description packets, the routers compare the database of their neighbor with their own database. At this point the router may find that parts of the neighbor's database may be more up-to-date than its own. If so, the router requests these pieces using a link state request packet. At this point the state of the adjacency is loading.

After the link state update requests have all been satisfied RouterA and RouterB databases are deemed synchronized and the routers are fully adjacent.

46. Which of the following is not an OSPF network type?

    a. Broadcast

    b. Non-broadcast

    c. Point-to-point

    d. Multiple access

Answer D is not an OSPF network type. OSPF has four network types or models: broadcast, non-broadcast, point-to-point, and point-to-multipoint. Depending on the network type, OSPF works differently. Understanding how OSPF works on each network model is essential in designing a stable and robust OSPF network.

The broadcast network type is the default type on LANs (Token Ring, Ethernet, and FDDI).

However, any interface can be configured as broadcast using the **ip ospf network** interface command.

- On a broadcast model, a DR and BDR is elected and all routers form adjacencies with the DR and BDR. This achieves optimal flooding because all LSAs are sent to the DR and the DR floods them to each individual router on the network.

- Neighbors do not need to be defined.

- All routers are on the same subnet.

- Care must be taken if the broadcast model is used on NMBA networks such as Frame Relay or ATM. Because a DR is elected, all routers must have physical connectivity to the DR. A fully meshed environment should be used or the DR should be statically configured using the priority command to ensure physical connectivity.

- The hello timer is 10 seconds, the dead interval is 40 seconds, and the wait interval is 40 seconds.

The non-broadcast network type is the default type on serial interfaces configured for Frame Relay encapsulation. However, any interface can be configured as non-broadcast using the **ip ospf network** interface command.

- With the non-broadcast model, a DR and BDR are elected and all routers form adjacencies with the DR and BDR. This achieves optimized flooding because all LSAs are sent to the DR and the DR floods them to each individual router on the network.

- Due to the lack of broadcast capabilities, neighbors must be defined using the neighbor command.

- All routers are on the same subnet.

- Similar to the broadcast model, a DR is elected. Care must be taken to ensure that the DR has logical connectivity to all routers on the network.

- The hello timer is 30 seconds, the dead interval is 120 seconds, and the wait interval is 120 seconds.

The network type point-to-point is the default type on serial interfaces that are not using Frame Relay encapsulation or can be selected as a subinterface type point-to-point. A subinterface is a logical way of defining an interface. The same physical interface can be split into multiple logical interfaces. This was originally created to deal with issues caused by split horizons on NBMA networks.

The point-to-point model can be configured on any interface using the **ip ospf network point-to-point** interface command.

- With a point-to-point model, no DR and BDR are elected and directly connected routers form adjacencies.

- Each point-to-point link requires a separate subnet.

- The hello timer is 10 seconds, the dead interval is 40 seconds, and the wait interval is 40 seconds.

The network type point-to-multipoint can be configured on any interface using the **ip ospf network point-to-multipoint** interface command.

- No DR is elected.

- Neighbors do not need to be defined because additional LSAs are used to convey neighbor router connectivity.

- One subnet is used for the whole network.

- The hello timer is 30 seconds, the dead interval is 120 seconds, and the wait interval is 120 seconds.

47. The OSPF cost is calculated using which of the following formulas?
    a. cost = (10,000,000 / bandwidth of the interface in bits per second)
    b. cost = (bandwidth of the interface in bits per second)
    c. cost = (100,000,000×bandwidth of the interface in bits per second)
    d. cost = (100,000,000 / bandwidth of the interface in bits per second)

The correct answer is D. The OSPF path cost is calculated using the following formula: cost = (100,000,000 / bandwidth in bits per second). The cost is inversely proportional to the bandwidth of the link; the higher the bandwidth, the lower the cost.

48. You want to make sure that RouterA is always elected the DR for the OSPF network. What should you do?

    a. Reload all of the routers and make sure RouterA is the first to come up.

    b. Set the OSPF priority on RouterA to one and all of the other routers to zero.

    c. Set the OSPF priority on RouterA lower than all of the other routers.

    d. None of the above

The correct answer is B. The **ip ospf priority interface** configuration command is used to set the priority of the router interface, which is used for DR election. The router with the highest priority will be elected the DR for the multi-access network. If two routers have the same OSPF priority, the router with the highest router ID will be elected the DR. A router with a priority of zero is ineligible to become the DR or BDR.

49. What is wrong with the network scenario in the following Illustration?

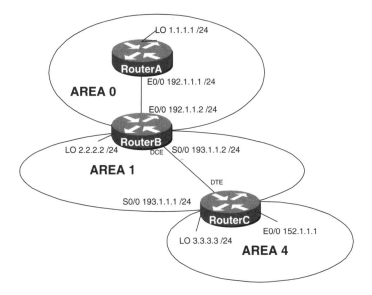

    a. RouterB cannot be in two areas.

    b. The addressing is not valid.

    c. A virtual link needs to be configured between area 1 and area 4.

    d. A virtual link needs to be configured between area 0 and area 4.

The correct answer is D. Area 0 needs to be at the center of all areas. All areas need to have physical connectivity to the backbone area 0. In our case area 4 does not, so a virtual link is needed to provide area 4 with a logical connection to the backbone area 0.

50. When you display the routing table on a Cisco router, you see a destination address followed by two numbers (2.2.2.2 [110/120] via 192.1.1.2, 00:02:22, Serial0/0). What does the first number indicate?

    a. The cost of the route

    b. The administrative distance of the route

    c. The local process number

    d. None of the above

The correct answer is B. After the destination address are two numbers: 110/120. The first number, 110, is the administrative distance of OSPF, which is used to compare multiple routes to the same destination. The lower the administrative distance, the more trustworthy the route. For example, RIP has an administrative distance of 120, so if RouterA learned the same route from RIP and OSPF, the OSPF route is preferred because it has the lower administrative distance.

The second number, 120, is the metric or cost of using the route. This is used to compare routes that are learned via the same routing protocol. The route with the lowest cost is preferred.

51. Which of the following is false regarding a point-to-multipoint OSPF interface?

    a. A DR and BDR are elected on a point-to-multipoint interface.

    b. Neighbors do not need to be defined.

    c. Any interface can be configured as a point-to-multipoint interface using the **ip ospf network point-to-multipoint** interface command.

    d. The hello timer is 30 seconds and the dead interval is 120 seconds.

Answer A is false. A point-to-multipoint network type is treated as a numbered point-to-point interface having one or more neighbors. When an interface is configured for point-to-multipoint, no DR and BDR are elected and neighbors do not need to be defined, greatly simplifying configuring OSPF over NBMA network.

52. While debugging on ip ospf events, you received the following message. What is most likely the problem?

```
OSPF: Send with youngest Key 5
OSPF: Rcv pkt from 193.1.1.1, Serial0/0 : Mismatch Authentica-
tion Key - No message digest key 1 on interface
```

    a. Only one router is configured for authentication.

    b. Message digest is not configured on interface s0/0.

    c. One router is configured with a message digest key of 5 the other with a key of 1.

    d. None of the above

The correct answer is C. Notice that the router is receiving an message digest key of 1 and sending an message digest key of 5 causing an authentication key mismatch.

Because the neighbor authentication does not match, the router simply disregards the OSPF packets from its neighbor. The authentication key and the message digest 5 password must match or the routers will not exchange OSPF information.

53. In the following Illustration what command would you use to configure RouterA for ospf process 64 and place interface s0 in area 0?

a. router ospf 64
   network 192.1.1.1 255.255.255.255 area 0
b. router ospf 64
   network 192.1.1.1 255.255.255.255
   area 0
c. router ospf 64
   network 192.1.1.0 0.0.0.255 area 0
d. router ospf 64
   network 192.1.1.0 0.0.0.255
   area 0

Answer C is correct. The network router configuration command defines what interface OSPF will run on and what OSPF area the interface will be in. A wild card mask is used in conjunction with the IP address, which enables the user to specify one or more interfaces in an area using only a single command. When using a wild card mask, a 0 means it must match and a 1 means it does not matter.

In the following example, OSPF process 64 is defined. Line 1 only enables OSPF on one interface 192.1.1.1. Line 2 enables OSPF on any interface with an IP address 132.10.x.x. Line 3 enables OSPF on all interfaces on the router.

```
router ospf 64
network 192.1.1.1 0.0.0.0 area 1
                ↑ Wild Card Mask of all zero specifies one particular address
network 132.10.0.0 0.0.255.255 area 2
                ↑ This Wild Card Mask specifies that only the first two Octets must match.
network 0.0.0.0 255.255.255.255 area 0
                ↑A wild card mask of all ones specifies any interface on the router.
```

54. RouterA is connected serially to RouterB. While debugging on ip ospf events on RouterB, you received the following message. What is most likely the problem?

```
RouterA#
OSPF: Mismatched hello parameters from 192.1.1.2
```

   a. Serial interface on RouterA is configured as OSPF network type point-to-point and RouterB serial interface is configured as OPSF network type broadcast.

   b. Serial interface on RouterA is configured as OSPF network type point-to-multipoint and RouterB serial interface is configured as OPSF network type non-broadcast.

   c. Serial interface on RouterA is configured as OSPF network type point-to-point and RouterB serial interface is configured as OPSF network type non-broadcast.

   d. None of the above

The correct answer is C. Notice that RouterA is receiving an OSPF packet from RouterB and the hello intervals do not match. The hello interval for OSPF network type point-to-point is 10 seconds and the hello interval for OSPF network type non-broadcast is 30 seconds.

If either the hello interval or the dead interval does not match, then the router will not form an adjacency with its neighbor.

55. An OSPF stub area _____.

   a. Prevents flapping within the domain from affecting the area

   b. Does not permit external LSAs

   c. Does not permit summary LSAs

   d. All of the above

The correct answer is B. In a stub area, no external LSAs are permitted; therefore, none are injected by the ABR. External LSAs are used to describe destinations outside the OSPF domain. For example, a route received from another routing protocol such as RIP and redistributed into OSPF is consider external and would be advertised in an external LSA.

Answer A is incorrect. Although stub areas prevent flapping outside of the domain from affecting the area, they do not prevent flapping that occurs within the domain from affecting the area. Because summary LSAs are still permitted, flaps that occur in other areas will still affect the stub area.

Answer C is incorrect. Totally stubby areas prevent external LSAs and summary LSAs. So flaps that occur within other areas will not affect the totally stubby area.

56. Which of the following is false regarding an NSSA area?

    a. An NSSA area can import external routes into the area.

    b. Routes are carried across the area as type 7 LSAs and converted to type 5 LSAs by the ABR.

    c. An NSSA area does not permit summary LSAs.

    d. None of the above

Answer C is false. NSSAs do not prevent flapping that occurs within the domain from affecting the area. Because summary LSAs are still permitted, flaps that occur in other areas will still affect the stub area. A NSSA area is similar to a stub area; however, it can import external routes into the area. The routes are carried across the area as type 7 LSAs and converted to type 5 LSAs by the ABR. A NSSA area would be used if, for example, you wanted to prevent external LSAs from entering the area, but you still needed to send external LSAs out of the area: for example, if one of the routers in the area was an ASBR.

57. Which OSPF command is used to summarize a set of external routes that have been injected into the domain?

    a. Summary address command applied to an ASBR

    b. Area range command applied to an ABR

    c. Summary address command applied to an ABR

    d. Area range command applied to an ASBR

The correct answer is A. Cisco enables you to summarize addresses in order to conserve resources by limiting the number of routes that need to be advertised between areas. Two types of address summarization are supported on a Cisco router: inter-area summarization and external route summarization. Inter-area summarization is used to summarize addresses between areas, whereas external summarization is used to summarize a set of external routes that have been injected into the domain. The area range command is applied to an ABR and the summary address command is applies to an ASBR.

58. Which of the following would cause OSPF neighbors not to form an adjacency? (multiple answers)

    a. The mask on the interface connecting the two routers does not match.

    b. Both of the routers have their OSPF priority set to zero.

    c. The hello interval on the routers does not match.

    d. None of the above

The correct answers are A and C. If the mask received in the hello packet does not match the mask of the interface on which the packet was received, the packet is dropped. If the sending and receiving routers do not have the same hello interval, they will not establish a neighbor relationship.

Answer B is incorrect. A router with an OSPF priority of zero is not eligible for DR election. However, this will not prevent the neighboring routers from forming an adjacency.

59. What is the significance of the N-bit in an OSPF hello packet?
  a. The N-bit is used to indicate that the router is capable of supporting OSPF demand circuits.
  b. The N-bit is used to indicate that the router is capable of supporting NSSA external LSAs.
  c. The N-bit is used to indicate that the router is capable of accepting AS external LSAs.
  d. The N-bit is used to indicate that the router is using authentication.

The correct answer is B. The N-bit in the options field is used to indicate if the router supports NSSA external LSAs. If the N-bit equals zero, the router will not accept or send these types of LSAs. If neighboring routers do not have the same N-bit setting, they will not form an adjacency.

Answer A is incorrect. The DC-bit is used to indicate whether or not a router is capable of supporting OSPF demand circuits.

Answer C is incorrect. The E-bit is used to indicate if the router is capable of accepting AS external LSAs.

Answer D is also incorrect. The AUType field is used to indicate which type of authentication is being used. Three types are available: null (no authentication), simple (clear text), and cryptographic (MD5).

60. Based on the following Illustration (assuming the OSPF priority of each router is set to 1), which router will be elected the DR and which will become the BDR?

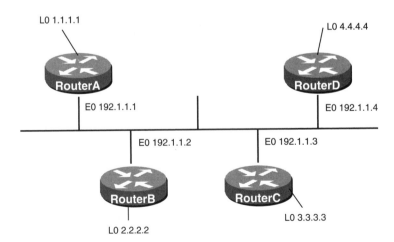

   a. RouterD will become the DR and RouterC will become the BDR.
   b. RouterA will become the DR and RouterB will become the BDR.
   c. RouterC will become the DR and RouterD will become the BDR.
   d. RouterB will become the DR and RouterA will become the BDR.

The correct answer is A. The DR and BDR are elected using the hello protocol. The election of the DR is determined by the router priority, which is carried in the hello packet. The router with the highest priority will be elected the DR; if a tie occurs, the router with the highest router ID is selected.

The router ID is the IP address of the loopback interface. If no loopback is configured, the router ID is the highest IP address on the router. RouterD has the highest router ID so it becomes the DR. RouterC has the second highest ID so it becomes the BDR.

All multi-access networks with two or more attached routers elect a DR. The DR concept enables a reduction in the number of adjacencies that need to be formed on a network. In order for OSPF-enabled routers to exchange routing information, they must form an adjacency with one another. If a DR was not used, then each router on a multi-access network would need to form an adjacency with every other router (because link State databases are synchronized across adjacencies). This would result in N-1 adjacencies.

Instead, all routers on a multi-access network form adjacencies only with the DR and BDR. Each router sends the DR and BDR routing information and the DR is responsible for flooding this information to all adjacent routers and originating a network link advertisement on behalf of the network. The BDR is used in case the DR fails. The reduction in adjacencies reduces the volume of routing protocol traffic as well as the size of the topological database.

When a router first becomes active on a multi-access network, the router checks to see if a DR is currently present for the network. If a DR is present, the router accepts the DR regardless of its priority. Once a DR is elected no other router can become the DR unless the DR fails. If no DR is present on the network, then the routers negotiate the DR based on router priority.

61. IS-IS is based on _____.
   a. Three levels of hierarchy
   b. Two levels of hierarchy
   c. One level of hierarchy
   d. Four levels of hierarchy

The correct answer is B. Like OSPF, IS-IS is based on two levels of hierarchy: level 1 and level 2 routing. Routing within an area is referred to as level 1 routing, and routing between areas is called level 2 routing. Level 2 routers connect multiple level 1 routers similar to area 0 in OSPF.

62. For routing IP, the IS-IS NSAP address is divided into which of the following?

    a. The area address, system-ID, and N-selector

    b. The area address and system-ID

    c. The area address and N-selector

    d. The system-ID, area address, and N-selector

The correct answer is A. For routing IP, the NSAP address is divided into three parts: the area address, the system-ID, and the N-selector.

The area address is a variable-length field that identifies the routing domain length of the area field and is associated with a single area within a routing domain. The system-ID is 6 bytes long and defines the ES or IS in an area. The NSAP selector is 1 byte long and identifies a particular network service at the network layer of a node. (See the following illustration.)A network service user can be a transport entity or the IS network itself.

Area number	System ID	N Sel
← Variable Length →	6 Bytes	1 Byte

63. The metric for Cisco IS-IS is _____.

    a. Dependent on the interface type

    b. Dependent on the delay of the interface

    c. Cisco assigns a metric of ten to every interface, regardless of the interface type.

    d. A composite of four metrics

The correct answer is C. The default metric for every IS-IS interface is set to ten regardless of the interface type. This can be changed with the interface command **isis metric**. If all interfaces are left at their default setting, the IS-IS metric becomes a simple measure of hop count.

IS-IS can use four metrics to calculate the shortest path and each metric can be an integer between 0 to 63. The metrics are **default**, which must be supported and understood by every router, **delay**, which reflects the delay of the transit network, **expense**, which reflects the cost of the link, and **error**, which is similar to IGRP/EIGRP and measures the error probability of the network. For each metric, a separate route is calculated resulting in an SPF calculation. So if a system is using all four metrics to calculate the cost, it will run the SPF algorithm four times for each destination network. Cisco only supports the default metric.

64. What is the maximum metric that can be assigned to any IS-IS route?

    a. 1,024

    b. 1,023

    c. 63

    d. 256

The correct answer is B. The maximum metric value that can be assigned to any route is 1,023. By limiting the metric to 1,023, the SPF algorithm is more efficient. The drawback is that the small value does not provide enough metric granularity in large networks.

65. BGP is _____.

    a. An interior gateway protocol

    b. A path vector protocol

    c. A link state protocol

    d. None of the above

The correct answer is B. Border Gateway Protocol (BGP) is a path vector interautonomous system routing protocol that is based on distance vector algorithms. The reason BGP is called a path vector protocol is that the BGP routing information carries a sequence of AS numbers, which indicate the path the route has traversed. This information is used to construct a graph of AS connectivity from which routing loops can be pruned. BGP was introduced to facilitate a loop-free exchange of routing information between autonomous systems, while controlling the expansion of routing tables through Classless Interdomain Routing (CIDR) and providing a structured view of the Internet through the use of AS.

66. CIDR is _____.

    a. A subnetting scheme

    b. An address allocation scheme that eliminates the concept of network class within BGP

    c. A summarization technique

    d. All of the above

The correct answer is B. CIDR was developed to address the explosive growth of IP addresses present in IP routing tables on Internet routers and the exhaustion of IP address space. CIDR is an address allocation scheme that eliminates the concept of network class within BGP. In CIDR, an IP network is represented by a prefix, which is the IP address and a number that indicates the left most contiguous significant bits in the address. For example, Figure 3-24 shows a number of Class C networks that are present on Service Provider A's network. Without CIDR, the service provider must advertise each network individually. With CIDR, as shown in Figure 3-25, Service Provider A can advertise all of these networks with one classless advertisement (200.10.0.0 /16).

67. The BGP rule of synchronization states that _____.

    a. All routers must have their databases synchronized.

    b. Before BGP can announce a route, the route must be present in the IP routing table.

Figure 3-24 Network advertisement without CIDR

Figure 3-25 Network advertisement with CIDR

    c. Before BGP can announce a route, the route must be present in the BGP table.

    d. The synchronization rule only applies to OSPF.

The correct answer is B. Before BGP can announce a route, the route must be present in the IP routing table. In other words, BGP and IGP must be in sync before the networks can be advertised. Cisco enables BGP to override the synchronization requirement with the router configuration command no synchronization. This enables BGP to announce routes that are known via BGP but are not in the routing table. The reason that this rule exists is because it is important that the AS be consistent with the routes it advertises.

For example, in the following Illustration RouterA and RouterB are the only routers running BGP. If synchronization is disabled on RouterB, it will advertise network 1.0.0.0 /8 to AS 200. When RouterD wants to send traffic to network 1.0.0.0, it sends the packet to RouterB, which does a recursive lookup in its IP routing table and forwards the packet to RouterC. Because RouterC is not running BGP, it has no visibility to network 1.0.0.0 and therefore drops the packet. This is why BGP requires synchronization between BGP and IGP. Care must be taken when disabling synchronization. If an AS is a transit, AS all routes should be running fully meshed IBGP before synchronization is disabled.

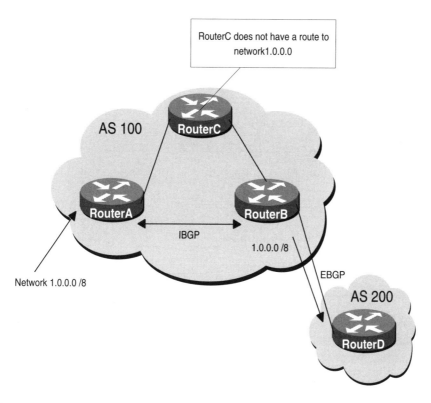

68. What protocol does BGP use?

    a. TCP port 83

    b. TCP port 179

    c. UDP port 179

    d. IP protocol number 179

The correct answer is B. BGP uses TCP as its transport protocol (port 179), which provides reliable data transfer.

69. What is the correct order of the states of BGP neighbor negotiation?

    a. Idle, Connect, Active State, OpenSent State, OpenConfirm, Established

    b. Idle, Active State, Connect, OpenSent State, OpenConfirm, Established

    c. Idle, Connect, OpenSent State, OpenConfirm, Active State ,Established

    d. Idle, Active State, OpenSent State, OpenConfirm, Connect, Established

The correct answer is A. Before BGP speakers can exchange network layer reachablity information (networks being advertised), a BGP session must be established. The following illustration states that BGP neighbor negotiation goes through before a connection becomes fully established.

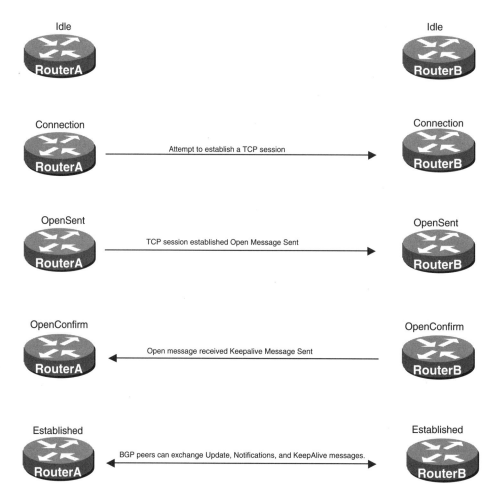

- **Idle**   Initially, BGP is in an Idle State until an operator initiates a start event, which is usually caused by establishing or restarting a BGP session.

- **Connect**   In this state, BGP is waiting for the transport protocol connection to be completed. If the transport protocol connection succeeds an OPEN message is sent to the peer router and the BGP state changes to OpenSent. If the connection fails, the local system changes to Active State and continues to listen for connections.

- **Active State**   In this state, BGP is trying to acquire a peer by initiating a transport protocol connection. If the connection is successful, an OPEN message is sent to the peer router. If the connection retry timer expires, the BGP state changes to connect and continues to listen for connections that may be initiated by the remote BGP peer.

- **OpenSent State**   In this state, BGP is waiting for an OPEN message from its peer. When an OPEN message is received, all fields are checked for correctness. If an error is detected, the local system sends a Notification message and changes its state to Idle. If no errors are detected, BGP starts sending keepalive messages to its peer.

- **OpenConfirm**   In this state, BGP waits for a keepalive or a Notification message. If the local system receives a keepalive message it changes its state to established. If the hold timer expires before a keepalive message is received, the local system sends a Notification message and changes its state to Idle.

- **Established**   This is the final stage of the neighbor negotiation. In the established state BGP peers can exchange Update, Notifications, and keepalive messages.

70. In the following Illustration both RouterB and RouterC are advertising network 1.0.0.0 /8 to RouterA. However, because RouterC is closer to this network, we would like all traffic destined to network 1.0.0.0 /8 from RouterA to be routed through RouterC. What should you do?

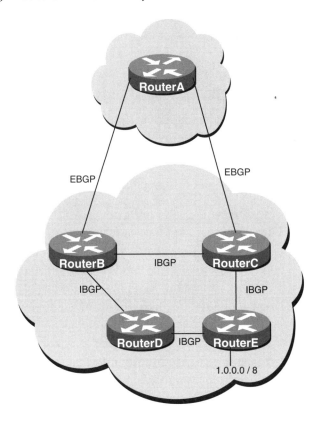

a. Set the Multi Exit Discriminator (MED) on route 1.0.0.0 /8 advertised from RouterC to 200 and the MED on route 1.0.0.0 /8 advertised from RouterB to 100. Because the MED coming from RouterC is higher, RouterA will prefer this route.

b. Set the MED on route 1.0.0.0 /8 advertised from RouterC to 100 and the MED on route 1.0.0.0 /8 advertised from RouterB to 200. Because the MED coming from RouterC is lower, RouterA will prefer this route.

c. Set the local preference on route 1.0.0.0 /8 advertised from RouterC to 200 and the MED on route 1.0.0.0 /8 advertised from RouterB to 100. Because the local preference coming from RouterC is higher, RouterA will prefer this route.

d. Set the local preference on route 1.0.0.0 /8 advertised from RouterC to 100 and the MED on route 1.0.0.0 /8 advertised from RouterB to 200. Because the local preference coming from RouterC is lower, RouterA will prefer this route.

The correct answer is B. To achieve this, we set the MED on route 1.0.0.0 /8 advertised from RouterC to 100 and the MED on route 1.0.0.0 /8 advertised from RouterB to 200. Because the MED coming from RouterC is lower, RouterA will prefer this route.

Answer A is incorrect. The router prefers the path with the lowest MED.

Answer C and D are incorrect. The local preference attribute is a degree of preference given to a route to compare it with other routes to the same destination. The higher local preference is the more preferred route. Local preference is not included in Update messages that are sent to BGP neighbors outside of the AS. If the attribute is contained in an update received from a BGP neighbor in a different AS, it is ignored.

71. What can be used to alleviate the full mesh requirement of IBGP?
   a. Turn off synchronization
   b. Route reflector
   c. Use BGP communities
   d. None of the above

The correct answer is B. In order to prevent routing loops within an AS, BGP will not advertise to internal BGP peers routes that it has learned via other internal BGP peers. This full mesh requirement of IBGP creates the need for neighbor statements to be defined for each IBGP router. In an AS of 100 routers, this would require 100 neighbor statements to be defined. As you can see, this does not scale well.

To get around this, a concept of a route reflector has been defined. A route reflector acts as a concentration router or focal point for all internal BGP (IBGP) sessions. Routers that peer with the route reflector are called route reflector clients. The clients peer with the route reflector and exchange routing information. The route reflector then exchanges or reflects this information to all clients, thereby eliminating the need for a fully meshed environment.

72. BGP uses a set of parameters (attributes) that describe the characteristics of a route. The attributes are sent in the BGP update packets with each route. The router uses these attributes to select the best route to the destination. Which of the following will BGP prefer over the rest?

   a. The route with the shortest AS path
   b. The route with the highest local preference
   c. The route with the lowest MED
   d. The route coming from the BGP router with the lowest router ID

The correct answer is B. The local preference attribute is a degree of preference given to a BGP route to compare it with other routes to the same destination. This is the second highest attribute used in the BGP decision process. (Cisco proprietary weight parameter is first.) The local preference attribute only is local to the autonomous system and does not get passed to EBGP neighbors. The higher the local preference, the more preferred the route. The following is the order of the BGP decision process used by the router in path selection.

1. If the next hop is unreachable, do not consider it.

2. Prefer the path that has the largest weight.

3. If the routes have the same weight, use the route with the highest local preference.

4. If the routes have the same local preference, prefer the route that was originated by BGP on this router.

5. If no route was originated, prefer the route with the shortest AS path.

6. If all paths are of the same AS length, prefer the route with lowest origin code (IGP < EGP < INCOMPLETE).

7. If the origin codes are the same, prefer the path with the lowest MED.

8. If the MEDs are the same, prefer external paths over internal paths.

9. If still the same, prefer the path through the closest IGP neighbor.

10. If still the same, prefer the path with the lowest BGP Router ID

73. BGP soft configuration _____.

   a. Enables policies to be configured and activated without resetting the BGP and TCP session
   b. Enables BGP neighbors to be configured but not activated
   c. Automatically disables synchronization
   d. None of the above

The correct answer is A. BGP soft configuration enables policies to be configured and activated without resetting the BGP and TCP session. This enables the new policy to take effect without significantly affecting the network. Without BGP soft configuration, BGP is required to reset the neighbor TCP connection in order for the new changes to take effect.

Two types of BGP soft reconfiguration are available: outbound reconfiguration, which will make the new local outbound policy take effect without resetting the BGP session, and inbound soft reconfiguration, which enables the new inbound policy to take effect.

The problem with inbound reconfiguration is that in order to generate new inbound updates without resetting the BGP session, all inbound updates (whether accepted or rejected) need to be stored by the router. This is memory intensive and wherever possible it should be avoided.

To avoid the memory overhead needed for inbound soft reconfiguration, the same outcome could be achieved by doing an outbound soft reconfiguration at the other end of the connection.

Outbound soft reconfiguration can be triggered with the command:

```
clear ip bgp [*|address | peer-group ] [soft out]
```

For inbound soft reconfiguration, an additional router command needs to be added before a soft reconfiguration can be issued. This is because this command tells the router to start storing the received updates.

```
neighbor [address | peer-group] soft-reconfiguration inbound
```

Inbound soft reconfiguration can be triggered with the following command:

```
clear ip bgp [*|address | peer-group ] [soft in]
```

74. AS100 peers directly with AS300. AS100 should only accept local routes from AS300. Which regular expression would you use to identify local routes from AS300?
    a. ^300$
    b. ^300*
    c. _300_
    d. ^300^

The correct answer is A. A regular expression is a pattern to match against an input string. When a regular expression is created, it specifies the pattern that a string must match. The caret means *begin with* and the dollar sign means *end with*. So the regular expression will match any string that begins with 300 and ends with 300. This regular expression will match any routes that originated in AS 300. Table 3-7 is a list of keyboard characters that have special meaning when used in regular expressions.

75. Which of the following is false regarding BGP confederations?

    a. BGP confederations are used to break an AS into multiple sub-ASs.

    b. Within a sub-AS, all IBGP rules apply.

    c. IBGP is used between sub-ASs.

    d. IBGP information such as next hop, MED, and local preference is preserved within the confederation.

Answer C is false. BGP confederations are used to break an AS into multiple sub-ASs. This is another way to deal with the full IBGP mesh requirement. Within in the sub-ASs, all IBGP rules apply. However, because each sub-AS is a different AS number, EBGP is used between them. This reduces the IBGP meshing in the domain.

Even though EBGP is used between sub-ASs, IBGP information such as next hop, MED, and local preference is preserved within the confederation. To the outside world, the confederation is seen as a single AS, the sub-ASs are hidden.

76. A BGP community is _____.

    a. The same as a confederation

    b. A group of routers that share a common property

    c. A group of routers within a confederation

    d. None of the above

Author: please supply table title

Table 3-7   Need Chapter Title

Character	Symbol	Meaning
Period	.	Matches any character including white space
Asterisk	*	Matches zero or more sequences of the pattern
Plus sign	+	Matches one or more sequences of the pattern
Question Mark	?	Matches zero or one occurrences of the pattern
Caret	^	Begins with
Dollar Sign	$	Ends with
Underscore	_	Matches the following
Brackets	[ ]	Matches an single value in range
Hyphen	-	Separates the endpoints of a range

The correct answer is B. A BGP community is a group of routers that share a common property. For example, a group of routers that are in the same AS that don't want to propagate network X outside of the AS could tag the prefix with the no-export community attribute. When a router receives a route tagged with the no-export attribute, the prefix will not be sent outside of the AS. The use of communities simplifies routing policies by identifying routes based on logical properties rather than the IP prefix.

The community attribute is optional and transitive. *Optional* means that all implementations of BGP may not recognize the community. *Transitive* means that the community value should be passed to BGP neighbors.

Two types of communities are available: well-known communities, which are reserved, and private communities, which are defined for local use.

An example of well-known communities are

- **NO_EXPORT** Routes that carry this community value should not be advertised outside of the local AS or local confederation.

- **NO_ADVERTISE** Routes that carry this community value should not be advertised to any BGP peer.

Private community attributes can also be defined. The common practice is to use the first two octets of the community for the AS number and the last two octets to define a policy. The community is written in decimal notation: for example, AS:policy.

77. What is the concept of BGP backdoor links?
    a. A way to force IGP routes to take precedence over EBGP routes
    b. A way to configure an alternate path which will only be used if the primary fails
    c. An opening in your security policy to all trusted networks direct connectivity
    d. None of the above

The correct answer is A. Cisco provides a way to force IGP routes to take precedence over EBGP routes. The concept is called backdoor links. EBGP routes can be tagged as backdoor routes, which sets the distance of these routes to the same as BGP local or 200. Because the distance is then higher than the IGP route, the backdoor IGP route is preferred.

78. On RouterC network, 1.0.0.0 is loaded in the BGP, but it is not in the IP routing table. The following shows the output from the **show ip bgp** and the **show ip route** commands on RouterC. RouterC has synchronization turned off. Based on the information provided, what is the problem?

```
RouterC#show ip bgp
BGP table version is 1, local router ID is 3.3.3.3
```

```
Status codes: s suppressed, d damped, h history, * valid, >
best, i - internal
Origin codes: i - IGP, e - EGP, ? - incomplete

 Network Next-Hop Metric LocPrf Weight Path
* i1.0.0.0 192.1.1.1 0 100 0 100 i

RouterC#show ip route
Codes: C - connected, S - static, I - IGRP, R - RIP, M - mobile,
B - BGP
 D - EIGRP, EX - EIGRP external, O - OSPF, IA - OSPF inter area
 N1 - OSPF NSSA external type 1, N2 - OSPF NSSA external type 2
 E1 - OSPF external type 1, E2 - OSPF external type 2, E - EGP
 i - IS-IS, L1 - IS-IS level-1, L2 - IS-IS level-2, * - candi-
date default
 U - per-user static route, o - ODR

Gateway of last resort is not set

 3.0.0.0/24 is subnetted, 1 subnets
C 3.3.3.0 is directly connected, Loopback0
C 193.1.1.0/24 is directly connected, Ethernet0/0
```

a. Synchronization should be turned on.

b. The BGP session needs to be restarted.

c. The next-hop to reach network 1.0.0.0 is via 192.1.1.1, which is not in RouterC's routing table.

d. None of the above

The correct answer is C. The reason that the route to network 1.0.0.0 is not in the IP routing table is the next-hop to reach network 1.0.0.0 is via 192.1.1.1 which is not in RouterC's routing table. The next-hop address is the IP address of the EBGP neighbor from which the route was learned. When routes are injected into the AS via EBGP, the next hop learned from EBGP is carried unaltered into IBGP. Care must be taken to ensure that reachability of the next hop is advertised via some IGP or static routing. If the next hop cannot be reached, the BGP route is considered inaccessible and will not be loaded in the routing table.

79. A route received for your peer is frequently going up and down causing BGP UPDATE and WITHDRAWN messages to be repeatedly propagated on the network. What should you do to prevent this?

a. Stop peering with this provider.

b. Filter out that particular route.

c. Apply route dampening.

d. Configure a static route to that network and redistribute it into BGP.

The correct answer is C. Cisco provides a mechanism to control route instability or flapping, with a feature called route dampening. A route that is unstable frequently going up and down will cause BGP UPDATE and WITHDRAWN messages to be repeatedly propagated on the network. This routing traffic can quickly use up link bandwidth and CPU cycles on the router.

The router will monitor a route and categorize it as either well behaved or ill behaved. The recent history of the route is used to estimate future stability; that is, a route that has gone up and down two times in the last three minutes is ill behaved and will be penalized in proportion to the expected future instability. Each time the route flaps, it is given a penalty. When the penalty reaches a predefined threshold, the route is suppressed. The more frequently a route flaps in a period of time, the faster it will be suppressed.

Once the route is suppressed the router continues to monitor its stability. An algorithm is put in place to reduce (decay) the penalty exponentially. Once the route is deemed stable, it is advertised.

The following set of terms and parameters applies to Cisco's implementation of route dampening:

- **Penalty**   An incremented numeric number that is assigned to the route each time it flaps.

- **Half-life-time**   A configurable numeric value that describes the amount of time that must pass to reduce the penalty by one half.

- **Suppress limit**   A numeric value that is compared with the penalty. If the penalty is greater than the suppress limit, the route is suppressed.

- **Reuse limit**   A numeric value that is compared with the penalty. If the penalty is less than the reuse limit, a suppressed route will no longer be suppressed.

- **Suppressed route**   A route that is not advertised even though it is up. If the penalty is greater than the suppress limit, the route is suppressed.

- **History entry**   An entry used to store flap information.

To apply route dampening to a specific network, use an access list to identify the match criteria and then apply the dampening using the route map.

80. How do you set the default route in OSPF?

    a. Create a static route and redistribute into OSPF.

    b. IP route 0.0.0.0 0.0.0.0

    c. Create a static route and use the default-information originate command to redistribute into OSPF.

    d. Nothing—if a default exists, it will automatically be loaded into OSPF.

The correct answer is C. An OSPF ASBR will not automatically advertise a default route into its routing domain even when one exists. The default-information originate command is needed to redistribute the default route into OSPF.

81. What command is used to force an OSPF router to advertise a default route regardless whether it actually has a route to 0.0.0.0?

    a. default-information originate

    b. default-network always

    c. default-information always

    d. default-network

The correct answer is C. The command default-information always, will force the router to advertise a default route into OSPF, regardless of whether it actually has a route to 0.0.0.0.

82. You want to enable IGRP on a Cisco router. Which of the following are the correct commands to enable IGRP on the router and have network 192.1.1.0 advertised in autonomous system 65.

    a. `router IGRP AS 65`
       `network 192.1.1.0`

    b. `router IGRP 65`
       `network 192.1.1.0 0.0.0.255`

    c. `router IGRP`
       `network 192.1.1.0 65`

    d. `router IGRP 65`
       `network 192.1.1.0`

The correct answer is D. The router IGRP 65 enables IGRP process 65 on the router. The command network 192.1.1.0 enables the sending of IGRP messages on that interface and advertises that network.

83. Given the following configuration, why aren't the IGRP learned routes being redistributed into EIGRP and vice versa?

```
!
router eigrp 100
 network 194.1.1.0
!
router igrp 200
 network 195.1.1.0
!
```

a. No redistribution command appears under the EIGRP process or the IGRP process.

b. The network numbers are different.

c. No metric is defined, so the router cannot redistribute the routes.

d. The AS numbers are not the same.

The correct answer is D. Because IGRP and EIGRP are similar routing protocols, route distribution is automatic. However, in order for mutual redistribution to be automatic, both EIGRP and IGRP must have the same AS number.

84. Given the following configuration, why aren't OSPF learned routes being redistributed into IGRP and vice versa?

```
router ospf 64
redistribute igrp
network 152.1.1.4 0.0.0.3 area 0
!
router igrp 100
 redistribute ospf 64
 network 153.1.0.0
```

a. The network numbers are different.

b. In order to redistribute between OSPF and IGRP, we need to tell the router what the metric will be used.

c. You cannot redistribute between a classful and a classless protocol.

d. None of the above

The correct answer is B. The reason that the routes are not being advertised is because no metrics are configured. OSPF and IGRP use totally different metrics to convey route preference.

IGRP uses five metrics to calculate the cost of the route (bandwidth, delay, reliability, load, and MTU). OSPF uses bandwidth as a metric for best path selection. When you redistribute OSPF into IGRP or IGRP into OSPF, you need to tell the router what the metric will be; otherwise, it marks the route as inaccessible.

85. OSPF has two equal cost paths to the same destination and fast switching is enabled. Which best describes the default behavior of OSPF?

a. By default, OSPF will only use one path.

b. OSPF will load balance across the two paths on a per-destination basis.

c. OSPF will load balance across the two paths on a packet-by-packet basis.

d. None of the above

The correct answer is B. By default, OSPF will load balance across four equal cost paths. If fast switching is enabled, the router will load balance on a per-destination basis. If process switching is being used, the router will load balance on a packet-by-packet basis.

86. Which of the following is false regarding load balancing?

    a. By default, RIP will load balance across four equal cost paths.

    b. By default, OSPF will load balance across four equal cost paths.

    c. By default, BGP will load balance across four equal cost paths

    d. The maximum equal paths that a Cisco router can be configured to use is six.

Answer C is false. By default, all IP routing protocols except BGP will use up to four equal cost paths for load balancing. You can configure a Cisco router to load balance on up to six equal cost paths, with the **max paths** command.

87. Which of following is true regarding policy routing? (multiple answers)

    a. Policy-based routing enables network administrators to select forwarding paths based on source address.

    b. Policy-based routing enables network administrators to select forwarding paths based on protocol type.

    c. Policy-based routing enables network administrators to select forwarding paths based on packet size.

    d. Policy-based routing enables network administrators to select forwarding paths based on application.

The correct answers are A, B, C, and D. Policy-based routing gives network administrators greater control over packet forwarding and routing that goes beyond the capabilities of traditional routing protocols. Traditionally, routers forward packets based on destination addresses using routing tables derived from routing protocols such as OSPF or RIP.

Policy-based routing goes far beyond traditional routing, enabling network administrators to select forwarding paths not only based on destination addresses, but also on protocol type, packet size, application, or source address. Policies can be defined to load balance traffic across multiple routers or provide Quality of Service (QOS) by forwarding packets over various links based on traffic profiles. Policy-based routing provides the network administrator with a mechanism to specify what path a packet will take. This freedom is greatly needed in today high-performance and complex internetworks.

88. Which of the following will be used to reach network 192.1.1.1?

    a. A static route to 192.1.1.1

    b. A connected route to 192.1.1.1

    c. A default route to 192.1.1.1

    d. A defined policy route map to 192.1.1.1

The correct answer is D. A policy route is considered first before the unicast routing table.

89. The Ethernet interface on your router is 152.1.1.1 /24, which is connected to another router that is configured as your gateway of last resort. You are trying to reach two networks, 9.9.9.9 and 152.1.2.1, both of which are directly connected to your gateway of last resort. You are able to reach 9.9.9.9, but not 152.1.2.1. You enable debugging on IP packets and notice that when you ping 9.9.9.9, the router forwards the packet to your gateway of last resort. However, when you ping 152.1.2.1, you get an error message that the packet is unroutable. What is the problem?

   a. The subnet does not exist.

   b. The gateway of last resort is down.

   c. Your router is configured for IP classless.

   d. Your router is configured for no IP classless.

The correct answer is D. IP classless is used if you have a gateway of last resort set and determines whether or not you forward traffic to the component of the major network that is not in the forwarding table. In this example, the major network is 152.1.0.0. We are trying to forward packets to 152.1.2.1, which is not in our forwarding table. If you have no IP classless configured, the packet is dropped regardless of whether or not you have a gateway of last resort. If you have IP classless on, the default gateway is used.

90. When you look at the routing table, you see an * next to one of the routes. What does * mean?

   a. The route best route to the destination

   b. The route has recently been removed from the table and can no longer be used.

   c. The route is candidate default.

   d. All of the above

The correct answer is C. An * next to a route in the IP routing table indicates that the route is a candidate default.

91. EIGRP uses which of the following algorithms to find the lowest metric loop-free path to each destination?

   a. DUAL

   b. Dijkstra algorithm

   c. Bellman-Ford algorithm

   d. Perlman algorithm

The correct answer is A. The Diffusing Update Algorithm (DUAL) uses the topology table to find the lowest metric loop free path to each destination. The next-hop router for the lowest cost path is referred to as the successor and is the next-hop IP address that is loaded in the routing table. The DUAL also tries to find a feasible successor, or the next best route, which is kept in the topology database.

92. Which of the following is not used as part of an IGRP configuration?

    a. Network address

    b. Subnet mask

    c. Autonomous system number

    d. Area number

    e. Both B and D

The correct answer is E. IGRP has no concept of mask or area. Two steps are involved to enable IGRP on a router. First an IGRP routing process is enabled on the router and then the network command is added specifying which interfaces will receive and send IGRP routing updates. It also specifies what networks will be advertised. The following command enables IGRP on R3. When enabling IGRP on a router, you specify which classful network the protocol will be run on.

```
R3(config)#router igrp 64
R3(config-router)#network 152.1.0.0
```

93. The configuration on your router is growing extremely large and approaching the limitation of NVRAM. Which command can be used to reduce the size of the configuration on the router?

    a. service compress-config

    b. compress-config

    c. no service config

    d. config-size

The correct answer is A. When the NVRAM is not large enough to store the router configuration, Cisco provides an option, which allows the configuration to be compressed. This option should only be used if the configuration file is bigger than the memory available in NVRAM. To compress the file you use the **service compress-config router** configuration command.

94. Which of the following routes will be used to reach 192.1.1.1?

    a. An OSPF learned route to 192.1.1.0 /30

    b. A EBGP learned route to 192.1.0.0 /16

    c. A static route to 192.1.1.0 /24

    d. A EIGRP learned route to 192.1.1.0 /30

The correct answer is D. The routing table is searched for a routing entry that contains the most specific match to the destination network. This is referred to as longest match routing. The routing table can contain host-specific addresses, subnets, summary routes, major network numbers, supernets, or a default address (Table 3-8, which also appears earlier in the chapter). If the router cannot match the destination address to any entry in the routing table, the packet is dropped and an ICMP host unreachable message is sent to the source address.

Answer A is incorrect. EIGRP has a lower administrative distance than OSPF (90 vs. 110). So the EIGRP route is preferred.

Answer B is incorrect. Although EBGP has a lower administrative distance than EIGRP (20 vs. 90), EIGRP has the more specific route to host 192.1.1.1. The router always uses the most specific route to a destination, regardless of its administrative distance.

Answer C is also incorrect. Although a static route has a lower administrative distance than EIGRP (1 vs. 90), EIGRP has the more specific route to host 192.1.1.1. The router always uses the most specific route to a destination, regardless of its administrative distance.

95. Which of the following is false regarding IS-IS?

    a. IS-IS routers discover and form adjacencies by exchanging IS-IS hello packets.

    b. Once an adjacency is formed the routers use an update process to construct the L1 and L2 link state databases.

    c. On broadcast networks, the LSPs are multicast to all neighbors.

    d. Like OSPF, IS-IS routers on a broadcast network form adjacencies with only the DR.

Answer D is false. Unlike OSPF, IS-IS routers on a broadcast network form adjacencies with every router on the broadcast network, not just the DR.

IS-IS routers discover and form adjacencies by exchanging IS-IS hello packets, which are transmitted every ten seconds. Like OSPF, an IS-IS hello packet is used to identify its capabilities to a router and describe the interface that it was sent over. If both routers

Table 3-8 Longest Match Routing

192.1.1.1 /32	Host-specific route
192.1.1.0 /30	Subnet
192.1.1.0 /25	Summary
192.1.1.0/24	Major network
192.1.0.0/16	Supernet
0.0.0.0	Default network

agree on the capabilities and interface parameters they become adjacent. Once they become adjacent, the hello packets act as keepalives. If the router does not receive a keepalive within the dead interval, the router declares its neighbor dead. The default dead interval is three times the keepalive interval, or 30 seconds.

Once an adjacency is formed, the routers use an update process to construct the L1 and L2 link state databases. L1 LSPs are flooded throughout the area and L2 LSPs are flooded over all L2 adjacencies. Like OSPF, IS-IS ages each LSP in the database, and the LSA must be refreshed every 15 minutes.

IS-IS uses SNPs to acknowledge the receipt of LSPs and to maintain link state database synchronization. On point-to-point links if an SNP is not received for a transmitted LSP in five seconds, a new LSP is generated. The IS-IS retransmission interval can be set on a per-interface basis with the command **isis retransmit-interval**. On a broadcast network, LSPs are not acknowledged by each router; instead, the DR periodically multicasts a CSNP that describes every LSP in the link state database. When a router receives a CSNP, it compares it with the LSP in its database. If the router's database does not contain a copy of all of the LSP listed in the CSNP update, the router multicasts an SNP listing the LSP that it requires. The DR then responds with the appropriate LSP.

Once the update process has built the link state database, it is used to calculate the shortest path tree. From this tree, a forwarding database is constructed and this is what is used to route packets.

96. Which of the following is true regarding CDP? (multiple answers)

  a. CDP runs on all Cisco routers and switches.

  b. CDP-enabled router will be able to learn directly connected neighbor port and hostname information.

  c. CDP-enabled router will be able to learn directly connected neighbor hardware model number and capabilities.

  d. CDP cannot be disabled on the router.

The correct answers are A, B, and C. CDP runs on all Cisco routers and switches. It can run over any physical media and over any protocol. Unlike a routing protocol, which shows a next-hop destination port for all known networks, CDP will only show information for directly connected neighbors. It is most useful for verifying that a router is connected to the proper port of its neighbor. A CDP-enabled router will be able to learn directly connected neighbor port and hostname information. Additional information such as the neighbor's hardware model number and capabilities are also reported.

A CDP-enabled router sends out a periodic multicast packet containing a CDP update. The time between these CDP updates is determined by the **cdp timer** command; the timer value default is 60 seconds. To disable the sending of CDP updates, use the **no cdp run** global command on all of the routers.

97. How can you change the OSPF cost of using an Ethernet interface from 10 to 90, without using the OSPF cost command?

    a. Change the bandwidth on the interface.

    b. Change the clock rate on the interface.

    c. Change the reference bandwidth form 100M to 900M.

    d. None of the above

The correct answer is C. OSPF calculates the cost of an interface by dividing the reference bandwidth by the speed of the interface. By default, the reference bandwidth is set to 100M so normally the OSPF cost of a 10M Ethernet is the (Reference bandwidth / 10M) = 100M / 10M = 10.

Changing the reference bandwidth can then change the OSPF cost of the interface. The question states that the cost of an Ethernet interface should be 90. To accomplish this, we need to set the reference bandwidth to 900M.

OSPF cost of an Ethernet interface = 900M / 10M = 90

98. A distribute list in OSPF _____.

    a. Prevents the filtered routes from being put in the routing table

    b. Prevents the filtered routes from being put in the OSPF LSA database

    c. Prevents the routes from being flooded to each neighbor

    d. All of the above

The correct answer is A. One common misconception is that a distribute list filters the routing updates. This is not true; the command prevents the filtered routes from being put in the routing table. The OSPF LSA database still contains the routes and therefore floods them to each neighbor. So each downstream router will still see all of the routes.

99. RouterA is not forming an OSPF adjacency with RouterB. The following is the output from the **debug ip ospf** events command on RouterA. What is most likely the problem?

```
03:07:28: OSPF: Hello from 152.1.1.77 with mismatched NSSA
option bit
03:07:35: OSPF: service_maxage: Trying to delete MAXAGE LSA
```

    a. RouterB is configured as stub area and RouterA is not.

    b. The max age timer does not match between the two routers.

    c. RouterA and RouterB are not on the same subnet.

    d. NSSA bit is set for encryption on RouterB but not RouterA.

The correct answer is A. Notice from the debug that RouterA is receiving a hello packet with the NSSA bit set, indicating that RouterB is a NSSA router. Remember from the earlier discussion that if the options in the hello packet do not match, the routers will not form an adjacency.

100. ISDN is being used for backup between a hub and a spoke. What can be done to prevent OSPF hello messages and LSAs from bringing the link up, while still allowing the benefits of OSPF over the entire domain?

   a. Do not define OSPF as interesting traffic.
   b. Configure the router for snap shot routing.
   c. Make the ISDN interface passive.
   d. Use OSPF demand circuits.

The correct answer is D. To prevent periodic hellos and LSAs from causing the ISDN link from coming up, the OSPF demand circuit is used. The OSPF on-demand circuit is an enhancement to the OSPF protocol that provides efficient operation over demand circuits like ISDN, X.25 SVCs, and dial-up lines. This feature supports RFC 1793, Extending OSPF to Support Demand Circuits.

If demand circuits are not used, OSPF periodic hello and LSA updates would be exchanged between routers that connected the on-demand link, even when no changes occurred in the hello or LSA information.

OSPF demand circuit suppresses periodic hellos and periodic refreshes of LSAs are not flooded over the demand circuit. Therefore, the link is only brought up when LSAs are exchanged for the first time, or when a change occurs in the information they contain.

This enables the underlying Data Link layer to be closed when the network topology is stable.

This feature is useful when you want to connect telecommuters or branch offices to an OSPF backbone at a central site. In this case, OSPF for on-demand circuits provide the benefits of OSPF over the entire domain, without excess connection costs. Periodic refreshes of hello updates, LSA updates, and other protocol overhead are prevented from enabling the on-demand circuit when no real data is available to transmit.

Overhead protocols such as hellos and LSAs are transferred over the on-demand circuit only upon initial setup and when they reflect a change in the topology. This means that critical changes to the topology that require new SPF calculations are transmitted in order to maintain network topology integrity. Periodic refreshes that do not include changes, however, are not transmitted across the link.

Answer A is incorrect. By not defining OSPF as interesting traffic, you will only prevent OSPF LSA and hello from causing the router to dial out and prevent the messages from keeping the link active.

Answer B is incorrect. Snapshot routing enables an ISDN hub-and-spoke network to be built without configuring and maintaining static routes. Snapshot routing is only supported on distance vector protocols such as RIP and IGRP for IP traffic. Without snapshot routing, running RIP on an ISDN circuit would mean that RIP packets would reset the ISDN idle time out every 30 seconds causing the ISDN interface to remain active, even if no user traffic is present. Snapshot defines an active and a quiet period. During the active period, an RIP-enabled snapshot router will exchange routing updates. If no active calls are present, the snap shot router will initiate an ISDN call during the active period to send routing updates. During the quiet period, a snapshot router will not send routing updates. Snapshot routing freezes entries in the routing table during the quiet period. The active and quiet periods are user defined. The minimum active period is five minutes and the minimum quiet period is eight minutes.

Answer C is incorrect. The passive interface command disables the sending and receiving of OSPF router information. The specified interface address appears as a stub network in the OSPF domain.

CHAPTER 4

CCIE Qualification Exam 3 (Cisco-Specific Technology)

This chapter will cover

- Router operation
- Router components
- Management
- Security.

Introduction

This chapter focuses on Cisco-specific topics including device operation, router commands, router components, performance management, and security. The exam contains questions on nonvolatile random access memory (NVRAM), flash memory, CPU, file system management, and configuration register settings. The exam also contains questions on the queuing techniques, traffic management techniques, command-line knowledge, and local area network (LAN) switching basics. The goal is to test the student's aptitude on Cisco device operation and architecture as well as the student's knowledge of router commands and his or her ability to interpret the output of those commands.

Router Memory

Depending on the router platform, the motherboard can contain up to four types of memory: dynamic random access memory (DRAM), read-only memory (ROM), NVRAM, and Flash. The DRAM is used by the router to process packets and run the operating system. ROM is used to store a bootstrap image. This image or file can be used to boot the router if all else fails. In small-end routers, the ROM holds only a subset of the Internetworking Operating Systems (IOS) image. In the larger platforms like the 7500, a full copy of the IOS image is contained on the ROM.

The NVRAM memory is nonvolatile, meaning that it will retain its information after a reload. Thismemory is used to store a copy of the router configuration. Flash memory is also nonvolatile and is used to store one or more copies of the IOS image. The capability to store multiple images is useful because it gives network administrators the ability to stage upgrades and back off an image if a problem occurs.

You can determine the amount of NVRAM and Flash on a router using the **show version** command. The following is the truncated output of the command on a 4500 router.

```
128K bytes of non-volatile configuration memory.
4096K bytes of processor board System flash (Read/Write)
4096K bytes of processor board Boot flash (Read/Write)
```

Notice that the router has 128K of NVRAM and 4096K of system and boot flash. The following is the truncated output of the command on a 2500 router.

```
32K bytes of non-volatile configuration memory.
16384K bytes of processor board System flash (Read ONLY)
```

Notice that the router has only has NVRAM and ROM no Flash.

Shared Memory Architecture

Several Cisco router models fall under this category including the 1600, 2500, 4000, 4500, and the 4700 series. All of these platforms have two things in common: they have a centralized processor and use system buffers for packet buffering. Shared memory routers only have one region of memory and it is shared between all of the interface controllers and the centralized processor.

A shared memory platform consists of three components: processor (CPU), memory (DRAM), and interface controllers. The CPU and the interfaces are connected to the shared memory via a data bus.

The processor is responsible for running the IOS and switching packets through the router. The processor used depends on the router platform, and can easily be determined by looking at the output of the **show version** command.

The memory used by these platforms is DRAM. The DRAM is divided into to two regions: local memory and IO memory (iomem). Iomem is often called shared memory because it is shared between the CPU and the interfaces.

The local memory is used for storing routing tables, caches, and running IOS code, but not for storing packets; the iomem is used for this purpose.

You can determine the amount of memory on a router using the **show version** command. The following shows the output of the command on a 4700 router.

```
cisco 4700 (R4K) processor (revision C) with 32768K/4096K bytes of memory.
Processor board ID 03386984
R4700 processor, Implementation 33, Revision 1.0 (Level 2 Cache)
```

Notice that there are two numbers separated by a slash. The first number is the amount of local memory on the router. The number after the slash is the amount of iomem memory. The two numbers combined indicate the total amount of DRAM on the router.

ISO creates two memory pools that are used to manage the available memory in the two regions. The pools are processor memory, which manages the memory in the local memory region, and I/O pool, which manages the memory in the iomem region. You can determine the amount of memory being used by the router using the **show memory** command. The following shows the output of the command on a 4500 router.

```
Cisco4500#sho memory
            Head        Total(b)    Used(b)    Free(b)    Lowest(b)   Largest(b)
Processor   60A999A0    22439520    1842556    20596964   20423628    20532796
      I/O   40000000    4194304     1532588    2661716    2500344     2488740
```

Notice that the total I/O memory is equal to the total iomem in the previous example. (Note that in the output of the **show version** command, the memory is given in kilobytes, so you need to multiple by 1,024. So 4,096×1,024 + 4,194,304.) However, the processor memory is much smaller than the local memory in the previous example. The reason for this is the processor pool can only use a subset of the memory, because part of it is used for running IOS and, on some platforms, storing the IOS image.

Run-from-RAM and Run-from-Flash Routers

Depending on the router model, the IOS image is run from RAM or Flash. In the run-from-RAM routers, software is stored in flash memory and executed in RAM. In run-from-Flash routers, the software is both stored and executed in flash memory.

The Cisco 2500 series uses the run-from-Flash memory architecture. The major drawback of this is that a new IOS image cannot be loaded to the router while it is running the current IOS image. This would require the Flash to overwrite itself, and the router would not operate. If the router has dual banks of Flash, you can download the new software image into a different flash memory partition.

To download a new software image without using Dual Flash Bank memory, a boot-helper image is used. The boot-helper image is a small subset of Cisco IOS software that supports a limited subset of the interfaces and the wide area network (WAN) protocols. The boot-helper image boots the router using the ROM image. This enables the flash memory to be overwritten because the Cisco IOS software that is stored in flash memory is not being used to run the router.

IOS Naming Convention

Cisco uses an IOS image naming convention to identify the platform or board for which the binary software is built. The naming convention also identifies the feature content of the image, and the area of memory used by the image at run time.

The IOS image name follows a three-part format; each part is separated by a dash. The first part identifies the platform, the second part identifies the features, and the last part identifies the run time memory and the compression format (pppp-fffff-mm).

Platform Identifiers

The first part of the image name (pppp) identifies the platform the image runs on. Table 4-1 is a list of IOS platform identifiers.

Cisco IOS Feature Identifier

The second part of the image name (ffff) identifies the software features that the image supports. Table 4-2 is a list of IOS feature identifiers.

Cisco Run Time
and Memory Space Identifier

The third part of the ISO image name (mm) is two letters. The first letter identifies the memory area where the Cisco IOS image is executed at run time. The second letter indicates the method used to compress the Cisco IOS binary image. Table 4-3 is a list of run-time identifiers and compression identifiers.

Table 4-1   IOS Platform Identifiers

Identifier	Platform
as5200	5200
ca1003	Cisco Advantage 1003
ca1005	Cisco Advantage 1005
cpa1003	CiscoPro 1003, 1004
cpa1005	CiscoPro 1005
cpa25	CiscoPro 2500
cpa3620	CiscoPro 3620
cpa3640	CiscoPro 3640
cpa45	CiscoPro 4500
*cs	Communication server
cs500	CS500
c1000	Cisco 1003, 1004
c1005	Cisco 1005
c1600	Cisco 1600
c2600	Cisco 2600 Quake
c2800	Catalyst 2800
c2900	Catalyst 2910, 2950
c29atm	Catalyst 2900 ATM
c3620	Cisco 3620
c3640	Cisco 3640
c3800	Cisco 3800
c4000	Cisco 4000 (11.2 and later; earlier releases use xx)
c4500	Cisco 4500, 4700
c5rsfc	Catalyst 5000 series
c5rsm	Catalyst 5000 RSP
c5atm	Catalyst ATM
c6400	cisco 6400 NSP

continued

Table 4-1   IOS Platform Identifiers (*continued*)

Identifier	Platform
c6400r	Cisco 6400 NRP
c6msm	Catalyst
c7000	Cisco 7000, 7010 (11.2 and later only)
c7200	Cisco 7200
Igs	IGS, 25xx, 3xxx, 5100, AP
gs3	Gateway server (AGS, AGS+)
gs7	Gateway server (7000, 7010)
Gsr	Gigabit Switch Router (12000)
ls1010	LightStream 1010
mc3810	Ardent Multiservice Cisco 3810
p<n	Partners' platform n
*pt	Protocol translator
rpm	MGX 8850
rsp	Cisco 75xx
ubr7200	Universal Broadband Router 7200
ubr900	Universal Broadband Router 900
ubr920	Universal Broadband Router 920
vcw	Voice Card Ware
xx	Cisco 4000
Igsetx	Cusci 2500 (media-specific image that supports only Ethernet, Token Ring

Table 4-2   IOS Feature Identifiers

Identifier	Features Supported
a	APPN
a2	ATM
a3	APPN replacement called SNA Switch (12.0(4)XN and 12.1)
b	AppleTalk

Boot	Boot image
C	Comm-server/remote access server (RAS) subset (SNMP, IP, Bridging, IPX, AppleTalk, DECnet, frame relay, HDLC, PPP, X.25, ARAP, TN3270, PT, XRemote, LAT) (non-CiscoPro)
c2	Comm-server/remote access server (RAS) subset (SNMP, IP, Bridging, IPX, AppleTalk, DECnet, frame relay, HDLC, PPP, X.25, ARAP, TN3270, PT, XRemote, LAT) (CiscoPro)
c3	Clustering
d	Desktop subset (SNMP, IP, Bridging, WAN, Remote Node, Terminal Services, IPX, AppleTalk, ARAP) (11.2 - DECnet)
d2	Reduced Desktop subset (SNMP, IP, IPX, AppleTalk, ARAP)
diag	Cisco IOS-based diagnostic images
e	IPeXchange (prior to 11.3)
eboot	Ethernet boot image for MC3810 platform
f	FRAD subset (SNMP, frame relay, PPP, SDLLC, STUN)
f2	Modified FRAD subset, EIGRP, PCbus, LAN Mgr removed, OSPF added
g	ISDN subset (SNMP, IP, Bridging, ISDN, PPP, IPX, AppleTalk)
g2	Gatekeeper proxy, voice, and video
g3	ISDN subset for c800 (IP, ISDN, frame relay)
h	For Malibu (2910), 8021D, switch functions, IP host
hdiag	Diagnostics image for Malibu (2910)
i	IP subset (SNMP, IP, Bridging, WAN, Remote Node, Terminal Services)
i2	Subset similar to IP subset for system controller image (3600)
i3	Reduced IP subset with BGP/MIB, EGP/MIB, NHRP, DIRRESP removed
i4	Subset of IP (available on 5200)
j	Enterprise subset (formerly BPX, includes protocol translation) *** not used until 10.3 ***
k	Kitchen sink (enterprise for high-end) (same as bx) (not used after 10.3)
k1	Baseline privacy key encryption (11.3 and later)
k2	High-end enterprise with CIP2 ucode (not used after 10.3)

continued

Table 4-2   IOS Feature Identifiers (*continued*)

Identifier	Features Supported
k2	Triple DES (11.3 and later)
k3	56-bit encryption with secured shell (SSH)
k4	168-bit encryption with SSH
k5	Reserved for future encryption capabilities (11.3 and later)
k6	Reserved for future encryption capabilities (11.3 and later)
k7	Reserved for future encryption capabilities (11.3 and later)
k8	Reserved for future encryption capabilities (11.3 and later)
k9	Reserved for future encryption capabilities (11.3 and later)
l	IPeXchange IPX, static routing, gateway
m	RMON (11.1 only)
m	For 11.2, Catalyst 2820-kernel, parser, ATM signaling, LANE Client, Bridging
n	IPX
o	Firewall (formerly IpeXchange Net Management)
o2	Firewall (3xx0)
o3	Firewall with SSH (36x0 26x0)
p	Service provider (IP RIP/IGRP/EIGRP/OSPF/BGP, CLNS ISIS/IGRP)
p2	Service provider with CIP2 ucode
p3	AS5200 service provider
p4	5800 (Nitro) service provider
q	Async
q2	IpeXchange Async
r	IBM base option (SRB, SDLLC, STUN, DLSW, QLLC), used with i, in, d (see note below)
r2	IBM variant for 1600 images
r3	IBM variant for Ardent images (3810)
r4	Reduced IBM subset with BSC/MIB, BSTUN/MIB, ASPP/MIB, RSRB/MIB removed
s	Source-route switch (SNMP, IP, Bridging, SRB) (10.x releases)
t	Telco return (12.0)
u	IP with VLAN RIP (Network Layer 3 Switching Software, RSRB, SRT, SRB, SR/TLB)

v	VIP and dual RSP (HSA) support
v2	Voice V2D
v3	Voice Feature Card
w	WBU Feature Sets (11.3WA and 12.0W5 releases)
I	IISP
I	LANE and PVC
p	PNNI
v	PVC traffic shaping
w2	Cisco Advantage ED train Feature Sets
a	IPX, static routing, gateway
b	Net management
c	FR/X.25
y	Async
w3	Distributed Director Feature Sets
x	X.25 in 11.1 and earlier releases. Also available in 12.0T on c800 series.
x	Frame relay/X.25 in 11.2 (IpeXchange)
x	H.323 Gatekeeper/Proxy in 11.3 and later releases for 2500, 3620, 3640,
y	Reduced IP (SNMP, IP RIP/IGRP/EIGRP, Bridging, ISDN, PPP)
y	Reduced IP (SNMP, IP RIP/IGRP/EIGRP, Bridging, WAN - X.25) (C1005) (11.2 - includes X.25) (c1005)
y	IP variant (no Kerberos, Radius, NTP, OSPF, PIM, SMRP, NHRP)
y2	IP variant (SNMP, IP RIP/IGRP/EIGRP, WAN - X.25, OSPF, PIM) (C1005)
y2	IP Plus variant (no Kerberos, Radius, NTP, and so on) (c1600)
y3	IP/X.31
y4	Reduced IP variant (Cable, MIBs, DHCP, EZHTTP)
y5	Reduced IP variant (Cable, MIBs, DHCP, EZIP) Home Office
y6	Reduced IP variant (c800)
z	Managed modems
40	40-bit encryption
56	56-bit encryption
56i	56-bit encryption with IPSEC

Table 4-3 Run-Time Identifiers and Compression Identifiers

Identifier	Execution Area
f	Image runs in Flash
m	Image runs in RAM
t	Image runs in ROM
l	Image will be relocated at run time.

Identifier	Compression Type
z	Image is Zip-compressed (lowercase z)
X	Image is Mzip-compressed
w	Image is Stac-compressed

Password Recovery

Situations occur when it is necessary to recover a lost password from a router. Password recovery requires gaining access to the configuration file and either viewing the password if it is not encrypted or replacing it with a new value if it is encrypted. The problem is that in order to gain access to the configuration file, you must have enable mode access to the IOS, which is password-protected.

In order to recover a lost password, you must tell the router to ignore the contents of NVRAM (the configuration file) when booting up. The router goes through a predefined startup sequence. At power up, the router performs a basic self-test, loads the IOS image the router, and then tries to load its configuration information from NVRAM.

NVRAM contains all of user-defined information, such as IP addresses routing protocols and any passwords.

In order to have the router ignore NVRAM during startup, you must modify the router's configuration register, a 16-bit register located in the router's NVRAM. In older Cisco routers, the register was set using physical jumpers; all newer models use a software jumper called a configuration register. Once the configuration register is changed, the router will boot using a blank configuration, enabling the user to log into the router without entering a password. At this point, the user can either view or change the password.

Password recovery techniques vary by router platform. The following is the format for recovering a password on the 2500, 4000, and 7000 series:

1. Attach a terminal or PC running terminal emulation software to the console port of the router. The auxiliary (AUX) port is not active during the boot sequence of a

router. Therefore, sending a break through the AUX port does not work. You must be connected to the console port and have the following settings:

- A 9,600 baud rate

- No parity

- Eight data bits

- One stop bit

- No flow control

2. Reboot the router by turning the power off and on again.

3. Press the Break key on your terminal within 60 seconds after the reboot; the rommon> prompt should appear.

4. At the rommon> prompt, enter o/r0x42, which tells the router to boot up without reading the contents of NVRAM.

5. Reload the router using the **reload** command or I depending on the platform.

6. After the router reloads without reading NVRAM, there will not be any passwords configured on the router. Get into privileged mode and either view, change, or delete the NVRAM passwords. You can then copy the startup configuration to the running configuration and change or view the password.

7. After successfully viewing or changing the password, go into configuration mode and set the router to boot from NVRAM, setting the configuration register back to its original setting.

8. Reload the router. You now know the password.

Password recovery techniques vary by router platform. The following is the format for recovering a password on the 1003, 1600, 3600, 4500, and 7500 series:

1. Attach a terminal or PC running terminal emulation software to the console port of the router. The AUX port is not active during the boot sequence of a router. Therefore, sending a break through the AUX port does not work. You must be connected to the console port and have the following settings:

- A 9,600 baud rate

- No parity

- Eight data bits

- One stop bit

- No flow control

2. Reboot the router by turning the power off and on again.

3. Press the Break key on your terminal within 60 seconds after the reboot; the rommon> prompt should appear. At the rommon> prompt, enter **confreg** command, which tells the router to boot up without reading the contents of NVRAM.

4. When the "do you wish to change the configuration" prompt appears, answer yes.

5. Answer no to all of the prompts until you get to "ignore system config info" and then answer yes.

6. Reload the router.

7. After the router reloads without reading NVRAM, there will not be any passwords configured on the router. Get into privileged mode and either view, change, or delete the NVRAM passwords. You can then copy the startup configuration to the running configuration and change or view the password.

8. After successfully viewing or changing the password, go into configuration mode and set the router to boot from NVRAM, setting the configuration register back to its original setting.

9. Reload the router. You now know the password.

Questions

1. The **ip host** command is used to _____.
   a. Define a default gateway in the router.
   b. Map a hostname to an IP address in the router.
   c. Configure the router name.
   d. Configure the DHCP addressing.

2. How many framing bits are in a DS1 frame?
   a. 193
   b. 192
   c. 1
   d. None

3. When configuring a 2511 terminal server, which commands should be applied under the lines 0 through 16 in order enable reverse telnetting to the connected device? (multiple answers)
   a. no exec
   b. transport input all

    c. login

    d. exec

4. When trying to telnet to a router, you receive the error message "password required but not set". What does this mean?

    a. Login is enabled on the VTY and no password is set.

    b. Login is disabled on the VTY and no password is set.

    c. No enable password is set.

    d. All of the above

5. The following is the output from the **show flash** command on a Cisco 7500. What does the *E* in the ED field mean?

```
HCFA_7507#show flash
-#- ED --type-- --crc--- -seek-- nlen -length- -----date/time------ name
1 e. image 1D0600C5 75EBFC 12 7596924 May 14 2001 08:07:28 rsp-jsv-.112
```

    a. The image has been erased.

    b. The file has an error.

    c. The file is executable.

    d. None of the above

6. The ones density requirement _____.

    a. Ensures that no more than one consecutive zero occurs in data

    b. Ensures that a minimum number of zeros are present in data

    c. Ensures that a minimum number of ones are present in data

    d. None of the above

7. You want to load a new image to a flash card on a 7500 router; however, an image already exists and there is not enough space available. What steps must be taken to load the new image?

    a. The flash card must be partitioned.

    b. The old image should be deleted and the router reloaded.

    c. The old image should be marked for deletion and then removed with the **squeeze** command.

    d. The old image should be deleted using the **delete** command.

8. You have been asked to recover an unknown password on a Cisco router. The configuration register should be set to _____.

    a. boot using NVRAM contents

    b. ignore NVRAM contents

    c. boot from ROM

    d. None of the above

9. By default, a serial interface running at T1 speed will use what queuing mechanism?
   a. FIFO
   b. WFQ
   c. WRED
   d. Priority queuing

10. Which of the following is the correct configuration register setting to set the console speed on a Cisco 3600 series router to 1,200 bps?
    a. 0x2102
    b. 0x2142
    c. 0x2902
    d. 0x1200

11. You have been asked to configure HSRP on RouterA and RouterB. RouterA should be the active router for the group. Which of the following configurations will accomplish this?
    a. Set the standby priority on RouterA to 150 and the standby priority on RouterB to 100.
    b. Set the standby priority on RouterA to 100 and the standby priority on RouterB to 150.
    c. Set the standby preempt on RouterA to 150 and the standby preempt on RouterB to 100.
    d. Set the standby preempt on RouterB to 150 and the standby preempt on RouterA to 100.

12. The serial interface is down and the line protocol is down on an HDLC link. What is most likely the problem?
    a. Keepalives are not being received from the remote router.
    b. The IP addresses are configured wrong.
    c. No cable is present.
    d. None of the above

13. Which of the following is false regarding HSRP?
    a. HSRP can be configured to enable the router to track interfaces; if the interface goes down, the HSRP standby priority is changed.
    b. If the standby router does not receive a hello packet from the active router within the default hold time, the standby router becomes active.
    c. Routers can be in multiple HSRP groups at a time.
    d. Once a router is active, no other router can become active until that router fails.

14. What is RTP?

    a. A unit that expresses one hour of traffic on a trunk or trunk group

    b. A traffic model used to determine the number of trunks required to service a specific amount of traffic

    c. A trunking protocol used between voice switches

    d. An Internet-standard protocol for the transport of real-time data, including audio and video

15. Which of following can be determined from the IOS code c7200-jo3s56i-mz.121-3.bin? (multiple answers)

    a. The file is an IOS image for a Cisco 7200 router.

    b. It supports firewall.

    c. It is compressed and designed to run from RAM.

    d. It is relocatable code.

16. A Cisco 2500 runs its IOS image in _____.

    a. RAM

    b. ROM

    c. Flash

    d. TFTP server

17. A Cisco 3600 runs its image in _____.

    a. RAM

    b. ROM

    c. Flash

    d. TFTP server

18. Which of the following is the correct numerical range for an extended access list?

    a. 1 to 99

    b. 100 to 199

    c. 800 to 899

    d. 900 to 999

19. If you had six voice calls with a duration of ten minutes each, how many Erlangs would that be?

    a. 6

    b. 1

    c. 60

    d. 30

20. In Figure 4-1, RouterA wants to deny all traffic from host 150.1.1.2 destined for PCA (152.1.1.2). Which of the following would accomplish this? (multiple answers)

    a. An inbound access list applied on the serial interface of RouterA

    b. An outbound access list applied to the Ethernet interface of RouterA

    c. An outbound access list applied on the serial interface of RouterA

    d. An inbound access list applied to the Ethernet interface of RouterA

21. Which of the following is false regarding access lists?

    a. Access lists can be used to control access, policy routing, DDR, CAR, and IOS firewall by the time of day.

    b. The **access-class** command is used to create a temporary access list entry in a dynamic access list.

    c. The **ip access-group** command is used to permit or deny incoming or outgoing packets on a particular interface.

    d. Access lists use wildcard masks.

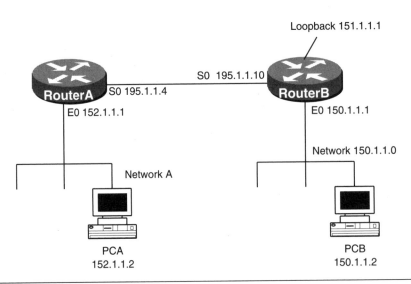

Figure 4-1   Network diagram

22. Which of the following queuing methods are used on a Cisco router? (multiple answers)

    a. WFQ

    b. FIFO

    c. Priority queuing

    d. Cut-through queuing

23. The following access list is configured on the router and applied to the serial interface using the command **ipx output-sap-filter 1000**. What will the access list prevent?

```
RouterB(config)#access-list 1000 deny -1 7
RouterB(config)#access-list 1000 permit -1
```

    a. The access list will prevent SAP entries for all network file servers from being sent.

    b. The access list will prevent SAP entries for all network print servers from being sent.

    c. Nothing—it is configured wrong; the permit statement will allow SAP entries.

    d. Both A and B

24. What will happen if an SAP update is received and the router does not have a route to the destination?

    a. The SAP entry will be added to the SAP table but not advertised.

    b. The SAP entry will be added to the SAP table.

    c. The router will not insert the entry in the SAP table.

    d. None of the above

25. How do you forward IPX/NetBIOS broadcast traffic across a router?

    a. Use an **ipx helper address**.

    b. Enable ipx-type-20 propagation.

    c. Use the command **ip forward UDP**.

    d. None of the above

26. The CPU utilization on your router is very high. You notice that the IP input process is using the majority of your CPU cycles. What is most likely the problem?

    a. A large number of packets are being process-switched.

    b. A large number of packets are being dropped.

    c. Packets are overflowing the buffers.

    d. None of the above

27. The serial interface is up, but the line protocol is down on an HDLC link. What is most likely the problem?

    a. Keepalives are not being received from the remote router.

    b. IP addresses are configured wrong.

    c. No clock is present.

    d. None of the above

28. You display the interface statistics with the **show interface** command, and notice a large number of output drops on the serial interface. What is most likely the problem?

    a. Packets are discarded because they exceed the medium's maximum packet size.

    b. The input rate to the serial interface exceeds the bandwidth available on the serial link.

    c. The serial receiver hardware was unable to hand received data to a hardware buffer because the input rate exceeded the receiver's capability to handle the data.

    d. An illegal sequence of one bits is received on a serial interface.

29. Which of the following is not a valid VTP mode?

    a. Server

    b. Client

    c. Transparent

    d. Spanning

30. What is the purpose of the **ethernet-transit-oui** command?

    a. It specifies the OUI code used in the encapsulation of Ethernet Type II frames.

    b. It is used to identify the vendor.

    c. It specifies the OUI code used on the Ethernet LAN.

    d. None of the above

31. The command **multiring all** is used to _____.

    a. Enable multiple rings.

    b. Enable a routed protocol to enter an SRB environment.

    c. Enable SRB on Ethernet.

    d. None of the above

32. The following is the output from the **show process cpu** command. What do the first and second number mean in the five-second average?

```
CPU utilization for five seconds: 15% / 5%; one minute: 0%; five minutes: 0%
PID Runtime(ms) Invoked uSecs 5Sec 1Min 5Min TTY Process
```

```
1 0 173 0 0.00% 0.00% 0.00% 0 Load Meter
2 0 15 0 0.00% 0.00% 0.00% 0 TACACS+
3 180 30 6000 0.24% 0.02% 0.00% 0 Check heaps
4 0 2 0 0.00% 0.00% 0.00% 0 Pool Manager
5 0 2 0 0.00% 0.00% 0.00% 0 Timers
```

    a. The first number is the instantaneous value and the second number is average total utilization during last five seconds.

    b. The first number is the average total utilization during last five seconds and the second number is the average utilization due to processor interrupts during last five seconds.

    c. The first number is the average total utilization during last five seconds and the second number is the instantaneous utilization.

    d. None of the above

33. The network administrator has asked you to translate the unregistered IP addresses on the Ethernet network attached to RouterA to globally unique addresses before sending the packets out to the Internet (see Figure 4-2). Which of the following would you use to accomplish this?

    a. An IP NAT inside source translation on RouterA

    b. An IP NAT inside source translation on RouterB

    c. An IP NAT outside source translation on RouterA

    d. An IP NAT outside source translation on RouterB

34. In Figure 4-2, IP address 10.1.1.1 is considered the _____.

    a. Inside global address

    b. Inside local address

    c. Outside local address

    d. Outside global address

35. Which of the following is false regarding dynamic inside source translation?

    a. Dynamic inside source translation establishes a mapping between a group of inside local addresses and a pool of global addresses.

    b. Unless overloading is used, you require a global IP address for each workstation that wants to communicate outside the private network.

    c. Dynamic address translation is more scalable and efficient than static translations.

    d. Outside users can establish a connection to inside addresses.

36. In Figure 4-3, Company X has multiple FTP servers hanging off of RouterA. Your network administrator has asked you to use NAT to ensure that FTP connections are load balanced equally across both servers. Which of the following configurations would accomplish this?

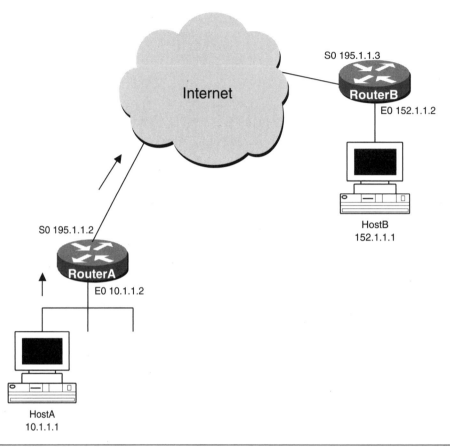

Figure 4-2 Network diagram

    a. A rotary pool is used in conjunction with an inside destination translation on RouterA.

    b. Overload is used along in conjunction with an inside destination translation on RouterA.

    c. A rotary poll is used in conjunction with an outside destination translation on RouterA.

    d. None of the above—NAT cannot be used for load balancing connections.

37. Which of the following is used on a Cisco router to prevent global synchronization from occurring?

    a. FIFO

    b. WFQ

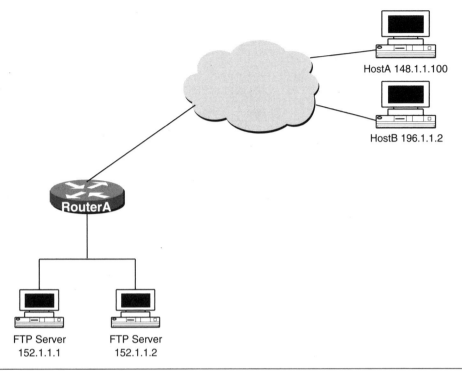

HostA 148.1.1.100

HostB 196.1.1.2

RouterA

FTP Server
152.1.1.1

FTP Server
152.1.1.2

Figure 4-3   Network diagram

    c.   WRED

    d.   PQ

38. The output from the **show buffers** command on the router indicates large numbers in the trims and created fields for the large buffer pool. What should you do?

    a.   Configure priority queuing.

    b.   Increase the maximum number of free system buffers allowed.

    c.   Prevent the router from trimming the buffers.

    d.   Increase the amount of memory on the router.

39. Which of the following is true regarding TACACS+? (multiple answers)

    a.   It is Cisco proprietary.

    b.   TACACS+ encrypts the entire body of the packet.

    c.   TACACS+ uses UDP.

    d.   TACACS+ only supports TCP/IP.

40. Which of the following configurations would give telnet traffic higher priority than FTP traffic?

   a. `priority-list 1 protocol ip low tcp telnet`

   b. `priority-list 1 protocol ip medium tcp telnet`

   c. `priority-list 1 protocol ip normal tcp telnet`
      `priority-list 2 protocol ip low tcp ftp`
      `priority-list 2 protocol ip low tcp ftp-data`

   d. None of the above

41. Based on the following configuration, what percentage of bandwidth will telnet traffic receive if no other traffic is present in queue 1?

```
queue-list 1 protocol ip 1 tcp www
queue-list 1 protocol ip 2 tcp telnet
queue-list 1 queue 1 byte-count 3000
queue-list 1 queue 2 byte-count 3000
```

   a. 30 percent

   b. 20 percent

   c. 50 percent

   d. 100 percent

42. Based on the following configuration, what percentage of bandwidth will FTP traffic receive?

```
queue-list 1 protocol ip 2 tcp www
queue-list 1 protocol ip 3 tcp telnet
queue-list 1 queue 2 byte-count 3000
queue-list 1 queue 3 byte-count 1500
```

   a. 25 percent

   b. 0 percent

   c. 50 percent

   d. None of the above because FTP is not defined in a queue list

43. Which of the following is false regarding queuing?

   a. Queuing allows congestion control by determining the order in which packets are sent out of an interface.

   b. With FIFO, packets are sent out of the interface in the same order that they arrive.

   c. WFQ is the default queuing mechanism on interfaces running at speeds of 2 Mbps and below.

   d. With custom queuing, care must be taken so that routing protocol updates are not starved by other protocol packets in queue 1.

44. Based on the following configuration, what best describes the action the router will take?

```
interface Ethernet0/0
ip address 135.25.7.2 255.255.255.224
rate-limit input 96000 16000 16000 conform-action transmit exceed-action drop
```

    a. Interface Ethernet 0/0 will limit input traffic to 96,000 bps.

    b. Interface Ethernet 0/0 will limit input traffic to 112,000 bps.

    c. Interface Ethernet 0/0 will limit input traffic to 112,000 bps.

    d. Interface Ethernet 0/0 will limit input traffic to 96,000 bps.

45. When implementing VoIP, it is important to minimize the end-to-end delay within a network. Which of the following causes delay in a network? (multiple answers)

    a. Serialization delay

    b. Propagation delay

    c. Jitter

    d. Echo

46. A Cisco router can network boot using which of the following protocols? (multiple answers)

    a. TFTP

    b. RCP

    c. MOP

    d. IGMP

47. In the following configuration, the router is set to timestamp all long messages and the current date and time is configured on the router. However, the log files are not timestamped with the correct time. What is the problem?

```
logging buffered
service timestamps log
```

    a. NTP is not configured.

    b. The system is using the uptime as the clock reference.

    c. Logging timestamps should be added to the configuration.

    d. None of the above

48. Which of the following configurations enables read-only SNMP access from host 192.1.1.1?

    a. `snmp-server community cisco ro 192.1.1.1`

    b. `snmp-server community cisco ro`
       `snmp-server 192.1.1.1`

   c. snmp-server community cisco ro 99
      access-list 99 permit 192.1.1.1 0.0.0.0

   d. snmp-server community cisco ro
      snmp-server 99
      access-list 99 permit 192.1.1.1 0.0.0.0

49. Which of the following configurations sets a login password on the console port of the router?

   a. line con 0
      password cisco

   b. line con 0
      login password cisco

   c. line con 0
      login
      password cisco

   d. You cannot set a password on a console port. Passwords can only be set on AUX and VTY ports.

50. How can you configure the router for the first time? (multiple answers)

   a. SNMP

   b. CLI

   c. The setup command facility

   d. SLARP

51. Which of the following is not a valid enable password?

   a. good4now

   b. two words

   c. 1moretime

   d. CiScO

52. You have a subset of users who do not have enable access to the router but need to be able to view the configuration for troubleshooting purposes. Which of the following commands will enable the users to view the entire configuration?

   a. privilege exec level 2 show running-config

   b. privilege exec level 2 write terminal

   c. privilege exec level 2 show startup-config

   d. All of the above

53. When RouterA pings address 192.1.1.1, the ping fails. The following is the output from the **debug frame-relay** packet command on RouterA. Based on the information provided, what is most likely the problem?

```
Serial0/0:Encaps failed--no map entry link 7(IP)
Serial0/0:Encaps failed--no map entry link 7(IP).
Serial0/0:Encaps failed--no map entry link 7(IP).
Serial0/0:Encaps failed--no map entry link 7(IP)
```

    a. RouterA does not have a route to network 192.1.1.1.

    b. Frame relay inverse ARP is disabled.

    c. The wrong encapsulation type is being used on the interface.

    d. None of the above

54. Based on the following output of the **show version** command, how much memory is on this router?

```
cisco 4700 (R4K) processor (revision C) with 32768K/4096K bytes of memory.
Processor board ID 03386984
R4700 processor, Implementation 33, Revision 1.0 (Level 2 Cache)
G.703/E1 software, Version 1.0.
Bridging software.
SuperLAT software copyright 1990 by Meridian Technology Corp).
X.25 software, Version 2.0, NET2, BFE and GOSIP compliant.
TN3270 Emulation software (copyright 1994 by TGV Inc).
2 Ethernet/IEEE 802.3 interface(s)
2 Token Ring/IEEE 802.5 interface(s)
4 Serial network interface(s)
128K bytes of non-volatile configuration memory.
4096K bytes of processor board System flash (Read/Write)
4096K bytes of processor board Boot flash (Read/Write)
```

    a. 32M of main memory and 4M of shared memory

    b. 36M of main memory and 4M of shared memory

    c. 36M of main memory and 4M of flash

    d. 32M of shared memory and 4M of flash

55. What does it mean when a BRI interface is spoofing?

    a. The interface is configured wrong.

    b. The SPID is configured wrong.

    c. The interface is awaiting interesting packets in order to place a call.

    d. The interface is administratively down.

56. What is the difference between Rxboot and BootROM?

    a. Rxboot is a full set image, whereas BootROM is a subset image.

    b. Rxboot is used on higher-end platforms, whereas BootROM is used on the lower-end platforms.

    c. Rxboot is a subset image, whereas BootROM is full image.

    d. None of the above

57. How do you configure the router so that it records the date and time of the last configuration change?

a. Enable the service configuration change.

b. Enable user level access.

c. Ensure that the clock is set on the router.

d. None of the above

58. Based on the following output from the show interface command, what is the five-minute outbound utilization of the interface?

```
TokenRing0 is up, line protocol is up
  Hardware is TMS380, address is 0006.f4c5.df18 (bia 0006.f4c5.df18)
  Description: Lab Inside Ring #59
  Internet address is 164.120.59.67/24
  MTU 4464 bytes, BW 16000 Kbit, DLY 630 usec, rely 255/255, load 64/255
  Encapsulation SNAP, loopback not set, keepalive set (10 sec)
  ARP type: SNAP, ARP Timeout 04:00:00
  Ring speed: 16 Mbps
  Multiring node, Source Route Transparent Bridge capable
  Group Address: 0x00000000, Functional Address: 0x08000000
  Ethernet Transit OUI: 0x000000
  Last input 00:00:00, output 00:00:00, output hang never
  Last clearing of "show interface" counters never
  Queueing strategy: fifo
```

a. 50 percent

b. 25 percent

c. 64 percent

d. 100 percent

59. When the established keyword is used in conjunction with an access list, a match occurs if the _____.

a. TCP datagram has the SYN bit set.

b. TCP datagram has the SYN or ACK bits set.

c. TCP datagram has the ACK or RST bits set.

d. TCP datagram has the SYN or RST bits set.

60. Which of the following access list entries will permit TCP connections to host 192.1.1.1 for port numbers greater than 1,023?

a. access-list 101 permit tcp any 192.1.1.1 0.0.0.0 gt 1023

b. access-list 101 permit tcp any 192.1.1.1 0.0.0.0 eq 1023

c. access-list 101 permit tcp any 192.1.1.1 0.0.0.0 lt 1023

d. access-list 101 permit tcp any 192.1.1.1 0.0.0.0 neq1023

61. Which of the following commands will encrypt the enable password on the router?

  a. enable password 0 test

  b. enable password 7 test

  c. service password-encryption

  d. None of the above

62. What registry value is used to cause the router to reboot without loading the startup configuration?

  a. 0x2102

  b. 0x2142

  c. 0x2101

  d. None of the above

63. Which of the following is not a valid way to configure a new router?

  a. Use the CLI.

  b. Boot the configuration from a server using BOOTP and SLARP.

  c. Use the setup dialog.

  d. SNMP

64. Which of the following is false regarding ED releases of IOS software?

  a. There are four types of ED releases.

  b. ED releases are vehicles that bring new development to the marketplace.

  c. ED maintenance releases do not accept the addition of features or platforms.

  d. ED releases are generally not as stable as main releases.

65. In IOS version 12.0(1), what does the number in parentheses stand for?

  a. The main release number

  b. The version number

  c. The maintenance release number

  d. The ED number

66. Which of the following is false regarding loopback interfaces?

  a. Loopback interfaces are always up unless the router goes down.

  b. Loopback interfaces are often used by BGP for peering sessions.

  c. If a loopback is configured with an IP address, the router will use this address as the router ID even if other interfaces have higher IP addresses.

  d. OSPF will use the first loopback interface configured as its router ID.

67. What is the significance of SC0 on a Catalyst 5500?
    a. SC0 is an internal logical interface used to telnet into the Catalyst for configuration and monitoring.
    b. SC0 is the interface used to provide trunking between Catalyst switches.
    c. SC0 is used to provide port security.
    d. None of the above

68. Which of the following statements is false regarding a Catalyst switch?
    a. After the Catalyst has been reset, all ports are defined to be on a single VLAN: VLAN 100.
    b. The Catalyst will automatically sense that an active LAN is connected to one of its ports and set the corresponding port parameters correctly.
    c. The Catalyst switch must have a domain name before it can use VLAN numbers other than 1.
    d. A Catalyst switch can be configured to block input to an Ethernet port when the MAC address of a station attempting to access the port is different from the configured MAC address.

69. When configuring a PRI interface on a Cisco router, which interface is the D channel?
    a. S0:0
    b. S0:24
    c. S0:23
    d. None of the above

70. How do you perform password recovery on a Catalyst switch?
    a. Change the configuration register to ignore NVRAM.
    b. Enter the break character within 30 seconds.
    c. The password on the Catalyst is not valid for the first 30 seconds after reload, so you can log on and change it.
    d. None of the above

71. How can you establish inter-VLAN communication?
    a. Use ISL.
    b. Use VTP.
    c. Use RTP.
    d. None of the above—inter-VLAN communication is not allowed.

72. What is the purpose of the range of MAC addresses assigned to the supervisor on a Catalyst? (multiple answers)
    a. It is used as the VLAN ID.

    b. It is used as the bridge ID for the box.

    c. It is used for the IP address of the SC0 interface.

    d. It is used for ISL connection.

73. What is the IOS command to create a shortcut so that you can type "sr" instead of "show ip route"?

    a. router(config)# ip alias exec sr show ip route

    b. router(config)#alias exec sr show ip route

    c. router(config)# shortcut exec sr show ip route

    d. router(config)# ip shortcut exec sr show ip route

74. Which of the following is true regarding a VLAN? (multiple answers)

    a. A VLAN is an administratively defined broadcast domain.

    b. Each port in a VLAN is in its own collision domain.

    c. All end stations in the same VLAN must be attached to the same switch.

    d. Each port in a VALN is in its own broadcast domain.

75. By default, on a Catalyst switch all ports are _____. (multiple answers)

    a. Disabled

    b. In VLAN1

    c. In a single broadcast domain

    d. In a single collision domain

76. You have just converted all of your workstations connected to your Catalyst for DHCP. What must you do to the switch interfaces connecting to the workstations to ensure that the DHCP requests don't time out? (multiple answers)

    a. Turn on port fast.

    b. Turn off trunking.

    c. Turn off port fast.

    d. Turn on auto negotiation.

77. You issue a **show port** command on a Catalyst switch and notice that you have a large number of delay exceeded errors. What is most likely the problem?

    a. This is an indication that the receive buffer is getting full.

    b. A device connected to this port is jabbering.

    c. This is an indication that the send buffer is getting full.

    d. None of the above

78. What is the maximum diameter of a Catalyst network with 10M or higher links?

    a. 4 hops

    b. 5 hops

    c. 7 hops

    d. 12 hops

79. What command would you use on a Catalyst switch to erase all the configuration information stored in NVRAM?

    a. write erase reload

    b. clear configuration

    c. clear configuration all

    d. clear NVRAM

80. When a Catalyst switch transfers frames between ports without buffering the entire frame in memory, it is operating in what mode?

    a. Store-and-forward mode

    b. Fast-switching mode

    c. Process-switching mode

    d. Cut-through mode

81. In which VTP mode you can create or delete VLANs?

    a. Active

    b. Server

    c. Spanning

    d. Client

82. Which of the following interface IP addresses would be used as the OSPF router ID if there were two serial interfaces, one Ethernet, and two loopback interfaces configured on a router?

    a. The interface with the highest IP address

    b. The interface with the lowest IP address

    c. The loopback interface with the highest IP address

    d. The loopback interface with the lowest IP address

83. Three routers running OSPF are connected via Ethernet. How can you ensure that RouterA becomes the designated router (DR) for the network?

    a. Set the ip ospf priority to 0 on RouterA.

    b. Set the ip ospf priority to 0 on RouterB and RouterC.

    c. Set the standby priority to 100 on RouterA.

    d. None of the above—a DR is not elected on an Ethernet network.

84. Which of the following is false regarding VTP pruning?

    a. VLAN 1 through 1,000 can be pruned.

    b. VTP pruning reduces unnecessary flooding.

    c. By default, VTP pruning is disabled.

    d. None of the above

85. Which of the following is false regarding RADIUS?

    a. Usernames and passwords are encrypted.

    b. RADIUS is not Cisco proprietary.

    c. RADIS uses TCP as its transport protocol.

    d. Both A and C

86. One Erlang is equal to how many CCS per hour?

    a. 36

    b. 63

    c. 10

    d. 100

87. What is Erlang B?

    a. It is a traffic model used to determine the number of trunks required to service a specific amount of traffic.

    b. It is a unit that expresses one hour of traffic on a trunk or trunk group.

    c. It is a voice-encoding technology.

    d. None of the above

88. Which of the following is false regarding VTP?

    a. VTP is a layer 2 messaging protocol.

    b. Using VTP, changes are automatically communicated to all the other switches in the network.

    c. A switch can only operate in server mode.

    d. VTP pruning reduces the unnecessary flooding of traffic.

89. Which of the following is false regarding CGMP?

    a. CGMP is Cisco proprietary.

    b. CGMP dynamically configures Catalyst switch ports so that IP multicast traffic is forwarded only to those ports associated with IP multicast hosts.

    c. When a router receives an IGMP message, it creates a CGMP messages and forwards it to the switch.

    d. CGMP runs on the switches only.

90. How would you gain access to a router whose password is not known?

    a. Reload the router and copy the startup configuration to the running configuration.

    b. Reload the router, issue the **break** command within the first 60 seconds, change the register value to ignore NVRAM, reload the router again, copy the startup configuration to the running configuration, change the password, change the configuration register back, and copy the running configuration to the startup configuration.

c. Reload the router, issue the **break** command within the first 60 seconds, change the register value to ignore NVRAM, reload the router again, and copy the running configuration to the startup configuration reload the router.

d. Reload the router, issue the **break** command within the first 60 seconds, change the register value to ignore NVRAM, reload the router again, copy the startup configuration to the running configuration, and change the password.

91. What are the primary modes used by the Cisco command interpreter EXEC? (Choose the best two answers.)
   a. Exec mode
   b. Privileged mode
   c. User mode
   d. Configuration mode

92. The serial interface is down, but the line protocol is up on an HDLC link. What is most likely the problem?
   a. Keepalives are not being received from the remote router.
   b. IP addresses are configured wrong.
   c. No clock is present.
   d. None of the above

93. Which of the following is false regarding access lists?
   a. There is an implied deny all at the end of all access lists.
   b. Access lists are applied in permit deny manner (all permit statements are applied first then deny statements).
   c. Access lists are used to control virtual terminal access.
   d. An access list is a sequential collection of permit and deny conditions.

94. What command can be used to determine the hardware configuration of a router? (multiple answers)
   a. show version
   b. show accounting
   c. show hardware
   d. None of the above

95. Which of the following passwords can be encrypted on a router?
   a. enable password
   b. enable secret

   c. chap secrets

   d. All of the above

96. What happens if a Catalyst switch receives a frame with a destination MAC address that is not in the CAM table?

   a. The frame is dropped.

   b. The frame is sent out all ports on the Catalyst.

   c. The frame is sent out all ports of the VLAN.

   d. The frame is routed.

97. Which of the following statements is false regarding DDR?

   a. DDR is implemented in two ways: DDR with dialer profiles and legacy DDR.

   b. Dialer profiles separate logical configurations from the physical interfaces.

   c. Legacy DDR enables physical interfaces to take on different characteristics based on incoming or outgoing call requirements.

   d. Dialer profiles enable BRIs to belong to multiple dialer pools.

98. Which of the following is true regarding legacy DDR? (multiple answers)

   a. With legacy DDR, all ISDN B channels inherited the physical interface's configuration.

   b. With legacy DDR, one dialer map is required per dialer per protocol.

   c. With legacy DDR, BRIs can belong to multiple dialer pools.

   d. Legacy DDR enables physical interfaces to take on different characteristics based on incoming or outgoing call requirements.

99. What must be done to allow a VLAN to span two or more switches?

   a. Set up pruning.

   b. Set up routing.

   c. Set up a trunk connection.

   d. None of the above

100. Which of the following configuration register values would force a router to boot from ROM?

   a. 0x2102

   b. 0x2142

   c. 0x2101

   d. 0x2104

Answer Key

1. B

2. C

3. A and B

4. A

5. B

6. C

7. C

8. B

9. B

10. C

11. A

12. C

13. D

14. D

15. A, B, and C

16. C

17. A

18. B

19. B

20. A and B

21. B

22. A, B, and C

23. B

24. C

25. B

26. A

27. A

28. B

29. D

30. A

31. C

32. B

33. A

34. B

35. D

36. A

37. C

38. B

39. A and B

40. B

41. C

42. A

43. D

44. A

45. A and B

46. A, B, and C

47. B

48. C

49. C

50. B, C, and D

51. C

52. C

53. B

54. A

55. C

56. C

57. C

58. B

59. C

60. A

61. C

62. B

63. D

64. C

65. C

66. D

67. A

68. A

69. C

70. C

71. A

72. B and C

73. B

74. A and B

75. B and C

76. A and B

77. B

78. C

79. C

80. D

81. B

82. C

83. B

84. A

85. C

86. A

87. A

88. C

89. D

90. B

91. B and C

92. D

93. B

94. A and C

95. D

96. C

97. C

98. A and B

99. C

100. C

Answer Guide

1. The **ip host** command is used to _____.
   a. Define a default gateway in the router.
   b. Map a hostname to an IP address in the router.
   c. Configure the router name.
   d. Configure the DHCP addressing.

The correct answer is B. The **ip host** command is used to define a static hostname-to-address mapping in the router's host cache. The Cisco IOS software maintains a table of hostnames and their corresponding addresses. Similar to a DNS server, you can statically map hostnames to IP addresses. This is very useful and saves a lot of keystrokes when you have multiple devices connected to the terminal server.

2. How many framing bits are in a DS1 frame?
   a. 193
   b. 192
   c. 1
   d. None

The correct answer is C. A DS1 frame has 193 bits, of which 192 are used for user data and one bit is used for framing.

3. When configuring a 2511 terminal server, which commands should be applied under the lines 0 through 16 in order enable reverse telnetting to the connected device? (multiple answers)
   a. no exec
   b. transport input all
   c. login
   d. exec

The correct answers are A and B. A terminal server is very simple to set up and requires minimal configuration. The only two commands needed are **transport input all** and **no exec**.

The command **transport input all** specifies the input transport protocol by default on IOS 11.1 and later the transport input is set to none. Prior to 11.1, the default was all. If the transport input is left to none, you will receive an error stating that the connection is refused by remote host, as shown in the following output:

```
terminal_server# telnet 1.1.1.1 2001 ←(Reverse Telnet)
Trying 1.1.1.1, 2001 ...
% Connection refused by remote host
```

The command **no exec** allows only outgoing connections for the line. This prevents an exec session from being started if the device attached to the terminal server sends out unsolicited data. Without this command, if the terminal server line receives unsolicited data, an EXEC process starts making the line unavailable.

Answer C is incorrect. The **login** command is used to enable password checking on the particular line.

Answer D is incorrect. The **exec** command enables exec sessions to start if the device attached to the terminal server sends out unsolicited data.

4. When trying to telnet to a router, you receive the error message "password required but not set". What does this mean?
   a. Login is enabled on the VTY and no password is set.
   b. Login is disabled on the VTY and no password is set.
   c. No enable password is set.
   d. All of the above

The correct answer is A. When login is enabled on a VTY line, password checking is performed. If no password is set, the router responds to the attempted connection by displaying an error message and resetting the connection.

Answer B is incorrect. When login is disabled on a VTY line, no password checking is performed, so you would not receive the error message.

Answer C is incorrect. The router has two levels of security: user and privileged. The commands available at the user level are a subset of those available at the privileged level. The privileged commands are password-protected to prevent unauthorized use. This is accomplished by setting up an enable password. An enable password gives a user access to the privileged command level.

5. The following is the output from the **show flash** command on a Cisco 7500. What does the *E* in the ED field mean?

```
HCFA_7507#show flash
-#- ED --type-- --crc--- -seek-- nlen -length- -----date/time------ name
1 e. image 1D0600C5 75EBFC 12 7596924 May 14 2001 08:07:28 rsp-jsv-.112
```

   a. The image has been erased.
   b. The file has an error.
   c. The file is executable.
   d. None of the above

The correct answer is B. The *E* in the ED field indicates that the file has an error.

Answer A is incorrect. The *D* in the ED field indicates that the file has been deleted.

Answer C is incorrect. The type field indicates if the file is an executable image a configuration file or unknown.

6. The ones density requirement _____.
   a. Ensures that no more than one consecutive zero occurs in data
   b. Ensures that a minimum number of zeros are present in data
   c. Ensures that a minimum number of ones are present in data
   d. None of the above

The correct answer is C. The term "ones density" refers to the fact that some telephone systems require a minimum number of one bits per time unit in a data stream. This enables repeaters to maintain timing.

7. You want to load a new image to a flash card on a 7500 router; however, an image already exists and there is not enough space available. What steps must be taken to load the new image?
   a. The flash card must be partitioned.
   b. The old image should be deleted and the router reloaded.
   c. The old image should be marked for deletion and then removed with the **squeeze** command.
   d. The old image should be deleted using the **delete** command.

The correct answer is C. Deleting a file from a flash card is a two-step process. First, the **delete** command is used to mark the file that you want to delete and then the **squeeze** command is used to actually remove the file.

8. You have been asked to recover an unknown enable password on a Cisco router. The configuration register should be set to _____.
   a. boot using NVRAM contents
   b. ignore NVRAM contents
   c. boot from ROM
   d. None of the above

The correct answer is B. The configuration register should be set to ignore the contents in NVRAM. When a router first loads, it boots its configuration file stored in NVRAM. This file contains all of the router's configuration information including the enable password. By changing the configuration register to ignore NVRAM, the router will boot with no configuration information. The user can then log into the router because no passwords are set, and either read the old password from NVRAM or change it.

9. By default, a serial interface running at T1 speed will use what queuing mechanism?

    a. FIFO

    b. WFQ

    c. WRED

    d. Priority queuing

The correct answer is B. Weighted fair queuing (WFQ) is the default queuing mechanism on interfaces running at speeds of 2 Mbps and below.

10. Which of the following is the correct configuration register setting to set the console speed on a Cisco 3600 series router to 1,200 bps?

    a. 0x2102

    b. 0x2142

    c. 0x2902

    d. 0x1200

The correct answer is C. A Cisco router has a 16-bit virtual register, which is written into the NVRAM. This processor configuration register is used for the following purposes:

- Set and display the configuration register value.

- Force the system into the bootstrap program.

- Select a boot source and default boot filename.

- Enable or disable the break function.

- Control broadcast addresses.

- Set the console terminal baud rate.

- Load operating software from ROM.

- Enable booting from TFTP server.

Bits 11 and 12 in the configuration register determine the baud rate of the console port on a 2500. Table 4-4 shows the bit settings for the four available baud rates. The factory-set default baud rate is 9,600.

To set the console speed to 1,200 bps, bit position 12 is set to 1 and 11 is set to 0. Answer C is the only one with the bit position set correctly.

Table 4-4 System Console Terminal Baud Rate Settings

Baud	Bit 12	Bit 11
9,600	0	0
4,800	0	I
1,200	I	0
2,400	I	I

11. You have been asked to configure HSRP on RouterA and RouterB. RouterA should be the active router for the group. Which of the following configurations will accomplish this?

    a. Set the standby priority on RouterA to 150 and the standby priority on RouterB to 100.

    b. Set the standby priority on RouterA to 100 and the standby priority on RouterB to 150.

    c. Set the standby preempt on RouterA to 150 and the standby preempt on RouterB to 100.

    d. Set the standby preempt on RouterB to 150 and the standby preempt on RouterA to 100.

The correct answer is A. Hot Standby Router Protocol (HSRP) enables the network administrator to configure a set of routers to work together to present the appearance of a single default gateway. The routers in an HSRP group share a virtual MAC address and IP address. The hosts on the LAN use this address as the default gateway. The HSRP protocol selects which router is active, and the active router receives and routes packets that are destined for the group's MAC address. The HSRP standby priority of an interface determines which router becomes the active router for the group. The HSRP member with the highest standby priority (assuming preemption is enabled) becomes the active router.

Answer B is incorrect. Because RouterB has the higher standby priority, it would be the active router for the group.

Answers C and D are incorrect. Standby preempt indicates that when the local router's standby priority is higher than the current active router, the local router should attempt to assume control as the active router. There is no value associated with this command.

12. The serial interface is down and the line protocol is down on an HDLC link. What is most likely the problem?

   a. Keepalives are not being received from the remote router.

   b. The IP addresses are configured wrong.

   c. No cable is present.

   d. None of the above

The correct answer is C. This status indicates that the router is not sensing a Carrier Detect (CD) signal. Possible causes of this are no cable is present or the cabling is bad.

13. Which of the following is false regarding HSRP?

   a. HSRP can be configured to enable the router to track interfaces; if the interface goes down, the HSRP standby priority is changed.

   b. If the standby router does not receive a hello packet from the active router within the default hold time, the standby router becomes active.

   c. Routers can be in multiple HSRP groups at a time.

   d. Once a router is active no other router can become active until that router fails.

Answer D is false. If the HSRP group is configured for standby preempt, the router with the highest standby priority will become the active router. This occurs regardless of the state of the current active router.

Answer A is true. The track option under HSRP enables the router to track other interfaces, so that if one of the other interfaces goes down, the device's standby priority is lowered. When the priority is lowered below that of the router in standby, the standby router becomes active. This is critical if the primary router loses its connection to the Internet or the company's intranet. Without tracking, the primary router would still receive packets from the hosts on the LAN even though it does not have a route to the outside world. If the two routers are running an Interior Gateway Protocol (IGP), the primary router will route the packets via the secondary router, but no Internet Control Message Protocol (ICMP) redirects will occur; if they are not running an IGP, the packets will be dropped.

Answer B is true. If the standby router does not receive a hello packet from the active router in ten seconds (which is the default hold time), the standby router becomes active.

Answer C is true. The router can be in multiple HSRP groups at one time. This enables the LAN administrator to load balance across all of the routers while still providing redundancies in case of a failure. In Figure 4-4, each PC on the LAN uses a different default gateway. HostA uses default gateway 192.1.1.10, which is the IP address of HSRP Group 1, and HostB uses 192.1.1.11, which is the IP address of HSRP Group 2.

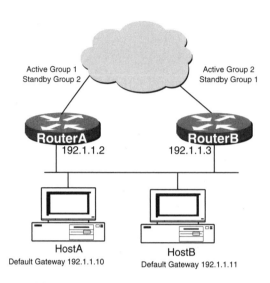

Figure 4-4 Multiple HSRP groups

When there are no failures, the traffic on the LAN is split equally between both routers. However, when a failure occurs, the standby router becomes active for that group and all traffic is routed to that interface.

14. What is RTP?
    a. A unit that expresses one hour of traffic on a trunk or trunk group
    b. A traffic model used to determine the number of trunks required to service a specific amount of traffic
    c. A trunking protocol used between voice switches
    d. An Internet-standard protocol for the transport of real-time data, including audio and video

The correct answer is D. Real-Time Protocol (RTP) is an Internet-standard protocol for the transport of real-time data, including audio and video.

15. Which of following can be determined from the IOS code c7200-jo3s56i-mz.121-3.bin? (multiple answers)
    a. The file is an IOS image for a Cisco 7200 router.
    b. It is an IP subset code load.
    c. It is compressed and designed to run from RAM.
    d. It is relocatable code.

The correct answers are A, B, and C. Cisco uses an IOS image naming convention to identify the platform or board for which the binary software is built. The naming convention also identifies the feature content of the image, and the area of memory used by the image at run time.

The IOS image name follows a three-part format; each part is separated by a dash. The first part identifies the platform, the second part identifies the features, and the last part identifies the run time memory and the compression format (pppp-fffff-mm).

The first part of the image name (pppp) identifies the platform the image runs on. Table 4-1, which appeared earlier in the chapter, is a list of IOS platform identifiers.

The second part of the image name (fffff) identifies the software features the image supports.

The third part of the ISO image name (mm) is two letters. The first letter identifies the memory area where the Cisco IOS image is executed at run time. The second letter indicates the method used to compress the Cisco IOS binary image.

The IOS code filename c7200-jo3s56i-mz.121-3.bin can be interpreted as follows:

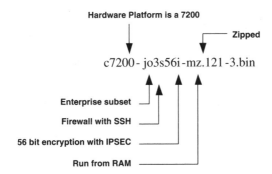

This file is an IOS image for a Cisco 7200 router. It is an Enterprise subset code load with firewall and encryption support. The image is compressed and is designed to run from RAM. The IOS version is 12.1 maintenance release 3.

16. A Cisco 2500 runs its IOS image in _____.

    a. RAM

    b. ROM

    c. Flash

    d. TFTP server

The correct answer is C. Depending on the router model, the IOS image is run from RAM or Flash. In the run-from-RAM routers, software is stored in flash memory and executed in RAM. In run-from-Flash routers, the software is both stored and executed in flash memory.

The Cisco 2500 series uses the run-from-Flash memory architecture. The major drawback of this is that a new IOS image cannot be loaded to the router while it is running the current IOS image. This would require the flash to overwrite itself, and the router would not operate. If the router has dual banks of flash, you can download the new software image into a different flash memory partition.

To download a new software image without using Dual Flash Bank memory, a boot-helper image is used. The boot-helper image is a small subset of Cisco IOS software that supports a limited subset of the interfaces and the WAN protocols. The boot-helper image boots the router using the ROM image. This enables the flash memory to be overwritten because the Cisco IOS software that is stored in flash memory is not being used to run the router.

17. A Cisco 3600 runs its image in _____.
   a. RAM
   b. ROM
   c. Flash
   d. TFTP server

The correct answer is A. The Cisco 7500 series routers run their image in RAM. Run-from-RAM routers store their IOS image in flash memory (usually in compressed form), and then load the image into RAM before it is used to operate the router. The running software image then resides in RAM, which enables new software images to be downloaded and copied over the existing software image stored in flash memory.

18. Which of the following is the correct numerical range for an extended access list?
   a. 1 to 99
   b. 100 to 199
   c. 800 to 899
   d. 900 to 999

The correct answer is B. An access list defined with a number ranging from 100 to 199 is an extended access list. An extended access list can be configured to be dynamic or static. Static is the default and can be changed using the keyword dynamic. Both static and dynamic access lists will be covered in detail later in this chapter.

An extended access list is used to permit or deny packets based on multiple factors (protocol, source IP address, destination IP address, precedence, TOS, and port number), providing much more granularity than a standard access list.

The extended access list permits logging, which creates an informational logging message about any packet that matches the list. This option is very useful when troubleshooting extended access lists.

Answer A is incorrect. An access list defined with a number ranging from 1 to 99 is a standard access list. A standard access list is used to permit or deny packets solely based on source IP address. The source address is the number of the network or host from which the packet is being sent.

The source address is followed by a wildcard mask, which is used to specify what bit positions are ignored and what positions must match. The wildcard mask is defined in more detail later in this chapter. This is a global configuration command.

Answer C is incorrect. An access list defined with a number ranging from 800 to 899 is an IPX-standard access list.

Answer D is incorrect. An access list defined with a number ranging from 900 to 999 is an IPX-extended access list.

19. If you had six voice calls with a duration of ten minutes each, how many Erlangs would that be?

    a. 6

    b. 1

    c. 60

    d. 30

The correct answer is B. An Erlang is a unit that expresses one hour of traffic on a trunk or trunk group. For example, six calls each of ten-minute duration equals one Erlang of traffic, while five one-hour duration calls equal five Erlangs of traffic.

20. In Figure 4-5, RouterA wants to deny all traffic from host 150.1.1.2 destined for PCA (152.1.1.2). Which of the following would accomplish this? (multiple answers)

    a. An inbound access list applied on the serial interface of RouterA

    b. An outbound access list applied to the Ethernet interface of RouterA

    c. An outbound access list applied on the serial interface of RouterA

    d. An inbound access list applied to the Ethernet interface of RouterA

The correct answers are A and B. There are two places that an access list could be applied on RouterA; an inbound access list could be applied on the serial interface or an outbound access list could be applied to the Ethernet interface. It is good design to apply the access lists closest to the traffic that will be denied.

Answers C and D are incorrect. When applying an access list to an interface, the user specifies whether the access list is applied to inbound or outbound or both traffic. The direction of traffic flow is relative to the router interface. So you need an inbound access list on the serial interface or an outbound access list on Ethernet interface.

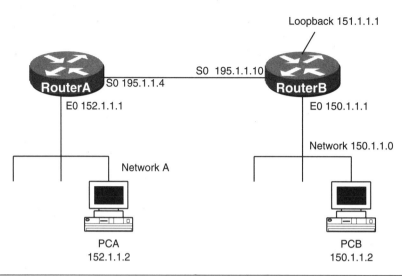

Figure 4-5 Network diagram

21. Which of the following is false regarding access lists?

    a. Access lists can be used to control access, policy routing, DDR, CAR, and IOS firewall by the time of day.

    b. The **access-class** command is used to create a temporary access list entry in a dynamic access list.

    c. The **ip access-group** command is used to permit or deny incoming or outgoing packets on a particular interface.

    d. Access list use wildcard masks.

Answer B is false. The **access-class** command is used to restrict incoming and outgoing VTY connections between a particular VTY line on a Cisco router and a specific address defined by the access list. This line configuration command applies a specific access list (1 to 99) to a VTY line. Incoming connects are restricted using the keyword **in** and outgoing connections are restricted using the keyword **out**.

The **access-enable** command is used to create a temporary access list entry in a dynamic access list based on predefined criteria. The host keyword tells the IOS only to allow access for the particular host that originated the telnet session. The timeout keyword specifies an idle timeout period. If the access list entry is not used within this period of time, the access entry is deleted. If the entry is deleted, the user will have to re-authenticate in order to gain access to the network.

Answer A is true. Time-of-day access lists, available in IOS 12.0, enable you to control access, policy routing, DDR, CAR, and IOS firewall by the time of day. The time range enables the network administrator to define when the permit or deny statements in the access list are in effect. Prior to this feature, access list statements were always in effect once they were applied. This new feature provides the administrator with greater flexibility in controlling resources.

To enable time-of-day access lists, you create a time range that defines specific times of the day and week. This range, which is identified by name, can then be referenced by a function (such as CAR), so that those time restrictions are imposed on the function itself.

Answer C is true. The **ip access-group** command is used to permit or deny incoming or outgoing packets on a particular interface based on criteria defined in the access list.

This interface configuration command applies a specific access list (1 to 199) to a router interface. Incoming packets are filtered using the keyword **in** and outgoing connections are filtered using the keyword **out**.

Answer D is true. A wildcard mask specifies which bits in an IP address should be ignored when comparing that address with another IP address. A 1 in the wildcard mask means to ignore that bit position when comparing to another IP address and a 0 specifies that the bit position must match.

22. Which of the following queuing methods are used on a Cisco router? (multiple answers)
    a. WFQ
    b. FIFO
    c. Priority queuing
    d. Cut-through queuing

The correct answers are A, B, and C. Cisco supports many queuing mechanisms including WFQ, FIFO, and priority queuing.

23. The following access list is configured on the router and applied to the serial interface using the command **ipx output-sap-filter 1000**. What will the access list prevent?

```
RouterB(config)#access-list 1000 deny -1 7
RouterB(config)#access-list 1000 permit -1
```

    a. The access list will prevent SAP entries for all network file servers from being sent.
    b. The access list will prevent SAP entries for all network print servers from being sent.
    c. Nothing—it is configured wrong; the permit statement will allow SAP entries.
    d. Both A and B

The correct answer is B. The syntax for an SAP access list is access list number, permit/deny, source network (a -1 signifies all networks), and the last field is service type. Two common IPX service types are NetWare file servers, specified by a 4, and NetWare print servers, specified by a 7. This access list will deny all network print server's SAPs from being sent.

Answer A is incorrect. In order to prevent file server SAPs from being sent, a 4 would need to be specified instead of a 7.

24. What will happen if an SAP update is received and the router does not have a route to the destination?

    a. The SAP entry will be added to the SAP table but not advertised.

    b. The SAP entry will be added to the SAP table.

    c. The router will not insert the entry in the SAP table.

    d. None of the above

The correct answer is C. If the router does not have a route to the destination when the SAP broadcast is received, it will not insert the SAP entry into the table.

25. How do you forward IPX/NetBIOS broadcast traffic across a router?

    a. Use an **ipx helper address**.

    b. Enable ipx-type-20 propagation.

    c. Use the command **ip forward UDP**.

    d. None of the above

The correct answer is B. NetBIOS over IPX uses type 20 propagation broadcast packets to get information about the named nodes on the network. By enabling type 20 packet propagation, IPX interfaces on the router may accept and forward type 20 propagation packets.

Answer A is incorrect. Routers normally block all broadcast requests and do not forward them to other network segments. The **ipx helper address** command can be used to enable the forwarding of broadcast messages (except type 20 broadcasts) to other networks and forward all other unrecognized broadcast messages.

26. The CPU utilization on your router is very high. You notice that the IP input process is using the majority of your CPU cycles. What is most likely the problem?

    a. A large number of packets are being process-switched.

    b. A large number of packets are being dropped.

    c. Packets are overflowing the buffers.

    d. None of the above

The correct answer is A. The IP input process deals with incoming IP frames that are process-switched. If you are seeing a large number of CPU cycles being used by this process, the router is process-switching a large number of packets. An IP frame will be processed-switched if it is a broadcast, is routed out the same interface it was received on, or if it is destined for the router itself (SNMP, telnet, or ping).

27. The serial interface is up, but the line protocol is down on an HDLC link. What is most likely the problem?

   a. Keepalives are not being received from the remote router.

   b. IP addresses are configured wrong.

   c. No clock is present.

   d. None of the above

The correct answer is A. The line protocol indicates whether the software processes that handle the line protocol consider the line usable (that is, whether keepalives are successful). The line protocol is goes down if you miss three keepalives.

28. You display the interface statistics with the **show interface** command, and notice a large number of output drops on the serial interface. What is most likely the problem?

   a. Packets are discarded because they exceed the medium's maximum packet size.

   b. The input rate to the serial interface exceeds the bandwidth available on the serial link.

   c. The serial receiver hardware was unable to hand received data to a hardware buffer because the input rate exceeded the receiver's capability to handle the data.

   d. An illegal sequence of one bits is received on a serial interface.

The correct answer is B. Output drops are seen when the router is attempting to hand off a packet to a transmit buffer but no buffers are available, which is most likely because the input rate to serial interface exceeds bandwidth available on serial link.

Answer A is incorrect. Giants are seen when packets are discarded because they exceed the medium's maximum packet size.

Answer C is incorrect. Overruns occur when the serial receiver hardware is unable to hand received data to a hardware buffer because the input rate exceeds the receiver's capability to handle the data.

Answer D is incorrect. Aborts occur when an illegal sequence of one bits is received on the serial interface.

29. Which of the following is not a valid VTP mode?

   a. Server

   b. Client

   c. Transparent

   d. Spanning

The correct answer is D. You can configure a switch to operate in server, client, or transparent VTP mode.

30. What is the purpose of the **ethernet-transit-oui** command?
   a. It specifies the OUI code used in the encapsulation of Ethernet Type II frames.
   b. It is used to identify the vendor.
   c. It specifies the OUI code used on the Ethernet LAN.
   d. None of the above

The correct answer is A. The ethernet-transit-oui command chooses the OUI code to be used in the encapsulation of Ethernet Type II frames and Ethernet SNAP frames across Token Ring networks. It also tells the router how to translate Token Ring frames into Ethernet frames. By default, the router uses the 0x0000F8 OUI when converting Ethernet Type II frames into Token Ring SNAP frames, and leaves the OUI as 0x000000 for Ethernet SNAP frames. So, the router knows whether a Token Ring SNAP frame should be converted back to Ethernet Type II or an Ethernet SNAP frame just by looking at the OUI in the Token Ring frame.

31. The command **multiring** all is used to _____.
   a. Enable multiple rings.
   b. Enable a routed protocol to enter an SRB environment.
   c. Enable SRB on Ethernet.
   d. None of the above

The correct answer is B. The **multiring all** command adds an RIF to IP packets going into the ring and deletes the RIF for packets leaving the ring. This enables a routed protocol to enter an SRB environment. This is necessary when the ring the router is attached to has embedded SRBs (bridging all protocols).

32. The following is the output from the **show process cpu** command. What do the first and second number mean in the five-second average?

```
CPU utilization for five seconds: 15% / 5%; one minute: 0%; five minutes: 0%
PID Runtime(ms) Invoked uSecs 5Sec 1Min 5Min TTY Process
 1 0 173 0 0.00% 0.00% 0.00% 0 Load Meter
 2 0 15 0 0.00% 0.00% 0.00% 0 TACACS+
 3 180 30 6000 0.24% 0.02% 0.00% 0 Check heaps
 4 0 2 0 0.00% 0.00% 0.00% 0 Pool Manager
 5 0 2 0 0.00% 0.00% 0.00% 0 Timers
```

   a. The first number is the instantaneous value and the second number is average total utilization during last five seconds.
   b. The first number is the average total utilization during last five seconds and the second number is the average utilization due to processor interrupts during last five seconds.

    c. The first number is the average total utilization during last five seconds and the second number is the instantaneous utilization.

    d. None of the above

The correct answer is B. The first number is the average total utilization during last five seconds and the second number is the average utilization due to processor interrupts during last five seconds. CPU interrupts are primarily caused by fast switching of traffic. Interrupts are also generated anytime a character is output from the console or auxiliary ports of a router. However, universal asynchronous receivers/transmitters (UARTs) are slow compared to the processing speed of the router, so it's not likely that console or auxiliary interrupts can cause a high CPU utilization on the router.

33. The network administrator has asked you to translate the unregistered IP addresses on the Ethernet network attached to RouterA to globally unique addresses before sending the packets out to the Internet (see Figure 4-6). Which of the following would you use to accomplish this?

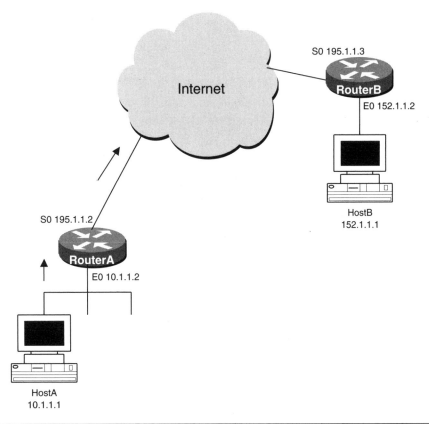

Figure 4-6   Network diagram

   a. An IP NAT inside source translation on RouterA
   b. An IP NAT inside source translation on RouterB
   c. An IP NAT outside source translation on RouterA
   d. An IP NAT outside source translation on RouterB

The correct answer is A. An IP NAT inside source translation would be used to translate the unregistered source address on Ethernet 0 to a globally unique address.

Answer B is incorrect. The translation needs to be done on RouterA, not RouterB.

Answers C and D are incorrect. The outside source address is used to translate the outside global address to an outside local address. This is often used in scenarios where overlapping occurs when an inside local address overlaps with an address of the destination that you are trying to reach.

34. In Figure 4-6, IP address 10.1.1.1 is considered the _____.
   a. Inside global address
   b. Inside local address
   c. Outside local address
   d. Outside global address

The correct answer is B. The inside local address is the IP address that is assigned to a host on the inside network, which will be translated. In most cases, this address is an unregistered IP address, meaning that it was not assigned by the Network Information Center (NIC).

Answer A is incorrect. The inside global address is the address that is used to represent one or more inside local IP addresses to the outside world. In most cases, this is an NIC-registered IP address.

Answer C is incorrect. The outside local address is an address of an outside host as it appears to the inside network. This is not necessarily a legitimate address; however, it is routable from the inside. In Figure 4-6, host address 152.1.1.1 is an outside local address.

Answer D is incorrect. The outside global address is an address assigned to a host on the outside network by the host's owner. The address was allocated from a globally routable address or network space.

35. Which of the following is false regarding dynamic inside source translation?
   a. Dynamic inside source translation establishes a mapping between a group of inside local addresses and a pool of global addresses.
   b. Unless overloading is used, you require a global IP address for each workstation that wants to communicate outside the private network.
   c. Dynamic address translation is more scalable and efficient than static translations.

   d. Outside users can establish a connection to inside addresses.

Answer D is false. Dynamic translation establishes a mapping between a group of inside local addresses and a pool of global addresses. This is very useful when you have a large group of unregistered users who want to access off-Net services.

Dynamic inside address translation dynamically translates an unregistered IP address to a registered IP address, using a predefined pool. This is a one-to-one relationship. As an outside connection is requested, an IP address is used from the pool. When the connection is finished, the globally significant IP address is released back into the pool, where it can be used for another connection.

Dynamic address translation is very efficient because the same global IP address can be used over and over as needed by multiple end stations. This is in contrast to the static translations where only one particular end station can use the global address.

Although dynamic address translation is more scalable, efficient, and simpler to administer, outside users cannot access inside addresses because there is no static mapping between IP address. After each session is closed, the global IP address is released back into the pool, where it can be used by other sessions. Each end station can and most likely will be mapped to a different global address when it opens a new connection. Therefore, it is impossible to reference a particular inside address with a global address.

36. In Figure 4-7, Company X has multiple FTP servers hanging off of RouterA. Your network administrator has asked you to use NAT to ensure that FTP connections are load balanced equally across both servers. Which of the following configurations would accomplish this?

   a. A rotary pool is used in conjunction with an inside destination translation on RouterA.

   b. Overload is used along in conjunction with an inside destination translation on RouterA.

   c. A rotary poll is used in conjunction with an outside destination translation on RouterA.

   d. None of the above—NAT cannot be used for load balancing connections.

The correct answer is A. A rotary pool used in conjunction with an inside destination translation on RouterA can be used as a means to provide load sharing among multiple highly utilized hosts. Figure 4-8 illustrates how this would work. Company X has multiple FTP servers that are accessed by customers to download software. The NAT translation is transparent to the user; they simply FTP to the virtual IP address 152.1.1.10.

When RouterA receives a packet destined for the virtual IP address, it translates the destination address to the first FTP server. When the next FTP connection is established

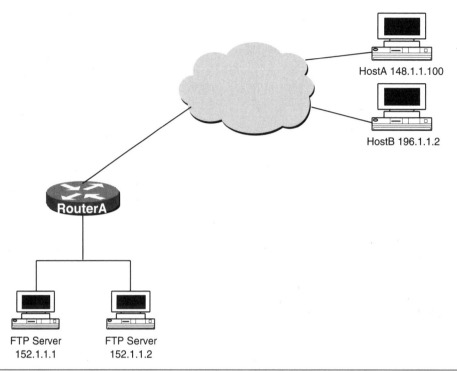

HostA 148.1.1.100

HostB 196.1.1.2

RouterA

FTP Server
152.1.1.1

FTP Server
152.1.1.2

Figure 4-7   Network diagram

to the virtual IP address, RouterA translates the destination address to the second FTP server. These translations occur in a round-robin fashion, providing equal load balancing across multiple FTP servers.

RouterA takes the following steps when translating rotary address:

1. Host A (148.1.1.100) establishes a connection to virtual host 152.1.1.10.

2. RouterA receives the packet destined for the virtual host 152.1.1.10, and translates the destination address to next real host from the pool: in this case, FTP server 152.1.1.1.

3. FTP server 152.1.1.1 receives the packet and responds.

4. RouterA receives the response packet from FTP server 152.1.1.1 and performs an NAT table lookup using the inside local address and port number, and the outside address and port number as the key.

5. The RouterA then translates the source address to the address of the virtual host and forwards the packet.

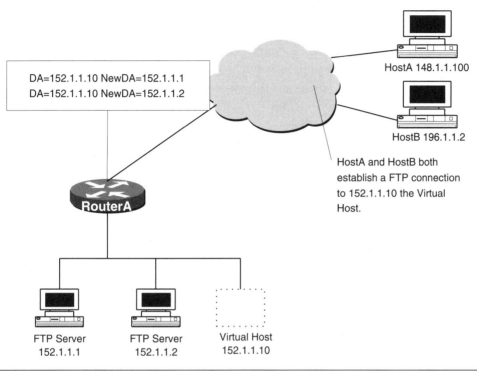

DA=152.1.1.10 NewDA=152.1.1.1
DA=152.1.1.10 NewDA=152.1.1.2

HostA 148.1.1.100

HostB 196.1.1.2

HostA and HostB both
establish a FTP connection
to 152.1.1.10 the Virtual
Host.

RouterA

FTP Server
152.1.1.1

FTP Server
152.1.1.2

Virtual Host
152.1.1.10

Figure 4-8 IP NAT rotary pool

6. Host B (196.1.1.2) establishes a connection to virtual host 152.1.1.10.

7. RouterA receives the packet destined for the virtual host 152.1.1.10, and translates the destination address to next real host from the pool: in this case, FTP server 152.1.1.2.

8. RouterA receives the response packet from FTP server 152.1.1.2 and performs the NAT lookup, translates the source address to the virtual address, and forwards the packet.

37. Which of the following is used on a Cisco router to prevent global synchronization from occurring?

   a. FIFO

   b. WFQ

   c. WRED

   d. PQ

The correct answer is C. Global synchronization is the event when congestion occurs in the network and multiple Transmission Control Protocol (TCP) streams reduce their transmission rates in response. As congestion is reduced, the TCP hosts increase their transmission rates until congestion is reach. When congestion occurs, the TCP hosts reduce their transmission rate again. This synchronization causes waves of congestion followed by periods during which the transmission link is not fully utilized.

A congestion avoidance algorithm called weighted random early detect (WRED) can be used to alleviate this problem. WRED is used to selectively discard low-priority traffic when the interface becomes congested. WRED predicts congestion and then avoids it by dropping packets from a single TCP connection. Because the packets are being dropped in a controlled manner, global synchronization can be avoided.

Without WRED, output buffers fill during periods of congestion. This results in queue tail drops where all packets are dropped for the tail of the queue. Because the packets are dropped all at once, multiple TCP streams are affected. This causes multiple streams to reduce their transmission rate. The streams then increase their transmission rates until congestion is reach again, causing the buffers to overfill and tail drops to happen again. This result in periods of congestion followed by periods when all of the TCP sessions slow and the link is not fully utilized.

38. The output from the **show buffers** command on the router indicates large numbers in the trims and created fields for the large buffer pool. What should you do?

   a. Configure priority queuing.

   b. Increase the maximum number of free system buffers allowed.

   c. Prevent the router from trimming the buffers.

   d. Increase the amount of memory on the router.

The correct answer is B. When the number of available buffers in the free list falls below the configured minimum number, the router attempts to create new buffers. The created field indicates the number of buffers that the router created.

The router is configured to have a maximum number of free buffers available. If the number of free buffers available exceeds this value, the router will trim the additional buffers. The trims field is incremented each time this occurs. You can reduce the number of creates and trims by increasing the maximum number of free system buffers allowed.

39. Which of the following is true regarding TACACS+? (multiple answers)

   a. It is Cisco proprietary.

   b. TACACS+ encrypts the entire body of the packet.

   c. TACACS+ uses UDP.

   d. TACACS+ only supports TCP/IP.

The correct answers are A and B. TACACS+ is a Cisco proprietary protocol that provides authentication and authorization support. TACACS+ is similar to RADIUS in the services that are provided; however, the implementation is quite different.

TACACS+ uses TCP as its transport layer, whereas RADIUS uses UDP. Another key difference is that RADIUS encrypts only the password in the access-request packet from the client to the server. The remainder of the packet is in the clear. TACACS+ encrypts the entire body of the packet but leaves a standard TACACS+ header. TACACS+ supports TCP/IP, AppleTalk remote access (ARA), NetBIOS frame protocol control, Novell Asynchronous Services Interface (NASI), and packet assembler/disassembler (PAD) connection.

40. Which of the following configurations would give telnet traffic higher priority than FTP traffic?

    a. `priority-list 1 protocol ip low tcp telnet`

    b. `priority-list 1 protocol ip medium tcp telnet`

    c. `priority-list 1 protocol ip normal tcp telnet`
       `priority-list 2 protocol ip low tcp ftp`
       `priority-list 2 protocol ip low tcp ftp-data`

    d. None of the above

The correct answer is B. Cisco's priority queuing mechanism enables traffic control based on protocol or interface type. There are four priority queues—high, medium, normal, and low—listed in order from highest to lowest priority. Datagrams that are not classified by the priority list mechanism are assigned to the normal queue. Answer B sets telnet traffic to the medium priority. By default, all other traffic will be assigned to the normal priority; therefore, telnet traffic will have higher priority than FTP traffic.

Answer A is incorrect. By default, FTP traffic will be set to normal priority, which is higher than low priority, which telnet is set to.

Answer C is incorrect. An interface can only be configured for one priority group.

41. Based on the following configuration, what percentage of bandwidth will telnet traffic receive if no other traffic is present in queue 1?

```
queue-list 1 protocol ip 1 tcp www
queue-list 1 protocol ip 2 tcp telnet
queue-list 1 queue 1 byte-count 3000
queue-list 1 queue 2 byte-count 3000
```

    a. 30 percent

    b. 20 percent

    c. 50 percent

    d. 100 percent

The correct answer is C. Custom queuing enables the user to define up to 16 traffic queues. The byte count indicates how many bytes can be transmitted from the queue before the next queue is serviced. Because the byte counts are the same, each queue will receive 50 percent of the bandwidth.

42. Based on the following configuration, what percentage of bandwidth will FTP traffic receive?

```
queue-list 1 protocol ip 2 tcp www
queue-list 1 protocol ip 3 tcp telnet
queue-list 1 queue 2 byte-count 3000
queue-list 1 queue 3 byte-count 1500
```

   a. 25 percent

   b. 0 percent

   c. 50 percent

   d. None of the above because FTP is not defined in a queue list

The correct answer is A. By default, all packets that do not match the any of the allocations specified by the queue list will be placed in queue 1. So FTP traffic will be placed in queue 1. Because the default byte count for a queue is 1,500, FTP will receive 25 percent of the bandwidth. WWW traffic will receive 50 percent and telnet traffic will receive the remaining 25 percent.

43. Which of the following is false regarding queuing?

   a. Queuing allows congestion control by determining the order in which packets are sent out of an interface.

   b. With FIFO, packets are sent out of the interface in the same order that they arrive.

   c. WFQ is the default queuing mechanism on interfaces running at speeds of 2 Mbps and below.

   d. With custom queuing, care must be taken so that routing protocol updates are not starved by other protocol packets in queue 1.

Answer D is false. In custom queuing queue, number 0 is reserved by IOS for keepalives, signaling, and other system critical functions. It is serviced before any other queues 1 through 16 are processed.

43. Based on the following configuration, what best describes the action the router will take?

```
interface Ethernet0/0
ip address 135.25.7.2 255.255.255.224
rate-limit input 96000 16000 16000 conform-action transmit exceed-action drop
```

    a. Interface Ethernet 0/0 will limit input traffic to 96,000 bps.

    b. Interface Ethernet 0/0 will limit input traffic to 112,000 bps.

    c. Interface Ethernet 0/0 will limit input traffic to 112,000 bps.

    d. Interface Ethernet 0/0 will limit input traffic to 96,000 bps.

The correct answer is A. Committed access rate (CAR) uses a token bucket algorithm to accurately measure network traffic. As each packet has the CAR limit applied, tokens are removed from the bucket in accordance with the byte size of the packet. Tokens are replenished at regular intervals, in accordance with the configured committed rate. The maximum number of tokens that can ever be in the bucket is determined by the normal burst size. Now, if a packet arrives and the available tokens are less than the byte size of the packet, the extended burst comes into play. If there is no extended burst capability, which can be achieved by setting the extended burst value equal to the normal burst value, then the operation is in a standard token bucket (that is, the packet will be dropped if tokens are unavailable). However, if extended burst capability is configured (that is, the extended burst is greater than the normal burst), then the stream is allowed to borrow more tokens. In this example, because there is no extended burst capability (extended burst value equal to the normal burst value), the input will be rate limited to 96,000 bps.

45. When implementing VoIP, it is important to minimize the end-to-end delay within a network. Which of the following causes delay in a network? (multiple answers)

    a. Serialization delay

    b. Propagation delay

    c. Jitter

    d. Echo

The correct answers are A and B. Packet delay can cause voice quality degradation if the end-to-end voice latency is too high, or even packet loss if the delay is variable. If the end-to-end voice latency becomes too long (250 ms, for example), the conversation begins to sound like a bad cell phone connection. There are several types of delay that you need to be aware of when calculating your delay budget. The first is propagation delay, which is the length of time it takes information to travel the distance of the line. This period is mostly determined by the speed of light; therefore, the propagation delay factor is not affected by the networking technology in use. The next type of delay is serialization delay, which is the amount of time it takes a router to process a voice packet, compress the packet, and move the packet to the output queue.

Answer C is incorrect. Jitter is delta between the end-to-end delay of two voice packets. If the end-to-end delay, the time it takes for a packet to reach the receiving endpoint after being transmitted, for packet x is 10 and packet $x + 1$ is 20, the jitter is 10.

Answer D is incorrect. Echo is when you hear your own voice in the telephone receiver while you are talking. Some echo is important; when timed properly, it is reassuring to the speaker. However, if the echo exceeds approximately 25 ms, it can be distracting and cause breaks in the conversation.

46. A Cisco router can network boot using which of the following protocols? (multiple answers)

    a. TFTP

    b. RCP

    c. MOP

    d. IGMP

The correct answers are A, B, and C. A Cisco router can boot from a server using the Trivial File Transfer Protocol (TFTP), the DEC Maintenance Operation Protocol (MOP), or the Remote Copy Protocol (RCP) across any of the supported media type.

47. In the following configuration, the router is set to timestamp all long messages and the current date and time is configured on the router. However, the log files are not timestamped with the correct time. What is the problem?

```
logging buffered
service timestamps log
```

    a. NTP is not configured.

    b. The system is using the uptime as the clock reference.

    c. Logging timestamps should be added to the configuration.

    d. None of the above

The correct answer is B. By default, the service timestamp uses the uptime as the clock reference. To have it use the current time, use service timestamps log datetime.

48. Which of the following configurations enables read-only SNMP access from host 192.1.1.1?

    a. `snmp-server community cisco ro 192.1.1.1`

    b. `snmp-server community cisco ro`
       `snmp-server 192.1.1.1`

    c. `snmp-server community cisco ro 99`
       `access-list 99 permit 192.1.1.1 0.0.0.0`

    d. `snmp-server community cisco ro`
       `snmp-server 99`
       `access-list 99 permit 192.1.1.1 0.0.0.0`

The correct answer is C. The Simple Network Management Protocol (SNMP) is made up of three components: an SNMP manager, an SNMP agent, and a management information base (MIB). SNMP provides a message format for sending and receiving information between the manager and the agent. The manager is typically part of a Network Management System (NMS) such as HP OpenView or NetView 6K. The agent and MIB reside on the router or device that will be managed.

The agent contains the MIB variables, which the SNMP manager can request or change. The manager can request a value from an agent (Read\Get) or change a value on an agent (Write\Set).

The question specifies that we only want to permit server 192.1.1.1 SNMP read access.

The first step is to specify a community string and permit read-only access. The community string is used as a password to permit access to the agent on the router. Because we only want to permit access from server 192.1.1.1, an access list is defined. Apply this to the SNMP community string.

49. Which of the following configurations sets a login password on the console port of the router?

    a. `line con 0`
       `password cisco`

    b. `line con 0`
       `login password cisco`

    c. `line con 0`
       `login`
       `password cisco`

    d. You cannot set a password on a console port. Passwords can only be set on AUX and VTY ports.

The correct answer is C. In order to do password checking on a console port, login must be enabled and a password must be set.

50. How can you configure the router for the first time? (multiple answers)

    a. SNMP

    b. CLI

    c. The **setup** command facility

    d. SLARP

The correct answers are B, C, and D. A router can be configured for the first time using the command-line interface (CLI), the **setup** command facility, or through SLARP. SNMP cannot be used because the router has no configuration information on it.

51. Which of the following is not a valid enable password?

    a. good4now

    b. two words

    c. 1moretime

    d. CiScO

Answer C is correct. An enable password can consist of upper- and lowercase alphanumeric characters including spaces, which are valid password characters. However, a password cannot have a numeric value as the first character.

52. You have a subset of users who do not have enable access to the router but need to be able to view the configuration for troubleshooting purposes. Which of the following commands will enable the users to view the entire configuration?

    a. `privilege exec level 2 show running-config`

    b. `privilege exec level 2 write terminal`

    c. `privilege exec level 2 show startup-config`

    d. All of the above

Answer C is correct. The **write terminal** and **show running-config** commands will only display the commands that the current user is able to modify (all the commands at or below the user's current privilege level). It will not display any of the commands above the user's current privilege level. So answers A and B would only enable the user to see the part of the configuration that they have access to change. The **startup-config** command will enable the user to view the entire startup configuration.

53. When RouterA pings address 192.1.1.1, the ping fails. The following is the output from the **debug frame-relay packet** command on RouterA. Based on the information provided, what is most likely the problem?

```
Serial0/0:Encaps failed--no map entry link 7(IP)
Serial0/0:Encaps failed--no map entry link 7(IP)
Serial0/0:Encaps failed--no map entry link 7(IP)
Serial0/0:Encaps failed--no map entry link 7(IP)
```

    a. RouterA does not have a route to network 192.1.1.1.

    b. Frame relay inverse ARP is disabled.

    c. The wrong encapsulation type is being used on the interface.

    d. None of the above

Answer B is correct. The output of the failed ping shows that the encapsulation has failed on interface $S^0/0$. This is caused because there is no frame relay map entry for the IP address.

54. Based on the following output of the **show version** command, how much memory is on this router?

```
cisco 4700 (R4K) processor (revision C) with 32768K/4096K bytes of memory.
Processor board ID 03386984
R4700 processor, Implementation 33, Revision 1.0 (Level 2 Cache)
G.703/E1 software, Version 1.0.
Bridging software.
SuperLAT software copyright 1990 by Meridian Technology Corp).
X.25 software, Version 2.0, NET2, BFE and GOSIP compliant.
TN3270 Emulation software (copyright 1994 by TGV Inc).
2 Ethernet/IEEE 802.3 interface(s)
2 Token Ring/IEEE 802.5 interface(s)
4 Serial network interface(s)
128K bytes of non-volatile configuration memory.
4096K bytes of processor board System flash (Read/Write)
4096K bytes of processor board Boot flash (Read/Write)
```

  a. 32M of main memory and 4M of shared memory

  b. 36M of main memory and 4M of shared memory

  c. 36M of main memory and 4M of flash

  d. 32M of shared memory and 4M of flash

Answer A is correct. The output from the show version command indicates 32MB of main memory and 4M of shared memory (indicated by "32768/4096 K bytes of memory" line at the top of the output). There is also 4M of Flash (see the bottom line of the output).

55. What does it mean when a BRI interface is spoofing?

  a. The interface is configured wrong.

  b. The SPID is configured wrong.

  c. The interface is awaiting interesting packets in order to place a call.

  d. The interface is administratively down.

Answer C is correct. When an ISDN interface is spoofing, it is awaiting interesting traffic in order to place a call. The D channel is active, but no layer connection has been established.

56. What is the difference between Rxboot and BootROM?

  a. Rxboot is a full set image, whereas BootROM is a subset image

  b. Rxboot is used on higher-end platforms, whereas BootROM is used on the lower-end platforms

  c. Rxboot is a subset image, whereas BootROM is full image.

  d. None of the above

Answer C is correct. Rxboot is used in Cisco 2500 family of routers. It is a subset image to boot up the router in case the system image (flash) fails. BootROM is a full image used in the high-end routers like the 7500 in case the system image (flash) fails.

57. How do you configure the router so that it records the date and time of the last configuration change?

    a. Enable the service configuration change.

    b. Enable user level access.

    c. Ensure that the clock is set on the router.

    d. None of the above

The correct answer is C. As long as the clock is set on the router, the date and time will be recorded for each configuration change.

58. Based on the following output from the **show interface** command,, what is the five-minute outbound utilization of the interface?

```
TokenRing0 is up, line protocol is up
 Hardware is TMS380, address is 0006.f4c5.df18 (bia 0006.f4c5.df18)
 Description: Lab Inside Ring #59
 Internet address is 164.120.59.67/24
 MTU 4464 bytes, BW 16000 Kbit, DLY 630 usec, rely 255/255, load 64/255
 Encapsulation SNAP, loopback not set, keepalive set (10 sec)
 ARP type: SNAP, ARP Timeout 04:00:00
 Ring speed: 16 Mbps
 Multiring node, Source Route Transparent Bridge capable
 Group Address: 0x00000000, Functional Address: 0x08000000
 Ethernet Transit OUI: 0x000000
 Last input 00:00:00, output 00:00:00, output hang never
 Last clearing of "show interface" counters never
 Queueing strategy: fifo
```

    a. 50 percent

    b. 25 percent

    c. 64 percent

    d. 100 percent

Answer B is correct. The load is the five-minute outbound utilization of the interface expressed as a fraction of 255. In this example, the load is 64/255 or 25 percent.

59. When the established keyword is used in conjunction with an access list, a match occurs if the _____.

    a. TCP datagram has the SYN bit set.

    b. TCP datagram has the SYN or ACK bits set.

    c. TCP datagram has the ACK or RST bits set.

    d. TCP datagram has the SYN or RST bits set.

The correct answer is C. The **extended access-list** command can be used to permit any packets returning to machines from already established connections. With the established keyword, a match occurs if the TCP datagram has the acknowledgment (ACK) or reset (RST) bits set.

60. Which of the following access list entries will permit TCP connections to host 192.1.1.1 for port numbers greater than 1,023?

    a. `access-list 101 permit tcp any 192.1.1.1 0.0.0.0 gt 1023`

    b. `access-list 101 permit tcp any 192.1.1.1 0.0.0.0 eq 1023`

    c. `access-list 101 permit tcp any 192.1.1.1 0.0.0.0 lt 1023`

    d. `access-list 101 permit tcp any 192.1.1.1 0.0.0.0 neq1023`

The correct answer is A. When the gt keyword is used, the router will match only packets with a greater port number.

Answer B is incorrect. When the eq keyword is used, the router will match only packets on a given port number.

Answer C is incorrect. When the lt keyword is used, the router will only match packets with a lower port number.

Answer D is incorrect. When the neq keyword is used, the router will only match packets not on the given port.

61. Which of the following commands will encrypt the enable password on the router?

    a. enable password 0 test

    b. enable password 7 test

    c. service password-encryption

    d. None of the above

The correct answer is C. The **service password-encryption** command encrypts all passwords in the router configuration.

Answer B is incorrect. An encryption type can be specified in the **enable password** command. Currently, the only encryption type supported by Cisco is type 7. If you specify encryption type, the next argument you supply must be an encrypted password (a password already encrypted by a Cisco router). This would be a password that you cut and pasted out of another router configuration.

If you specify an encryption type and then enter a clear text password, you will not be able to reenter enable mode on the router. The 7 indicates to the router that the password already has been encrypted. So when you enter your password, it will execute the encryption algorithm that you entered and compare it with the password in the command. Because the router thinks this is also encrypted, the comparison will fail and you will not be able to gain access to the router using the password that you entered.

Answer A is incorrect. The 0 specifies that the password is unencrypted. This is command that should be used if you are entering a clear text password.

62. What registry value is used to cause the router to reboot without loading the startup configuration?

    a. 0x2102

    b. 0x2142

    c. 0x2101

    d. None of the above

The correct answer is B. A Cisco router has a 16-bit register known as the virtual configuration register. This register resides in NVRAM. When bit 6 is set to 1 (0x2142), the router will ignore the contents of NVRAM when it boots. This is the bit that we set when doing password recovery.

63. Which of the following is not a valid way to configure a new router?

    a. Use the CLI.

    b. Boot the configuration from a server using BOOTP and SLARP.

    c. Use the setup dialog.

    d. SNMP

The correct answer is D. A new router has no configuration information on it, like an IP address or community strings, so SNMP cannot be used to configure it. The router can be configured via CLI, BOOTP, or setup dialog.

64. Which of the following is false regarding ED releases of IOS software?

    a. There are four types of ED releases.

    b. ED releases are vehicles that bring new development to the marketplace.

    c. ED maintenance releases do not accept the addition of features or platforms.

    d. ED releases are generally not as stable as main releases.

Answer C is false. Each ED maintenance release includes not only bug fixes, but also a set of new features, new platform support, and general enhancements to protocols and the Cisco IOS infrastructure.

Answer A is true. There are four types of ED releases, each with a slightly different release model and life cycle milestones. The ED releases can be classified as the following:

- Consolidated Technology Early Deployment (CTED) releases

- Specific Technology Early Deployment (STED) releases

- Specific Market Early Deployment (SMED) releases

- Short-lived Early Deployment releases, also known as X Releases (XED)

Answer B is true. Unlike main Cisco IOS releases, ED releases are vehicles that bring new development to the marketplace.

Answer D is true. Because ED releases added additional features and functionality, they are generally not as stable as main line releases. Cisco IOS main releases seek greater stability and quality. For that reason, main releases do not accept the addition of features or platforms.

65. In IOS version 12.0(1), what does the number in parentheses stand for?
   a. The main release number
   b. The version number
   c. The maintenance release number
   d. The ED number

The correct answer is C. The number in parentheses is the maintenance release number. So IOS version 12.0(1) is the first maintenance release for the main line release 12.0.

66. Which of the following is false regarding loopback interfaces?
   a. Loopback interfaces are always up unless the router goes down.
   b. Loopback interfaces are often used by BGP for peering sessions.
   c. If a loopback is configured with an IP address, the router will use this address as the router ID even if other interfaces have higher IP addresses.
   d. OSPF will use the first loopback interface configured as its router ID.

Answer D is false. OSPF automatically prefers a loopback interface over any other kind, and it chooses the highest IP address among all loopback interfaces in the router, not necessarily the first.

Answer A is true. Because loopback interfaces are virtual and not tied to any physical media, they are always up unless the router itself is down.

Answer B is true. Interior Border Gateway Protocol (IBGP) peers often use loopback interfaces. The advantage of using loopback interfaces is that they eliminate a dependency of a physical interface being up. In most cases, the router will have multiple paths to reach a peer address. If the BGP peer is tied to a physical interface and that interface goes down, the peer session is down. By tying the peer address to a loopback interface, the peer session will remain active as long as the router can reach that address.

Answer C is true. If a loopback interface is configured with an IP address, the router will use this IP address as its router ID, even if other interfaces have larger IP addresses. Because loopback interfaces never go down, greater stability in the routing table is achieved.

67. What is the significance of SC0 on a Catalyst 5500?

    a. SC0 is an internal logical interface used to telnet into the Catalyst for configuration and monitoring.

    b. SC0 is the interface used to provide trunking between Catalyst switches.

    c. SC0 is used to provide port security.

    d. None of the above

The correct answer is A. The SC0 interface is an internal logical interface on the switch and is accessible via any of the physical ports. Before you can telnet to the switch or use Simple Network Management Protocol (SNMP) to manage the switch, you must assign an IP address to either the in-band (SC0) logical interface or the management Ethernet (ME1) interface.

68. Which of the following statements is false regarding a Catalyst switch?

    a. After the Catalyst has been reset, all ports are defined to be on a single VLAN: VLAN 100.

    b. The Catalyst will automatically sense that an active LAN is connected to one of its ports and set the corresponding port parameters correctly.

    c. The Catalyst switch must have a domain name before it can use VLAN numbers other than 1.

    d. A Catalyst switch can be configured to block input to an Ethernet port when the MAC address of a station attempting to access the port is different from the configured MAC address.

Answer A is false. When the Catalyst first powered on, it is in a state where all ports are in VLAN 1.

Answer B is true. The Catalyst acts as a large multiport LAN switch. The Catalyst will automatically sense that an active LAN is connected to one of its ports and set the corresponding port parameters correctly.

Answer C is true. When a Catalyst switch is first powered on all of its ports are assigned to VLAN 1. The Catalyst switch must have a domain name before it can use VLAN numbers other than 1.

Answer D is true. Catalyst Media Access Control (MAC) address security enables the Catalyst switch to block input to an Ethernet port when the MAC address of a station attempting to access the port is different from the configured MAC address. When a port receives a frame, the Catalyst compares the source address of that frame to the secure source address learned or configured for the port. By default, when port security is enabled, the Catalyst will learn the first device that attaches to the port; this will be the MAC address that the Catalyst will permit. When a source address change occurs, the port is disabled, and the LED for that port turns orange. When the port is re-enabled, the port LED turns green. If the MAC address is not given, the command turns on learning mode so that the first MAC address seen on the port becomes the secure MAC address.

69. When configuring a PRI interface on a Cisco router, which interface is the D-channel?

    a. S0:0

    b. S0:24

    c. S0:23

    d. None of the above

The correct answer is C. When configuring a Primary Rate Interface (PRI), you must first define a T1 controller interface and specify the proper T1 framing and line coding. The PRI gets configured as a serial interface:23, specifying the D channel of the PRI interface.

70. How do you perform password recovery on a Catalyst switch?

    a. Change the configuration register to ignore NVRAM.

    b. Enter the break character within 30 seconds.

    c. The password on the Catalyst is not valid for the first 30 seconds after reload, so you can log on and change it.

    d. None of the above

The correct answer is C. The enable password on a Catalyst switch is not valid for the first 30 seconds after reload. To change the password, perform the following steps:

 NOTE You must complete these steps within 30 seconds of reloading the switch.

1. Attach a terminal or PC running a terminal emulation program to the console port of the switch. Set the terminal speed to 9,600 baud rate, no parity, eight data bits, and one stop bit.

2. Power the switch off and then on.

3. Press ENTER at the password prompt to enter a null password.

4. Type enable at the prompt to enter enable mode.

5. Press ENTER at the password prompt to enter a null password.

6. Change the password using the **set password** command or the **set enable pass** command.

71. How can you establish inter-VLAN communication?
    a. Use ISL.
    b. Use VTP.
    c. Use RTP.
    d. None of the above—inter-VLAN communication is not allowed.

The correct answer is A. To allow data to traverse between two VLANs (or broadcast domains), a layer 3 device must be used to route between the VLANs. To accomplish this, an ISL trunk is often configured between the switch and a router. VLAN-trunking enables 100-Mbps Fast Ethernet or 1,000-Mbps Gigabit Ethernet interfaces to place a tag on the packet that identifies the VLAN to which the packet belongs. This enables packets from multiple VLANs to be sent on the same interface, while still maintaining separation. When the other end of the Inter-Switch Link (ISL) trunk receives this tagged packet, it will place it in the correct VLAN.

72. What is the purpose of the range of MAC addresses assigned to the supervisor on a Catalyst? (multiple answers)
    a. It is used as the VLAN ID.
    b. It is used as the bridge ID for the box.
    c. It is used for the IP address of the SC0 interface.
    d. It is used for ISL connection.

The correct answers are B and C. The MACs on each port are used for bridge port IDs for spanning tree. The range of MACs on the supervisor is used to identify the bridge ID for the box. The last MAC in the range is used for the IP address for SC0.

73. What is the IOS command to create a shortcut so that you can type "sr" instead of "show ip route"?
    a. router(config)# ip alias exec sr show ip route
    b. router(config)#alias exec sr show ip route
    c. router(config)# shortcut exec sr show ip route
    d. router(config)# ip shortcut exec sr show ip route

The correct answer is B. You can create aliases for commonly used or complex commands. The format of the **alias** command is alias keyword, followed by where the command is issued (exec, configuration, or interface), followed by the name given to the shortcut followed lastly by the actual command.

74. Which of the following is true regarding a VLAN? (multiple answers)
    a. A VLAN is an administratively defined broadcast domain.
    b. Each port in a VLAN is in its own collision domain.
    c. All end stations in the same VLAN must be attached to the same switch.
    d. Each port in a VLAN is in its own broadcast domain.

The correct answers are A and B. A VLAN is an administratively defined broadcast domain. This means all end stations that reside in a common VLAN will receive broadcast packets that are sent by other end stations that reside in the same VLAN. Each port in VLAN is in its own collision domain.

Answer C is incorrect. One of the main advantages of VLAN technology is its capability to have interfaces on different switches as part of the same VLAN.

Answer D is incorrect. Each port in a VLAN is in its own collision domain, not broadcast domain. The entire VLAN is the broadcast domain.

75. By default, on a Catalyst switch all ports are _____. (multiple answers)
   a. Disabled
   b. In VLAN1
   c. In a single broadcast domain
   d. In a single collision domain

The correct answers are B and C. By default, all ports on a Catalyst switch are in a single VLAN (VLAN1), which is a single broadcast domain.

Answer A is incorrect. All ports on a Catalyst switch are enabled by default.

Answer D is incorrect. Each physical port on the switch is in its own collision domain.

76. You have just converted all of your workstations connected to your Catalyst for DHCP. What must you do to the switch interfaces connecting to the workstations to ensure that the DHCP requests don't time out? (multiple answers)
   a. Turn on port fast.
   b. Turn off trunking.
   c. Turn off port fast.
   d. Turn on auto negotiation.

The correct answers are A and B. Connectivity delays can occur through a switch when workstations first come online. It can take close to a minute before a switch will start servicing a directly connected workstation. Because the DHCP client software is not persistent during the startup procedure, the clients give up trying to connect to a server before the switch has even allowed traffic to pass through the switch to the client.

The features in the Catalyst that cause this initial delay are Spanning Tree Protocol (STP), EtherChannel negotiation, trunking negotiation, and link speed/duplex negotiation between the switch and the workstation. To reduce this delay, port fast should be enabled. Port fast speeds up STP by immediately moving to the forwarding state, without going through the blocking, listening, or learning states. Trunking can also be turned off to reduce delay.

77. You issue a **show port** command on a Catalyst switch and notice that you have a large number of delay exceeded errors. What is most likely the problem?

   a. This is an indication that the receive buffer is getting full.

   b. A device connected to this port is jabbering.

   c. This is an indication that the send buffer is getting full.

   d. None of the above

The correct answer is B. A delay exceed error occurs when the transmitting MAC waits too long for traffic on the network to stop before transmitting. The switch drops the packet and goes to the next one. A high number of delay exceeded errors is an indication of a cable problem or that another device on the network connected to this port is jabbering.

Answer A is incorrect. A receive error counter indicates that the receive buffer is getting full.

78. What is the maximum diameter of a Catalyst network with 10M or higher links?

   a. 4 hops

   b. 5 hops

   c. 7 hops

   d. 12 hops

The correct answer is C. The maximum diameter is the maximum number of bridge hops between any two end stations in the layer 2 network. The maximum diameter for network with 10M bits links or higher is 7.

79. What command would you use on a Catalyst switch to erase all the configuration information stored in NVRAM?

   a. write erase reload

   b. clear configuration

   c. clear configuration all

   d. clear NVRAM

The correct answer is C. The **clear configuration all** command deletes all modules and system information stored in NVRAM on a Catalyst switch.

80. When a Catalyst switch transfers frames between ports without buffering the entire frame in memory, it is operating in what mode?

   a. Store-and-forward mode

   b. Fast-switching mode

   c. Process-switching mode

   d. Cut-through mode

The correct answer is D. In cut-through mode, the Catalyst transfers non-broadcast packets between ports without buffering the entire frame into memory. Instead, when a port on the Catalyst that is operating in cut-through mode receives the first few bytes of a frame, it analyzes the packet header to determine the destination of the frame and establishes a connection between the input and output ports.

Answer A is incorrect. Store-and-forward mode is the traditional mode of operation for a bridge. In store-and-forward mode, the port adapter reads the entire frame into memory and then determines whether the frame should be forwarded. At this point, the frame is also examined for any errors (frames with errors are not forwarded). If the frame contains no errors, it is sent to the destination port for forwarding.

81. In which VTP mode can you create or delete VLANs?

    a. Active

    b. Server

    c. Spanning

    d. Client

The correct answer is B. In VTP server mode, you can create, modify, and delete VLANs. VTP servers advertise their VLAN configuration to other switches in the same VTP domain and synchronize their VLAN configuration with other switches based on advertisements received over trunk links. VTP server is the default mode.

Answers A and C are incorrect. Active and spanning are not VTP modes.

Answer D is incorrect. In VTP client mode, you cannot create, change, or delete VLANs on a VTP client.

82. Which of the following interface IP addresses would be used as the OSPF router ID if there were two serial interfaces, one Ethernet, and two loopback interfaces configured on a router?

    a. The interface with the highest IP address

    b. The interface with the lowest IP address

    c. The loopback interface with the highest IP address

    d. The loopback interface with the lowest IP address

The correct answer is C. The router ID is the IP address of the loopback interface. If no loopback is configured, the router ID is the highest IP address on the router.

83. Three routers running OSPF are connected via Ethernet. How can you ensure that RouterA becomes the designated router (DR) for the network?

    a. Set the ip ospf priority to 0 on RouterA.

    b. Set the ip ospf priority to 0 on RouterB and RouterC.

    c. Set the standby priority to 100 on RouterA.

    d. None of the above—a DR is not elected on an Ethernet network.

The correct answer is B. The router with the highest priority will be elected the DR; if a tie occurs, the router with the highest router ID is selected. The router ID is the IP address of the loopback interface. If no loopback is configured, the router ID is the highest IP address on the router. The router priority can be configured on the router interface with the **ip ospf priority** command. If the ospf priority is set to zero, the router is cannot become the DR. So by setting the opsf priority to zero on RouterB and RouterC, we ensure that RouterA becomes the DR for the network.

84. Which of the following is false regarding VTP pruning?

    a. VLAN 1 through 1,000 can be pruned.

    b. VTP pruning reduces unnecessary flooding.

    c. By default, VTP pruning is disabled.

    d. None of the above

Answer A is false. Enabling VTP pruning on a VTP server enables pruning for the entire management domain. By default, VLANs 2 through 1,000 are pruning-eligible. VTP pruning does not prune traffic from VLANs that are pruning-ineligible. VLAN 1 is always pruning-ineligible; traffic from VLAN 1 cannot be pruned.

85. Which of the following is false regarding RADIUS?

    a. Usernames and passwords are encrypted.

    b. RADIUS is not Cisco proprietary.

    c. RADIUS uses TCP as its transport protocol.

    d. Both A and C

The correct answer is C. The major difference between TACACS+ and RADIUS is the network transport protocol that each uses. The RADIUS protocol uses UDP to exchange information, not TCP.

86. One Erlang is equal to how many CCS per hour?

    a. 36

    b. 63

    c. 10

    d. 100

The correct answer is A. Centum call seconds (CCS) is a unit that expresses the amount of time that a particular line is in use. The CCS measurement is made per 100 seconds of usage. For example, a telephone with 18 CCS per hour means that it is off-hook (in use) 1,800 seconds per hour. One Erlang equals 36 CCS per hour.

87. What is Erlang B?

    a. It is a traffic model used to determine the number of trunks required to service a specific amount of traffic.

    b. It is a unit that expresses one hour of traffic on a trunk or trunk group.

    c. It is a voice-encoding technology.

    d. None of the above

The correct answer is A. Erlang B traffic mode used to determine how many lines are required between a telephone system and a central office or between multiple locations.

88. Which of the following is false regarding VTP?

    a. VTP is a layer 2 messaging protocol.

    b. Using VTP, changes are automatically communicated to all the other switches in the network.

    c. A switch can only operate in server mode.

    d. VTP pruning reduces the unnecessary flooding of traffic.

Answer C is false. You can configure a switch to operate as a server, client, or in transparent mode. In server mode, the switch can create, modify, and delete VLANs and specify other configuration parameters (such as VTP version and VTP pruning) for the entire VTP domain. VTP servers advertise their VLAN configuration to other switches in the same VTP domain and synchronize their VLAN configuration with other switches based on advertisements received over trunk links. VTP server is the default mode.

In client mode, the switch cannot create, change, or delete VLANs on a VTP client. In transparent mode, switches do not participate in VTP. A VTP transparent switch does not advertise its VLAN configuration and does not synchronize its VLAN configuration based on received advertisements. However, in VTP version 2, transparent switches do forward VTP advertisements that they receive out of their trunk ports.

Answer A is true. VTP is a layer 2 messaging protocol that manages the addition, deletion, and renaming of VLANs on a networkwide basis. VTP minimizes misconfigurations and configuration inconsistencies that can result in a number of problems, such as duplicate VLAN names, incorrect VLAN-type specifications, and security violations.

Answer B is true. With VTP, you can make configuration changes centrally on one or more switches and those changes are automatically communicated to all the other switches in the network.

Answer D is true. VTP pruning reduces the unnecessary flooding of traffic, such as broadcast, multicast, unknown, and flooded unicast packets. VTP pruning increases available bandwidth by restricting flooded traffic to those trunk links that the traffic must use to access the appropriate network devices.

89. Which of the following is false regarding CGMP?

    a. CGMP is Cisco proprietary.

    b. CGMP dynamically configures Catalyst switch ports so that IP multicast traffic is forwarded only to those ports associated with IP multicast hosts.

    c. When a router receives an IGMP message, it creates a CGMP message and forwards it to the switch.

    d. CGMP runs on the switches only.

Answer D is false. CGMP software components run on both the Cisco router and the Catalyst 5000 series switch. A CGMP-capable IP multicast router sees all IGMP packets and can inform the Catalyst series switch when specific hosts join or leave IP multicast groups.

90. How would you gain access to a router whose password is not known?

    a. Reload the router and copy the startup configuration to the running configuration.

    b. Reload the router, issue the **break** command within the first 60 seconds, change the register value to ignore NVRAM, reload the router again, copy the startup configuration to the running configuration, change the password, change the configuration register back, and copy the running configuration to the startup configuration.

    c. Reload the router, issue the **break** command within the first 60 seconds, change the register value to ignore NVRAM, reload the router again, and copy the running configuration to the startup configuration reload the router.

    d. Reload the router, issue the **break** command within the first 60 seconds, change the register value to ignore NVRAM, reload the router again, copy the startup configuration to the running configuration, and change the password.

The correct answer is B. When password recovery is necessary, the steps in answer C should be done to change the password without losing configuration information.

91. What are the primary modes used by the Cisco command interpreter EXEC? (Choose the best two answers.)

    a. Exec mode

    b. Privileged mode

    c. User mode

    d. Configuration mode

The correct answers are B and C. The command interpreter is called the EXEC. The EXEC interprets the commands you type and carries out the corresponding operations. For security purposes, the EXEC has two levels of access: user and privileged. The commands available at the user level are a subset of the commands available at the privileged level.

92. The serial interface is down, but the line protocol is up on an HDLC link. What is most likely the problem?

   a. Keepalives are not being received from the remote router.

   b. IP addresses are configured wrong.

   c. No clock is present.

   d. None of the above

The correct answer is D. This is not a possible state to have the serial interface down and the protocol up.

93. Which of the following is false regarding access lists?

   a. There is an implied deny all at the end of all access lists.

   b. Access lists are applied in permit deny manner (all permit statements are applied first then deny statements).

   c. Access list are used to control virtual terminal access.

   d. An access list is a sequential collection of permit and deny conditions.

The correct answer is B. Access lists are a sequential collection of permit and deny conditions. They are evaluated sequentially by the router is a top-down manner. Cisco IOS software tests addresses against the conditions in an access list one by one. The first match determines whether the software accepts or rejects the address. Because the software stops testing conditions after the first match, the order of the conditions is critical. If no conditions match, the software rejects the address.

94. What command can be used to determine the hardware configuration of a router? (multiple answers)

   a. show version

   b. show accounting

   c. show hardware

   d. None of the above

The correct answers are A and C. Both the **show hardware** and **show version exec** commands can be used to display the hardware configuration of the router.

95. Which of the following passwords can be encrypted on a router?

   a. enable password

   b. enable secret

   c. chap secrets

   d. All of the above

The correct answer is D. The **service password-encryption** command will encrypt all passwords that are saved in its configuration file. This prevents passwords from being read from the configuration file. The problem is that the algorithm used by service password-encryption is a simple Vigenere cipher, which can easily be reversed.

96. What happens if a Catalyst switch receives a frame with a destination MAC address that is not in the CAM table?

   a. The frame is dropped.

   b. The frame is sent out all ports on the Catalyst.

   c. The frame is sent out all ports of the VLAN.

   d. The frame is routed.

The correct answer is C. If a frame is received with a destination MAC address that is not in the CAM table, the switch will forward the frame out all outbound ports of a VLAN.

97. Which of the following statements is false regarding DDR?

   a. DDR is implemented in two ways: DDR with dialer profiles and legacy DDR.

   b. Dialer profiles separate logical configurations from the physical interfaces.

   c. Legacy DDR enables physical interfaces to take on different characteristics based on incoming or outgoing call requirements.

   d. Dialer profiles enable BRIs to belong to multiple dialer pools.

Answer C is false. DDR is implemented in two ways: DDR with dialer profiles and legacy DDR. Dialer profiles enable logical and physical configurations to be bound together dynamically on a per-call basis. This enables physical interfaces to take on different characteristics based on incoming or outgoing calls.

98. Which of the following is true regarding legacy DDR? (multiple answers)

   a. With legacy DDR, all ISDN B channels inherited the physical interface's configuration.

   b. With legacy DDR, one dialer map is required per dialer per protocol.

   c. With legacy DDR, BRIs can belong to multiple dialer pools.

   d. Legacy DDR enables physical interfaces to take on different characteristics based on incoming or outgoing call requirements.

The correct answers are A and B. One of the major disadvantages of legacy DDR is that all ISDN B channels inherited the physical interface's configuration. Another drawback of legacy DDR is one dialer map is required per dialer per protocol. This makes multiprotocol configurations very complex.

Answer C is false. Dialer profiles are required in order for Basic Rate Interfaces (BRIs) to belong to multiple dialer pools.

Answer D is false. Dialer profiles enable physical interfaces to take on different characteristics based on incoming or outgoing call requirements.

99. What must be done to allow a VLAN to span two or more switches?

    a. Set up pruning.

    b. Set up routing.

    c. Set up a trunk connection.

    d. None of the above

The correct answer is C. In order for VLANs to span across multiple switches a trunk connection must be established. Trunk ports recognize frame tags and are therefore able to carry VLAN information between switches.

Answer A is incorrect. VTP pruning reduces the unnecessary flooding of traffic, such as broadcast, multicast, unknown, and flooded unicast packets. VTP pruning increases available bandwidth by restricting flooded traffic to those trunk links that the traffic must use to access the appropriate network devices.

Answer B is incorrect. VTP domain is not necessary for switches to share VLAN information.

100. Which of the following configuration register values would force a router to boot from ROM?

    a. 0x2102

    b. 0x2142

    c. 0x2101

    d. 0x2104

The correct answer is C. A configuration with a value of 0x2101 forces a router to boot from ROM. Only when the boot field has a value of 0 or 1 will the router boot from ROM.

Answers A, B, and D are incorrect. These configuration register settings will cause the router to look at the boot commands in the configuration file to determine what IOS to load.

CCIE Qualification Exam 4 (Desktop Protocols and Bridging)

This chapter will cover:

- Desktop protocols
- Bridging and DLSw
- Local area networking technologies

Introduction

This chapter focuses on desktop protocols and bridging and local area network (LAN) technologies. The practice exam contains questions on all bridging types such as Data Link Switching (DLSw), the routing information field (RIF) format, the Internetwork Packet Exchange (IPX), and LAN technologies. The goal is to test the user's aptitude on bridging technologies and concepts such as Data Link addressing, Media Access Control (MAC), and Logical Link Control (LLC).

Technology Overview

In the following section, we'll examine various bridging methods in detail, including source-route bridging (SRB), the spanning tree algorithm, the Routing Information Field (RIF), source-route transparent bridging (SRT), translational bridging, DLSw, Novell NetWare, IPX and its routing protocols, and the Service Advertisement Protocol (SAP).

317

Bridging

Bridges operate at layers 1 and 2 of the OSI model. Bridges work with lower-layer protocols such as MAC layer services and are more complex than repeaters because they function with two layers of protocols.

A bridge is a device that enables devices on different LAN segments to communicate as if they were on the same switch, HUB, or concentrator. Because bridges operate at the Data Link layer of the OSI reference model, they are concerned only with the addresses of network devices and not the actual paths between them. For this reason, high-level protocols, which provide functionality at the Network layer and above in the OSI reference model, are totally transparent to bridging—hence, the term transparent bridging.

Several types of bridging methods are used in today's networks. This chapter will focus on the following:

- Transparent bridging (TB)
- Source-route bridging (SRB)
- Source-route transparent bridging (SRT)
- Source-route translational bridging (SRTB)

Transparent Bridging

Transparent bridging provides an interconnection of LANs transparent to stations communicating across a bridge. Any station can communicate with any other station in the network as though both stations were on the same LAN. All frame-forwarding functions are handled entirely within the transparent bridge based on a path determined by the spanning tree algorithm.

Transparent refers to the fact that the bridge silently forwards non-local traffic to attached LANs in a way that is transparent to the user. End-station applications do not know about the presence of the bridge. The bridge learns about the presence of end stations by listening to traffic passing by. From this listening process, the bridge builds a database of end-station addresses attached to its LANs. For each frame it receives, the bridge checks the frame's destination address against the addresses in its database. If the destination is on the same LAN, it does not forward the frame. If the destination is on another LAN, it forwards the frame. If the destination address is not present in the database, the bridge forwards the frame to all the LANs connected to the bridge except the LAN from which it originated. All Transparent bridges use the spanning tree protocol and algorithm.

Transparent bridging, the type used in Ethernet and documented in Institute of Electrical and Electronic Engineers (IEEE) 802.1, is based on the concept of a spanning tree.

This tree of Ethernet links and bridges spans the entire bridged network. The tree originates at a root bridge, which is determined by election, based on bridge priority and either Ethernet addresses or engineer-defined preference. The tree expands outward from there. Any bridge interfaces that would cause loops to form are shut down. If several interfaces could be deactivated, the one with the lowest-path cost to the root is chosen for activation. This process continues until the entire network has been traversed, and every bridge interface is either assigned a role in the tree or deactivated.

Spanning Tree Algorithm

The spanning tree algorithm produces and maintains a loop-free topology in a bridged network, which may contain loops in its physical design. In a mesh topology, where more than one bridge is connected between two LANs, data packets can bounce back and forth between two LANs' parallel bridges. This creates a redundancy in data traffic and produces the phenomenon known as looping. Without spanning tree, when looping occurs, you must configure the local and/or remote LAN to remove the physical loop. With spanning tree, a self-configuring algorithm enables a bridge to be added anywhere in the LAN without creating loops. When you add the new bridge, the spanning tree transparently reconfigures all bridges on the LAN into a single loop-free spanning tree.

Spanning tree never has more than one active data route between two end stations, thus eliminating data loops. For each bridge, the algorithm determines which bridge ports to use to forward data and which ones to block to form a loop-free topology. The spanning tree protocol enables the automatic backup of data paths, and the bridges connecting to the redundant paths enter backup mode automatically. When a primary bridge fails, a backup bridge becomes active.

Source-Route Bridging (SRB)

The main differences between transparent bridging and source-route bridging are how the bridge forwards the packet and the structure of the packet itself. These differences make the two bridging schemes incompatible. The Source-Routing scheme operates at the LLC sublayer of the Data Link layer, but takes a different approach to determine the path. Source-Routing bridges are not considered transparent because they rely on the end stations for determining the route the packet should take through the network. A process called route discovery is used to find the optimal path for the communications session. Through this process, the route is discovered using broadcast packets sent between the source and destination end stations.

Source-route bridging is a means of determining the path used to transfer data from one workstation to another. Workstations that use Source-Routing participate in route discovery and specify the route used for each transmitted packet. The source-route bridge merely carries out the routing instructions placed into each data packet when the packet is assembled by the sending workstation—hence the name Source-Routing. Although it includes the term routing, Source-Routing is a part of bridging technology at layer 2, not layer 3, routing using network addresses such as IP 32-bit Classes A, B, and C.

Source-route bridging is used on Token Ring networks and is installed in a large number of major networks throughout the world. Source-route bridging also offers very good throughput when designed properly.

Unlike transparent bridging, SRB puts most of the smarts in the hosts and uses simple bridges to forward the packets. Within the SRB frame is a routing information field (RIF). The RIF is a list of rings and bridges that a packet should traverse to reach its final destination. Each bridge/ring pair that the frame transverses, from source to destination, is represented by a route designator (RD) in the RIF.

The source station determines the path to the destination by sending out an all-route explorer. This frame is forwarded through every path in the network towards the destination. As the frame passes through the network, bridges add their RDs to the end of the all-route explorer RIF field. As the frame passes through the network, the RIF compiles a list of bridge and ring numbers describing the path to the destination. When the all-route explorer arrives at the destination, the RIF contains an RD, which is the exact sequence of addresses from the source to the destination. When the destination end station receives the frame, it generates a response frame to the source. This response frame includes the route path the source station should use to reach the destination.

Routing Information Field (RIF)

The information contained in an RIF consists of a 2-byte routing control field and multiple RD fields, each of which are 2 bytes long.

Routing Control Field

The routing control field consists of five subfields: a 3-bit type field, a 5-bit length field, a 1-bit direction field, a 3-bit largest frame field, and a 4-bit reserved field. The bits in the reserved field are transmitted as all zeros. The following is a description of each field:

- **Type field** The type field is 3 bits long and is the broadcast indicator. It contains three possible values: a directed frame binary 000, an all-route explorer frame binary 100, and a single-route explorer frame binary 110. A directed frame indicates that the frame contains the defined path across the network, and no change is needed on the RIF. An all-route explorer frame goes through the whole network. All source-route bridges must copy the frame to every port except the one that has a destination ring that is already in the RIF. A single-route explorer frame is a frame that passes through a predetermined path constructed by a spanning tree algorithm in the bridges. A station should receive only one single-route explorer from the network.

- **Length field**   The length field is 5 bits long and contains the length of the routing information field in bytes.

- **Direction field**   The direction field is 1 bit long and determines how source-route bridges in the network read the RIF. If the bit is set to 0, the RIF should be read left to right; if the bit is set to 1, the RIF should be read right to left.

- **Largest frame field**   The largest frame field is 3 bits long and indicates the size in bytes of the largest frame that can transverse the network. Table 5-1 is a chart of the possible values.

Route Designator Field

The route designator (RD) field is a list of rings and bridges that a packet should traverse to reach its destination. The 2-byte RD field consists of two subfields: a 12-bit ring number and a 4-bit bridge number. The 12-bit ring number ranges from 0x001 to 0xfff, supporting decimal ring numbers from 1 to 4,095. The bridge number ranges from 0x1 to 0xf, supporting decimal bridge numbers from 1 to 15.

Table 5-1   Largest Frame Size Values

Value	Largest Frame Size
000	516 bytes
001	1,500 bytes
010	2,052 bytes
011	4,472 bytes
100	8,191 bytes
101	11,407 bytes
110	17,800 bytes
111	Used in all-route explorers

On an SRB network, each ring is assigned a unique ring number and each bridge is also assigned a number. When an all-route broadcast frame is transmitted, each bridge that forwards the frame to another ring adds its bridge number and the ring number to the frame's RIF. When a bridge receives a frame to forward, it compares the route designators in the RIF with its attached ring and bridge numbers:

- If a target ring number match is in an all-route or single-route broadcast frame, the bridge discards the frame because it has already circled the target ring.

- If a target ring number match is not in an all-route or single-route broadcast frame, the bridge adds its route designator to the frame's RIF and forwards it.

- If a ring-number, bridge-number, and ring-number combination match is in a non-broadcast frame, the bridge forwards the frame to the indicated ring.

- If no ring-number, bridge-number, and ring-number combination match is in a nonbroadcast frame, the bridge discards the frame.

When the frame reaches its destination, the route designator describes the path from the source ring to the destination ring.

Source-Route Transparent Bridging (SRT)

Although both transparent and source-route bridging methods work well in their own environments, they are not particularly well suited to work in each other's environments. In addition, because these bridging schemes are not compatible, they do not interoperate in a mixed environment. Source-route bridges cannot operate in a transparent environment simply because the packets do not contain routing information. Without routing information, a source-route bridge has no way to recognize that the packet should be forwarded.

Bridges function differently in Token Ring and Ethernet networks. Aside from the differences in bit ordering, packet size, and acknowledgment bits, bridging methods are another obstacle. Ethernet bridges use transparent bridging in which the bridges determine the route of the traffic through the network. Token Ring networks use transparent bridging in some instances, but generally depend on Source-Routing as the primary bridging method.

A source-route transparent bridge (SRT) combines both bridging schemes on a single platform. This enables both source-routing and transparent data to use the same bridged environment. An SRT bridge source-routes any frames that contain routing information and transparently bridges packets that do not contain routing information. Whether the packet contains routing information or not is determined by the routing information bit in the frame. If the routing information bit is set to 0 (RII = 0), no routing information is contained and the frame is transparently bridged. If the routing information bit is set to 1 (RII = 1), the frame is source-routed.

Translational Bridging

Translational bridging enables you to bridge between dissimilar LANs, commonly Ethernet and Token Ring, or Ethernet and FDDI. In the case of Ethernet/Token Ring bridging, Translational bridging only enables connectivity for nonroutable protocols like LAT, the Maintenance Operations Protocol, and NetBIOS.

The translation for bridging between Ethernet/Token Ring and Ethernet/FDDI requires bit order reversal because the internal representation of MAC addresses is different on Ethernet, Token Ring, and FDDI. Ethernet is little endian (it transmits the least order bit first) and Token Ring and FDDI are big endian (they transmit the high order bit first). For example, the address 0000.0cxx.xxxx on Ethernet would appear as 0000.30yy.yyyy on Token Ring because every byte needs to be bit-swapped.

Both Ethernet and Token Ring use the first transmitted bit of a frame's destination address to determine whether the frame is unicast or multicast. With no address conversion, a unicast frame (a frame that has only one destination) on one network may appear as a multicast address (an address for more than one station) on another network. Remember that Ethernet/Token Ring bridging is only possible with nonroutable protocols. The reason for this is that routable protocols often carry MAC addresses in the data portion of a frame. For example, the Address Resolution Protocol (ARP) places the hardware address in the data portion of the link-layer frame. It is simple to convert source and destination addresses in the header, but the conversion of hardware addresses that may appear in the data portion is more difficult. When performing source-route transparent or source-route translational bridging between Ethernet and Token Ring, Cisco does not search for instances of hardware addresses in the data portion. So, only nonroutable protocols are supported when bridging between Ethernet and Token Ring.

Translational bridging between Ethernet/FDDI carries the issue of bit reversal a little further because few protocols work across the FDDI/Ethernet barrier. One reason for this is the concept of a canonical address above the MAC layer; any address above the MAC layer on FDDI should be ordered canonically according to Ethernet order. This is how IP is done on FDDI, and it's why Cisco can bridge IP when going from Ethernet to FDDI. Unfortunately, other protocols don't necessarily do this.

Data Link Switching (DLSw)

Data Link Switching (DLSw) provides a means to transport nonroutable traffic such as SNA and NetBIOS over an IP network. IBM first introduced it in 1992 to provide a common method of transporting SNA data across an IP network. Prior to DLSw, remote source-route bridging (RSRB) was used to provide wide area transport between LANs.

The main difference between RSRB and DLSw is support for local data link control termination. Both SNA and NetBIOS are connection-oriented protocols. Both protocols rely on link-layer acknowledgments and keepalive messages to ensure the integrity of connections and the delivery of data.

DLSw terminates the data link control at the local node for connection-oriented data, as shown in Figure 5-1. The advantage of this is the link-layer acknowledgments and keepalive messages do not have to traverse a wide area network (WAN). In addition, local termination reduces the likelihood of link-layer timeouts across WANs. RSRB does not terminate the data link control locally, resulting in an increased potential for data link control timeouts over WAN connections (see Figure 5-2). In addition, RSRB is limited to a seven-hop count, which limits the diameter of the network. With

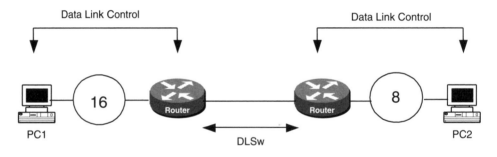

Figure 5-1   DLSw uses a local acknowledgment to control data flow.

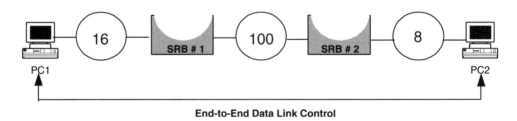

Figure 5-2   RSRB provides an end-to-end connection over an IP WAN.

DLSw, the RIF is terminated at the local router. Because of this, DLSw is not limited to seven hops, allowing for larger diameter networks.

Novell NetWare

Novell NetWare is a network operating system that provides transparent remote file access, printer sharing, and support for various applications such as electronic mail transfer and database access. Novell, Inc. developed NetWare in the early 1980s. It was derived from Xerox Network Systems (XNS), which was created by Xerox Corporation in the late 1970s, and is based on a client-server architecture.

Internetwork Packet Exchange (IPX)

NetWare uses IPX to route packets through an internetwork similar to the way TCP/IP uses IP. Like IP, IPX is a connectionless datagram-based network protocol.

IPX Addressing

An IPX address specifies the location of a particular entity in a network or internetwork. Addresses enable two entities not directly connected to communicate. Each entity in a network or Internet, such as a host, server, communication device, or printer, must have a unique identifier or address.

These addresses are represented in hexadecimal format and consist of two parts: a network number and a node number. The IPX network number is assigned by the network administrator and is 32 bits long. The node number is usually the MAC address of network interface cards (NICs). The node portion of the address is 48 bits long.

Because IPXs use the MAC address for the node number, this enables the sending stations to predict what MAC address to use on a data link. No layer 3 to layer 2 ARP is needed. This is different from IP addressing where there is no correlation between the MAC address and the IP address. Because of this, IP must use ARP to determine the destination MAC address for a particular IP address.

IPX Encapsulation Types

Novell NetWare IPX supports four different IPX Ethernet encapsulation types on a LAN. In order for two workstations on a LAN to communicate directly, they must use the same encapsulation type. When assigning network numbers to an interface that supports multiple networks, you must specify a different encapsulation type for each network. Because multiple networks share the physical medium, this enables the communication server to determine which packets belong to which network. For example, you can configure up to four IPX networks on a single Ethernet cable because four encapsulation types are supported for Ethernet. When you use secondary IPX networks, you can configure up to four IPX networks. Each IPX network must be a different and unique Ethernet frame type. The following is a list of the encapsulation types supported:

- **Novell Ethernet_802.3** Cisco refers to this as Novell-Ether encapsulation. It includes an IEEE 802.3 length field but not an IEEE 802.2 (LLC) header. The IPX header immediately follows the 802.3 length field.

- **Novell_802.2** Cisco refers to this as Service Advertisement Protocol (SAP) encapsulation. It uses the standard IEEE 802.3 frame format.

- **Ethernet Version 2** Cisco refers to this as ARPA encapsulation. Ethernet Version 2 includes the standard Ethernet Version 2 header, which consists of destination and source address fields followed by an EtherType field.

- **SNAP** SNAP extends the IEEE 802.2 header by providing a type code similar to that defined in the Ethernet Version 2 specification.

Service Advertisement Protocol (SAP)

SAP is an IPX protocol, which is used to advertise network resources such as file and print servers. The SAP advertisements are sent out every 60 seconds. The SAP advertisement contains a list of services that are identified by a hexadecimal number called an SAP identifier.

Each router in the network exchanges SAP updates and builds a table containing all known services along with their network addresses. The table is used to service Novell clients that request particular services through the use of the Get Nearest Server (GNS) query.

IPX Routing Protocols

IPX can use the distance vector routing protocol Routing Information Protocol (RIP), the Enhanced Interior Gateway Routing Protocol (EIGRP), or the routing protocol NetWare Link State Protocol (NLSP) to advertise network reachability.

IPX RIP

IPX/RIP is a distance vector protocol. In distance vector algorithms, a router maintains a table that contains only the distance to the target network and the direction or vector a packet must travel to reach the destination network. The vector usually takes the form of a router's address through which a packet must traverse to reach its ultimate destination. With distance vector algorithms, the best-cost routes can be computed when the only information exchanged by routers is a list of reachable networks along with their distances. Each router can calculate a route and its associated distance to each network by choosing the neighbor with the shortest path available.

In an internetwork using distance vector routing, routers periodically determine whether the internetwork configuration has changed. They also periodically broadcast packets to their immediate neighbors; these packets contain all the information they currently have about the internetwork's topology.

After receiving an update, distance vector routers consolidate the information and pass summarized data along to other routers, servers, and end devices. Through this periodic checking and broadcasting, which is performed at regular intervals regardless of whether the internetwork has changed, all routers are kept updated with correct internetwork addresses. Because RIP is a distance vector protocol, routers configured for NetWare RIP work in the same way: performing periodic checking and information exchange while updating their routing tables with new information. IPX RIP sends routing updates every 60 seconds. To calculate the best-path IPX, RIP uses a "tick" as the metric, which represents the delay expected when using a particular path. One tick is one-eighteenth of a second. In the case of two paths with an equal tick count, IPX RIP uses the hop count as a tie-breaker.

Enhanced Interior Gateway Routing Protocol (EIGRP)

EIGRP is a Cisco proprietary advanced distance vector routing protocol, which was first released in 1994 (IOS 9.21) to address the limitations of traditional distance vector protocols and link state protocols.

Traditional distance vector protocols such as RIP forward routing updates to all attached neighbors, which in turn forward the updates to their neighbors. This hop-by-hop propagation of routing information creates large convergence times and looped topology problems.

Link state protocols such as NLSP have been offered as an alternative to the traditional distance vector protocols. The problem with link state protocols is that they solve the convergence problems of traditional distance vector protocols by replicating the topology information across the entire domain. This replication becomes undesirable in large networks and greatly affects CPU utilization due to the number of SPF calculations that need to be run.

In addition, EIGRP supports incremental SAP updates, extends the maximum network diameter to 224 hops, and provides optimal path selection through the use of metrics based on delay, bandwidth, reliability, and load. EIGRP also enables automatic redistribution between RIP/SAP and EIGRP.

NetWare Link Services Protocol (NLSP)

NLSP is a link state routing protocol. This type of protocol derives its name from the fact that link state routers track the status of other routers and links. Link state protocols adapt more quickly to network topology changes than distance vector protocols. Thus, they are better than distance vector protocols for managing internetworking on large, complex internetworks.

Link state protocols significantly reduce the communication overhead required for routing. NLSP can significantly improve network performance because it frees the resources to be used for transferring data packets, rather than routing information. NLSP is particularly efficient for WAN routing, in which available communication bandwidth is limited.

NLSP is designed to be functional only with routers. It does not require that workstations report their statuses to a router, and a workstation does not know that the network is working with the NLSP or IPX RIP protocol.

NLSP enables large NetWare internetworks to be designed and implemented, and it is not constrained by the limitations of the IPX RIP protocol. In addition to the elimination of RIP/SAP broadcasts, NLSP provides load balancing across equally weighted segments. NLSP updates and converges the network three to four times faster than RIP. Faster convergence increases the reliability and efficiency of your network. It is designed as a hierarchical topology.

Questions

1. Using the information in the following Illustration what would the RD field of the RIF be for PC1 to reach PC2?

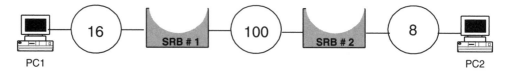

PC1   PC2

    a. 0161.1002.0080

    b. 0101.0642.0080

    c. 1001.6402.0800

    d. 1601.1002.8000

2. Which of the following do IPX clients use to locate the nearest active server for a particular service?

  a. SAP

  b. GNS

  c. IPX RIP

  d. NLSP

3. How many networks are carried in an IPX RIP update?

  a. 25

  b. 10

  c. 30

  d. 50

4. If an Ethernet station detects a collision during transmission, it _____.

  a. Retransmits the frame

  b. Sends a beacon

  c. Waits a random period of time before attempting retransmission

  d. None of the above—collisions are possible on an Ethernet network.

5. Given the RIF value 1290.0011.0022.0080, what is the correct path?

  a. Ring 1, Bridge 1 to Ring 2, Bridge 2 to Ring 8

  b. Ring 8, Bridge 2 to Ring 2, Bridge 1 to Ring 1

  c. Ring 129, Bridge 1 to Ring 1, Bridge 22 to Ring 8

  d. Ring 1, Bridge 1 to Ring 0, Bridge 22 to Ring 80

6. Which of the following is true regarding DLSw?

  a. DLSw terminates the data link control session at the router and provides local ACKs.

  b. DLSw overcomes the seven-hop limit inherent in source-route bridging.

  c. DLSw reduces the amount of explorer traffic that is sent across the network.

  d. All of the above.

7. Given the following RIF c820.0011.0022.0080, which type of packet is this?

  a. Single-route explorer

  b. All-route explorer

  c. Directed frame

  d. STP frame

8. What does the router use to determine the nearest server for IPX Get Nearest Server response?
   a. Tick count
   b. Hop count
   c. Bandwidth
   d. First service on the list

9. Which of the following is false regarding source-route bridging?
   a. By default, Cisco routers use RIF information for routed protocols.
   b. Bridge numbers must be unique only between bridges that connect the same two Token Rings.
   c. Each ring in an SRB network must be unique.
   d. Source-Route bridging enables multiple, active paths through the network.

10. In Token Ring, what does it mean when a frame returns to the source with the A and C bits set to 0?
    a. The destination station does not exist or it is not active.
    b. The end station exists, but the frame was not copied.
    c. The destination received the frame.
    d. None of the above—the A and C bits are used in Ethernet.

11. What does CSMA/CD stand for?
    a. Carrier Sense Multiple Access Contention Detection
    b. Carrier Sense Media Access Contention Detection
    c. Carrier Sense Multiple Access Collision Detect
    d. Carrier Sense Media Access Collision Detect

12. Given the RIF routing control field c820, what is the RD length?
    a. 2 bytes
    b. 4 bytes
    c. 8 bytes
    d. 20 bytes

13. Which of the following bridging types supports mixed media? (multiple answers)
    a. Transparent bridging
    b. Source-Route bridging
    c. Translation bridging
    d. Source-Route Transparent bridging

14. Using the information in the following Illustration what would the RD field of the RIF be on PC1 to reach PC2?

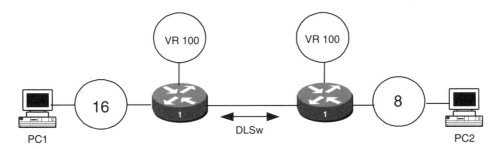

a. 1601.1000

b. 0101.0640

c. 0101.0648

d. 1601.1001.0080

15. In SRB, what does the RIF define?

a. The translation between Ethernet and Token Ring

b. The topology of the network

c. The path for SRB frames to transverse the network

d. The bridge type

16. Ethernet networks are laid out in a _____.

a. Physical ring logical bus

b. Physical ring logical star

c. Physical star logical bus

d. Physical star logical ring

17. Which of the following is true regarding bridges and LAN switches?

a. Bridges operate at layer 2 of the OSI model; LAN switches operate at layer 3.

b. LAN switches enable multiple physical LAN segments to be interconnected into a single, larger network; bridges do not.

c. Switches forward and flood traffic based on MAC addresses; bridges do not.

d. Switches are much faster than bridges because the forwarding is performed in hardware versus software.

18. Which of the following is false regarding the RIF?

a. When using DLSw, the RIF is terminated at the router.

b. The RIF is always read from left to right.

c. Until recently, IBM only supported a maximum of eight RD fields in an RIF.

d. The RD field of the RIF contains alternating sequences of ring and bridge numbers that start and end with ring numbers.

19. Which of the following LAN protocols use a token-passing media access scheme? (multiple answers)
    a. FDDI
    b. Ethernet
    c. Fast Ethernet
    d. Token Ring

20. Given the RIF routing control field c820, what is the largest frame size that can be supported?
    a. 200 bytes
    b. 1,500 bytes
    c. 4,000 bytes
    d. None of the above

21. Which type of packet consists of a single data packet that is copied and sent to a specific subset of nodes on the network?
    a. Broadcast
    b. Unicast
    c. Multicast
    d. Direct-broadcast

22. Which of the following are valid SRB explorer packets? (multiple answers)
    a. All-route explorer packet
    b. Single-route explorer packet
    c. All-RIF explorer packet
    d. Local explorer packet

23. Which IEEE specifies the implementation of the physical layer and the MAC sub-layer used by Ethernet?
    a. 802.3
    b. 802.4
    c. 802.5
    d. None of the above

24. Which of the following is false regarding IPX?
    a. The network address consists of a network number and a node number expressed in the following format: network.node.
    b. IPX uses ARP.
    c. IPX network addresses must be unique.
    d. IPX can use RIP or NLSP for routing.

25. The spanning tree protocol provides _____.
  a. Loop detection
  b. Automatic backup of data paths
  c. Trunking between VLANs
  d. Both A and B

26. In an STP environment, the root bridge is selected based on what?
  a. Highest bridge ID
  b. Lowest bridge ID
  c. Highest priority
  d. Lowest priority

27. Which of the following data link media access protocols uses a 48-bit MAC address?
  a. Token Ring
  b. Ethernet
  c. FDDI
  d. All of the above

28. With respect to the Spanning Tree algorithm, a bridge that forwards traffic on behalf of a LAN is said to be the _____.
  a. Root bridge
  b. Non-designated bridge
  c. Designated bridge
  d. Transparent bridge

29. In a Transparent bridge environment, if a frame is received and the destination address is not in the bridge's table, the frame is _____.
  a. Dropped
  b. Flooded back out the inbound port
  c. Flooded to all ports except the inbound port
  d. Flooded to all ports

30. The specification for STP is _____.
  a. 802.1d
  b. 802.3
  c. 802.4
  d. 802.5

31. In IPX, a tick is calculated based on what?
  a. Hop count
  b. Cost

    c. Delay

    d. All of the above

32. Which bridging technique will enable you to route between a bridged interface and routed interface?

    a. Concurrent Routing and Bridging (CRB)

    b. Integrated Routing and Bridging (IRB)

    c. Transparent bridging

    d. Source-route bridging

33. In a source-route transparent bridged (SRT) environment, frames with the RII bit equal to zero will be _____.

    a. Source-route bridged

    b. Transparently bridged

    c. Dropped

    d. None of the above

34. Which of the following is false?

    a. IP can be bridged between Ethernet and Token Ring.

    b. When bridging from Ethernet to Token Ring, the MAC addresses must be bit-swapped.

    c. Bridges running SRT never add or remove RIFs from a frame.

    d. In an SRT environment, only packets with an RIF field are source-routed.

35. Transparent bridges exchange configuration messages and topology change messages using _____.

    a. LSAs

    b. BLSAs

    c. VTP

    d. BPDUs

36. What will the destination MAC address be if PC1 on LAN 1 sends a frame to PC2 on LAN2?

    a. PC1's MAC address

    b. Bridge 2's MAC address

    c. Bridge 1's MAC address

    d. PC2's MAC address

37. What will the destination MAC address be if PC1 on LAN1 sends a frame to PC2 on LAN2?

    a. PC1's MAC address

    b. Router 2's MAC address

    c. Router 1's MAC address

    d. PC2's MAC address

38. If more than one bridge is connected to the same LAN, which bridge is elected as the designated bridge?

    a. The bridge with the smallest path cost to the root bridge

    b. The bridge with the lowest priority

    c. The bridge with the highest priority

    d. None of the above

39. With respect to the spanning tree algorithm, a bridge ID comprises a _____.

    a. Bridge priority and serial number

    b. Bridge priority and port priority

    c. Bridge priority and interface number

    d. Bridge priority and bridge MAC address

40. The command **multiring all** is used to _____.

    a. Enable multiple rings

    b. Enable a routed protocol to enter an SRB environment

    c. Enable SRB on Ethernet

    d. None of the above

41. Transparent bridging bases its forwarding decision on _____.

    a. An RIF field

    b. A MAC address

    c. An all-route explorer

    d. A single-route explorer

42. Ethernet uses _____ bit ordering.
    a. Non-canonical
    b. Canonical
    c. Reverse
    d. Byte-oriented

43. An FDDI single-attached station (SAS) attaches to _____.
    a. Both rings
    b. The secondary ring
    c. The primary ring through a concentrator
    d. None of the above

44. Which of the following is false regarding FDDI?
    a. FDDI uses a dual-ring architecture.
    b. DAS attaches to concentrators.
    c. Single-attached station attaches to primary ring.
    d. FDDI MAC address is non-canonical.

45. Which IEEE standard defines Token Ring?
    a. 802.5
    b. 802.3
    c. 802.1Q
    d. 802.2

46. Which of the following is false regarding Token Ring?
    a. Only the station in possession of the token is allowed to transmit.
    b. Data is removed from the ring by the sending station.
    c. Token Ring supports priorities.
    d. Collisions are inherent in a Token Ring environment.

47. What happens if a dual-attached station (DAS) device is powered down?
    a. The ring will wrap.
    b. The ring will beacon.
    c. Nothing because it is attached to both rings
    d. Nothing because it is attached to a concentrator

48. In Token Ring, what does it mean when a frame returns to the source with the A and C bits set to 1?
    a. The frame was not received by the destination.
    b. The frame contains an error.

    c. The receiving station recognized its address as the destination address and has copied the frame.

    d. The destination station is not active on the ring.

49. DLSw+ always transfers data in _____ format.

    a. Canonical

    b. Non-canonical

    c. FIFO

    d. None of the above—it depends on the media attached.

50. A router is being used as a translational bridge between an Ethernet network and a Token Ring network. Host X on the Ethernet sends a packet to Host Y on the Token Ring. The source MAC address of the packet is 4000.A089.0002. How would the MAC address be interpreted in a Token Ring environment?

    a. 2000.980A.0004

    b. 0040.89A0.2000

    c. 0200.0591.0040

    d. 0200.0500.0840

51. The active monitor in Token Ring is responsible for what? (multiple answers)

    a. Providing the master clock for data transmission

    b. Removing any constantly circulating data packets

    c. Correcting errors

    d. Detecting a loss token and initiating a new token

52. What is the token-passing scheme where a device can pass its token without having received its original frame back?

    a. Fast Token Ring

    b. FDDI

    c. Token passing

    d. Early token release

53. Which types of devices would be found on an FDDI network? (multiple answers)

    a. CAS

    b. DAS

    c. SAS

    d. FAS

54. Token Ring networks are laid out in a _____.

    a. Physical ring logical bus

    b. Physical ring logical star

  c. Physical star logical bus

  d. Physical star logical ring

55. Which type of packet consists of a single data packet that is copied and sent to all nodes on the network?

  a. Broadcast

  b. Unicast

  c. Multicast

  d. Direct-broadcast

56. What happens if an SAP entry is received and no routing entry exists?

  a. Nothing—routing entries are not needed for SAP entries.

  b. The router will load the SAP entry.

  c. The router will drop an SAP update.

  d. The router will advertise the SAP entry.

57. Which of the following access lists could be used to filter a Novell file server SAP from being sent?

  a. RouterB(config)#access-list 1000 deny -1 7

  b. RouterB(config)#access-list 1000 deny -1 4

  c. RouterB(config)#access-list 1000 deny -1 3

  d. RouterB(config)#access-list 1000 deny -1 32

58. The standby monitor on a Token Ring is responsible for what?

  a. Providing the master clock for data transmission

  b. Removing any constantly circulating data packets

  c. Correcting errors

  d. Detecting monitor failures and starting the monitor contention process

59. Novell SAP is _____.

  a. Used to provide mail services

  b. A protocol used by network resources to advertise their addresses

  c. Used to provide dynamic routing

  d. None of the above

60. Which media access method does Ethernet use?

  a. CSMA/CD

  b. Token passing

  c. EtherType

  d. None of the above

61. In IPX RIP, which route is preferred?
   a. The route with the highest tick value
   b. The route with the lowest tick value
   c. The route with the highest hop count
   d. The route with the lowest hop count

62. CRB enables you to _____.
   a. Route only
   b. Route between bridged and routed interfaces
   c. Bridge and route on the same interface
   d. Bridge and route on different interfaces

63. Which of the following is false regarding beaconing in a Token Ring environment?
   a. A station will send a beacon out if it does not hear from its upstream neighbor in seven seconds.
   b. The station that is beaconing is the station that has the problem.
   c. The station that is beaconing is the station that has detected the problem.
   d. When a station receives a beacon frame, it removes itself from the ring and performs internal diagnostics.

64. Token Ring uses _____ bit ordering.
   a. Non-canonical
   b. Canonical
   c. Reverse
   d. Byte-oriented

65. What is the primary difference between DSLw and bridging?
   a. DLSw terminates data link control; bridging does not.
   b. DLSw can transport NetBIOS traffic; RSRB cannot.
   c. DSLw can transport bridge traffic across a wide area network; RSRB cannot.
   d. All of the above

66. Which of the following bridging techniques can be used to bridge between mixed media? (multiple answers)
   a. Transparent bridging
   b. SRB
   c. RSRB
   d. DLSw

67. What does format error mean in the show ipx traffic display?
    a. An SAP was received for a service that already exists.
    b. A packet was received on an interface using a different encapsulation type.
    c. An IPX buffer was not available.
    d. None of the above

68. What does uses mean in the IPX routing table?
    a. It indicates the number of times a particular route is used.
    b. It is the number of packets that have been successfully sent using the route.
    c. It is the number of times the router fast-switched the packet.
    d. None of the above

69. What must you do in order to support multiple IPX network numbers on an Ethernet interface?
    a. Use secondary interfaces, each one with a network number.
    b. Use subinterfaces.
    c. Use secondary interfaces; each network must run a different Ethernet frame type.
    d. None of the above

70. What is the major difference between 100BaseT and 10BaseT?
    a. The access and collision detection used
    b. The frame format
    c. The length requirement
    d. The network diameter

71. A router and a Novell file/print server are attached to the same LAN. A client on the LAN sends a Get Nearest Server (GNS) request. Who will respond?
    a. The router
    b. The server
    c. Both
    d. None of the above

72. Which of the following are valid transport protocols used between DLSw+ routers? (multiple answers)
    a. Promiscuous
    b. FST
    c. TCP/IP
    d. Border peer

73. The Token Ring station with the _____ will be elected the active monitor for the ring.
   a. Highest MAC address
   b. Lowest MAC address
   c. Highest router ID
   d. Lowest router ID

74. The MTU on a 4MB Token Ring network is _____.
   a. 1,500
   b. 4,352
   c. 2,002
   d. None of the above

75. What happens when a router receives an IPX broadcast packet?
   a. The router forwards the packet to all destinations.
   b. The router forwards the packet to all destinations on that network.
   c. The router drops the packet.
   d. None of the above

76. A router is being used as a bridge between an Ethernet network and an FDDI network. Host X on the Ethernet sends a packet to Host Y on the FDDI. The source MAC address of the packet is 2000.980A.0004. How would the MAC address be interpreted in an FDDI environment?
   a. 0400.1950.0020
   b. 4000.0000.0001
   c. 2000.980A.0004
   d. 0200.0500.0840

77. Given the following RIF 4820.0011.0022.0080, what type of packet is this?
   a. Single-route explorer
   b. All-route explorer
   c. Directed frame
   d. STP frame

78. Assume a datagram is sent from a Cisco router/bridge on Ring 21, across Bridge 5 to Ring 256, and then across Bridge 10 to Ring 1365 for delivery to a destination host on that ring. What would the RIF look like in the router describing this path?
   a. 0830.0155.a100.0555
   b. 0830. 1055.100a.0555
   c. 0830.0025.2510.1365
   d. 0830.0155.100a.5550

79. Which of the following do IPX servers use to broadcast the services that they offer to hosts?
    a. SAP
    b. GNS
    c. IPX RIP
    d. NLSP

80. Which of the following is a Cisco IPX encapsulation type?
    a. ARPA
    b. SAP
    c. Novell-Ether
    d. All of the above

81. Which of the following is not a valid IPX routing protocol?
    a. NLSP
    b. IPX RIP
    c. EIGRP
    d. OSPF

82. Which type of packet consists of a single data packet that is copied and sent from the source to a single destination on a network?
    a. Broadcast
    b. Unicast
    c. Multicast
    d. Direct-broadcast

83. In Token Ring, what does it mean when a frame returns to the source with the A bit set to 1 and the C bit set to 0?
    a. The destination station does not exist or is not active.
    b. The end station exists, but the frame was not copied.
    c. The destination received the frame.
    d. None of the above—the A and C bits are used in Ethernet.

84. On a Token Ring network, which station will become the standby monitor?
    a. The station with the highest MAC address
    b. The station with the lowest MAC address
    c. The station with the highest router ID
    d. All stations on the ring except the station that is the active monitor

85. An IPX network address consists of _____.
    a. A network number and a node number

    b. A network and subnet work number

    c. A network number and port number

    d. A network number

86. What is the purpose of the **ethernet-transit-oui** command?

    a. It specifies the OUI code used in the encapsulation of Ethernet Type II frames.

    b. It is used to identify the vendor.

    c. It specifies the OUI code used on the Ethernet LAN.

    d. None of the above

87. A type 2 beacon on a Token Ring means what?

    a. A station is sending claim tokens, but is not seeing them come back around the ring.

    b. A station is seeing an upstream neighbor transmitting all of the time.

    c. There is a physical break in the ring topology.

    d. None of the above

    e. All of the above

88. What is Fast EtherChannel?

    a. A trunking technology

    b. A LAN protocol

    c. A media access scheme

    d. None of the above

89. What is IPXWAN?

    a. A routing protocol

    b. A link startup and negotiation protocol

    c. A service advertisement protocol

    d. None of the above

90. What sets the RIF indicator bit?

    a. The source station

    b. The destination station

    c. The router

    d. The bridge

91. What is the destination MAC address of a BPDU?

    a. 8001.4300.0000

    b. C000.0000.0100

    c. 8007.7802.0200

    d. All of the above

92. Which of the following is not a valid bridge port state?
   a. Listening
   b. Blocking
   c. Learning
   d. Spanning

93. What is 4B/5B in FDDI?
   a. An encoding scheme
   b. A contention scheme
   c. A carrier sense scheme
   d. A token-passing scheme

94. What is the command used to configure IPX load balancing?
   a. IPX load
   b. IPX load interval
   c. IPX maximum-paths
   d. IPXWAN

95. What does a Token Ring device do if it detects the absence of tokens or data from its upstream neighbor?
   a. It polls the station to see if it is alive.
   b. It raps the ring.
   c. It sends a beacon frame.
   d. It shuts down.

96. What is the purpose of a jam signal on an Ethernet network?
   a. It is used to detect collisions on a network.
   b. It is used to detect if another station is transmitting.
   c. It causes the receivers to discard the frame due to a CRC error.
   d. None of the above

97. What does IPX split horizon do?
   a. It prevents routing and SAP updates from being advertised back to the router from which they were learned.
   b. It filters SAP updates.
   c. It filters RIP updates.
   d. It provides a transport for IPX over Frame Relay.

98. What is an RIF used for?
   a. It is used to transport SNA traffic across an IP backbone.
   b. It is used to indicate the priority of a packet.

    c. It is used to indicate the path that an SRB frame should take from the source to destination.

    d. None of the above

99. What is the ipx helper used for?

    a. It defines an IPX default gateway in the router.

    b. It maps a service to an ipx address in the router.

    c. It converts broadcast packets to unicast packets.

    d. It configures the DHCP addressing.

100. What is SSRP?

    a. A fault-tolerance mechanism for LAN

    b. A spanning tree protocol

    c. A VTP protocol

    d. None of the above

Answer Key

  1. B

  2. B

  3. D

  4. C

  5. B

  6. D

  7. A

  8. A

  9. A

10. A

11. C

12. C

13. C and D

14. B

15. C

16. C

17. D

18. B

19. A and D

20. B

21. C

22. A, B, and D

23. A

24. B

25. D

26. D

27. D

28. C

29. C

30. A

31. C

32. B

33. B

34. A

35. D

36. D

37. C

38. A

39. D

40. B

41. B

42. B

43. C

44. B

45. A

46. D

47. A

48. C

49. B

50. C

51. A, B, and D

52. D

53. B and C

54. D

55. A

56. C

57. B

58. D

59. B

60. A

61. B

62. D

63. B

64. A

65. A

66. C and D

67. B

68. A

69. C

70. D

71. B

72. B and C

73. A

74. C

75. C

76. A

77. B

78. D

79. A

80. D

81. D

82. B.

83. B

84. D

85. A

86. A

87. C

88. A

89. B

90. A

91. D

92. D

93. A

94. C

95. C

96. C

97. A

98. C

99. C

100. A

Answer Guide

1. Using the information in the illustration below, what would the RD field of the RIF be for PC1 to reach PC2?

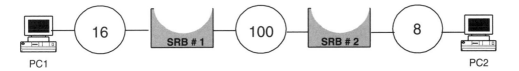

PC1   PC2

   a. 0161.1002.0080
   b. 0101.0642.0080
   c. 1001.6402.0800
   d. 1601.1002.8000

The correct answer is B. The information contained in an RIF consists of the routing control field and multiple route designation (RD) fields, each of which are 2 bytes long. The 2-byte RD field consists of two subfields, a 12-bit ring number, and a 4-bit bridge number. The 12-bit ring number ranges from 0x001 to 0xfff, supporting decimal ring numbers from 1 to 4,095. The bridge number ranges from 0x1 to 0xf, supporting decimal bridge numbers from 1 to 15.

The RD is represented in hexadecimal format, so the decimal values in the figure need to be converted. The decimal value 16 becomes 0x010, 1 becomes 0x1, 100 becomes 0x064, 2 becomes 0x2, 8 becomes 0x008, and the last bit is 0. Therefore, the RD would be written as 0101.0642.0080.

2. Which of the following do IPX clients use to locate the nearest active server for a particular service?
   a. SAP
   b. GNS
   c. IPX RIP
   d. NLSP

The correct answer is B. A Get Nearest Server (GNS) request packet is sent by a client on an IPX network to locate the nearest active server of a particular type. An IPX network client issues a GNS request to solicit either a direct response from a connected server or a response from a router that tells it where on the internetwork the service can be located.

Answer A is incorrect. The Service Advertisement Protocol (SAP) is an IPX protocol through which network resources advertise their addresses and the services they provide. Advertisements are sent via SAP every 60 seconds. IPX services are identified by a hexadecimal number, which is called an SAP identifier.

Answer C is incorrect. IPX RIP is a distance vector routing protocol used to advertise IPX network reachability.

Answer D is also incorrect. NetWare link state protocol (NLSP) is a link state routing protocol used to advertise IPX network reachability.

3. How many networks are carried in an IPX RIP update?
   a. 25
   b. 10
   c. 30
   d. 50

The correct answer is D. By default, a router running IPX RIP sends out one routing update per minute. Each routing update packet can include up to 50 entries. If many networks exist on the internetwork, the router sends out multiple packets per update. For example, if a router has 130 entries in the routing table, it would send three routing update packets per update. The first routing update packet would include the first 50 entries, the second packet would include the next 50 entries, and the last routing update packet would include the last 30 entries.

4. If an Ethernet station detects a collision during transmission, it _____.
   a. Retransmits the frame
   b. Sends a beacon
   c. Waits a random period of time before attempting retransmission
   d. None of the above—collisions are not possible on an Ethernet network.

The correct answer is C. If a station detects a collision during transmission, it stops sending data and immediately transmits a 32-bit jam sequence. The purpose of the jam sequence is to ensure that all stations receiving this frame will receive the jam signal in place of the correct 32-bit MAC CRC. This causes the receivers to discard the frame due to a CRC error. To avoid additional collisions, each station waits a random period of time before attempting retransmission.

5. Given the RIF value 1290.0011.0022.0080, what is the correct path?
   a. Ring 1, Bridge 1 to Ring 2, Bridge 2 to Ring 8
   b. Ring 8, Bridge 2 to Ring 2, Bridge 1 to Ring 1
   c. Ring 129, Bridge 1 to Ring 1, Bridge 22 to Ring 8
   d. Ring 1, Bridge 1 to Ring 0, Bridge 22 to Ring 80

The correct answer is B. The information contained in an RIF consists of a 2-byte routing control field and multiple route designation (RD) fields, each of which are 2 bytes long. The routing control field consists of five subfields, a 3-bit type field, a 5-bit length field, a 1-bit direction field, and a 3-bit largest frame field, the remaining 4 bits are reserved and transmitted as all zeros. The following is a description of each field:

- **Type field**   The type field is 3 bits long and is the broadcast indicator. It contains three possible values: a directed frame binary 000, an all-route explorer frame binary 100, and a single-route explorer frame binary 110. A directed frame indicates that the frame contains the defined path across the network, and no change is needed on the RIF. An all-route explorer frame goes through the whole network. All source-route bridges must copy the frame to every port except the one that has a destination ring that is already in the RIF. A single-route explorer frame is a frame that passes through a predetermined path constructed by a spanning tree algorithm in the bridges. A station should receive only one single-route explorer from the network.

- **Length field**   The length field is 5 bits long and contains the length of the routing information field in bytes.

- **Direction field**   The direction field is 1 bit long and determines how source-route bridges in the network read the RIF. If the bit is to 0, the RIF should be read left to right; if the bit is set to 1, the RIF should be read right to left.

- **Largest frame field**   The largest frame field is 3 bits long and indicates the size in bytes of the largest frame that can transverse the network. Table 5-2, which was shown earlier in the chapter, is a chart of the possible values:

Table 5-2 Largest Frame Size Values

Value	Largest Frame Size
000	516 bytes
001	1,500 bytes
010	2,052 bytes
011	4,472 bytes
100	8,191 bytes
101	11,407 bytes
110	17,800 bytes
111	Used in all-route explorers

In our case, the routing control field is 0x1290 written as binary 1001010010000000. Notice that the sixth bit is a 1, indicating that the RIF should be read right to left. The correct path is Ring 8, Bridge 2 to Ring 2, Bridge 1 to Ring 1.

6. Which of the following is true regarding DLSw?
   a. DLSw terminates the data link control session at the router and provides local ACKs.
   b. DLSw overcomes the seven-hop limit inherent in source-route bridging.
   c. DLSw reduces the amount of explorer traffic that is sent across the network.
   d. All of the above

The correct answer is D. Data Link Switching (DLSw) terminates the data link control (LLC2) session at the router and provides local acknowledgements for LLC2 traffic. Logical Link Control type 2 (LLC2) is a connection-oriented protocol that operates at the Data Link layer, providing sequencing for MAC layer frames, error control, and flow control between end stations. SNA generates a large number of non-data control messages that need to be acknowledged in a predefined amount of time. If a response is not received, the message is retransmitted. By performing local acknowledgements, the overhead traffic sent across the backbone is greatly reduced.

Because DLSw also terminates the RIF at the router, it overcomes the seven-hop count limit inherent in source-route bridging. Up to six hops are supported on either side of the DLSw backbone, which can be an unlimited number of hops. When the router receives the RIF, it terminates it and translates the packet into a TCP datagram. The packet is then routed over the backbone to a DLSw router attached to the destination source-route bridged network. When the DLSw packet is received by the remote router, it is translated back to an LLC2 packet and the hop count is set to 1. The packet is then Source-Route bridged to the destination using the route information stored in the DSLw router.

When a DLSw router receives an explorer packet, it terminates it and it sends a CANUREACH packet to all known DLSw peer routers in the network. When the remote routers receives the CANUREACH packet, they translate them into local explorer packets and send them out over their attached LANs. If the destination end station is found, the end station sends an explorer response packet to the router. The router then sends an ICANREACH packet to the originating DLSw router. The router caches all of the responses so the next time the cache is used, no messages need to be sent, greatly reducing the amount of explorer traffic sent across the network.

7. Given the following RIF c820.0011.0022.0080, which type of packet is this?
   a. Single-route explorer
   b. All-route explorer
   c. Directed frame
   d. STP frame

The correct answer is A. The frame type is identified by the first three bits of the RIF. It contains three possible values: a directed frame binary 000, an all-route explorer frame binary 100 and a single-route explorer frame binary 110. A directed frame indicates that the frame contains the defined path across the network and no change is needed on the RIF. An all-route explorer frame goes through the whole network. All source-route bridges must copy the frame to every port except the one that has a destination ring that is already in the RIF. A single-route explorer frame is a frame that passes through a predetermined path constructed by a spanning tree algorithm in the bridges. A station should receive only one single-route explorer from the network.

We need to convert the hex value c820 to binary; this comes out to be 1100100000100000. The value of the first three bits is 110, which indicates that the frame is a single-route explorer.

8. What does the router use to determine the nearest server for IPX Get Nearest Server response?
   a. Tick count
   b. Hop count
   c. Bandwidth
   d. First service on the list

The correct answer is A. The selection of nearest server is based on the tick count. The service with the lowest tick count is used. If the tick counts are the same, then the service with the lowest hop count is used. If the hop counts are the same, then the hop count for the service itself is used. If another tie exists, the first service in the list is used.

9. Which of the following is false regarding Source-Route Bridging?

   a. By default, Cisco routers use RIF information for routed protocols.
   b. Bridge numbers must be unique only between bridges that connect the same two Token Rings.
   c. Each ring in an SRB network must be unique.
   d. Source-route bridging enables multiple, active paths through the network.

Answer A is false. The Cisco software default is to not collect and use RIF information for routed protocols. This enables operation with software that does not understand or properly use RIF information, such as versions of Novell. In order for a router to send datagrams across a source-route bridge network, it must be able to collect and use RIF information. You can configure a Cisco router to use RIF information for routed protocols with the **multiring** command, enabling Cisco routers with Token Ring interfaces to connect to a source-bridged Token Ring network.

Answers B and C are true. A ring is a single Token Ring network segment. Each ring in the extended Token Ring network is designated by a unique 12-bit ring number. Each bridge between two Token Rings is designated by a unique 4-bit bridge number. Bridge numbers must be unique only between bridges that connect the same two Token Rings.

Answer D is also true. Unlike transparent bridging, which requires time to recomputed topology in the event of failures, source-route bridging enables multiple, active paths through the network. This greatly reduces the time it takes to switch over to alternate routes in the event of failure.

10. In Token Ring, what does it mean when a frame returns to the source with the A and C bits set to 0?

   a. The destination station does not exist or it is not active.
   b. The end station exists, but the frame was not copied.
   c. The destination received the frame.
   d. None of the above—the A and C bits are used in Ethernet.

The correct answer is A. The Token Ring frame contains a field used to indicate the status of the frame. If the A and C bits are set to 0, it means that the end station does not exist or is not active on the ring. If the destination address receives and successfully copies the frame, it set the A and C bits to 1. If the A bit is set to 1 and the C bit is set to 0, it means that the end station exists, but the frame was not copied.

11. What does CSMA/CD stand for?

   a. Carrier Sense Multiple Access Contention Detection
   b. Carrier Sense Media Access Contention Detection
   c. Carrier Sense Multiple Access Collision Detect
   d. Carrier Sense Media Access Collision Detect

The correct answer is C. Carrier Sense Multiple Access Collision Detect (CSMA/CD) is a media access scheme where network devices contend for use of the physical network medium. An Ethernet station wanting to transmit a packet must listen to the cable to determine if any other station is transmitting (Carrier Sense). All nodes wanting to transmit packets have an equal chance to do so. (Multiple Access). If two nodes transmit at the same time, they detect this, and stop transmitting (Collision Detection.)

12. Given the RIF routing control field c820, what is the RD length?
   a. 2 bytes
   b. 4 bytes
   c. 8 bytes
   d. 20 bytes

The correct answer is C. The length field is 5 bits long and contains the length of the routing information field in bytes. The length field identified by the bit positions 4 through 8 of the RIF. We need to convert the hex value c820 to binary; this comes out to be 1100100000100000. The value of the bits is binary 01000, which is 8 decimal; therefore, the RD length is 8 bytes.

13. Which of the following bridging types supports mixed media? (multiple answers)
   a. Transparent bridging
   b. Source-Route bridging
   c. Translation bridging
   d. Source-Route Transparent bridging

The correct answers are C and D. Several bridging technologies are used to interconnect devices. Transparent bridging is used between homogeneous networks and is found primarily in Ethernet environments. Source-route bridging (SRB) is used between homogeneous networks and occurs primarily in Token Ring environments. Translational bridging provides translation between the formats and transit principles of different media types such as Ethernet and Token Ring. Source-Route Transparent bridging combines the algorithms of transparent bridging and source-route bridging to enable communication in mixed Ethernet/Token Ring environments.

14. Using the information in the Illustration below what would the RD field of the RIF be on PC1 to reach PC2?

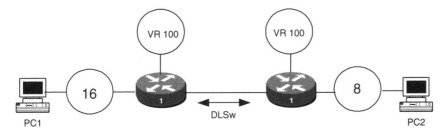

    a. 1601.1000
    b. 0101.0640
    c. 0101.0648
    d. 1601.1001.0080

The correct answer is B. Unlike RSRB, which passes the RIF through the network, DLSw always terminates the RIF in a source-route bridge frame. So the RIF on PC1 would be Ring 16, Bridge 1 to Ring 100. The decimal values need to be converted to hex; the end result is 0101.0640.

15. In SRB, what does the RIF define?
    a. The translation between Ethernet and Token Ring
    b. The topology of the network
    c. The path for SRB frames to transverse the network
    d. The bridge type

The correct answer is C. The RIF in the IEEE 802.5 header is used by a source-route bridges to determine through which ring/bridge segments a frame must transit to reach the destination. The RIF is inserted into the MAC header immediately following the source address field in every frame by the source station, giving this style of bridging its name. The destination station reverses the routing field to reach the originating station. Routing information is contained in the RD field of the RIF. The RD contains all of the ring and bridge numbers that the frame must transfer to reach the destination.

16. Ethernet networks are laid out in a _____.
    a. Physical ring logical bus
    b. Physical ring logical star
    c. Physical star logical bus
    d. Physical star logical ring

The correct answer is C. Ethernet networks are laid out as a physical star but operate as a logical bus. A star topology is a LAN architecture in which the endpoints on a network are connected to a common central hub, or switch, by dedicated links. Ethernet devices connect to a centralized hub, making it a physical star; however, it operates as a logical bus.

17. Which of the following is true regarding bridges and LAN switches?
    a. Bridges operate at layer 2 of the OSI model LAN switches operate at layer 3.
    b. LAN switches enable multiple physical LAN segments to be interconnected into a single, larger network; bridges do not.
    c. Switches forward and flood traffic based on MAC addresses; bridges do not.
    d. Switches are much faster than bridges because the forwarding is performed in hardware versus software.

The correct answer is D. Bridging and switching occur at the link layer (layer 2) of the OSI model. Bridges and switches analyze incoming frames, make forwarding decisions based on information contained in the frames, and forward the frames toward the destination. Both bridges and switches enable multiple physical LAN segments to be interconnected into a single, larger network. Similar to bridges, switches forward and flood traffic based on MAC addresses. Because switching is performed in hardware instead of in software, however, it is significantly faster.

18. Which of the following is false regarding the RIF?

    a. When using DLSw, the RIF is terminated at the router.

    b. The RIF is always read from left to right.

    c. Until recently, IBM only supported a max of eight RD fields in an RIF.

    d. The RD field of the RIF contains alternating sequences of ring and bridge numbers that start and end with ring numbers.

Answer B is false. Each RIF contains a 1-bit direction field, which determines how the RIF should be read by source-route bridges in the network to follow the path to reach the end station. If the bit is to 0, the RIF should be read left to right; if the bit is set to 1, the RIF should be read right to left.

Answer A is true. Unlike RSRB, which passes the RIF through the network, DLSw always terminates the RIF in a source-route bridge frame.

Answer C is true. A single RIF can contain more than one RD field. The IEEE specifies a maximum of 14 RD fields (a maximum of 13 bridges or hops because the last bridge number always equals 0). Until recently, IBM specified a maximum of eight RD fields (a maximum of seven bridges or hops. Newer IBM bridge software programs combined with new LAN adapters support 13 hops.

Answer D is true. Bridges add to the frame their bridge number and the ring number onto which the frame is forwarded. The first bridge also adds the ring number of the first ring. The routes in the RD field of an RIF frame are alternating sequences of ring and bridge numbers that start and end with ring numbers.

19. Which of the following LAN protocols use a token-passing media access scheme? (multiple answers)

    a. FDDI

    b. Ethernet

    c. Fast Ethernet

    d. Token Ring

The correct answers are A and D. In the token-passing media access scheme, network devices access the physical medium based on possession of a token. Examples of LANs that use the token-passing media access scheme are Token Ring and FDDI.

Answers B and C are incorrect. Both Ethernet and Fast Ethernet use the CSMA/CD media access scheme. In the CSMA/CD media access scheme, network devices contend for use of the physical network medium.

20. Given the RIF routing control field c820, what is the largest frame size that can be supported?

    a. 200 bytes

    b. 1,500 bytes

    c. 4,000 bytes

    d. None of the above

The correct answer is D. The routing control field of the RIF indicates the largest frame size that can be handled along a designated route. The largest frame field is identified by the bit positions 10 through 12 of the RIF routing control field. In order to determine the largest frame that is supported, you need to convert the hex value c820 to binary; this comes out to be 1100100000100000. The largest frame supported is 2,052 bytes. Table 5-3, which is shown earlier in the chapter, is a chart of the possible values:

21. What type of packet consists of a single data packet that is copied and sent to a specific subset of nodes on the network?

    a. Broadcast

    b. Unicast

    c. Multicast

    d. Direct-broadcast

Table 5-3 Largest Frame Size Values

Value	Largest Frame Size
000	516 bytes
001	1,500 bytes
010	2,052 bytes
011	4,472 bytes
100	8,191 bytes
101	11,407 bytes
110	17,800 bytes
111	Used in all-route explorers

The correct answer is C. A multicast transmission consists of a single data packet that is copied and sent to a specific subset of nodes on the network. A broadcast transmission consists of a single data packet that is copied and sent to all nodes on the network. A unicast transmission consists of a single packet that is sent from the source to a destination on a network. An IP directed broadcast is a datagram that is sent to the broadcast address of a subnet to which the sending machine is not directly attached.

22. Which of the following are valid SRB explorer packets? (multiple answers)

   a. All-route explorer packet

   b. Single-route explorer packet

   c. All-RIF explorer packet

   d. Local explorer packet

The correct answer is A, B, and D. Bridge uses a system of explorer packet marking to propagate routing information through an SRB network. The end stations send an explorer packet as the packet is forwarded to the destination and each bridge that it traverses updates the RIF. By accumulating this information, the explorer packet gathers a hop-by-hop description of a path through the SRB network.

There are three types of explorer packets that are used: local explorer packets, single-route explorer packets, and all-route explorer packets. The major difference between an all-route broadcast frame and a single-route broadcast frame is in the number of frames that appear on the destination ring. An all-route frame appears on the destination ring the same number of times as there are routes to that ring. In contrast, a single-route frame appears on the destination ring as many times as there are single-route broadcast routes to that ring.

A local explorer packet is generated by some end systems (either NetBIOS or SNA) to find a host connected to the local ring. Single-route explorers are explorers that pass through a predetermined path constructed by a spanning tree algorithm in the bridge. A station should receive only one single-route explorer from the network. An all-route explorer frame goes through the whole network. All source-route bridges must copy the frame to every port except the one that has a destination ring that is already in the RIF.

23. Which IEEE standard specifies the implementation of the physical layer and the MAC sublayer used by Ethernet?

   a. 802.3

   b. 802.4

   c. 802.5

   d. None of the above

The correct answer is A. IEEE 802.3 is a LAN protocol that specifies an implementation of the physical layer and the MAC sublayer. IEEE 802.3 uses CSMA/CD access at a variety of speeds over a variety of physical media. Extensions to the IEEE 802.3 standard specify implementations for Fast Ethernet.

Answer B is incorrect. IEEE 802.4 is a LAN protocol that specifies an implementation of the physical layer and the MAC sublayer. IEEE 802.4 uses token-passing access over a bus topology and is based on the token bus LAN architecture.

Answer C is incorrect. IEEE 802.5 is a LAN protocol that specifies an implementation of the physical layer and MAC sublayer. IEEE 802.5 uses token-passing access at 4 or 16 Mbps over STP cabling and is similar to IBM Token Ring.

24. Which of the following is false regarding IPX?
   a. The network address consists of a network number and a node number expressed in the following format: network.node.
   b. IPX uses ARP.
   c. IPX network addresses must be unique.
   d. IPX can use RIP or NLSP for routing.

Answer B is false. IPX's use of a MAC address for the node number enables the system to send nodes to predict what MAC address to use on a data link. In IP, the network address has no correlation to the MAC address, so IP nodes must use ARP to determine the destination address.

Answer A is true. An IPX network address consists of a network number and a node number expressed in the following format: network.node. The network number identifies a physical network. It is a 4-byte (32-bit) quantity that must be unique throughout the entire IPX internetwork. The network number is expressed as hexadecimal digits. The maximum number of digits allowed is eight. The node number identifies a node on the network. It is a 48-bit quantity, represented by dotted triplets of four-digit hexadecimal numbers.

Answer C is also true. Like other network addresses, Novell IPX network addresses must be unique. These addresses are represented in hexadecimal format and consist of two parts: a network number and a node number.

Answer D is true. IPX uses dynamic protocols to advertise reachability. It can use both distance vector routing protocols like the Routing Information Protocol (RIP) or link state routing protocols like the NetWare Link State Protocol (NLSP).

25. The spanning tree protocol provides _____.
   a. Loop detection
   b. Automatic backup of data paths
   c. Trunking between VLANs
   d. Both A and B

The correct answer is D. The spanning tree algorithm produces and maintains a loop-free topology in a bridged network, which may contain loops in its physical design. With spanning tree, a self-configuring algorithm enables a bridge to be added anywhere in the LAN without creating loops. When you add the new bridge, the spanning tree transparently reconfigures all bridges on the LAN into a single loop-free spanning tree.

Spanning tree never has more than one active data route between two end stations, thus eliminating data loops. For each bridge, the algorithm determines which bridge ports to use to forward data and which ones to block to form a loop-free topology. The spanning tree protocol enables automatic backup of data paths; the bridges connecting to the redundant paths enter backup mode automatically. When a primary bridge fails, a backup bridge becomes active.

26. In an STP environment, the root bridge is selected based on what?
   a. Highest bridge ID
   b. Lowest bridge ID
   c. Highest priority
   d. Lowest priority

The correct answer is D. The root bridge is selected based on priority. The lower the value of number, the more likely the bridge will be chosen as root. The default priority is 128. If the priority is equal, the bridge with the lowest bridge ID is selected as the root.

27. Which of the following data link media access protocols uses a 48-bit MAC address?
   a. Token Ring
   b. Ethernet
   c. FDDI
   d. All of the above

The correct answer is D. All MAC addressing for LANs use a 48-bit address expressed in 6 bytes for both source and destination addresses. The first three bytes of the physical address indicate the vendor organization unit identification (OUI). This OUI provides the basis for the unique MAC address. Originally, Xerox handed out these addresses. Now, assigning the addresses is the responsibility of the IEEE. The purpose of centralizing this activity is to ensure that duplicate addresses will not occur among network interface cards (NICs). Each vendor of an NIC must register its use with the IEEE. IEEE will assign the vendor a 3-byte address, which is the first three bytes of the physical address. For example, 00-00-0c-00-00-00 is assigned to Cisco; 02-60-8C-00-00-00 is assigned to 3Com Corporation; 08-00-20-00-00-00 is assigned to Sun

Microsystems. Having all 0's in the last three bytes only indicates a range. The owner of the first three bytes assigns the last three bytes of the address, which means he or she is allowed to assign up to 2^{24} addresses (16,777,215) to his or her NICs.

28. With respect to the Spanning Tree algorithm, a bridge that forwards traffic on behalf of a LAN is said to be the _____.
    a. Root bridge
    b. Non-designated bridge
    c. Designated bridge
    d. Transparent bridge

The correct answer is C. The spanning tree algorithm selects a designated bridge for each LAN. This bridge is responsible for forwarding traffic on behalf of the LAN to the root bridge. If more than one bridge is connected to the same LAN, the bridge with the smallest path cost to the root is selected as the designated bridge. In the case of duplicate path costs, the bridge with the lowest bridge ID is selected as the designated bridge.

29. In a Transparent bridge environment, if a frame is received and the destination address is not in the bridge's table, the frame is _____.
    a. Dropped
    b. Flooded back out the inbound port
    c. Flooded to all ports except the inbound port
    d. Flooded to all ports

The correct answer is C. Transparent bridges use a table for traffic forwarding. When a frame is received on one of the bridge's interfaces, the bridge looks up the frame's destination address in its internal table. If the table contains an association between the destination address and any of the bridge's ports with the exception of the port on which the frame was received, the frame is forwarded out the indicated port. If no association is found, the frame is flooded to all ports except the inbound port.

30. The specification for STP is _____.
    a. 802.1d
    b. 802.3
    c. 802.4
    d. 802.5

The correct answer is A. The spanning tree protocol is a layer 2 protocol designed to run on bridges and switches. The spanning tree protocol is implemented to prevent loops in a bridged environment. The IEEE specification for the spanning tree protocol is 802.1d.

Answer B is incorrect. IEEE 802.3 is a LAN protocol that specifies an implementation of the physical layer and the MAC sublayer. IEEE 802.3 uses CSMA/CD access at a variety of speeds over a variety of physical media. Extensions to the IEEE 802.3 standard specify implementations for Fast Ethernet.

Answer C is incorrect. IEEE 802.4 is a LAN protocol that specifies an implementation of the physical layer and the MAC sublayer. IEEE 802.4 uses token-passing access over a bus topology and is based on the token bus LAN architecture.

Answer D is incorrect. IEEE 802.5 is a LAN protocol that specifies an implementation of the physical layer and MAC sublayer. IEEE 802.5 uses token-passing access at 4 or 16 Mbps over STP cabling and is similar to IBM Token Ring.

31. In IPX, a tick is calculated based on what?
   a. Hop count
   b. Cost
   c. Delay
   d. All of the above

The correct answer is C. The tick value is based on the interface delay. The actual algorithm used by Cisco to determine the tick value is ([interface delay + 333] / 334). Each tick is about one-eighteenth of a second. The default tick value on serial interface is 6 and on LAN interface is 1. The path with the lowest tick count is selected first, and hop count is used as a tie-breaker.

32. What bridging technique will enable you to route between a bridged interface and routed interface?
   a. Concurrent routing and bridging (CRB)
   b. Integrated routing and bridging (IRB)
   c. Transparent bridging
   d. Source-route bridging

The correct answer is B. IRB provides the capability to route between a bridge-group and a routed interface using a concept called Bridge-Group Virtual Interface (BVI). When you enable routing for a given protocol on the BVI, packets coming from a routed interface destined for a host on the bridged interface are routed to the BVI and are forwarded to the corresponding bridged interface. All traffic routed to the BVI is forwarded to the corresponding bridge group as bridged traffic.

33. In a source-route transparent bridged (SRT) environment, frames with the RII bit equal to zero will be _____.
   a. Source-route bridged
   b. Transparently bridged
   c. Dropped
   d. None of the above

The correct answer is B. When enabled for source-route bridging, the router will look at the RII field of each frame. Packets without an RIF field (RII = 0) are transparently bridged. Packets with an RIF field (RII = 1) are passed to the source-route bridging module for handling.

34. Which of the following is false?

    a. IP can be bridged between Ethernet and Token Ring.

    b. When bridging from Ethernet to Token Ring, the MAC addresses must be bit-swapped.

    c. Bridges running SRT never add or remove RIFs from a frame.

    d. In an SRT environment, only packets with an RIF field are source-routed

Answer A is false. When bridging between Token Ring and Ethernet packet transformations must occur. Ethernet uses canonical bit ordering; this means that the least significant bit in a byte is translated or read first. Non-canonical bit ordering is used by Token Ring, which means the most significant bit in a byte is translated first. It is important to understand that the concepts of canonical and non-canonical do not refer to the 0's and 1's in a MAC address being in different order on the wire itself. It is how the NICs read the 0's and 1's that is different. Because the MAC addresses are bit-swapped, protocols such as IP, XNS, and Novell IPX that use a MAC address in any portion of their data cannot successfully be bridged between Token Ring and Ethernet, and vice versa. For example, MAC addresses are carried in the data portion of a frame. For example, ARP places the hardware address in the data portion of the link-layer frame. It is simple to convert source and destination addresses in the header, but conversion of hardware addresses that may appear in the data portion is more difficult. When performing source-route transparent or source-route translational bridging between Ethernet and Token Ring, Cisco does not search for instances of hardware addresses in the data portion. So, only nonroutable protocols work with Ethernet/Token Ring bridging.

Answer B is true. When bridging for Ethernet to Token Ring, the MAC addresses are bit-swapped because the bit ordering on Token Ring is different from other media.

Answer C is true. When running SRT, frames that did not have an RIF when they were produced by their generating host will never gain an RIF, and frames that did have an RIF when they were produced will never lose that RIF.

Answer D is true. As specified by the SRT specification, only packets without an RIF field (RII = 0) will be transparently bridged. Packets with an RIF field (RII = 1) are passed to the source-route bridged.

35. Transparent bridges exchange configuration messages and topology change messages using _____.

    a. LSAs

    b. BLSAs

    c. VTP

    d. BPDUs

The correct answer is D. A spanning-tree calculation occurs when the bridge is powered up and whenever a topology change is detected. The calculation requires communication between the spanning-tree bridges. This is accomplished through configuration messages called Bridge Protocol Data Units (BPDUs). Configuration messages contain information identifying the root bridge (root identifier) and the distance from the sending bridge to the root bridge (root path cost). Configuration messages also contain the bridge and port identifier of the sending bridge and the age of information contained in the configuration message.

The fields of the BPDU Transparent bridge configuration message are as follows:

- **Protocol identifier** This field contains the value 0 that identifies the spanning tree algorithm and protocol.

- **Version** 0 value specified by standard.

- **Message type** 0 value.

- **Flag** A 1-byte field, of which only the first two bits are used. The topology change (TC) bit signals a topology change. The topology change acknowledgment (TCA) bit is set to acknowledge the receipt of a configuration message with the TC bit set.

- **Root ID** Identifies the root bridge by listing its 2-byte priority followed by its 6-byte ID.

- **Root path cost** Contains the cost of the path from the bridge sending the configuration message to the root bridge. The root path cost can be adjusted.

- **Bridge ID** Identifies the priority and ID of the bridge sending the message.

- **Port ID** Identifies the port from which the configuration message was sent. This field enables loops created by multiple attached bridges to be detected and dealt with.

- **Message age** Specifies the amount of time since the root sent the configuration message on which the current configuration message is based.

- **Maximum age** Two bytes that indicate when the current configuration message should be deleted.

- **Hello time** Provides the time period between root bridge configuration messages.

- **Forward delay** Provides the length of time that bridges should wait before transitioning to a new state after a topology change. If a bridge transitions too soon, not all network links may be ready to change their state, and loops can result.

36. What will the destination MAC address be if PC1 on LAN 1 sends a frame to PC2 on LAN2?

a. PC1's MAC address

b. Bridge 2's MAC address

c. Bridge 1's MAC address

d. PC2's MAC address

The correct answer is D. Bridges interconnect LANs by relaying data frames between the separate MAC entities of the bridged LANs. MAC frames provide the necessary forwarding information in the form of source and destination addresses. This information is essential for the successful transmission and reception of data. In a bridged environment, a local station can communicate with a remote bridged station as if they were on the same local LAN. Although the networks connected by a bridge remain physically separate, they appear as one network to the rest of the devices on the Internet. So when PC1 sends a packet to PC2, the destination MAC address is the MAC address of PC2, just like it would be if the two PCs where on the same physical LAN.

37. What will the destination MAC address be if PC1 on LAN 1 sends a frame to PC2 on LAN2?

a. PC1's MAC address

b. Router 2's MAC address

c. Router 1's MAC address

d. PC2's MAC address

The correct answer is C. The destination MAC address will be the MAC address of Router 1. When PC1 wants to send a frame to PC2, it must send it to Router 1 (its default gateway) because the two PCs are on different LANs. The router will then route the packet across the network using the layer 3 address.

38. If more than one bridge is connected to the same LAN, which bridge is elected as the designated bridge?

   a. The bridge with the smallest path cost to the root bridge
   b. The bridge with the lowest priority
   c. The bridge with the highest priority
   d. None of the above

The correct answer is A. The spanning tree algorithm selects a designated bridge for each LAN. If more than one bridge is connected to the same LAN, the bridge with the smallest path cost to the root is selected as the designated bridge. In the case of duplicate path costs, the bridge with the lowest bridge ID is selected as the designated bridge. The non-designated bridges on the LANs put each port that has not been selected as a root port into a blocked state. In the blocked state, a bridge still listens to hello BPDUs so that it can act on any changes made in the network (for example, if a designated bridge fails) and change its state from blocked to forwarding (forwarding data).

39. With respect to the spanning tree algorithm, a bridge ID comprises a _____.
   a. Bridge priority and serial number
   b. Bridge priority and port priority
   c. Bridge priority and interface number
   d. Bridge priority and bridge MAC address

The correct answer is D. The bridge ID is a unique ID used by the spanning tree algorithm to determine the spanning tree. Each bridge in the network is assigned a unique bridge identifier comprised of a bridge priority and bridge MAC address.

40. The command **multiring all** is used to _____.
   a. Enable multiple rings
   b. Enable a routed protocol to enter an SRB environment
   c. Enable SRB on Ethernet
   d. None of the above

The correct answer is B. The **multiring all** command adds an RIF to IP packets going into the ring and deletes the RIF for packets leaving the ring. This enables a routed protocol to enter an SRB environment. This is necessary when the ring the router is attached to has embedded SRBs (bridging all protocols).

41. Transparent bridging bases its forwarding decision on _____.
   a. An RIF field
   b. A MAC address
   c. An all-route explorer
   d. A single-route explorer

The correct answer is B. Transparent bridges are so named because their presence and operation are transparent to network hosts. Transparent bridging provides an interconnection of LANs transparent to stations communicating across the bridge. Any station can communicate with any other station in the network as though both stations were on the same LAN. Transparent bridges base their forwarding decision on the layer two MAC address.

Transparent bridging requires that the bridges dynamically maintain a source address database for each of their LAN connections. Each bridge LAN interface operates in promiscuous mode so that every frame on the LAN is received and processed. The source address from each frame is saved in the database. The database then is searched to determine whether the destination address of the frame is located in the database. If so, the frame is forwarded to the appropriate LAN segment. If both the source and destination stations are on the same LAN, the frame is discarded. If, however, the frame destination is not found in the database, the bridge forwards the frame to the all other LAN segments.

Transparent bridging is used on MAC bridges that interconnect IEEE 802.3 or Ethernet LANs or IEEE 802.5 Token Ring LANs. Bridging is a method of switching packets. In a bridged network, no correspondence is required between addresses and paths; addresses don't imply anything about where hosts are physically attached to the network. Any address can appear at any location. In contrast, routing requires more thoughtful address assignment, corresponding to physical placement.

Bridging relies heavily on broadcasting. Because a packet may contain no bridging information other than the destination address, which implies nothing about the path that should be used, the only option may be to send the packet everywhere! This is one of bridging's most severe limitations because this method of data delivery is very inefficient and can trigger broadcast storms. In networks with low-speed links, this method can introduce crippling overhead.

42. Ethernet uses _____ bit ordering.
    a. Non-canonical
    b. Canonical
    c. Reverse
    d. Byte-oriented

The correct answer is B. Ethernet uses canonical bit ordering. This means that the least significant bit in a byte is translated or read first. Non-canonical bit ordering is used by Token Ring, which means the most significant bit in a byte is translated first.

43. An FDDI single-attached station (SAS) attaches to _____.
    a. Both rings
    b. The secondary ring
    c. The primary ring through a concentrator
    d. None of the above

The correct answer is C. FDDI defines three types of devices: single-attachment station (SAS), dual-attachment station (DAS), and a concentrator. A SAS attaches to the primary ring through a concentrator. The advantage of this is that the devices will not have any effect on the FDDI ring if they are disconnected or powered off. The concentrator attaches directly to both the primary and secondary rings. A DAS attaches two both rings through ports A and B. Each port provides a connection for both the primary and the secondary ring. Devices using DAS connections will affect the ring, causing it to wrap if they are disconnected or powered off.

44. Which of the following is false regarding FDDI?
   a. FDDI uses a dual-ring architecture.
   b. DAS attach to concentrators
   c. Single-attach stations attach to primary Ring
   d. FDDI MAC address is non-canonical

Answer B is false. The FDDI address is 48 bits long; bits 0 and 1 of the first byte are the I/G bit and the U/L bit. In the destination address, the I/G bit indicates whether the address is an individual (unique) address or a group (multicast) address. The next bit, U/L, indicates whether the address is universally administered (assigned by the IEEE to a vendor, called the prom address) or are locally administered address.

In the source address 0 of the first byte is the RII bit, which displaces the I/G bit because all source addresses are individual addresses. This bit indicates whether source-route information is in the field. Source-routing generally is not used with FDDI, but the option is there. Bridges that encapsulate frames onto FDDI use source-routing if the received packet is originally a source-route frame (meaning the bridge forwarded to FDDI from a Token Ring network).

Answer A is true. FDDI uses a dual-ring architecture. The dual ring is comprised of two rings (the primary and the secondary ring) that normally operate independently. Data can travel on each ring, in opposite directions. Although data is allowed to travel on both rings, data commonly is transmitted only on the primary ring until a certain fault occurs, in which the two rings may become one ring. When a fault does occur, such as if a DAS is powered down or a cable break occurs, the two rings wrap to form one ring.

Answer C is true. A SAS attaches to the primary ring through a concentrator. The advantage of this is that the devices will not have any effect on the FDDI ring if they are disconnected or powered off. The concentrator attaches directly to both the primary and secondary rings.

Answer D is true. The addressing for FDDI is similar to the IEEE 802.5 MAC addressing. The addresses are 48 bits long and are in non-canonical order.

45. Which IEEE standard defines Token Ring?
   a. 802.5
   b. 802.3
   c. 802.1Q
   d. 802.2

The correct answer is A. Token Ring is a first and second layer protocol in the OSI seven-layer model. Token Ring was first developed by IBM as a LAN protocol. It was standardized in IEEE 802.5 and published in 1985.

Answer B is incorrect. IEEE 802.3 is the specification for Ethernet.

Answer C is incorrect. IEEE 802.1Q is the specification for VLANs.

46. Which of the following is false regarding Token Ring?
   a. Only the station in possession of the Token Ring is allowed to transmit.
   b. Data is removed from the ring by the sending station.
   c. Token Ring supports priorities.
   d. Collisions are inherent in a Token Ring environment.

Answer D is false. Token Ring deals with the problem of collisions by controlling access to the network via a token-passing scheme. Because only the station is possession of a token is allowed to transmit data, collisions cannot occur.

When a station wants to send a frame, it waits for the token. Once in possession of the token, the station initiates transmission of the frame to the destination. The frame is repeated by each station until it reaches the destination. During this process, the frame is checked for errors and any jitter is removed. The destination station copies the frame and repeats it on the ring. The frame circles back to the source where it is removed.

47. What happens if a dual-attached station (DAS) device is powered down?
   a. The ring will wrap.
   b. The ring will beacon.
   c. Nothing because it is attached to both rings
   d. Nothing because it is attached to a concentrator

The correct answer is A. When a DAS device is powered down or fails, the devices on either side of the station wrap, forming a single ring. Network operation continues for the remaining stations on the ring. However, if two stations wrap, you will have a segmented ring. This is one of the main disadvantages of dual-attached devices; if they are powered off or fail, they cause the ring to wrap. With SAS, each station is connect to a concentrator, which attaches directly to both the primary and secondary rings. The concentrator ensures that the failure or power-down of any SAS does not bring down the ring. This is particularly useful when PCs or devices that often powered off connect to the ring.

An optical bypass switch can be used with DAS devices to provide continuous dual-ring operation if a device on the dual ring fails. This is used both to prevent ring segmentation and to eliminate failed stations from the ring. The optical bypass switch performs this function through the use of optical mirrors that pass light from the ring directly to the DAS device during normal operation. In the event of a failure of the DAS device, such as a power-off, the optical bypass switch will pass the light through itself by using internal mirrors and thereby maintain the ring's integrity. The benefit of this capability is that the ring will not enter a wrapped condition in the event of a device failure.

48. In Token Ring, what does it mean when a frame returns to the source with the A and C bits set to 1?

    a. The frame was not received by the destination.

    b. The frame contains an error.

    c. The receiving station recognized its address as the destination address and has copied the frame.

    d. The destination station is not active on the ring.

The correct answer is C. At the end of each Token Ring frame is a frame status byte. Within this field are the A and C bits. The A bit is the address-recognized bit. This bit is set to 0 by the transmitting station and is set to 1 by any station that recognized its address as the destination address. The C bit is the frame-copied bit. This bit is also set to 0 by the transmitting station and is set to 1 by the station that copies the frame. When a frame is successfully received by the end station, both the A and C bits are set to 1.

49. DLSw+ always transfers data in _____ format.

    a. Canonical

    b. Non-canonical

    c. FIFO

    d. None of the above—it depends on the media attached.

The correct answer is B. DLSw+ always transfers data in non-canonical format. DLSw will automatically make the correct MAC address conversion depending on the destination media. When DLSw+ receives a MAC address from an Ethernet-attached device, it assumes it is canonical and converts it to non-canonical for transport to the remote peer. At the remote peer, the address is either passed unchanged to Token Ring-attached end systems or converted back to canonical if the destination media is Ethernet.

50. A router is being used as a translational bridge between an Ethernet network and a Token Ring network. Host X on the Ethernet sends a packet to Host Y on the Token Ring. The source MAC address of the packet is 4000.A089.0002. How would the MAC address be interpreted in a Token Ring environment?

    a. 2000.980A.0004

    b. 0040.89A0.2000

    c. 0200.0591.0040

    d. 0200.0500.0840

The correct answer is C. Ethernet uses canonical bit ordering; this means that the least significant bit in a byte is translated or read first. Non-canonical bit ordering is used by Token Ring, which means the most significant bit in a byte is translated first. It is important to understand that the concepts of canonical and non-canonical do not refer to the 0's and 1's in a MAC address being in different order on the wire itself. It is how the NICs read the 0's and 1's that is different.

Based on this, to find the conical address, break down the packet in hexadecimal, take groupings of two hex digits (8 bits), look up their opposite in Table 5-4, and then swap them. It is a good idea to create a table like Table 5-4 before you begin converting the address. The table is created by taking the nibble, which is half a byte, and reversing the order of the bits. For example, decimal value 1 is written as binary 0001. This becomes 1000 or decimal 8.

1. Break down the packet into hexadecimal.

4000.A089.0002 = 40 00 A0 89 00 02

2. Take the hexadecimal values and covert them to the opposite value using Table 5-4. So for the first hexadecimal value, 4 becomes 2 and 0 remains 0.

40 00 A0 89 00 02 becomes 20 00 50 19 00 04

Table 5-4   Finding Conical Addresses

0=0	8=1
1=8	9=9
2=4	A=5
3=C	B=D
4=2	C=3
5=A	D=B
6=6	E=7
7=E	F=F

3. Now swap the two numbers in each hexadecimal grouping. For example, 20 becomes 02. Do this for all of the hexadecimal groupings. The result is the conical address.

20 00 50 19 00 04 becomes 02 00 05 91 00 40

51. The active monitor in Token Ring is responsible for _____. (multiple answers)
    a. Providing the master clock for data transmission
    b. Removing any constantly circulating data packets
    c. Correcting errors
    d. Detecting a loss token and initiating a new token

The correct answers are A, B, and D. On a Token Ring network, one station is elected the active monitor for the ring. The active monitor is responsible for monitoring and controlling the ring.

It is responsible for providing the ring master clock, which ensures that all stations on the ring are synchronized. In Ethernet, a preamble bit pattern is sent before each frame, which enables all receiving stations to synchronize their receivers to the incoming signal. With Token Ring, the active monitor provides the clock for the entire ring; there is no need for a preamble.

The active monitor is also responsible for preventing unclaimed frames for continually circulating the ring. This typically happens if the sending device fails, and its frame subsequently continues to circle the ring. The unclaimed frame prevents other stations from transmitting. The active monitor detects the frame, removes it, and generates a new token.

Another function of the active monitor is detecting a lost token. The active monitor determines what the longest possible time is for a token to travel the full path of the ring. The active monitor uses this as the basis of determining if a token is lost. If the active monitor does not see a token in the predetermined time interval, it assumes the token is lost and purges the ring. This typically happens when the source leaves the ring before removing its own frame.

52. What is the token-passing scheme where a device can pass its token without having received its original frame back?
    a. Fast Token Ring
    b. FDDI
    c. Token passing
    d. Early token release

The correct answer is D. To enable greater use of the bandwidth of a Token Ring network, early token release is used. A station can transmit a token even without receiving its original frame back. The station releases the token after transmitting the ending delimiter of the frame. This enables more efficient use of the available bandwidth.

53. Which types of devices would be found on an FDDI network? (multiple answers)
   a. CAS
   b. DAS
   c. SAS
   d. FAS

The correct answers are B and C. An FDDI network has two types of devices: dual-attached stations (DAS) and signal-attached stations (SAS). DAS devices connect to both FDDI rings and SAS devices connect to a concentrator that attaches to both FDDI rings.

54. Token Ring networks are laid out in a _____.
   a. Physical ring logical bus
   b. Physical ring logical star
   c. Physical star logical bus
   d. Physical star logical ring

The correct answer is D. Token Ring networks are laid out as a physical star but operate as a logical ring. A star topology is a LAN architecture in which the endpoints on a network are connected to a common central hub, or switch, by dedicated links. Token Ring devices connect to a multistation access unit (MAU) similar to Ethernet in which all stations connect to a hub. Token Ring operates as a logical ring because the token is passed from station to station.

55. Which type of packet consists of a single data packet that is copied and sent to all nodes on the network?
   a. Broadcast
   b. Unicast
   c. Multicast
   d. Direct-broadcast

The correct answer is A. A broadcast transmission consists of a single data packet that is copied and sent to all nodes on the network. In these types of transmissions, the source node addresses the packet by using the broadcast address.

Answer B is incorrect. A unicast transmission consists of a single packet that is sent from the source to a destination on a network. The source station addresses the packet by using the address of the destination node. The package is then sent onto the network and the network passes the packet to its destination.

Answer C is also incorrect. A multicast transmission consists of a single data packet that is copied and sent to a specific subset of nodes on the network. The source station addresses the packet using a multicast group address. The packet is then sent into the network, which makes copies of the packet and sends a copy to each node that is part of the multicast group.

Answer D is incorrect. An IP directed broadcast is a datagram that is sent to the broadcast address of a subnet to which the sending machine is not directly attached.

56. What happens if an SAP entry is received and no routing entry exists?
   a. Nothing—routing entries are not needed for SAP entries.
   b. The router will load the SAP entry.
   c. The router will drop an SAP update.
   d. The router will advertise the SAP entry.

The correct answer is C. The router will drop an SAP update if it does not have a routing entry for it. If the router has the SAP entry and the dynamic route that is associated with a static SAP is lost or deleted, the static SAP will not be announced until the route is relearned.

57. Which of the following access lists could be used to filter a Novell file server SAP from being sent?
   a. RouterB(config)#access-list 1000 deny -1 7
   b. RouterB(config)#access-list 1000 deny -1 4
   c. RouterB(config)#access-list 1000 deny -1 3
   d. RouterB(config)#access-list 1000 deny -1 32

The correct answer is B. The syntax for an SAP access list is access list number, permit/deny, source network (a -1 signifies all networks), and service type. Two common IPX service types are NetWare file servers, specified by a 4, and NetWare print servers, specified by a 7. This access list will deny all network file servers SAP updates from being sent.

Answer A is incorrect. This access list will deny all network print servers SAP updates from being sent.

Answer C is incorrect. This access list will deny all network print queue or print group SAPs updates from being sent.

Answer D is also incorrect. This access list will deny all network NetBIOS SAPs updates from being sent.

58. The standby monitor on a Token Ring is responsible for what?
   a. Providing the master clock for data transmission
   b. Removing any constantly circulating data packets

   c. Correcting errors

   d. Detecting monitor failures and starting the monitor contention process

The correct answer is D. The standby monitor is responsible for detecting active monitor failures and starting the monitor contention process. The active monitor is responsible for monitoring and controlling the ring. It is responsible for providing ring master clock, which ensures that all stations on the ring are synchronized.

59. Novel SAP is _____.

   a. Used to provide mail services

   b. A protocol used by network resources to advertise their address

   c. Used to provide dynamic routing

   d. None of the above

The correct answer is B. The Service Advertisement Protocol (SAP) is an IPX protocol through which network resources advertise their addresses and the services they provide. Advertisements are sent via SAP every 60 seconds. IPX services are identified by a hexadecimal number, which is called an SAP identifier. Two common IPX service types are NetWare file servers, specified by a 4, and NetWare print servers, specified by a 7.

Routers listen to SAP updates and build a table of all known services along with their network address. Routers then send their SAP table every 60 seconds. Novell clients send a query to a router requesting a service. The local router responds to the query with the network address of the requested service, and then the client can contact the service directly.

60. Which media access method does Ethernet use?

   a. CSMA/CD

   b. Token passing

   c. EtherType

   d. None of the above

The correct answer is A. LAN protocols typically use one of two methods to access the physical network medium: carrier sense multiple access collision detect (CSMA/CD) or token passing. Ethernet uses CSMA/CD for media access, whereas Token Ring uses token passing. In the CSMA/CD media access scheme, network devices contend for use of the physical network medium.

When an Ethernet attached device has data to transmit, it first listens to the cable to see if a carrier (signal) is being transmitted by another node. This is achieved by monitoring whether a current is flowing in the cable. If no signal (current) is present, the node is allowed to transmit its data. If a signal is present, the station must wait to transmit its data.

To ensure that no collisions occur during data transmission, the sending station monitors the cable during the entire transmission. A collision occurs when two stations listen for traffic, hear none, and then transmit simultaneously. The end station detects a collision by excessive current on the cable.

If a collision is detected, the station stops transmitting data and immediately transmits a 32-bit jam sequence. The purpose of the jam signal is to ensure that all stations receiving this frame will receive the jam signal in place of the correct 32-bit MAC CRC. This causes the other receivers to discard the frame due to a CRC error. To avoid additional collisions, each station waits a random period of time before attempting etransmission.

61. In IPX, RIP which route is preferred?
  a. The route with the highest tick value
  b. The route with the lowest tick value
  c. The route with the highest hop count
  d. The route with the lowest hop count

The correct answer is B. IPX RIP uses a tick as the metric to determine the best path to the destination. A tick is the delay expected when using a particular length. One tick is one-eighteenth of a second. In the case of two paths with an equal tick count, IPX RIP uses the hop count as a tie-breaker.

62. CRB enables you to _____.
  a. Route only
  b. Route between bridged and routed interfaces
  c. Bridge and route on the same interface
  d. Bridge and route on different interfaces

The correct answer is D. Cisco routers have three different ways of implementing bridging: Default Behavior, Concurrent Routing and Bridging (CRB), and Integrated Routing and Bridging (IRB). Before IRB and CRB, you could only bridge or route a protocol on a platform basis. For example, if the **ip route** command was used, and then IP routing was done on all interfaces, it could not bridged. CRB gives you the flexibility to bridge or route a protocol on an interface basis. You can route a given protocol on some interfaces and bridge the same protocol on bridge-group interfaces within the same router. The router can then be both a router and a bridge for a given protocol on the same interface; CRB does routing and bridging on separate interfaces.

63. Which of the following is false regarding beaconing in a Token Ring environment?
  a. A station will send a beacon out if it does not hear from its upstream neighbor in seven seconds.
  b. The station that is beaconing is the station that has the problem.
  c. The station that is beaconing is the station that has detected the problem.

   d. When a station receives a beacon frame, it removes itself from the ring and performs internal diagnostics.

Answer B is false. The station that is beaconing is not the station with the problem. It is the station that has detected that its upstream neighbor has the problem. Any ring station that detects an error can generate a beacon MAC frame. The frame is addressed to all other stations on the ring. A beacon frame contains the address of the station that discovered the error, its Nearest Active Upstream Neighbor (NAUN) address and the type of beacon condition. When a workstation receives the beaconing message, it will respond by removing itself from the ring and going through an internal diagnostic to determine if it is the cause of the problem.

64. Token Ring uses _____ bit ordering.

   a. Non-canonical

   b. Canonical

   c. Reverse

   d. Byte-oriented

The correct answer is A. Token Ring uses non-canonical bit ordering. This means that the most significant bit in a byte is translated first. Ethernet uses canonical bit ordering, which means the least significant bit in a byte is translated or read first.

65. What is the primary difference between DSLw and bridging?

   a. DLSw terminates data link control; bridging does not.

   b. DLSw can transport NetBIOS traffic; RSRB cannot.

   c. DSLw can transport bridge traffic across a wide area network; RSRB cannot.

   d. All of the above

The correct answer is A. The principal difference between DLSw and bridging is that for connection-oriented data, DLSw terminates the data link control, whereas bridging does not. DLSw defines a reliable means of transporting SNA and NetBIOS traffic in a multiprotocol router network using TCP/IP encapsulation. DLSw is an alternative to Cisco's remote source-route bridging (RSRB).

66. Which of the following bridging techniques can be used to bridge between mixed media? (multiple answers)

   a. Transparent bridging

   b. SRB

   c. RSRB

   d. DLSw

The correct answers are C and D. Both RSRB and DLSw can be used to bridge between mixed media.

67. What does format error mean in the show ipx traffic display?

    a. An SAP was received for a service that already exists.

    b. A packet was received on an interface using a different encapsulation type.

    c. An IPX buffer was not available.

    d. None of the above

The correct answer is B. A format error occurs when a router receives an IPX packet with a different IPX encapsulation type than the router's interface, or when the length of the received packet is smaller than 30 bytes or larger than the interface maximum transmission unit (MTU).

68. What does uses mean in the IPX routing table?

    a. It indicates the number of times a particular route is used.

    b. It is the number of packets that have been successfully sent using the route.

    c. It is the number of times the router fast-switched the packet.

    d. None of the above

The correct answer is A. The uses counter associated with each route is incremented each time that route is chosen as the path for an IPX packet. It doesn't necessarily mean that that many packets have been successfully sent using that route; rather, it means that the route was chosen that many times. It is possible after the uses counter is incremented that the packet was discarded.

69. What must you do in order to support multiple IPX network numbers on an Ethernet interface?

    a. Use secondary interfaces, each one with a network number.

    b. Use subinterfaces.

    c. Use secondary interfaces, each network must run a different Ethernet frame type.

    d. None of the above

The correct answer is C. When assigning network numbers to an interface that supports multiple networks, you must specify a different encapsulation type for each network. Because multiple networks share the physical medium, the communication server can determine which packets belong to which network. For example, you can configure up to four IPX networks on a single Ethernet cable, because four encapsulation types are supported for Ethernet. When you use secondary IPX networks, you can configure up to four IPX networks. Each IPX network must be a different and unique Ethernet frame type. IPX networks having different frame types (Novell-Ether, SAP, ARPA, and SNAP).

70. What is the major difference between 100BaseT and 10BaseT?

    a. The access and collision detection used

    b. The frame format

    c. The length requirement

    d. The network diameter

The correct answer is D. Both 100BaseT and 10BaseT use the same IEEE 802.3 MAC access and collision detection methods, and they also have the same frame format and length requirements. The main difference between 100BaseT and 10BaseT other than the speed is the network diameter. With100BaseT, the maximum network diameter is 205 meters; with 10BaseT, it is 2,000 meters.

Reducing the 100BaseT network diameter was necessary because it uses the same collision-detection mechanism as 10BaseT. With 10BaseT, distance limitations are defined so that a station will be able to detect if a collision has occurred within the first 64 bytes of transmission. If the network diameter is too large, the propagation delay across the media would be longer than the transmission delay. To achieve the increased throughput of 100BaseT, the size of the collision domain had to shrink. A station transmitting ten times faster must have a maximum diameter that is ten times less.

71. A router and a Novell file/print server are attached to the same LAN. A client on the LAN sends a Get Nearest Server (GNS) request. Who will respond?

    a. The router

    b. The server

    c. Both

    d. None of the above

The correct answer is B. The router will not respond to a Get Nearest Server (GNS) request when there is a local server on the segment. If a server for the service type sent in the GNS by the client exists on the local cable the client is on, or the best server for that service type is out the same interface, a Cisco will *never* answer the GNS request because of the split horizon rule. If that server happens to have GNS responses turned off, then the client will never get a response.

72. Which of the following are valid transport protocols used between DLSw+ routers? (multiple answers)

    a. Promiscuous

    b. FST

    c. TCP/IP

    d. Border peer

The correct answers are B and C. Cisco supports five different transport protocols between DLSw+ routers:

- **TCP/IP** Transports SNA and NetBIOS traffic across WANs providing local acknowledgment to minimize unnecessary traffic and prevent data link control timeouts.

- **TCP/IP with RIF Passthru** Transports SNA and NetBIOS traffic across WANs but does not terminate the RIF. This solution enables multiple active paths between FEPs.

- **Fast Sequence Transport (FST)/IP** Transports SNA and NetBIOS traffic across WANs with an arbitrary topology. This option does not support local acknowledgment of frames.

- **Direct** Transports SNA and NetBIOS traffic across a point-to-point HDLC or point-to-point Frame Relay connections. This option does not support local acknowledgment of frames.

- **DLSw Lite** Transports SNA and NetBIOS traffic across a point-to-point Frame Relay connection providing local acknowledgment and reliable transport.

Answer A is incorrect. Promiscuous mode is used on a router to enable it to accept peer connection requests from routers that are not preconfigured. If promiscuous mode is not used, the router must define which remote peers are allowed to connect to it. This feature is commonly used in hub environments to minimize changes when branch offices are added or deleted.

Answer D is incorrect. With DLSw+, a cluster of routers in a network can be combined into a peer group. Peer groups are designed to address the broadcast replication that occurs in a fully meshed network. SRB and standard DLSw implementations require peer connections between every pair of routers. This full mesh configuration is difficult to configure and results in each router having to replicate search requests for each peer connection.

By grouping routers in peer groups, a designated focal router is responsible for broadcast replication. Within a peer group, one or more of the routers is designated to be the border peer. Instead of all routers peering to one another, each router within a group peers to the border peer and border peers establish peer connections with other border routers.

73. The Token Ring station with the _____ will be elected the active monitor for the ring.
   a. Highest MAC address
   b. Lowest MAC address
   c. Highest router ID
   d. Lowest router ID

The correct answer is A. A token claiming process is the method used in determining the active monitor on the LAN. All stations on the ring can participate in the token claiming process. Ring stations detecting the absence of an active monitor enter into claim token transmit mode by broadcasting a Claim_Token MAC frame containing its MAC address. Each ring station participating in the token claiming process analyzes the source address field of the Claim_Token MAC frame against its own address. If the source address in the claim token is greater than the station's address, the station enters claim token repeat mode. If the source address is less than the station's' address, the station transmits its own Claim_Token MAC frames using its MAC address. A network node is selected to be the active monitor if it has the highest MAC address on the ring.

74. The MTU on a 4MB Token Ring network is _____.

    a. 1,500

    b. 4,352

    c. 2,002

    d. None of the above

The correct answer is C. The maximum transmission unit (MTU) is the maximum packet size, in bytes, that a particular interface can handle. The 4MB Token Ring networks have an MTU of 2,002. FDDI networks and 16 Mbps Token Ring networks have an MTU of 4,352. For Ethernet, the MTU value is 1,500 data bytes excluding the local network header.

75. What happens when a router receives an IPX broadcast packet?

    a. The router forwards the packet to all destinations.

    b. The router forwards the packet to all destinations on that network.

    c. The router drops the packet.

    d. None of the above

The correct answer is C. By default, the router will block all broadcast requests and does not forward them to other network segments. This prevents the degradation of performance over the entire network. The **ipx helper-address** command enables broadcasts to be forwarded to other networks. The command lets you forward the broadcasts to a server, network, or networks that can process them.

76. A router is being used as a bridge between an Ethernet network and an FDDI network. Host X on the Ethernet sends a packet to Host Y on the FDDI. The source MAC address of the packet is 2000.980A.0004. How would the MAC address be interpreted in an FDDI environment?

    a. 0400.1950.0020

    b. 4000.0000.0001

   c. 2000.980A.0004

   d. 0200.0500.0840

The correct answer is A. Ethernet uses canonical bit ordering. This means that the least significant bit in a byte is translated or read first. Non-canonical bit ordering is used by FDDI, which means the most significant bit in a byte is translated first. It is important to understand that the concepts of canonical and non-canonical do not refer to the 0's and 1's (in a MAC address being in different order on the wire itself. It is how the NICs read the 0's and 1's that is different.

Based on this, to find the canonical address, take the groupings of two hex digits (8 bits), look up their opposite in Table 5-5, and then swap them. The result is the non-canonical address 0400.1950.0020.

It is a good idea to create a table like Table 5-5 before you begin converting the address. The table is created by taking the nibble, which is half a byte, and reversing the order of the bits. For example, decimal value 1 is written as binary 0001. This becomes 1000 or decimal 8.

1. Break down the packet into hexadecimal.

2000.980A.0004 = **20 00 98 0A 00 04**

2. Take the hexadecimal values and covert them to the opposite value using Table 5-5. So for the first hexadecimal value, 2 becomes 4, and 0 remains 0.

20 00 98 0A 00 04 becomes 40 00 91 05 00 02

Table 5-5 Finding Canonical Addresses

0=0	8=1
1=8	9=9
2=4	A=5
3=C	B=D
4=2	C=3
5=A	D=B
6=6	E=7
7=E	F=F

3. Now swap the two numbers in each hexadecimal grouping. For example, 40 becomes 04. Do this for all of the hexadecimal groupings. The result is the conical address.

40 00 91 05 00 02 becomes 0400.1950.0020

77. Given the following RIF 4820.0011.0022.0080, what type of packet is this?
   a. Single-route explorer
   b. All-route explorer
   c. Directed frame
   d. STP frame

The correct answer is B. The frame type is identified by the first three bits of the RIF. You need to convert the hex value 4,820 to binary, this comes out to be 1001000000100000. The value of the first three bits is 100, which indicates that the frame is an all-route explorer frame. Three values are possible: a directed frame binary 000, an all-route explorer frame binary 100 and a single-route explorer frame binary 110. A directed frame indicates that the frame contains the defined path across the network and no change is needed on the RIF. An all-route explorer frame goes through the whole network. All source-route bridges must copy the frame to every port except the one that has a destination ring that is already in the RIF. A single-route explorer frame is a frame that passes through a predetermined path constructed by a spanning tree algorithm in the bridges. A station should receive only one single-route explorer from the network.

78. Assume a datagram is sent from a Cisco router/bridge on Ring 21, across Bridge 5 to Ring 256, and then across Bridge 10 to Ring 1365 for delivery to a destination host on that ring. What would the RIF look like in the router describing this path?
   a. 0830.0155.a100.0555
   b. 0830. 1055.100a.0555
   c. 0830.0025.2510.1365
   d. 0830.0155.100a.5550

The correct answer is D. The information contained in an RIF consists of the routing control field and multiple route designation (RD) fields each of which are 2 bytes long. The 2-byte RD field consists of two subfields, a 12-bit ring number and a 4-bit bridge number. The RD is represented in hex so the decimal ring/bridge values need to be converted. The decimal value 21 becomes 0x015, 5 becomes 0x5, 256 becomes 0x100, 10 becomes A, 1365 becomes 0x555, and the last bit is 0. The RD would be written as 0155.100a.5550.

79. Which of the following do IPX servers use to broadcast the services that they offer to hosts?

   a. SAP

   b. GNS

   c. IPX RIP

   d. NLSP

The correct answer is A. The Service Advertisement Protocol (SAP) is an IPX protocol through which network resources advertise their addresses and the services they provide. Advertisements are sent via SAP every 60 seconds. IPX services are identified by a hexadecimal number, which is called an SAP identifier.

Answer B is incorrect. A Get Nearest Server (GNS) request packet is sent by a client on an IPX network to locate the nearest active server of a particular type. An IPX network client issues a GNS request to solicit either a direct response from a connected server or a response from a router that tells it where on the internetwork the service can be located.

Answer C is incorrect. IPX RIP is a distance vector routing protocol used to advertise IPX network reachability.

Answer D is incorrect. NetWare link state protocol (NLSP) is a link state routing protocol used to advertise IPX network reachability.

80. Which of the following is a Cisco IPX encapsulation type?

   a. ARPA

   b. SAP

   c. Novell-Ether

   d. All of the above

The correct answer is D. Cisco supports four different IPX Ethernet encapsulation types on a LAN. The following Ethernet encapsulation types are supported: Novell-Ether (this is the default encapsulation on a Cisco Ethernet interface), ARPA, SAP, and SNAP.

81. Which of the following is not a valid IPX routing protocol?

   a. NLSP

   b. IPX RIP

   c. EIGRP

   d. OSPF

The correct answer is D. IPX can use three different routing protocols to propagate routing information: IPX RIP, NLSP, or EIGRP. OSPF does not support IPX.

IPX RIP is a distance vector protocol similar to IP RIP. The main disadvantage of IPX RIP is that it sends out large RIP and SAP updates every 60 seconds. This can consume substantial amounts of bandwidth. The RIP metric for route determination is based on ticks with hop count used as a tie-breaker.

EIGRP for a Novell IPX network is a Cisco proprietary protocol. It has the same fast rerouting and partial update capabilities as Enhanced IGRP for IP. In addition, EIGRP supports incremental SAP updates, extends the maximum network diameter to 220 hops, and provides optimal path selection through the use of metrics based on delay, bandwidth, reliability, and load.

NetWare Link Services Protocol (NLSP) is a link state routing protocol from Novell that overcomes some of the limitations associated with the IPX RIP and SAP.

82. Which type of packet consists of a single data packet that is copied and sent from the source to a single destination on a network?
   a. Broadcast
   b. Unicast
   c. Multicast
   d. Direct-broadcast

The correct answer is B. A unicast transmission consists of a single packet that is sent from the source to a destination on a network. The source station addresses the packet by using the address of the destination node. The package is then sent onto the network and the network passes the packet to its destination.

Answer A is incorrect. A broadcast transmission consists of a single data packet that is copied and sent to all nodes on the network. In these types of transmissions, the source node addresses the packet by using the broadcast address.

Answer C is incorrect. A multicast transmission consists of a single data packet that is copied and sent to a specific subset of nodes on the network. The source station addresses the packet using a multicast group address. The packet is then sent into the network, which makes copies of the packet and sends a copy to each node that is part of the multicast group.

83. In Token Ring, what does it mean when a frame returns to the source with the A bit set to 1 and the C bit set to 0?
   a. The destination station does not exist or is not active.
   b. The end station exists, but the frame was not copied.
   c. The destination received the frame.
   d. None of the above—the A and C bits are used in Ethernet.

The correct answer is B. The Token Ring frame contains a field used to indicate the status of the frame. If the A bit is set to 1 and the C bit is set to 0, it means that the end station exists, but the frame was not copied. If the A and C bits are set to 1, it means that the end station received and successfully copied the frame. If the A and C bits are set to 0, it means that the end station does not exist or is not active on the ring.

84. On a Token Ring network, which station will become the standby monitor?

    a. The station with the highest MAC address

    b. The station with the lowest MAC address

    c. The station with the highest router ID

    d. All stations on the ring except the station that is the active monitor

The correct answer is D. Two types of stations exist on a Token Ring network: the active monitor (AM) station and the standby monitor (SBM) stations. There is only one active monitor station per ring; all other stations on the ring are standby monitor stations. The active monitor is chosen during a process called the claim token process. After the active monitor is chosen, all other stations become standby monitors (SBMs).

85. An IPX network address consists of _____.

    a. Network number and node number

    b. Network and subnet work number

    c. Network number and port number

    d. Network number

The correct answer is A. An IPX network address consists of a network number and a node number expressed in the following format: network.node. The network number identifies a physical network. It is a 4-byte (32-bit) quantity that must be unique throughout the entire IPX internetwork. The network number is expressed as hexadecimal digits. The maximum number of digits allowed is eight. The node number identifies a node on the network. It is a 48-bit quantity, represented by dotted triplets of four-digit hexadecimal.

86. What is the purpose of the **ethernet-transit-oui** command?

    a. It specifies the OUI code used in the encapsulation of Ethernet Type II frames.

    b. It is used to identify the vendor.

    c. It specifies the OUI code used on the Ethernet LAN.

    d. None of the above

The correct answer is A. The **ethernet-transit-oui** command chooses the OUI code to be used in the encapsulation of Ethernet Type II frames and Ethernet SNAP frames across Token Ring networks. It also tells the router how to translate Token Ring frames into Ethernet frames. By default, the router uses the 0x0000F8 OUI when converting Ethernet Type II frames into Token Ring SNAP frames, and leaves the OUI as 0x000000 for Ethernet SNAP frames. So, the router knows whether a Token Ring SNAP frame should be converted back to Ethernet Type II or an Ethernet SNAP frame just by looking at the OUI in the Token Ring frame.

87. A type 2 beacon on a Token Ring means what?

    a. A station is sending claim tokens, but is not seeing them come back around the ring.

    b. A station is seeing an upstream neighbor transmitting all of the time.

    c. There is a physical break in the ring topology.

    d. None of the above

    e. All of the above

The correct answer is C. The IBM Token Ring architecture has four types of beacons. A beacon type 1 is used for recovery purposes. A beacon type 2 is the most common beacon, which indicates a physical break in the ring topology. A beacon type 3 is a claim token beacon and is sent by a station when it is sending claim tokens but is not seeing them come back around the ring. A beacon type 4 is a streaming beacon, which is sent by a station that is seeing an upstream neighbor transmitting all of the time.

88. What is Fast EtherChannel?

    a. A trunking technology

    b. A LAN protocol

    c. A media access scheme

    d. None of the above

The correct answer is A. EtherChannel is a trunking technology that groups together multiple full-duplex 802.3 Ethernet interfaces to provide fault-tolerant, high-speed links between switches, routers, and servers. EtherChannel is a logical aggregation of multiple Ethernet interfaces.

89. What is IPXWAN?

    a. A routing protocol

    b. A link startup and negotiation protocol

    c. A service advertisement protocol

    d. None of the above

The correct answer is B. IPXWAN is a link startup and negotiation protocol (specified by Novell in Informational RFC 1362) for use over serial lines and other wide area services. IPXWAN involves procedures that determine a master and a slave side of each WAN connection, and provide for dynamic assignment of Novell addresses, and determination of the link delay metric. Use of IPXWAN is required in order to interconnect Cisco routers with the Multiprotocol Router (MPR) product from Novell.

90. What sets the RIF indicator bit?

    a. The source station

    b. The destination station

    c. The router

    d. The bridge

The correct answer is A. The routing information field (RIF) contains the route to a particular destination and is included only in those frames destined for other LANs. The routing information indicator (RII) is bit 0 (left-most or most-significant bit) of the first byte of the source address. The RII bit, by being set, cues source-route bridges to look further into the frame for routing and control information contained in the RIF. The RII is set by the source station. Setting the RII bit equal to 1 indicates the presence of routing information within the frame. If the RII bit is not set (equal to 0), it means that no routing information is present.

91. What is the destination MAC address of a BPDU?

    a. 8001.4300.0000

    b. C000.0000.0100

    c. 8007.7802.0200

    d. All of the above

The correct answer is D. The destination address field of a BPDU indicates the destination address as specified in the Bridge Group Address table. For IEEE STP BPDU frames, the address is 0x800143000000. For IBM STP BPDU frames, the address is 0xC00000000100. For Cisco STP BPDU frames, the address is 0x800778020200.

92. Which of the following is not a valid bridge port state?

    a. Listening

    b. Blocking

    c. learning

    d. Spanning

The correct answer is D. Each port on a switch using STP exists in one of the following states:

- **Blocking** A port in the blocking state does not participate in frame forwarding. After initialization, a BPDU is sent to each port in the switch. A switch initially assumes it is the root until it exchanges BPDUs with other switches. This exchange establishes which switch in the network is the root. If there is only one switch in the network, no exchange occurs, the forward delay timer expires, and the ports move to the listening state. A switch always enters the blocking state following switch initialization.

- **Listening** The listening state is the first transitional state a port enters after the blocking state. The port enters this state when STP determines that the port should participate in frame forwarding.

- **Learning** A port in the learning state prepares to participate in frame forwarding. The port enters the learning state from the listening state.

- **Forwarding** A port in the forwarding state forwards frames. The port enters the forwarding state from the learning state.

- **Disabled** A port in the disabled state does not participate in frame forwarding or STP.

93. What is 4B/5B in FDDI?
   a. An encoding scheme
   b. A contention scheme
   c. A carrier sense scheme
   d. A token-passing scheme

The correct answer is A. To prevent continuous zeros from passing around the ring, 4B/5B encoding scheme is used. With 4B/5B encoding, no more than three consecutive zeros will ever be passed onto the ring (except for start and stop bits). Four data bits are represented by five transmission bits. For this reason, the true operating speed of an FDDI ring is 125 Mbps. FDDI also uses Non-Return to Zero Invert (NRZI) data-encoding scheme to generate the signal representing 4B/5B encoding bits onto the ring. With NRZI, a one bit is represented by a signal voltage change ($+7$ Volts to -7 Volts or -7 Volts to $+7$ Volts). A zero bit is represented by no voltage change. All signal changes are made at the cycle midpoint.

94. What is the command used configure IPX load balancing?
   a. IPX load
   b. IPX load interval
   c. IPX maximum-paths
   d. IPXWAN

The correct answer is C. The **IPX maximum-paths** command sets the maximum number of equal-cost paths the Cisco IOS software will use when forwarding packets.

95. What does a Token Ring device do if it detects the absence of tokens or data from its upstream neighbor?
   a. Polls the station to see if it is alive
   b. Raps the ring
   c. Sends a beacon frame
   d. Shuts down

The correct answer is C. If a station detects the absence of tokens or data from its upstream neighbor, the station will generate a beacon frame. Any ring station that detects an error can generate a beacon MAC frame. The frame is addressed to all other stations on the ring. A beacon frame contains the address of the station that discovered the error, its Nearest Active Upstream Neighbor (NAUN) address, and the type of beacon condition. When a workstation receives the beaconing message, it will respond by removing itself from the ring and going through an internal diagnostic to determine if it is the cause of the problem.

96. What is the purpose of a jam signal on an Ethernet network?
   a. It is used to detect collisions on a network.
   b. It is used to detect if another station is transmitting.
   c. It causes the receivers to discard the frame due to a CRC error.
   d. None of the above

The correct answer is C. If a station detects a collision during transmission, it stops sending data and immediately transmits a 32-bit jam sequence. The purpose of the jam sequence is to ensure that all stations receiving this frame will receive the jam signal in place of the correct 32-bit MAC CRC. This causes the receivers to discard the frame due to a CRC error. To avoid additional collisions, each station waits a random period of time before attempting retransmission.

97. What does IPX split horizon do?
   a. It prevents routing and SAP updates from being advertised back to the router from which they were learned
   b. It filters SAP updates
   c. It filters RIP updates
   d. It provides a transport for IPX over Frame Relay

The correct answer is A. IPX split horizon is a scheme used by the router to avoid problems caused by advertising routes or SAP back to the router from which they were learned. The split horizon scheme omits routes and SAPs learned from one neighbor in updates sent to that neighbor. When split horizon is enabled on a router's interface, the router records the interface over which routes and SAP updates was received and does not propagate information about that route or SAP back out that interface.

98. What is an RIF used for?
   a. It is used to transport SNA traffic across an IP backbone.
   b. It is used to indicate the priority of a packet.
   c. It is used to indicate path that a SRB frame should take from source to destination.
   d. None of the above

The correct answer is C. The RIF is a field in source-route bridged frames that indicates the SRB path the frame should take when traversing a Token Ring network. In the case of an explorer packet, the RIF is a field of the source-route bridged frame that indicates the SRB path that the SRB explorer has traversed so far. The information contained in an RIF consists of a 2-byte routing control field and multiple route designation (RD) fields, each of which are 2 bytes long. The routing control field consists of five subfields: a 3-bit type field, a 5-bit length field, a 1-bit direction field, and a 3-bit largest frame field. The remaining 4-bits are reserved and transmitted as all zeros.

99. What is the ipx helper used for?
  a. It defines an IPX default gateway in the router.
  b. It maps a service to an ipx address in the router.
  c. It converts broadcast packets to unicast packets.
  d. It configures the DHCP addressing.

The correct answer is C. IP helper addressing is a form of static addressing that uses directed broadcasts to forward local and all-nets broadcasts to desired destinations within the internetwork.

100. What is SSRP?
  a. A fault-tolerance mechanism for LAN
  b. A spanning tree protocol
  c. A VTP protocol
  d. None of the above

The correct answer is A. LANE relies on three servers: the LANE configuration server, the LANE server, and the BUS. If any one of these servers fails, the emulated LAN cannot fully function. Cisco has developed a fault-tolerance mechanism known as simple server redundancy that eliminates these single points of failure. Simple server redundancy uses multiple LANE configuration servers and multiple broadcast-and-unknown and LANE servers. You can configure servers as backup servers, which will become active if a master server fails. The priority levels for the servers determine which servers have precedence.

INDEX

Symbols

1003 routers, 245
1600 routers, 236, 245
2500 routers, 236–237, 244
3600 routers, 245
4000 routers, 236, 244
4500 routers, 236–237
4700 routers, 236–237
7000 routers, 244
7500 routers, 236, 245

A

AAL layer, ATM, 25
access-class command, 250
Acks, EIGRP, 128
active state, EIGRP, 127
addresses
    frame relay, 21–22
    IP, 31–32
    IPX, 325
adjacencies
    IS-IS, 152

    OSPF, 136, 143–145
advertising routes, IGRP, 122
answer explanations
    bridging, 349–392
    Cisco-specific router configuration, 272–313
    networking protocols, 63, 65
    routing protocols, 180–234
answers
    bridging, 345–349
    Cisco–specific router configuration, 268–270
    networking protocols, 61–63
    routing protocols, 176–179
Application layer, OSI reference model, 16
areas
    IS-IS, 151
    OSPF, 135–137
ARP (Address Resolution Protocol)
    frames, 34
    headers, 35
AS (autonomous system), OSPF, 135

INTERNATIONAL CONTACT INFORMATION

AUSTRALIA
McGraw-Hill Book Company Australia Pty. Ltd.
TEL +61-2-9417-9899
FAX +61-2-9417-5687
http://www.mcgraw-hill.com.au
books-it_sydney@mcgraw-hill.com

CANADA
McGraw-Hill Ryerson Ltd.
TEL +905-430-5000
FAX +905-430-5020
http://www.mcgrawhill.ca

GREECE, MIDDLE EAST,
NORTHERN AFRICA
McGraw-Hill Hellas
TEL +30-1-656-0990-3-4
FAX +30-1-654-5525

MEXICO (Also serving Latin America)
McGraw-Hill Interamericana Editores S.A. de C.V.
TEL +525-117-1583
FAX +525-117-1589
http://www.mcgraw-hill.com.mx
fernando_castellanos@mcgraw-hill.com

SINGAPORE (Serving Asia)
McGraw-Hill Book Company
TEL +65-863-1580
FAX +65-862-3354
http://www.mcgraw-hill.com.sg
mghasia@mcgraw-hill.com

SOUTH AFRICA
McGraw-Hill South Africa
TEL +27-11-622-7512
FAX +27-11-622-9045
robyn_swanepoel@mcgraw-hill.com

UNITED KINGDOM & EUROPE
(Excluding Southern Europe)
McGraw-Hill Education Europe
TEL +44-1-628-502500
FAX +44-1-628-770224
http://www.mcgraw-hill.co.uk
computing_neurope@mcgraw-hill.com

ALL OTHER INQUIRIES Contact:
Osborne/McGraw-Hill
TEL +1-510-549-6600
FAX +1-510-883-7600
http://www.osborne.com
omg_international@mcgraw-hill.com

LICENSE AGREEMENT

THIS PRODUCT (THE "PRODUCT") CONTAINS PROPRIETARY SOFTWARE, DATA AND INFORMATION (INCLUDING DOCUMENTATION) OWNED BY THE McGRAW-HILL COMPANIES, INC. ("McGRAW-HILL") AND ITS LICENSORS. YOUR RIGHT TO USE THE PRODUCT IS GOVERNED BY THE TERMS AND CONDITIONS OF THIS AGREEMENT.

LICENSE: Throughout this License Agreement, "you" shall mean either the individual or the entity whose agent opens this package. You are granted a non-exclusive and non-transferable license to use the Product subject to the following terms:

(i) If you have licensed a single user version of the Product, the Product may only be used on a single computer (i.e., a single CPU). If you licensed and paid the fee applicable to a local area network or wide area network version of the Product, you are subject to the terms of the following subparagraph (ii).

(ii) If you have licensed a local area network version, you may use the Product on unlimited workstations located in one single building selected by you that is served by such local area network. If you have licensed a wide area network version, you may use the Product on unlimited workstations located in multiple buildings on the same site selected by you that is served by such wide area network; provided, however, that any building will not be considered located in the same site if it is more than five (5) miles away from any building included in such site. In addition, you may only use a local area or wide area network version of the Product on one single server. If you wish to use the Product on more than one server, you must obtain written authorization from McGraw-Hill and pay additional fees.

(iii) You may make one copy of the Product for back-up purposes only and you must maintain an accurate record as to the location of the back-up at all times.

COPYRIGHT; RESTRICTIONS ON USE AND TRANSFER: All rights (including copyright) in and to the Product are owned by McGraw-Hill and its licensors. You are the owner of the enclosed disc on which the Product is recorded. You may not use, copy, decompile, disassemble, reverse engineer, modify, reproduce, create derivative works, transmit, distribute, sublicense, store in a database or retrieval system of any kind, rent or transfer the Product, or any portion thereof, in any form or by any means (including electronically or otherwise) except as expressly provided for in this License Agreement. You must reproduce the copyright notices, trademark notices, legends and logos of McGraw-Hill and its licensors that appear on the Product on the back-up copy of the Product which you are permitted to make hereunder. All rights in the Product not expressly granted herein are reserved by McGraw-Hill and its licensors.

TERM: This License Agreement is effective until terminated. It will terminate if you fail to comply with any term or condition of this License Agreement. Upon termination, you are obligated to return to McGraw-Hill the Product together with all copies thereof and to purge all copies of the Product included in any and all servers and computer facilities.

DISCLAIMER OF WARRANTY: THE PRODUCT AND THE BACK-UP COPY ARE LICENSED "AS IS." McGRAW-HILL, ITS LICENSORS AND THE AUTHORS MAKE NO WARRANTIES, EXPRESS OR IMPLIED, AS TO THE RESULTS TO BE OBTAINED BY ANY PERSON OR ENTITY FROM USE OF THE PRODUCT, ANY INFORMATION OR DATA INCLUDED THEREIN AND/OR ANY TECHNICAL SUPPORT SERVICES PROVIDED HEREUNDER, IF ANY ("TECHNICAL SUPPORT SERVICES"). McGRAW-HILL, ITS LICENSORS AND THE AUTHORS MAKE NO EXPRESS OR IMPLIED WARRANTIES OF MERCHANTABILITY OR FITNESS FOR A PARTICULAR PURPOSE OR USE WITH RESPECT TO THE PRODUCT. McGRAW-HILL, ITS LICENSORS, AND THE AUTHORS MAKE NO GUARANTEE THAT YOU WILL PASS ANY CERTIFICATION EXAM WHATSOEVER BY USING THIS PRODUCT. NEITHER McGRAW-HILL, ANY OF ITS LICENSORS NOR THE AUTHORS WARRANT THAT THE FUNCTIONS CONTAINED IN THE PRODUCT WILL MEET YOUR REQUIREMENTS OR THAT THE OPERATION OF THE PRODUCT WILL BE UNINTERRUPTED OR ERROR FREE. YOU ASSUME THE ENTIRE RISK WITH RESPECT TO THE QUALITY AND PERFORMANCE OF THE PRODUCT.

LIMITED WARRANTY FOR DISC: To the original licensee only, McGraw-Hill warrants that the enclosed disc on which the Product is recorded is free from defects in materials and workmanship under normal use and service for a period of ninety (90) days from the date of purchase. In the event of a defect in the disc covered by the foregoing warranty, McGraw-Hill will replace the disc.

LIMITATION OF LIABILITY: NEITHER McGRAW-HILL, ITS LICENSORS NOR THE AUTHORS SHALL BE LIABLE FOR ANY INDIRECT, SPECIAL OR CONSEQUENTIAL DAMAGES, SUCH AS BUT NOT LIMITED TO, LOSS OF ANTICIPATED PROFITS OR BENEFITS, RESULTING FROM THE USE OR INABILITY TO USE THE PRODUCT EVEN IF ANY OF THEM HAS BEEN ADVISED OF THE POSSIBILITY OF SUCH DAMAGES. THIS LIMITATION OF LIABILITY SHALL APPLY TO ANY CLAIM OR CAUSE WHATSOEVER WHETHER SUCH CLAIM OR CAUSE ARISES IN CONTRACT, TORT, OR OTHERWISE. Some states do not allow the exclusion or limitation of indirect, special or consequential damages, so the above limitation may not apply to you.

U.S. GOVERNMENT RESTRICTED RIGHTS: Any software included in the Product is provided with restricted rights subject to subparagraphs (c), (1) and (2) of the Commercial Computer Software-Restricted Rights clause at 48 C.F.R. 52.227-19. The terms of this Agreement applicable to the use of the data in the Product are those under which the data are generally made available to the general public by McGraw-Hill. Except as provided herein, no reproduction, use, or disclosure rights are granted with respect to the data included in the Product and no right to modify or create derivative works from any such data is hereby granted.

GENERAL: This License Agreement constitutes the entire agreement between the parties relating to the Product. The terms of any Purchase Order shall have no effect on the terms of this License Agreement. Failure of McGraw-Hill to insist at any time on strict compliance with this License Agreement shall not constitute a waiver of any rights under this License Agreement. This License Agreement shall be construed and governed in accordance with the laws of the State of New York. If any provision of this License Agreement is held to be contrary to law, that provision will be enforced to the maximum extent permissible and the remaining provisions will remain in full force and effect.